The Man Who Would Not Be Washington

★

Robert E. Lee's
Civil War and His Decision
That Changed American History

★

JONATHAN HORN

★

SCRIBNER

New York   London   Toronto   Sydney   New Delhi

SCRIBNER
A Division of Simon & Schuster, Inc.
1230 Avenue of the Americas
New York, NY 10020

For information about special discounts for bulk purchases,
please contact Simon & Schuster Special Sales at 1-866-506-1949
or business@simonandschuster.com.

The Simon & Schuster Speakers Bureau can bring authors to your live event.
For more information or to book an event, contact the Simon & Schuster Speakers Bureau
at 1-866-248-3049 or visit our website at www.simonspeakers.com.

Jacket design by Elena Giavaldi
Jacket photograph © John Parrot/Stocktrek Images/Getty Images

Manufactured in the United States of America

1 3 5 7 9 10 8 6 4 2

Library of Congress Cataloging-in-Publication Data is available.

ISBN 978-1-4767-4856-6
ISBN 978-1-4767-4858-0 (ebook)

To Caroline,
who went with me to the source
of the Potomac and helped me
find the way back home

Who looks at Lee must think of Washington;
In pain must think, and hide the thought,
So deep with grievous meaning it is fraught.
      —Herman Melville, "Lee in the Capitol"

Contents

Contents

PART IV
Postbellum

Maps

Cumberland

Potomac River

Chesapeake & Ohio Canal

South Branch Potomac R.

A L L E G H E N Y   M O U N T A I N S

North Fork Shenandoah R.

Shenandoah R.

South Fork Shenandoah R.

B L U E   R I D G E   M O U N T A I N S

Rapidan River

THE POTOMAC:

The River

GEORGE WASHINGTON

and

ROBERT E. LEE

called home

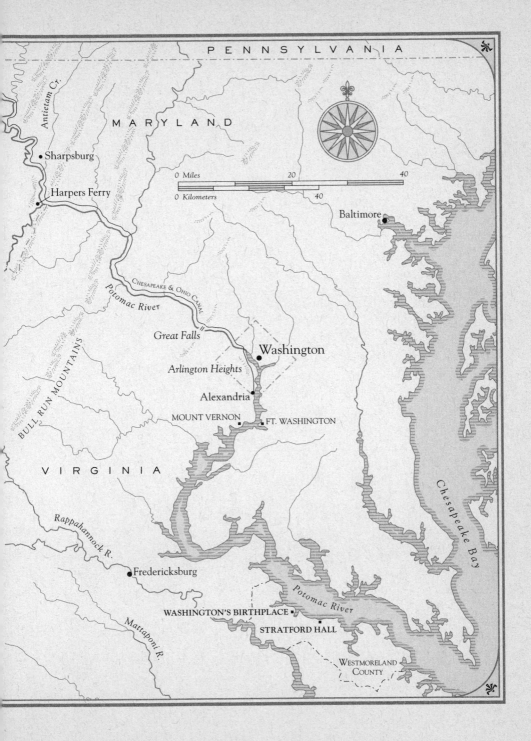

The View

The cadets at West Point might not have nicknamed Robert E. Lee the "Marble Model" had they seen the statue of George Washington in the rotunda in Richmond. Here was a real marble model. On April 23, 1861, as the fifty-four-year-old Lee looked up at the figure, he could see how his fellow Virginian had appeared around the same age. By that time in his life, General Washington had won the Revolutionary War and made the historic decision to surrender power to civilian authority. Now the man who would not be king, as rendered by the sculptor Jean-Antoine Houdon, stood on a pedestal beneath the round skylight crowning Virginia's capitol dome. Under his left hand lay thirteen rods, bound like the thirteen colonies themselves. A sword, no longer needed, dangled to the side. His body, stretching more than six feet from head to heel, faced away from the closed chamber his admirer waited to enter. If the men meeting behind those doors had their way, Lee would pick up the sword, cut the cords tying the rods, and secure Virginia's independence anew.

The delegates to the state convention had requested Lee's attendance at noon on this day. They had recently approved an ordinance removing Virginia from the Union. The vote transformed the Potomac River, whose banks generations of Washingtons and Lees had called home, into a fault line. "Will the present line of separation be the permanent one?" Lee now asked aloud. How often, when back home at dear Arlington House, he had admired the Potomac view: the current whisking past the Virginia hillside; the Washington Monument's unfinished shaft rising on the opposite bank; the columns atop the United States Capitol awaiting their dome in the distance.

Only five days earlier, Lee had crossed the Potomac for a meeting in the federal city. The new Lincoln administration had offered him command of the Union army being raised to crush the insurrection. Unable to imagine fighting against his native state but still unwilling to take sides against the Union George Washington had forged, Lee rejected the offer but did not yet surrender his commission in the army he had served for more than three decades. With his heart as divided as the riverbanks, he traveled back over the Long Bridge to Arlington House. Once behind the mansion's massive columns, he entered a hall lit by the old Mount Vernon lantern and lined with paintings, including the earliest portrait of George Washington. Locked among these relics and others—silver, china, and furniture—that had been a part of his life since marrying the daughter of the first president's adopted son, Lee at last reached his decision. He could see no other path. He would resign from the US Army. Soon he was on to Richmond. En route, crowds swarmed his train at every stop. "Lee, Lee," they chanted until he appeared on the rear platform with his hat tucked under his elbow. Strands of silver softened the dark hair sweeping over his wide forehead. A neat black mustache firmed up his lips. He stood just under six feet. Then, without uttering a word, he bowed and returned to his seat.

Now, once again, Lee heard his name. The double doors partitioning the chamber from the rotunda opened. An escort guided Lee into the old hall Thomas Jefferson had designed. The delegates stood as Lee entered. More than one noted his "manly bearing." He walked almost halfway down the aisle and then stopped, as if torn between the Washington statue behind him and the convention president occupying the rostrum ahead. Everyone agreed Lee belonged somewhere along this line—a link between the past and the future. "In the eyes of the world," one relative said, the wedding thirty years earlier had transformed Lee into "the representative of the family of the founder of American liberty." In requesting Lee's service, President Abraham Lincoln's emissary had appealed to Lee's Washington connections. That the Virginia convention planned to do the same would have surprised no one. The delegates considered their choice of a commander in chief to be as momentous as the Continental Congress's.

Convention president John Janney, a white-haired conservative who had opposed secession before accepting its inevitability, had prepared a formal address suitable to the occasion. He welcomed the new commander in chief of Virginia's armed forces as the heir to "soldiers and sages of by-gone days, who have borne your name, and whose blood now flows in your veins." Two Lees had signed the Declaration of Independence. Another, Lee's father, had served as one of Washington's most trusted lieutenants during the Revolution. Washington himself was a blood relative, albeit a third cousin twice removed. Near Washington's birthplace in Westmoreland County, Virginia, Lee had spent his first years toddling along the Potomac before moving upriver to Alexandria, the town closest to Washington's Mount Vernon plantation. "When the necessity became apparent of having a leader for our forces," said Janney, "all hearts and all eyes, by the impulse of an instinct which is a surer guide than reason itself, turned to the old county of Westmoreland." It was not just the pedigree that persuaded the delegates but also the commensurate talent Lee had shown since his days at West Point. The army's ranking general had proclaimed Lee "the very best soldier I ever saw in the field."

Lee, still standing in the aisle, must have thought about Arlington as Janney explained the convention's expectations. "And now, Virginia having taken her position, as far as the power of this Convention extends, we stand animated by one impulse, governed by one desire and one determination, and that is that she shall be defended; and that no spot of her soil shall be polluted by the foot of an invader." The charge was simple, sweeping, and impossible. Lee already knew he could not protect the home he had left. The view he cherished overlooking the nation's capital would render Arlington indefensible. Federal forces would cross the river, flood up the hillside, and seize the mansion. Unless his wife removed the relics soon, "the Mt. Vernon plate & pictures," as Lee called them, would be lost. Arlington would never be the same.

Yet whatever reservations Lee harbored about the convention's judgment, the delegates harbored no doubts about Lee. "Sir," Janney said toward the end:

> *we have, by this unanimous vote, expressed our convictions that you are, at this day, among the living citizens of Virginia, "first in war." We pray to God most fervently that you may so conduct the operations committed to your charge, that it will soon be said of you, that you are "first in peace," and when that time comes you will have earned the still prouder distinction of being "first in the hearts of your countrymen."*

No one, least of all Lee, could have missed Janney's allusion. Only one man had ever been "first in war, first in peace, and first in the hearts of his countrymen"—George Washington. It had been Lee's father, Henry "Light-Horse Harry" Lee, who coined the phrase in a funeral oration for his old general. So popular had the epitaph become that the words fused the Washington and Lee names long after Harry Lee had drifted into disgrace. As a commentator in Robert E. Lee's hometown newspaper put it, "The fact that these memorable words, as they were addressed and applied by the distinguished President of the Convention, were the outpourings of his Father's heart . . . must have been peculiarly touching and solemnizing to the newly appointed generalissimo." To be first in war, first in peace, and first in the hearts of his countrymen would make Robert E. Lee nothing short of George Washington.

What else Harry Lee said has been less remembered. At its climax, his funeral oration summoned Washington's spirit from the grave. "Methinks I see his august image, and hear falling from his venerable lips these deep sinking words." In Harry Lee's telling, Washington's ghost warned future generations to resist internal divisions.

Thus will you give immortality to that union, which was the constant object of my terrestrial labours; thus will you preserve undisturbed to the latest posterity, the felicity of a people to me most dear, and thus will you supply (if my happiness is now aught to you) the only vacancy in the round of pure bliss high Heaven bestows.

Speaking with one voice, Washington's ghost and Harry Lee had given future generations of Americans their marching orders. Providence, it seemed, could not have positioned Robert E. Lee any better to answer these pleas for union. But Lee made a different decision. He turned down the Union command. He cast his fortune south of the Potomac, and his legacy has divided Americans ever since.

On one side, southern traditionalists have claimed that the decision transformed Robert E. Lee into the "second coming" of George Washington. Even if the funeral oration suggested otherwise, rebellion against the Union and loyalty to Washington's memory went hand in hand. Had not Washington led a rebellion against union with the British? The comparisons began as soon as Lee made his choice. Janney prayed for a day when Lee would share the epitaph his father had given Washington. Lee's own eulogists made it so. An early biographer who had served on Lee's staff during the war described his chief as "one whom, like Washington, we may designate as 'first in war, first in peace, and first in the hearts of his countrymen.'" True, unlike Washington, Lee lost his revolution, but his demeanor in defeat made him all the more noble. "He was," according to a frequently quoted speech, "Washington without his reward." After seeing "two splendid equestrian statues" of George Washington and Robert E. Lee, Lee's nephew ventured, "Riding side by side in calm majesty, they are henceforth contemporaries in all the ages to come." Indeed, the two horsemen traveled together into the twentieth century. Douglas Southall Freeman, who won the 1935 and 1958 Pulitzer Prizes for biographies of Lee and Washington, concluded that only "modesty" prevented Lee himself "from drawing the very obvious analogy between his situation and that of Washington."

On the other side of the debate, writers have grumbled that such conclusions have twisted the pro-Union exhortations of the ghost Lee's father exhumed. How can Lee ride off into history with Washington after fighting to destroy the first president's "terrestrial labours"? The question confounded many even during Lee's time. After the Union army seized Arlington in the war's early days, a British correspondent visiting the home wondered how a rebel general could have lived among Washington's relics and be the son-in-law of Washington's adopted child. "Follow the train of thought," the correspondent wrote, "and you may become as perplexed as I am in reference to the possible status of the pater patriae." Modern-day debunkers chasing this train of thought have set out to detach Lee's car from Washington's by dismissing the links between the two men as "minutiae" cobbled together by Confederate apologists. A recent biographer mocks writers who "envision a mystical bond between" Washington and Lee.

So once more, Lee is trapped in the middle. More than a century and a half after secession forced him to choose sides, he has become a pawn in another conflict between two camps conceding no common ground. Either Lee's name must be united with Washington's, or it must be banished from all associations. Something has been lost in this polarization, and that something is the truth. The connections between Washington and Lee are neither mystic nor manufactured. Lee was not the second coming of Washington, but he might have been had he chosen differently. As Washington was the man who would not be king, Lee was the man who would not be Washington. The story that emerges when viewed in this light is more complicated, more tragic, and more illuminating. More complicated because the unresolved question of slavery—the driver of disunion—was among the personal legacies that Lee inherited from Washington. More tragic because the Civil War tore apart the bonds that connected Lee to Washington in wrenching ways that no one could have anticipated. More illuminating because the battle that raged over Washington's legacy shaped the nation that America has become.

The view from Arlington House today looks very different. The mansion once filled with Washington heirlooms has become the Robert E. Lee Memorial. Where trees once shaded the hillside, the sun now reflects off white tombstones lining the grass. A granite bridge guides the eye across the river to the city of Washington. In the foreground, the marble columns of the Lincoln Memorial, honoring the man who saved Washington's Union, anchor an axis that extends eastward: first toward the towering Washington Monument and then toward the Capitol dome, clad in iron and crowned by the Statue of Freedom. As the eye follows this axis, the mind wants to believe that harmony governs history. But this is Arlington's secret: the line connecting Lincoln to Washington and Freedom appears so straight because the house lies not upon it. Lee stares down from the flank, a river away on a path not taken.

PART I

★

Antebellum

CHAPTER ONE

Foundering Father

If an eighteen-year-old George Washington had gotten his way, there would have been no Robert E. Lee. Lee would never have married the daughter of Washington's adopted son, never have stared up at Washington's marble statue, and never have gone to war against Washington's Union. These events, of course, all lay in the unknowable future for Washington circa 1750. All he knew then was that he loved a girl who did not love him in return. He could not have imagined who her grandson might one day be.

History shines little light on the infatuation that stirred in Washington's adolescent mind. Only fragments of letters illuminate the tale. Apparently, even the mere sight of other women inflamed the crush. Once, while in the company of "a very agreeable young lady," Washington complained that her appearance revived his "former passion" for the "Low Land Beauty." How he longed, he said, to bury that "troublesome passion in the grave of oblivion." Legend holds that this lowland beauty was a blue-eyed blonde named Lucy Grymes. Though not all historians agree, Washington's moniker fits Lucy's description. She hailed from Virginia's lowlands, and her many suitors testified to her beauty. The evidence later persuaded her most famous grandson, Robert E. Lee. "I believe," he wrote, "there are grounds for the belief that Genl Washington in early life was pleased with the beauty." Whatever Washington's true interest, the match was not to be. In 1753, Lucy married a lawyer named Henry Lee II.

The Man Who Would Not Be Washington

That a country lawyer could snag the belle of the ball over the future Father of His Country might seem surprising until one considers that Washington at the time could not even present himself as master of his own home. In fact, a year earlier, the Lee family had come into possession of something else Washington coveted: the Potomac property known as Mount Vernon. When owner Lawrence Washington died in 1752, he left the estate first to his widow, Anne, and then upon her death to his favorite half brother, George Washington. Anne, as it turned out, chose not to dally at Mount Vernon. Within a year, she married one of Henry Lee II's cousins, George Lee. Choosing to live elsewhere, the new couple leased Mount Vernon to the man they knew would inherit it anyway. For more than six years, George Washington lived as a tenant of the Lee family. Not until Anne Lee died in 1761 did Washington take full ownership of Mount Vernon.

While Washington's greatness still lay in the future, the Lees had already established themselves as one of Virginia's finest families. Henry Lee II's great-grandfather Richard "The Emigrant" had arrived in Jamestown around 1640 as a clerk and died a quarter century later as a veritable baron, owning numerous African slaves and fifteen thousand acres of land, much of it on the Tidewater tract called the Northern Neck between the Potomac and Rappahannock Rivers. Richard Lee had gambled by moving up the Chesapeake Bay from the colony's first and more fashionable settlements around Jamestown to this still sparsely populated northern frontier. As late as 1653, the Potomac backlands contained only about a thousand colonists, but soon great houses would rise across the region.

On the fossil-rich white cliffs overlooking the river in Westmoreland County, Henry Lee II's uncle Thomas Lee built an imposing brick mansion called Stratford Hall. The commanding spot befitted the fortune he had made as a royal naval inspector on the river and as a land agent in the surrounding regions. As Thomas Lee explored the Potomac, he became convinced that it represented a water highway to the vast lands beyond the Appalachian Mountains. In 1744, he negotiated an Indian treaty opening the Ohio country for white settlement and then united fellow land speculators in a venture called the Ohio Company. When Thomas Lee died in 1750, Lawrence Washington took over as president of the company. For all that he had accomplished during his life, Thomas Lee achieved his greatest distinction posthumously: two of his sons, Richard Henry Lee and Francis Lightfoot Lee, would sign the Declaration of Independence.

As Thomas Lee's nephew, Henry Lee II would have disappeared under the shadow of his celebrated cousins if not for his marriage to beautiful Lucy. The couple settled not far downriver from Mount Vernon. In 1756, they named their first son Henry Lee III. A half century later, this boy, known as Harry, would father the most famous rebel general of the Civil War. But first he fought his own revolution. He would owe his success to a surprising benefactor: his father's old romantic rival, George Washington.

It was said that Harry Lee came "out of his mother's womb a soldier." Perhaps part of Washington still wished he had placed him there. More likely, Washington simply possessed avuncular feelings for the young neighbor who grew up calling Mount Vernon's mistress "Aunt Martha." Washington had married the rich widow Martha Dandridge Custis a few years after Harry's birth. Though Martha brought two children from her previous marriage to Mount Vernon, she never gave the Father of His Country a biological child of his own, a fact Washington would later use to quiet any talk of an American monarchy. The man who would not be king had no lineal heirs.

To fill the void, Washington seemed always on the lookout for the son he would never have. While commanding the Continental Army, he forged closer bonds with young officers than with his fellow generals. His military family included the brilliant Caribbean immigrant Alexander Hamilton, the principled South Carolinian John Laurens, and the idealistic Marquis de Lafayette of France. None of these aides had even been born when, in 1754, Washington fought the first battles of the French and Indian War while commanding militia loyal to the

British crown. But what the aides lacked in experience, they more than compensated for with vigor and intelligence. Washington especially prized their literary talents, which he needed to avoid drowning in the never-ending stream of correspondence that flowed into his camp.

Harry Lee fit the mold of a Washington protégé perfectly. As a student at Princeton (then the College of New Jersey), he earned accolades for his readings and literary translations. A family friend predicted he "will be one of the first fellows in this country." Graduating in 1773, he shelved plans to study law in London as the chasm between the mother country and the colonies widened. Soon from Williamsburg and Philadelphia came reports of his kinsmen agitating for independence. On June 1, 1776, at the Second Continental Congress, Richard Henry Lee proposed before anyone else, "That these United Colonies are, and of a right ought to be, free and independent states." Leaping to second the motion, Massachusetts delegate John Adams later saluted the Lees as a "band of brothers . . . in the defence of their country."

As these events transpired, Harry Lee traded his dream of a degree in the law for a commission as a captain in the dragoons. Swift and agile, these horsemen could gather forage, conduct reconnaissance, and carry out raids where infantry dared not go. Harry Lee made the transition from manor life to camp life seamlessly. By the fall of 1777, his signature had emerged as a familiar line at the bottom of intelligence reports addressed to Washington. He indulged the general's taste for tales from deserters and double agents. That winter, during one of his expeditions, a large British force surprised and surrounded him at the Spread Eagle Tavern near Valley Forge. With only a small force, Harry could not even guard all the tavern's windows. "The contest was very warm," he reported. "The British dragoons trusting to their vast superiority in number, attempted to force their way into the house." Trickery offered the sole hope. "Fire away, men," Harry blustered. "Here comes our infantry; we will have them all." Although he knew no reinforcements were on the way, he also knew his enemies could not be so sure. Taking no risk, the British retreated. Outgunned but not outsmarted, Harry Lee had prevailed.

Washington sent his personal congratulations. The triumph, small as it was, deepened his respect for the young Lee. "I needed no fresh proof of your merit," he wrote. "I waited only for the proper time and season to shew it—these I hope are not far off." As promised, the time and season soon arrived. In March, Harry Lee received an invitation to join Washington's military family. The offer was tempting for an ambitious twenty-two-year-old. Proximity to power meant power itself. As someone intent on martial fame, however, Harry could not stomach switching from a field officer engaged in battle to a staff officer engaged in correspondence. "To have possessed a post about your Excellency's person is certainly the first recommendation I can bear to posterity," he acknowledged in an artful yet awkward response declining the offer. A few days later, still determined to better employ the young Lee's "exemplary zeal, prudence and bravery," Washington settled on a more suitable promotion. He recommended—and Congress approved—making Harry Lee a major in "command of two troops of Horse," which together would "act as an independent partisan Corps."

The hundred horsemen in the new corps would operate outside the normal chain of command. The arrangement afforded Harry Lee an aura of autonomy that more experienced officers could only envy, and envy him they did. Rumors spread that the young Virginian owed his success more to the blood he shared with members of Congress than to the blood he risked on the battlefield. As complaints trickled into headquarters, Washington worried that others were "extremely jealous of the superior advantages and priviledges which Major Lee has somehow or other obtained." For Harry, there was no mystery. It was a matter of merit. As Washington had told Congress, "Capt. Lees genius peculiarly adapts him to a command of this nature."

Peculiar, indeed. Harry Lee possessed a mix of qualities not usually found in one person. Though tanned from his time in the field, his skin was "as fair as a lily." His blue eyes scanned the battlefield beneath arched brows. Though not large in stature, he commanded respect in the saddle. One observer fancied him a "little hero." Though a meticulous planner, he was quick in action. Though a stern disciplinarian, he showed devotion to his men. In their eyes and to the world, he became known as "Light-Horse Harry" Lee.

In 1779, the corps conducted a surprise attack against the British outpost at Paulus Hook, New Jersey. Approaching under the cover of night, Harry Lee threatened to execute any of his soldiers who "may violate in the slightest degree the silence he has ordered to be observed." The soldiers did not dare defy him. Just recently he had sentenced a deserter among them to be decapitated despite Washington's decrying the "inhumanity." Now, as the men charged through the final defensive ditch, discipline held. With their bayonets fixed, the attackers achieved complete surprise. The raid yielded more than 150 prisoners. Washington proclaimed it a "brilliant transaction." Not all of Harry Lee's fellow officers were so pleased. Some accused him of breaking the chain of command. A court-martial ensued. Enraged, the young officer could see no middle course between accepting dishonor and resigning. That he would even consider such extremes revealed a rashness that worried Washington. "I should be sorry you would suffer your sensibility to betray you into an error which on reflexion you would condemn," the general wrote. In the end, Harry received vindication three times over. The court-martial cleared him of the charges, Congress struck a gold medal in his honor, and Washington gave him permission to label their letters "private" so that other officers would not read their correspondence. The two had sealed a bond that would last for life.

Toward the end of the war, Washington sent "Lee's Legion," which now included infantry, to the conflict's southern theater, where the British had tightened their grip. Harry persuaded the American theater commander, Major General Nathanael Greene, to lead an offensive into South Carolina. It would prove a turning point. With Greene moving farther south, his British counterpart, General Charles Cornwallis, decided to head north to Virginia. That path would eventually pen the British into a place called Yorktown. There, in October 1781, Harry Lee watched the British surrender to a combined American-French force with Washington at its head. "The British army," Harry

Lee remembered many years later, "marched out of its lines with colors cased, and drums beating. . . . Certainly no spectacle could be more impressive."

Though another two years would pass before the signing of a peace treaty, Harry Lee chose not to remain in the field with his troops. A few months after Yorktown, he headed home. His youngest son, Robert, would later blame this shameful abdication on "broken health," which "depressed his spirits." Probably the reverse was true. Harry Lee's problems started in his head and spread from there. While deflecting General Greene's praise for his contributions to the overall strategy, he stewed over perceived slights in individual battle reports. More troubling were the old accusations that his success resulted from family connections instead of from individual merit. By early 1782, Harry Lee could no longer bear, as he put it, "the indifference with which my efforts to advance the cause of my country is considered by my friends . . . and my consciousness that it is not in my power to efface the disagreeable impression." Like Washington, Greene feared the young man would make an impetuous decision. "I believe few officers, either in America or Europe, are held in so high a point of estimation as you are," Greene wrote. "Envy is the best evidence in the world of great merit."

With depression clouding his mind, Harry Lee refused to see reason. His self-control disappeared in a storm of self-pity. "I am candid to acknowledge my imbecility of mind, and hope time and absence may alter my feelings: at present my fervent wish is for the most hidden obscurity," he wrote in a letter explaining his decision to leave the army. "I wish I could bend my mind to other decisions. I have tried much, but the sores of my wounds are only irritated afresh by such efforts. My poor soldiers are dear to me, most dear. I pray your patronage to them if I must part." And part he did.

At twenty-six years old, Harry Lee had fixed a new course that would lead to insolvency and ignominy. The dashing horseman, who had outmaneuvered his enemies on the battlefield, became a hopeless specula-tor, who bet his fortune on land and lost. The officer who had brought discipline to the ranks could apply none to himself. The prodigy, whose success had come so early and easily, degenerated into a pathetic per-sonification of failure. Of all the cruel reversals that visited Harry in this second act, the cruelest was Washington's unintentional role in the tragedy. The friendship that fueled Harry Lee's rise during the Revo-lution now hastened his demise. The more closely he followed Wash-ington, the more he courted misfortune.

As with so much in Harry's life, the trouble began on the Potomac. There was no greater apostle for the river's possibilities than George Washington. The river had enchanted Washington since boyhood. At age sixteen, he joined a surveying expedition that tramped over the mountains to the river's upper stretches. The journey took him over "the worst road that ever was trod by man or beast" into the dark woods where Indians performed the "war daunce" and "wild turkies" roamed. Washington's career started here, near where the Potomac begins, and their two paths never diverged. Like Thomas Lee, Wash-ington believed the Potomac, which flows eastward down the Appala-chians to the Chesapeake Bay, would serve as an artery for traders and settlers. Rather than divide north and south, the river would connect east and west.

Below present-day Washington, DC, the wide river that runs past Mount Vernon's bluff invites such optimism. But above the capital, this gentle tidal scene meets the stronger rock of the piedmont, a land-scape that has resisted change for millions of years. Across this time warp, the Potomac tumbles forty feet down in just two hundred yards. For the Potomac to connect east and west as Washington envisioned, a canal would have to bypass these rocky rapids known as Great Falls. After the Revolution, Washington was named president of a company that Maryland and Virginia incorporated to carry out the necessary improvements. He had "no doubt" that the project would succeed and "bring the Atlantic States & the Western Territory into close connex-ion, & be productive of very extensive commercial & political consequences." The confidence was contagious. One guest at Mount Vernon remembered "hearing little else for two days from the persuasive tongue of this great man" and left being "completely infected . . . with the canal mania." In 1786, Washington informed Harry Lee, "This business is progressing in a manner that exceeds our most sanguine expectations. Difficulties vanish as we proceed."

Harry Lee bought more than the rhetoric. In 1788, he purchased five hundred acres of land bordering Great Falls. If the river improvements succeeded—and Washington had said they would—the property's value would skyrocket. Harry imagined a bustling town with wharves and warehouses ready to serve the endless river traffic sure to follow. "The advantages," as he saw them, "infinitely exceed that of any spot of ground in the U. States." Already sounding like a swindler, he convinced his fellow Princeton graduate James Madison to join the venture. "I consider myself bound to let you have a part of the bargain with me." If Madison had any doubts about the deal, Washington could put them to rest. "No man more highly estimates it than General Washington who is one of the best judges of property & is intimately acquainted with the place."

The deal, however, was not as clear-cut as Harry claimed. Instead of dipping his toe, he had jumped into the deep end without a worry as to whether he could stay afloat. The audacity of his purchase surprised even the company's biggest backer. Washington advised Madison that the land "opens a field almost too extensive for imagination" but warned that "the profits . . . cannot be immediate." Not immediate became not ever. Legal disputes, fund-raising deficits, and engineering difficulties ensnared the project. The great metropolis never amounted to more than a handful of buildings. Before the reality of it all set in, Harry Lee named the town after his wife, Matilda. She was his second cousin, the granddaughter of that early prophet of the Potomac, Thomas Lee. When Harry gained her hand in 1782, he also gained possession of the family's iconic home at Stratford. It was a sad irony, then, that to pay off the debts for his misguided gambles on the Potomac, Harry Lee began selling off the labors of Thomas Lee's life. Piece by piece, he dismantled Stratford Hall. Matilda's health disappeared with her estate. As she lay dying in 1790, she attempted to save what was left—just over half of the 6,595 acres—by placing the property in a trust for their oldest son.

Washington's dreams for the Potomac had sucked Harry Lee into a whirlpool of debt. Excuses he had, but he could not talk his way out of the red. That he tried only tarred his reputation more. Even Washington could not escape the swindling. "Nothing but the untoward & unexpected course of fiscal concerns in this country could have produced delay in my payment of your debt," Harry assured Washington in early 1798. "I am pained in a great degree to hear of any inconvenience accruing to you." Nonetheless, a year later the sum remained unpaid. Harry vowed to right his wrongs. "I shall never recede from my exertions till I do accomplish the end, for no event of my life has given me more anguish," he promised in May 1799. But time was running short, and when George Washington died later that year, Harry Lee was still in his debt.

Harry Lee's political fortunes turned out much the same. Like many veterans of the Continental Army, he once again marched under Washington's banner during the fierce political struggles that shaped the early republic. The war veterans had seen firsthand that the survival of liberty depended on the strength of the union between the states. They worried that the Articles of Confederation adopted during the war could not hold. "The period seems to be fast approaching when the people of these U. States must determine to establish a permanent capable government or submit to the horrors of anarchy and licentiousness," Harry wrote Washington on September 8, 1786.

As Harry penned those words, Washington pressed for news from a convention on interstate commerce in Annapolis. The idea for the convention had been hatched at Mount Vernon the previous year during a summit regarding access to the Potomac River. Commissioners from Maryland and Virginia had proposed including more states in their negotiations. At Annapolis, as Washington would soon learn, talks among delegates from five states had yielded a similar result: a call for another follow-up meeting, this one to take place in Philadelphia the next year and include even more states. With George Washington presiding, it would be this convention that produced the Constitution. Washington's beloved Potomac had carried the country on the course to a more perfect union.

Whether the new document enhancing federal power would become the law of the land would depend on how each state voted at its own convention. Harry Lee championed the cause at Virginia's convention in 1788. The Constitution, he told his fellow delegates, "is now submitted to the people of Virginia. If we do not adopt it, it will be always null and void as to us." Then he explained why fighting beside Washington had convinced him that Virginians should embrace the document.

> *The people of America, Sir, are one people. I love the people of the North, not because they have adopted the Constitution; but, because I fought with them as my countrymen, and because I consider them as such. Does it follow from hence, that I have forgotten my attachment to my native State? In all local matters I shall be a Virginian: In those of a general nature, I shall not forget that I am an American.*

In the end, the "ayes" barely edged out the "noes." For the next seven decades, Virginia would submit to the Constitution. Harry next turned his persuasive powers toward recruiting the only conceivable candidate for president. "Without you," he told Washington, "the govt can have but little chance of success."

Yet no sooner had Washington sworn to "preserve, protect, and defend the Constitution" than he learned that Harry Lee had changed his opinion about the charter. Harry, according to a report that reached Washington's desk, was "one of the number" of Virginians "changing their sentiments, from a conviction of the impracticability of Union with States, whose interests are so dissimilar to those of Virginia." The tensions surfaced during the debate over Treasury Secretary Alexander Hamilton's fiscal reforms, which called for the federal government to assume the debts the states had accumulated during the war. James Madison, among other prominent Virginians, broke with the administration over the policy. His followers would become known as Republicans; Hamilton's would become known as Federalists. Harry Lee joined Madison in opposing the assumption scheme but only after trying to profit off insider information. He wanted to know whether the treasury secretary expected securities to rise in value. Hamilton did not indulge the request, which even Harry conceded might "be improper." Whether based on conviction or convenience, Harry's conversion to antifederalism paid dividends. In 1791, Harry Lee became governor of Virginia.

Had Harry remained on the path of Republicanism, his story might have reached a happier ending. But like the prodigal son, he veered back in the other direction and returned to Washington's camp as a committed Federalist. The transition was not hard to make. His friendship with the president had remained close even as their politics had drifted apart, and Harry harbored a reflexive dislike for the high priest of Republicanism, Thomas Jefferson. Moreover, a brewing rebellion on the Pennsylvania frontier reminded Harry of the dangers of disunion—the very reason he had supported the Constitution in the first place. The so-called Whiskey Rebellion began in 1794, when westerners revolted against the administration's excise tax on their favorite drink. With federal authority collapsing along the frontier, Harry shared Washington's fear that the revolt represented a "diabolical" plot "to destroy the best fabric of human government and happiness, that has ever been presented for the acceptance of mankind."

Even before the rebellion, Harry had his heart set on restarting his military career. In 1792, Washington had passed him over for command of a western army. To his cabinet, the president had confided that Harry Lee had "more resource" than any other candidate, but, alas, "no economy." In desperation, Harry considered going abroad to join the revolutionary struggle in France until Washington convinced him to avoid that "paroxysm of disorder." So when Washington called out the militia in the summer of 1794, he could not have been surprised to see a letter from his old friend. "The awful occasion demands united efforts," Harry wrote. "I beg leave to offer to you my services in any way or station you may deem them proper." Though Washington himself accompanied the army part of the way west, he entrusted Harry with command. Facing overwhelming federal force, the revolt quickly fizzled.

As opposition to federal authority on the frontier collapsed, opposition to Harry Lee back home mounted. Instead of returning to a hero's welcome in Virginia, he found himself, as he put it, "an object of the most virulent enmity." The now ex-governor was paranoid but not wrong. The politics of Virginia were no longer the politics of Washington. While Harry had realigned himself with the administration, the Old Dominion had swung the other way. Concerns about the growing reach of federal power had shifted loyalties from Washington's Mount Vernon to Jefferson's Monticello. And where Virginia had gone, the rest of the country would soon follow. The election of 1800 handed Thomas Jefferson the White House, swept the aging Federalists from power, and all but ended Harry Lee's public career.

Washington did not live to see what became known as the Revolution of 1800. He died a few weeks before the turn of the century. The occasion of his death gave Harry, then serving his one and only term in the House of Representatives, his last and most lasting glory: the honor of delivering Congress's official eulogy. On December 26 at Philadelphia's German Lutheran Church, he uttered the words that would forever connect his name to Washington's. As Henry "Light-Horse Harry" Lee dismounted the pulpit, he bade farewell to his hero and to any realistic hope for future success.

Failure after failure followed. Harry compounded the tragedy by dragging down Ann Hill Carter, his second wife. The two had married during his time as governor. Washington had congratulated his friend for having "exchanged the rugged & dangerous field of Mars, for the soft and pleasurable bed of Venus." Ann's father, the wealthy Charles Carter, had discouraged the match. His precious dark-haired daughter deserved better. But her heart was as fixed as the governor's was fickle. Harry wooed her only after his first choice for a second wife had spurned his advances. Ann warned the other woman, "Stop, stop . . . you do not know what you are throwing away." Just twenty years old, Ann soon realized that it was she who had thrown something away: the financial security and comforts that had shielded her childhood. As a relative later told the story, "One fortnight was her dream of happiness from which she awoke to a life of misery." By the time Charles Carter died in 1806, Harry could no longer afford to send a proper coach to drive Ann home from the funeral. With no carriage top to shield her from the elements, Ann, then pregnant with what would be her fourth surviving child, rode home to Stratford Hall. Sick and stripped of all illusions, she brought Robert E. Lee into the world on January 19, 1807.

Harry did not live with his new child for long. Instead, his debts landed him in prison. No longer a congressman, no longer a respected voice in the Tidewater, no longer even a free man, Harry's thoughts returned to the Revolution, that grand stage he had exited too soon. He produced a history of the war's southern theater. "Colonel Lee," a book reviewer noted, "has acquired for himself the reputation of an accurate observer and spirited writer, in addition to that which he had before merited, of a brave soldier." Leaving prison in 1810, he returned to Stratford. But Henry Lee IV, the oldest surviving son of his late first wife, had reached his majority, and the great house was now his. The town of Alexandria offered a refuge, and so the Lees packed their belongings and headed upriver. While in prison, Harry had assured his young wife that he would live out his days by her side, but now she knew better than to bank on her husband's promises.

By 1812, Harry Lee had returned to jail, this time by choice. A sharply split Congress had declared war against Britain. Republicans generally supported the decision; Federalists opposed it. In Baltimore, the streets belonged to the Republicans. When a Federalist newspaper in the city editorialized against the war, a mob demanded that the publishers pay for their ink with blood. Two decades earlier, such lawlessness had led Harry back to Washington's side during the Whiskey Rebellion. Now, for reasons unclear, it led him to Baltimore, where he holed up in a house with friends of the paper. Outside, the crowd swelled. City officials told the dissidents that their safety required moving to a nearby jail. The publisher protested, but Harry, who by virtue of his military experience had taken command, overrode the objections. On July 28, he led his followers into prison. As darkness descended, the guards defending the jailhouse melted away into the mob. The prison doors were flung open. Harry and his fellow dissidents extinguished the candles. Perhaps they could escape in the confusion. Some succeeded, but Harry Lee was too famous. The mob threw him down the jailhouse steps. Blows rained down on his body. Hands armed with knives jabbed at his face. As he lay helpless, the assailants dripped hot candle grease into the eyes that once looked up to Washington as a neighbor, as a general, as a president, and as a friend.

Somehow Harry returned to Alexandria alive. His vision slowly recovered, but his scars made him a sad sight for others to behold. Still in debt and now in chronic pain, he once again longed for a life of obscurity. The clear waters of the Caribbean called. To that end, in the summer of 1813, he sailed down the river of his ruin, never to see its banks again. The voyage would have given his weary eyes one last glimpse of Mount Vernon resting high above the Potomac. The image was fleeting but not forgotten.

CHAPTER TWO

A Potomac Son

The summer after Harry Lee sailed down the Potomac, a naval squadron flying the Union Jack headed upriver. Fort Washington on the Maryland bank opposite Mount Vernon had fallen.* The Americans guarding the position had chosen to blow up their own magazine for reasons no one could quite understand. Only diplomacy could save poor Alexandria from the British now. On the morning of August 29, 1814, the town faced a fearsome sight: two frigates, two rocket ships, two bomb ships, and a schooner formed a battle line stretching from one end of town to the other. Confronting more than a hundred guns, Alexandria's leaders realized their homes could be "laid in ashes in a few minutes." Any doubts about the enemy's willingness to open fire had disappeared days earlier when flames from Washington, DC, had illuminated the night sky. The British soldiers had torched the capital's public buildings. If Alexandria did not surrender, its rows of redbrick buildings would share the fate of the White House and Capitol.

Alexandria's Common Council had no choice but to accept humiliating terms of surrender. Before sailing away, the British loot grew to include ships, flour, tobacco, cotton, wine, and sugar. The invaders also stole what Alexandria's more than seven thousand residents held most dear: their pride. Alexandria was not just any Potomac port; it was General George Washington's hometown. Back in 1749, Washington

*At the time, Fort Washington was often called Fort Warburton.

helped lay out the town's first lots. Many years later, when Congress gave the president authority to draw the four ten-mile boundary lines forming the new diamond-shaped District of Columbia, Washington carefully tucked Alexandria into the bottom corner. No longer part of Virginia, Alexandria owed its prosperity to its position just below the falls of Washington's favorite river. Wagons from the west brought wheat to the wharves. Tobacco from the Tidewater filled the markets. By 1814, the wealth from this trade had filled Washington's grid with taverns and shops. Now British boots had defiled the streets. Alexandria had surrendered without a fight. "Thanks be to Almighty God that this degraded town no longer forms a part of the state of Virginia!" a Richmond newspaper editorialized. "We would scorn to live in the same State with men who would stoop to kiss the feet of a British officer."

The British admiral who led the attack on the nation's capital confessed that his success owed as much to who had not been present as to who was. "If General Washington had been president we should never have thought of coming here," he said. The family that Harry Lee left behind in Alexandria surely would have agreed.

Robert Edward Lee was seven years old when the War of 1812 humiliated Alexandria. Where exactly he spent the occupation, like so much else about his childhood, is unknown. Perhaps his family fled town; perhaps they huddled at what passed for home at 607 Oronoco Street, the redbrick house that a distant cousin had lent. Harry Lee had abandoned the five surviving children from his second marriage not only to the whims of war but also to the uncertainty of sleeping under roofs not their own. Forced to raise the brood alone, Ann Carter Lee had accepted more burdens than her body could bear. Time would turn her into an invalid.

That the younger children could hardly remember their father made the oldest brother, Charles Carter Lee, known as Carter, cherish his memories all the more. He could remember Harry sharing old letters from George Washington and other heroes of the Revolution. "I have read in their own manuscripts, on the paper touched and folded by their hallowed hands, their public and private communications, all breathing the ardor of patriotism and the counsels of wisdom." Carter clung to these pages for the rest of his life, as if revisiting nursery rhymes tucked into the first folds of the mind. The stories learned at childhood, he explained, "become entwined with ourselves and mingled with our self-esteem." Family history was American history. "It would but be mingling the flow of filial affection and patriotic feeling were I to run over our toils and our triumphs from the monumental heights around Boston to the unmarked battle fields of Georgia; for either by his sword or his pen, the memory of my father is connected with them all."

From the Caribbean, Harry sent Carter new letters filled with platitudes and advice he hoped would trickle down to Carter's younger brother, Sydney Smith Lee, known as Smith, and then to his youngest brother, Robert. "If he is rightly assisted & guided in his education," Harry wrote of Carter, "he will benefit Smith & Robert greatly." Some of these letters disappeared at sea, only to surface after the Lee boys had grown. Nevertheless, their contents offer a glimpse of the lessons Harry Lee wished to convey. "Dwell on the virtues, and imitate, as far as lies in your power, the great and good men whom history presents to our view," Harry advised. "Read therefore the best poets, the best orators, and the best historians."

Not surprisingly, Harry Lee hoped that the man he eulogized as first in war and first in peace would remain first in the hearts of the next generation. Throughout his troubles, Harry remained an apostle for Washington's glory. He allowed others to reprint the funeral oration at no cost despite desperately needing the money. He once urged Congress to appropriate funds for a Washington mausoleum, which "will impress a sublime awe" in future generations. "We are deeply interested in holding" up Washington's virtues "as illustrious models to our sons," he explained. He recommended his own sons read "Washington's official letters wherein the just good honorable man is plainly to be seen even by a young reader." The boys, Harry wrote, should train themselves to rise before the sun because "the great American soldier and statesman . . . told me himself, that had he not happily been from early life accustomed to rise early, he could never have executed the duty which devolved on him in the course of life." Regarding the vices that had ruined his own life, Harry instructed Carter, "Avoid debt, the sink of mental power and the subversion of independence, which draws into debasement even virtue, in appearance certainly, if not in reality. 'A man ought not only to be virtuous in reality, but he must also always appear so'; thus said to me the great Washington." While this balance had eluded Harry Lee, he hoped his sons might find it in Washington's example.

In writing about Washington's character, Harry stumbled on deep revelations about his own. In some ways, Washington's and Harry's personalities had been similar. Harry described Washington as "ardent" and "impetuous by nature." But where equally fiery emotions melted away Harry's public image and left him pleading "imbecility of mind," Washington somehow contained "his passions" with "reason." The secret, in Harry's opinion, was Washington's "habitual self-control." Washington could "repress his inclinations whenever his judgment forbade their indulgence." By extolling Washington's self-control, Harry pinpointed the virtue whose absence most explained his own disgrace. With self-control, Washington could hold together his passions as he held together a starving army and thirteen colonies. Without self-control, Harry succumbed to his worst impulses: speculating, swindling, and self-pitying. His mind came apart. Harry's sons would wonder which of these two courses their own lives would follow. "The rocks on which I am in the greatest danger of splitting a disposition [are] to aim too high, or at too much," Carter wrote. "It was this that ruined my great father in dispersing his mighty powers."

No one better understood Harry Lee's vices than his second wife, and she labored to offset them with virtues in her children. Ann taught her sons the "economy" that Washington once faulted their father for lacking. Every child might want something different for dinner—veal for the brothers, fowl for one sister, and fruit for another—but Ann refused to cater to individual tastes. "As there is to be but one dish, all cannot be pleased," she said. She urged her children to find "that noble independence of spirit, which would cause you to blush at incurring an expense, you could not in justice to your family afford." She did not hide the reality of their finances. "We cannot borrow money, because we cannot repay it." Unlike her husband, she dismissed quick fixes. She considered even friendly wagers as "wages of iniquity," which her children must avoid at all cost. "You must repel every evil and allow yourself to indulge in such habits only as are consistent with religion and morality," she wrote one son. "Oh that I could impart to you the knowledge gained from the experience of . . . years, then would you be convinced of the vanity of every pursuit not under the control of the most inflexible virtue." When Ann detected a slight stubbornness in young Robert, she wrote for advice to her sister, who recommended a remedy: "Whip and pray, and pray and whip."

Necessity was an even sterner teacher, driving out whatever vanity Ann could not exorcise. In 1818, letters arrived dashing whatever faint hopes the family held for Harry Lee's return. The old man had died on Cumberland Island, Georgia, while attempting to come home. By this time, Carter Lee had enrolled at Harvard, and Smith Lee would soon join the navy. Young Robert would have to assume the role of man of the house. He later recalled that before he progressed far enough in school to read the great poets, he had already become his mother's "outdoor agent & confidential messenger." This is not to say that Robert's childhood passed without pleasure. There were swims in the Potomac, romps around a yard filled with white-flowering snowball trees, and days spent hunting. But these fleeting scenes are not the dominant images of Robert's boyhood. Contemporaries described him as anything but a boy, as a "devoted daughter" nursing his mother, as a "housekeeper" doing the marketing, as "an old man" looking after his mother's finances and cheering her spirits.

In a sense, Robert gave up the indulgences of boyhood because his father turned down the responsibilities of manhood. "At the hour when the other school-boys went to play, he hurried home to order his mother's drive, and would then be seen carrying her in his arms to the carriage, and arranging her cushions with the gentleness of an experienced nurse," a family friend turned biographer wrote. During these rides, the boy would protect his mother from the elements and the cold. "He would pull from his pocket a great jack-knife and newspaper, and make her laugh with his efforts to improvise curtains, and shut out the intrusive wind which whistled through the crevices of the old family-coach." When her spirits sagged, he concocted amusements. "With the gravity of an old man," Robert would warn "that, unless she was cheerful, the drive would not benefit her." The moments they shared were for her pleasure, not his.

Thus, from an early age, Robert learned to put others' emotions before his own. Looking back on this childhood, he said, "I have been for so many years in the habit of repressing my feelings." The fixations of his father, the mores of his mother, and the austerity of his upbringing left little choice. Robert might want for much, but he would not want for the self-control that separated his father from Washington.

A boy growing up in Alexandria did not have to look far to see Washington. Young Robert studied at Alexandria Academy, which Washington had endowed in his will for educating children of "poor and indigent persons." Robert ran errands in the market where Washington had trained troops during the French and Indian War. He worshipped at the Episcopal church where Washington had owned a pew. For long stretches, he lived at 607 Oronoco Street, which Washington had supposedly visited more than almost any other home in town. As a baby, Robert even nursed from a mother known to wear a locket on her breast with Washington's picture. The pendant was a gift from the president. The question of how the immediacy of these images influenced Robert's development has divided biographers. What causes less debate—and matters more—is that almost everyone in nineteenth-century America revered Washington.

"The name of Washington is constantly on our lips," Walt Whitman explained, and for good reason. A conversation as simple as asking for directions inevitably led to his name. "Every thing great and good in America is called Washington; its capitol, its cities, towns, counties, and districts, all bear his name," a newspaper correspondent noted. Americans celebrated Washington's Birthday as a holiday akin to the Fourth of July. No house was complete without his picture. "The sculptor and the painter will be employed unceasingly to keep pace with the increasing demand," a congressman predicted. The great Charles Willson Peale alone produced sixty Washington portraits, one of which hung in the house where Robert's mother grew up.

In this adoration for Washington, visitors from Europe detected the lingering influence of Old World traditions. While touring New York's slums, English author Charles Dickens found tavern walls plastered with pictures of Washington and Queen Victoria. A French diplomat saw traces of the "magical power" of monarchy in "the force of opinion attached to his person throughout the whole of America." Yet for all the trappings of the Old World, the spread of the Washington cult reflected a distinctly New World ideal: that sons did not have to follow in the footsteps of their biological fathers, that they could instead follow the example of the father of their country. Of all the duties a mother owed her sons, a popular women's magazine wrote, "Especially should she instruct them to revere the memory of the sincerest patriot and wisest man whose deeds lent glory to our revolutionary struggle—the first President of the Republic."

Mothers looking for lesson plans had their pick of biographies. Hundreds of authors lifted their pens in Washington's honor. No one enjoyed greater success than a writer named Mason Locke Weems. After the president's death, Parson Weems, as he became known, fired off a note to a publisher: "Washington, you know is gone! Millions are gaping to read something about him." Whether that something was fact or fiction mattered little to Weems as he raced to publish what would be the first of many editions of his Washington biography. The book's popularity said less about Weems's knowledge of his subject and more about his understanding of how Americans hungered for stories that could humanize their departed hero. Where Weems could not cherry-pick anecdotes, he grew them on made-up cherry trees. Still, for decades, the Washington whom Weems created became the Washington whom Americans revered. By studying this Washington's virtues, "every youth," Weems promised, "may become a Washington." One Abraham Lincoln remembered devouring the book while growing up in the backwoods of Indiana in "the earliest days of my being able to read."

Boys who opened the editions sold during Robert's childhood would have connected Weems's tales with the Lee name. The title page boasted a glowing review attributed to Harry Lee. "The author has treated this great subject with admirable success in a new way. He turns all the actions of Washington to the encouragement of virtue, by a careful application of numerous exemplifications drawn from the conduct of the founder of our republic." In other words, Weems had fulfilled Harry Lee's hope of "holding . . . forth" Washington's virtues "as illustrious models to our sons." Robert would later write that the enormous demand for Washington biographies "speaks greatly in favour of the People . . . and must tend vastly to their benefit in every respect."

The most anticipated event of Robert's childhood occurred on October 16, 1824, when the Marquis de Lafayette visited Alexandria. Like his neighbors, Robert must have counted the days until this character from the pages of Washington lore materialized on the streets of town. The French nobleman had made his first voyage to the New World during the American Revolution. Of all the members of George Washington's military family, Lafayette had come closest to being a surrogate son. "Treat him as if he were my son," Washington instructed a surgeon after a musket ball had ripped through Lafayette's leg at the Battle of Brandywine. When Lafayette visited Mount Vernon in 1784 after the war, he found his portrait hanging above the mantel. Now the old hero had returned to America for what would become a more than six-thousand-mile triumphal tour.

Alexandria demanded a spot on the itinerary. "The citizens of Alexandria are persuaded that you will look upon them with no common interest," declared an official invitation reminding Lafayette that Alexandria had been where "as a neighbor and a citizen" Washington's "intercourse was most affectionate and intimate." How could Lafayette refuse? He understood why Alexandrians claimed his American father as their town father. And while in Alexandria, he could visit Ann Lee, the widow of the "enterprising" horseman he had admired during the Revolution.

Waiting to welcome the sexagenarian as soon as he crossed the Potomac, Alexandrians gathered at the end of the Long Bridge from Washington. Appointed an honorary marshal, seventeen-year-old Robert undoubtedly cut an impressive figure amid the crowd. The blue sash hugging his trim waist would have emphasized his deepening chest. Under the cap shielding his ruddy face, his dark eyes would have watched Lafayette's wigged and worn figure come into view. Fifteen hundred soldiers then led a parade into town. Around three o'clock in the afternoon, the four gray horses pulling Lafayette's coach reached the intersection of Washington and King Streets. Over the road, the town had erected a ceremonial hundred-foot arch, adorned with portraits of Washington and Lafayette. From a window perch, high above what a newspaper termed "the multitude in the streets," a certain young heiress noticed how handsome Robert appeared as he followed Lafayette through the arch. Her father, George Washington Parke Custis, the short, red-faced, balding man riding in the carriage behind Lafayette's, would not have approved.

It was not a grudge against the boy. Custis had heard all about the Lees' troubles. His wife, Mary Lee Fitzhugh, was the Lees' distant cousin, and her generous brother, William Fitzhugh, once owned their refuge at 607 Oronoco Street. Custis tried, as much as anyone, to fill the void Harry Lee had left. Often he would invite the Lee children to Arlington, the showy neoclassical mansion he had built just upriver from Alexandria. Robert would later credit Custis with being "all a father could." That, however, did not mean Custis wanted his daughter eyeing Harry Lee's boy, not in that way, and especially not on a day when her eyes should have been focused on her father. Custis was, as everyone knew, George Washington's adopted son, the child of Mount Vernon.

The next day, Custis led Lafayette and other dignitaries on a cruise down the Potomac to his old boyhood home. A couple of hours into the cruise, the cannons of Fort Washington fired a salute. There atop the bluff on the opposite bank sat Mount Vernon. A red roof sloped over a piazza offering views so magnificent that Washington had proclaimed his house the most "pleasantly situated" in America. Awed at the sight, the dignitaries fell to their knees. On the way up to the house, Custis and Lafayette stopped at a dilapidated burial vault wedged into the hillside and overgrown with trees. It was Washington's grave. The time had come for Custis to give a speech, and speech making was what he did best. "At this awful and impressive moment, when . . . you bend with reverence over the remains of Washington, the child of Mount Vernon presents you with this token," he declared. Then, to Lafayette, he presented a lock of Washington's hair set in a gold ring with the words "Pater Patriae" and "Mount Vernon" engraved on either side.

Memories flooded up the hillside as the two men approached the house. Lafayette remembered how Washington had welcomed him on the piazza forty years earlier and how Custis, then a blue-eyed, light-haired three-year-old, had waddled in his adoptive father's massive shadow. "It was in this portico, in 1784, that you were introduced to me by the general," Lafayette said. "You were a very little gentleman, with a feather in your hat, and holding fast to one finger of the good general's remarkable hand, which was all you could do, my dear sir, at that time." The story of how Custis came to Mount Vernon had begun long before his birth. In 1757, the death of his grandfather Daniel Parke Custis had transformed his grandmother Martha Dandridge Custis into one of Virginia's wealthiest widows. The ambitious George Washington had wooed and won her hand with the knowledge that the Custis estate included almost eighteen thousand acres of land and almost three hundred slaves. Because Daniel died without a will, common law granted Martha one-third of the estate while splitting the remainder between her two children, Jacky and Patsy. Marriage to the widow Custis placed Washington in control over her share and in charge of the children's trusts. The arrangement elevated Washington to the pinnacle of the planter elite and eventually provided the financial freedom needed to devote his energies to securing America's freedom.

For all its advantages, however, the union between George and Martha Washington was not perfect. It produced no children. More devastating, the children from Martha's first marriage, despite her coddling, did not survive the second. Patsy died in 1773 from complications related to epilepsy. Away at college, Jacky suffered from a different sort of disease: indolence. The young heir dropped out of school to marry his sweetheart. As Washington scouted battlefields during the Revolution, Jacky Custis looked for a home for his growing family. He overpaid for a tract above Alexandria. "Nothing," he explained, "could have induced Me to have given such Terms, but the unconquerable Desire I had, to live in the Neighbourhood of Mt Vernon." According to family lore, Jacky also desired to join Washington in the army. For some reason, he waited until Yorktown. Catching a fatal illness in camp, the raw soldier passed away in his wife's arms shortly after the British laid down theirs. Martha had lost her last child. Jacky's widow, meanwhile, faced a future of raising four children alone. As Washington embraced the two grieving women, he made a decision regarding the youngest of the children: a two-year-old girl named Nelly and the infant George Washington Parke Custis. "From this moment," Washington supposedly said, "I adopt his two youngest children as my own." George Washington Parke Custis would have no memories of this moment, but no one would have more memories of Mount Vernon afterward.

Now, escorting Lafayette through the familiar rooms, Custis could remember, as he put it, Washington's "domestic habits and manners; the routine of his methodical life; what he said and did, when he retired from public cares and duties." Custis had seen Washington the farmer, who woke early in the morning, rode around his farms, washed down a hearty dinner with Madeira, wrote in his library, sat with his family at the tea table in the evening, and went to bed at nine. He had seen the immaculate white horses that pulled the president's carriage, and the ceremony when Washington laid the cornerstone for the new Capitol building in the city that would bear his name. Custis had also seen Washington the father: caring but severe, distant yet demanding.

Custis could never measure up to his adoptive father's expectations. The influence of an "indulgent" adoptive mother may explain why. As his sister Nelly remarked, "Grandmamma always spoiled" Custis because he was "the pride of her heart." Washington worried as Custis squandered his time at Princeton. "You are now extending into that stage of life when good or bad habits are formed. When the mind will be turned to things useful and praiseworthy, or to dissipation and vice," he warned. Desperate as Custis claimed to be to please Washington, a diversion into "dissipation" of some sort led to his expulsion from the college. In 1798, Washington shipped the boy to St. John's College in Annapolis with a note that read, "Mr. Custis possesses competent talents to fit him for any studies, but they are counteracted by an indolence of mind." The experiment lasted less than a year. For all his adoptive father's hopes, Custis returned to Mount Vernon unable to manage even his own finances. Washington died recognizing his failure as a parent. "What is best to be done with him," he said of Custis in 1799, "I know not."

Where Custis should reside posed the most pressing question after Martha Washington followed her husband to the grave in 1802. Custis could not stay at Mount Vernon, because George Washington had left the property to a nephew, United States Supreme Court Justice Bushrod Washington. There were the hereditary Custis lands, including the valuable White House plantation in Virginia's New Kent County, but those were far from home. There was also the tree-covered hill that Jacky had purchased overlooking the Potomac, land now lying inside the new District of Columbia. Custis would eventually call the spot Arlington. After an attempt to buy Mount Vernon failed, Custis headed upriver. If he could not own Mount Vernon, he would bring its spirit to Arlington.

Now, as Custis and Lafayette finished touring Mount Vernon,

someone observed how "every thing in the house" was as it had been. But that was not so. Gone were the tea-and-table china designed for the veterans of the Revolution and adorned with the crest of their Society of the Cincinnati. Gone were the silver plate, the punch bowl, the family portraits, and even beds and curtains. Martha Washington had left these treasures to Custis in her will. Gone also were Washington's carriage and the tent that housed his headquarters during the war. Custis had bid $610 for the former and $161 for the latter at auction. Ironically, to buy these and other relics, Custis violated his adoptive father's warnings about debt.

At Arlington, Custis stashed the memorabilia in a dilapidated cottage near the river until the dampness destroyed two paintings. To save his collection, he decided to build a new home high on the hill. He hired architect George Hadfield to design a mansion that could serve as a "Washington treasury." Hadfield, who had spent several thankless years supervising the US Capitol's construction across the river, modeled Arlington House after a classical temple, complete with a faux-marble portico and pediment. The first bricks laid in 1803 might have dried in molds Custis had purchased from Mount Vernon. Fifteen years later, as the eight-columned front neared completion, the house made headlines when a lightning bolt ripped through the roof but caused little damage.

A Washington monument long before an obelisk across the river would steal that distinction, Arlington was the physical manifestation of Custis's life mission: to preserve his adoptive father's legacy. An amateur artist, Custis hung his own oversized Revolutionary battle paintings among a collection featuring Charles Willson Peale's 1772 portrait of George Washington. Though one room housed the bed where Washington died—Custis claimed to have left the bedding "in precisely the same condition"—Arlington House felt very much alive. Thousands tramped across the lawn for picnics every year. An annual sheep-shearing festival paid homage to Washington's oft-forgotten work as a pioneer of American agriculture. Custis awarded prizes and showcased his own efforts to produce fine wool from rams and ewes bred, in part, from the Mount Vernon flock. With the Washington war tent pitched on the lawn, guests sporting homespun clothes drank American wines while Custis gave his orations in a voice his daughter recalled as "melodious" but others found tedious. Out of these celebrations of Washington's spirit emerged an early vision of American nationalism. The view looking down from Arlington Heights somehow justified the vast but still mostly vacant grand avenues that the capital's designers had sketched out across the river.

Lafayette himself declared the view from Arlington's portico "the finest he had ever seen." At least a few times before returning to France, he visited the place. At least once, Robert E. Lee met him there. Hearing Custis's stories while peering into the relic-filled rooms left an indelible impression. Of Arlington, Robert said, "My affections & attachments are more strongly placed than at any other place in the World."

However strong his attachments, Robert could not stick around Arlington and Alexandria. Unlike Custis, he needed to earn a living. Shortly before dying, George Washington had reaffirmed his support for creating a national military academy. By 1824, the academy founded at West Point on the Hudson River north of New York City had sufficient funding to educate 250 cadets free of charge, a factor not inconsequential to the Lee family. Robert had rapidly advanced in mathematics. During a lesson on conic sections, a teacher admired how he "drew each one with as much accuracy and finish, lettering and all, as if it was to be engraved and printed." That aptitude suited him for a military education focused on engineering. Though Ann Lee opposed the idea—she could not imagine how she could live without her son—Robert requested a nomination. Unfortunately, so did many other young men. Applications poured in to the secretary of war, who was at that time South Carolina's John C. Calhoun. Not yet the staunch supporter of states' rights he would become, Calhoun oversaw an institution drawing students from across the country.

To distinguish Robert's application from the pile, his family and friends tapped every possible connection. William Fitzhugh, Custis's brother-in-law, arranged for Robert to personally deliver a recommendation to Calhoun. The letter asked that whatever Calhoun decide, he decide quickly. Given the Lees' financial struggles, Robert could afford to "lose no time in selecting the employment to which his future life is to be devoted." The letter also mentioned the debt that the United States owed the family. "He is the son of Genl Henry Lee, with whose history, you are, of course, acquainted; and who (whatever may have been the misfortune of his latter years) had certainly established, by his revolutionary services, a strong claim to the gratitude of his country." Other recommendations testified to Robert's "gentlemanly deportment" and "excellent disposition." If these testimonials proved wanting, the support of George Washington's adopted daughter, the lovely Nelly, may have clinched the case. Custis's sister was said to have "interested herself very much in obtaining his commission."

Such a connected, talented, and mature young man—who had come of age in Washington's hometown and learned the self-control Harry Lee lacked—belonged at West Point. Washington had envisioned the cadets as the next generation of military leaders, and, starting in the summer of 1825, Robert E. Lee would stand among them. As Robert bid farewell to the scenes of his childhood, he must have known he would one day return. His attachment to Arlington held strong not only because of what the house represented but also because of who lived there: Custis's daughter, Mary.

CHAPTER THREE

Lee's Union

The girl who lived up the hill had "engrossed" Robert E. Lee for as long as anyone could remember. Her visits to Alexandria lured him from other childhood playmates. His visits to Arlington planted the first seeds of romance. Together, their young hands buried a row of saplings in Arlington's soil. The look they shared during Lafayette's parade yielded a Christmas kiss weeks later.

Nevertheless, like Arlington Heights, Mary Anna Randolph Custis was a tall climb for a Lee. A glimpse of her portrait does not explain why. Her high cheekbones, severe brows, and prominent chin imitated her father's less-than-attractive and "rather irregular features." More flattering were the comparisons she inspired to her great-grandmother Martha Washington. Portraits of the two ladies hint at a "striking resemblance" that grew stronger with age. But while Martha received high marks for style, Mary often received shocked stares. Her disheveled appearance—dresses hemmed too high, clothes often mismatched—contrasted with outside expectations for the scion of one of America's great families. Despite these fashion faux pas, Mary's brown eyes beamed with confidence of the highest class. One admirer described her bearing as befitting her "rank and bringing up." Mary's personality also reflected her roots. She exhibited not only her father's artistic talent but also the indolence that Washington had failed to drive from two generations of Custises. Lee described her as "addicted to laziness and forgetfulness." Her strong opinions, owing to an elite education, amused her pen pals, but only when her letters actually arrived. More often, her tardiness left correspondents, including anxious suitors, in suspense.

As the Custises' sole surviving child, Mary stood in line to inherit the vast estate that had brought George Washington to her great-grandmother's doorstep. So powerful and sought after was the Custis family fortune that John Adams openly asked whether Washington would have been first in war and first in peace without it. "Would Washington have ever been commander of the revolutionary army or president of the United States, if he had not married the rich widow of Mr. Custis?" Though Mary's father had fiddled away some of the Custis fortune, he had done a better job preserving the Washington legacy. That, too, would one day belong to Mary. Whoever married Arlington's heiress would, indeed, be "the representative of the family of the founder of American liberty."

Lee was hardly alone in recognizing "the novel situation" awaiting the winner of Mary's hand. Among her suitors was an up-and-coming Tennessee congressman named Sam Houston. But like all the gentlemen callers who climbed Arlington Heights, the future first president of the Republic of Texas descended disappointed. One acquaintance called Mary an "impregnable fortress."

As the fortress held fast, Lee learned everything he could at West Point about military engineering, including the art of the siege. He adjusted better than most to the rigors of a schedule that filled almost every minute between reveille at dawn and lights out at ten o'clock in the evening with class, studying, drilling, and barely edible food. That he received no demerits, managed to save money on a small stipend, scored at the top of his class in artillery and tactics, earned the academy's highest honor of corps adjutant, and served, to his mother's pride, as an assistant mathematics professor spoke to his self-discipline, economy, and aptitude. Even his posture stood apart from the other cadets'. "Though firm in his position and perfectly erect, he had none of the stiffness so often assumed by men who affect to be very strict in their ideas of what is military," recalled a fellow cadet.

During the summer of 1827, Lee returned home on furlough to much fanfare. His "attractive manners" as he strode about in his gray cadet uniform impressed Mary's friends. Two years passed before they saw him again. By that time, he had graduated second in his class and joined the Army Corps of Engineers. The young women now proclaimed him "splendid-looking." They enjoyed his company, and he theirs. The self-deprecation that one would expect from Ann Lee's son tempered the bravado that one would expect from a young officer. His banter flowed with an upbeat and sometimes bawdy flirtatiousness. His humor could rib and reproach without offending. Mary's friend described him "as full of life, fun, and particularly of teasing, as any of us."

As full of life as Lee was, he was also full of despair. He suffered bouts of sadness that left him "wretched" or "miserable." He confessed that he was "naturally inclined" to "melancholy." A sense of fatalism had seeped into his thoughts, a chemical bond he could not understand to a father whom he could barely remember. Only later in life when watching his own son struggle with what he called "my gravity" would Lee allude to its hereditary quality. Trained to suppress rather than "vent" certain emotions, Lee could withdraw into himself. "I am not very accessible and am as niggardly of my friendship as if it was worth having," he explained. Often Lee described himself as playing a role in a script beyond his control. He liked to say that he could never have his "own way." His training at West Point had reinforced the central takeaway of his upbringing: duty before desire. Years before a religious awakening gave him the theology for explaining the difference between the two, Lee already strove for resignation.

This is not to say that acceptance always came easily. Robert was still a Lee. Never more so than when he lost the mother to whom, as he put it, he "owed every thing." It happened almost as soon as he returned to Virginia. With his mother sick, the newly minted second lieutenant once again reported for caregiver duty and almost never left her bedside. "If R[obert] left the room, she kept her eyes on the door until he returned," a cousin wrote. When Ann Carter Lee's eyes closed for the final time in July 1829, Robert suffered a breakdown severe enough to keep him from the funeral. He paced beside her empty bed while others laid her body to rest. The sorrow never subsided. As the years passed, Lee would still remember his mother's death as if it happened yesterday. Within weeks, however, he had hidden the scar from view.

Publicly, Lee seemed his playful self again. Privately, he had begun another vexing rite of passage: courtship. By August 22, he had asked his younger sister, Mildred Lee, to transmit a cryptic message to Mary Custis. "I remember his uttering as he left the room, confused sentences about beauty and size, how little could be added to the former and how much to the latter," Mildred wrote Mary. "You know when one is much agitated, their expressions are generally intricate and difficult to be understood." In the confusion, this much was clear: Lee was in love.

In the midst of these flirtations, a more serious note arrived. The Army Corps of Engineers ordered Lee to head to Georgia in November 1829 for duty on a remote island called Cockspur. His departure did not go unnoticed. Around the same time, Mary complained of mysterious "acute pangs." Mildred offered this advice: "Beware of the year 1830, suffer it not to commence before executing resolutions, which you have so long formed of repressing and softening a disposition hitherto so fatal to the beaux."

The first sight of Cockspur must have given Lee pangs of his own. Stuffed in the mouth of the Savannah River, the island was as much water as land, more fit for alligators than engineers. The tides regularly swept over the shore. The mud never dried. When work was possible between the tides, Lee oversaw the early stages of constructing a fort. An often absent superior left Lee as the sole officer much of the time. Although a team of laborers—some wageworkers, some slaves—performed the backbreaking work of cutting ditches, raising embankments, and clearing reeds, Lee sloshed through the mud alongside them. "Tell Cousin Mary Custis," he wrote his brother Carter, then staying near Arlington, "that if she thinks that I am going to stay here . . . without hearing any thing of her . . . she is very much mistaken." Lee kept his word. When construction on the island ended for the summer, he hurried to Arlington.

Mary had changed since their last meeting. In the spring of 1830, a family tragedy shook her assumptions about the world. William Fitzhugh, her charitable uncle who had sheltered the Lees, died unexpectedly amid what a newspaper called "the flower of his life." When Mary first heard the news, she thought only of how the mourning period would hinder her social life. This selfishness brought a stinging rebuke from her mother, a lesson that made sense as soon as Mary saw her uncle's widow grieving. Mary realized, at once, "the vanity of earthly things." On July 4, 1830, as America celebrated Independence Day, Mary pledged to mend her soul and rededicate her life. Her mother "wept" when she heard the news: Mary had opened her heart to God.

But Mary's heart also opened to the army lieutenant who called at her doorstep over and over again that summer. He must have told her about army life and teased her, as he often did, for being sheltered. She tried to reason with him about religion. While Lee had grown up attending church, the sermons had not yet stirred his soul. To play on her fears for his spirit, Lee delighted in exaggerating his religious shortcomings. Calling himself "sinful Robert," he warned her not to "expect miracles in my case." Though Mary could not expect a miracle, she prayed for one. "Oh draw him also to Thee that we may with one heart & one mind live to the glory of our Redeemer." Confident that she could make almost any other sacrifice God demanded, she doubted she could give up her love for Lee. "May He never draw my soul from Thee," she wrote in her journal. "If I am deceived by Satan open then my eyes."

One day that summer, in Arlington's main hall, where Washington's portrait hung and the cool river breeze divided the house in two, the pages of the book on Lee's lap fluttered. Reading aloud to Mary, his thoughts wandered. Mary's mother must have noticed, for she said, "Mary, Robert must be tired and hungry; go into the dining-room and get him some lunch." Lee followed Mary around the corner. When she bent to cut a slice of fruitcake, "he put his arm around her" and asked for something that would last even longer. Yes, Mary Custis said. She would be a Lee.

The news raced up and down the Potomac. The daughter of the child of Mount Vernon had made her choice. The impregnable fortress had all but fallen. Only one last defender remained, and that was George Washington Parke Custis. For now, his answer to the request for his daughter's hand was maybe. "I am engaged to Miss Mary," Lee wrote Carter shortly afterward. "She & her mother have given their consent. But the Father has not yet made up his mind, though it is supposed will not object."

The heir to Stratford Hall, Henry Lee IV, could see no cause for objection when word of the engagement reached him in Paris. He considered his half brother Robert's match advantageous but not undeserved. The distinctions that Robert had earned at West Point made him "good enough for any woman." Lost in Henry IV's analysis was his own public humiliation, the reason the heir to Stratford had ended up overseas. Several months before Lee's engagement, a Senate debate over Henry IV's nomination for ambassador to Algiers had turned an old family scandal into a national political scandal. Henry IV had slept with his wife's sister, then a ward in his care. To make matters worse, he had squandered the girl's inheritance. Even selling what remained of Stratford Hall did not erase his debts. Disgraced, he became known as Henry "Black-Horse Harry" Lee. Like his father, he longed for a new life overseas. Leaving America before knowing whether the Senate would confirm his nomination, he did not return after learning of its rejection.

The self-imposed exile of not one but two generations of Lees, the loss of their ancestral home at Stratford, and the questions surrounding their financial future gave Mary's father pause. He had grown up in a house where Washington had not been shy about sharing his views on marriage. Custis had once received a stern letter for making advances on a young lady instead of focusing on his studies. Washington wrote, "This is not a time for a boy of your age to enter into engagements which might end in sorrow and repentance." In a letter to one of Custis's sisters, Washington recommended subjugating passions to practical concerns. He warned not to "revel in an ocean of love" because "love is a mighty pretty thing; but like all other delicious things, it is cloying." Instead, Washington encouraged judging a prospective partner based on a three-part test: "good sense—good dispositions—and the means of supporting you in the way you have been brought up."

Lee could meet only two of Washington's prerequisites. A career in the military would never yield the third: the means of supporting Mary as she had been brought up. At times, Lee doubted his own desirability. He worried the "long years of expectancy" for marriage to Mary "would never have an end." As he once told Mary, "I thought & intended always to be one & alone in the World for I never expected You would be mine." Although Lee hoped that Custis would judge him on his own merits, he also subscribed to the traditional notion that a man's ancestors said much about the man. Advising a junior officer many years later, he said, "Never marry unless you can do so into a family which will enable your children to feel proud of both sides of the house."

Lee's cause was not without hope. If Washington had looked past Light-Horse Harry's sins, perhaps Custis could, too. In fact, Custis had suggested as much two years earlier in an article for the *Daily National Intelligencer* as part of a series on Washington's life. He recalled how Washington's "merit-discerning eye" had looked on young men like Harry Lee "with peculiar esteem and favor." Custis then praised Harry Lee for returning his mentor's affection "with a force and grandeur of eloquence wholly his own." The article recounted how "an unhappy rage for speculation" had stolen Harry Lee's fortune but not his "fondly cherished passion" for Washington. "When all else around him seemed cold and desolate," Harry still found "warmth" in Washington's memory. Custis closed by urging his fellow citizens to remember the good in the man and forget the bad. "Let the faults of Lee be buried in his distant grave."

Whether Mary's father would practice what he preached remained an open question when Robert E. Lee returned to Cockspur in November 1830. At least once before leaving, Lee broached the subject with Custis. The dramatic conversation hardened into a traumatic memory. "Whenever I think of that morning, the same feeling returns which I then had," Lee told Mary. "I know it must be very hard for him to give away his dear daughter, but he can't expect to have her with him always." Mary hoped prayer would sustain her fiancé as he sailed away for Cockspur, but she soon learned that his "mind was far otherwise engaged" during the long nights at sea. "Would you think that I was selfish enough to wish you to be with me in that dark, confined and crowded little cabin? And would even now give the world if you were here, on this desolate and comfortless Island," Lee wrote after his arrival.

Like everything else in the Cockspur mud, Lee's spirits sank. A tropical storm had destroyed most of the last year of labor. "Nearly all the embankments were broken down, ditches filled . . . and what was worse than all, the wharf which cost us so much time & money is destroyed," Lee reported. The new year did not bring better weather. "I can scarcely find a dry spot to work upon," he wrote Mary in January. "Rain, rain, rain, nothing but rain." The gloomy solitude Lee felt mirrored the world he saw. "I have not seen the moon for two weeks," he complained. "Whenever it rains or is even cloudy the moon never appears, which makes me as melancholy as a lover's lute or the drone of a Lincolnshire bagpipe." The rare clear night brought a strange serenity. "The nights are so bright & beautiful & still that I can almost distinguish the noise of a single wave from the roaring of the multitude." But could Custis distinguish one Lee from a long line?

When possible, Lee broke up the monotony with visits to Savannah. The Mackay family, whose son John had also graduated from West Point in 1829, opened their home to Lee. What attracted Lee most to the house was the company of John's sisters. Lee did not hide these friendships from Mary. In fact, he offered copious details, including his disappointment over not receiving kisses from the girls on Christmas. Lee either knew Mary would not be jealous or hoped to send a not-so-subtle message about the urgency of settling matters with her father.

The more time passed, the more impatient Lee grew. "If you choose or prefer to think it would not do injury, I will write to him, this would decide him at once," he wrote Mary in March. But what "if it should be the wrong way," he worried. "Tell me which is best, for I am the worst coward in this affair, & am almost afraid to think of it." At long last, in early spring, Mary sent the news that Lee had waited half a year to hear: Custis had consented. "If you 'felt so grateful' to your Father for his kindness, what must I feel," Lee responded. "I only wish that his 'approbation' in the one case was as well founded as his 'objections' in the other." No one could "be more sensible" to the shortcomings of Henry Lee III and IV. "But should I be able to escape the sins into which they have fallen, I hope the blame which is justly their due, will not be laid to me."

More good news followed. The army reassigned Lee "as soon as practicable" to Fort Monroe on the Chesapeake Bay at the end of the Virginia Peninsula, wedged between the York and James Rivers. At Fort Monroe, a lively community full of young officers awaited. In the warmer months, families flocked to the beaches for bathing and fishing. Plus, a steamboat shuttling up and down the bay made regular trips to the District of Columbia. His solitary existence on Cockspur had ended. Once at Fort Monroe, Lee moved into a building called the Engineer Quarters, which he shared with a "gentlemanly" superior officer who became a close friend, Captain Andrew Talcott. The quarters also housed Talcott's sister and her children. After the wedding, Mary would join the party.

Peppered with questions from Mary about what to expect, Lee worried how she would adapt. They would have two rooms of their own, but Lee described one as "a closet with a window in it." He joked that Mary could try her "hand at housekeeping," but he knew not to expect too much. "We will have to trust to you to pour out our coffee," he wrote. "But I expect I shall have to do it." Unlike Lee's childhood,

Mary's had not prepared her for the responsibilities of managing a household. Mildred Lee could have spoken for her brother when she told Mary, "Fortune has never frowned on you; all has been calm and serene . . . the sky has been uniformly bright, no clouds have yet overcast it." Growing up on the Arlington hill, Mary had breathed only the most rarefied air. The path down would be steep. "The change from Arlington to a Garrison of wicked & Blasphemous soldiers will be greater & more shocking to you than you are aware of," Lee warned in his last letter before the wedding. "I do not know that I should be so candid, was it not too late for you to change now."

When the bride-to-be awoke at Arlington on June 30, 1831, the sky outside her window appeared as bright and cloudless as ever. Lee had told Mary to watch for his steamboat coming up the Potomac. Past the swirling tides guarding the river's mouth, past the white cliffs concealing Stratford Hall, past the green slopes elevating Mount Vernon, the journey took Lee against the current. With every turn of the paddle wheel, he moved closer to resuscitating the surname that had sunk into scandal and to rebuilding the bridge that connected it with the greatest surname in the land. The bridesmaids awaiting his arrival on Arlington Heights gazed down at the city across the river. Little could they know that Washington would soon be as veiled from view as the path ahead for bride and groom.

The rain began in the afternoon and turned into a downpour. The Custises had offered to send the old Mount Vernon carriage, wobbling on what would be its last set of wheels, to meet Lee at the harbor in Alexandria. The Reverend Reuel Keith, traveling on horseback, was not as fortunate. So wet were the reverend's clothes when he arrived that he had to accept a fresh pair from Custis, who, as one bridesmaid noted, was a much shorter man "so far as inches were concerned." With a gap between his shoes and pants, the "woebegone" reverend could not hide his flesh, and the guests could not hide their laughter.

At the appointed time, Custis's sister Nelly, always Washington's favorite, started playing the piano. Father and daughter walked arm in arm into the family parlor and then down an aisle leading to Mary's future. Claps of thunder punctuated the wedding march as Mary approached Lee. Grasping her hand, Lee felt her palm tremble. The sensation made him anxious. His ruddy face turned white. Suddenly he felt as "bold as a sheep." In all the years that he had pictured this moment, he never imagined it this way. Standing before God with Mary was no more romantic than standing "at the Black Board at West Point." Though the reverend "had few words to say," Lee felt "he dwelt upon them as if he had been reading my Death warrant."

For days afterward, the revelers camped at Arlington. A bridesmaid remembered the men competing for the attentions of her friends. While playing billiards, the ladies neglected one "well-behaved" groomsman for "a very great scamp" who "was addicted to the tender habit of squeezing the finger tips of the young ladies as he passed them the balls." Each night, to ease conversation, Custis would have filled George Washington's grand punch bowl and "bounteously dispensed" the contents. On Sunday, July 3, the party rode to Alexandria for what proved a "hell-fire" sermon at Washington's church. "What can I say for this week," Mary wrote in her prayer journal, "but that in the circumstance with which I am surrounded my poor vain foolish heart has been too much drawn aside from Thee." When the party finally dispersed on July 5, Lee relished some private time with Mary. He left Talcott to draw his own conclusions. "I would tell you how the time passed, but fear, I am too much prejudiced to say anything more, but that it went very rapidly & still continues to do so."

However the time passed, Mary's parents could not hide their sadness when it ended and Mary moved with her new husband to Fort Monroe. "I have dictated I cannot tell how many letters in the silent hours of night, as well as in the leisure which the comparative solitude of our house now gives," Mrs. Custis wrote Mary on August 10. "I will not attempt to tell you how I felt at your departure. I hastened to turn from my own loss to a contemplation of your happiness—united to the man of your choice you could I am sure with him find enjoyment in far less favorable circumstances than those in which you are now placed." But enjoyment would not be so easy to find. As soon as the newlyweds arrived at Fort Monroe, bad omens for their future appeared on the horizon.

On August 13, people across the East Coast noticed a strange haze in the sky. Blues and greens emanated from the sun until a black mark emerged on its surface. Nine days later, a slave preacher named Nat Turner, convinced of his prophetic powers, led his followers on a murderous uprising against white families in Virginia's Southampton County. From home to home, they went spreading terror, hunting masters, and recruiting slaves. Their axes and hatchets sliced and chopped adults and children alike until finally meeting musket fire. By the time federal troops from Fort Monroe reached the county seat, local authorities had restored order. Sixty white men, women, and children died in the rebellion; more than three times that number of blacks died in reprisals. Lee, who stayed behind at Fort Monroe, reported how "the whites" even killed a loyal slave in "unwarrantable haste." In the months following, the specter of insurrection thrust the Old Dominion into a state of reflection. Sensing the danger in their midst, Virginia lawmakers debated whether to rid their commonwealth of slaves altogether or to pass new laws further oppressing blacks. That Virginia ultimately took the latter course would shape Lee's life in ways he could not imagine.

As Fort Monroe bustled with activity, Mary felt isolated. The other families did not share her religious fervor. While child-rearing duties occupied most of the women, military duties occupied her husband. Lee had "but little time" to accompany her on walks on the beach. "What would I give for one stroll on the hills at Arlington this bright day," she wrote her parents. Her mother made matters worse. "I took a short walk yesterday and thought of the pleasure it would give us all if you could partake."

Homesick, Mary did what she could to re-create the atmosphere of Arlington House. She hung curtains from the windows, studied the Bible with a slave named Cassy on loan from her parents, and waited for her mother to send delicacies—gingerbread, fruitcakes, and cheeses—that a lieutenant's wife could not obtain at Fort Monroe. The dependence on charity disgusted Lee. "We ought not to give others the trouble of providing for us always," he lectured. To no one's surprise, Mary's housekeeping also disgusted Lee. Her mother had predicted this clash from the beginning—the meticulous engineer versus the spoiled heiress. Although Mrs. Custis hoped her daughter would "profit by example," Mary evidently did not clean up her act enough to impress Lee. "He does scold me early & late," Mary whined to her mother during the fall. Speaking from "experience," Mrs. Custis told Lee that scolding Mary was "useless." Just as George Washington's scolding had not changed Custis, Lee's would not change Mary. She was her father's daughter.

Already there was talk that the engineer's organizational talents could compensate for the skills his new father-in-law had never developed. Though grateful for the paternal "affection" Custis had shown him during his fatherless childhood, Lee soon emerged as the adult in the relationship. He saw Custis as the same frivolous character whose future had worried Washington. Lee noted how his father-in-law neglected his farms and finances for playwriting and painting. Land rich but cash poor, Custis confessed himself "often in want of a single dollar." Trying to help, Lee advised Custis during that first year of marriage how to better manage a small island the family owned in the Chesapeake. "As I knew you objected to long letters, I have tried to make this as short as possible," Lee wrote, as if addressing a child. Seeing Lee's good sense, Mrs. Custis wondered whether her husband's financial mismanagement and her daughter's homesickness might not share a common solution. By October, she asked Mary a question that would linger for decades: Should Custis "withdraw Robert from his present profession and yield to him the management of affairs"?

Christmas could not come soon enough for Mary and her parents. Returning to Arlington for the holiday, the newlyweds found Custis already consumed in preparations for a celebration that would take place on February 22, 1832—Washington's centennial birthday. Custis had not only readied a play but also painted a battle scene showing Washington astride his horse. It was not a celebration, however, that reunited Washington's extended family at Mount Vernon early in the new year, but the death of Custis's older sister Eliza, who had always envied her younger siblings raised at Mount Vernon. With the rest of the Custis clan, Lee came out to pay his respects. The executors of Washington's will had lifted the president's body into a new vault the previous spring, around the same time Lee had started his journey back up the coast from Georgia. Now Lee watched Eliza's coffin being stacked on top of Washington's.

In a letter a couple of days afterward to one of the Mackay girls with whom he had flirted in Savannah, Lee described the scene at Mount Vernon. "There was a melancholy group of us & my black face looked longer than usual." But Lee joked that his thoughts had wandered from this awe-inspiring scene to a more irreverent image: the Mackay girl's wedding night. "And how did you deport yourself My child," he asked. "Did you go off well, like a torpedo cracker on Christmas morning?" Mary, who could not have missed her husband's colorful metaphor, added her congratulations at the bottom of the letter. Her tone was not uplifting. "I am now a wanderer on the face of the earth & know not where we are going next," she wrote. "I suppose you remain in Savannah near your Mother? What happiness? I am with mine now—the past & the future disregarded." If Lee read between the lines of Mary's scrawl, he could have predicted the future she disregarded. After the holiday, he returned to Fort Monroe alone. Mary planned to stay at Arlington until the first of May.

Distance strained the bonds of marriage. Lee noticed their letters growing shorter. Steamboat delays through the Chesapeake Bay and Potomac River slowed the mail between Fort Monroe and Arlington. Weeks passed without hearing from Mary. "This will never do Molly," he wrote. When Lee did hear from Mary, she wrote to push back her departure. Despairing, he did whatever he could to entice her to return.

He bragged about cavorting with other women. "Hasten down, if you do not want to see me turned out a Beaux again." He shamed her for not being on hand to comfort a woman whose son had died. He even kidded about cutting his own throat. When all else failed, he imposed a June first ultimatum. "I cannot consent to your remaining at Arlington longer."

Not until a couple of weeks past that deadline did Mary finally arrive. She looked fatter and rounder than Lee remembered. On September 17, 1832, he wrote her parents with the news they had anticipated for months: Mary had given birth to a boy. She had proposed a name, though Lee must have felt misgivings, for he added, "I do not know that it is a matter decided on." But like so much else, the matter had been decided. The boy's name would be George Washington Custis Lee.

PART II

★

Casus Belli

CHAPTER FOUR

Half Slave, Half Free

On June 29, 1848, Captain Robert E. Lee rode over the bridge from Washington. It was the last leg of his journey home from America's war in Mexico. He had not seen his wife and children since leaving them at Arlington almost two years earlier. Scouting attack routes through jagged lava fields had deepened the furrows on his face. Advising General Winfield Scott during late-night war councils had added the first white strands to his dark brown hair. Earning battlefield glory had accorded Lee a majestic stature that friends had not previously noticed. So much had the experience altered Lee that the family members assembled in Arlington's main hall did not realize the identity of the lone rider heading up the hillside until Spec, the family terrier, rushed out.

Lee's seven children could not hide their astonishment. The older children could remember only a younger-looking man who had taught them to swim, tended their bedsides when they were injured or ill, and sent them letters from afar admonishing them to study and behave. "Upon you," Lee had warned as he headed off to battle, "will depend whether I shall be happy or miserable on my return." The younger children had no memories of Lee at all. Not quite five years old, Robert E. Lee Jr. hoped to make a good first impression. A slave named Eliza had scrubbed his face, curled his hair, and clothed his body in a blue frock with white diamonds. "Where is my little boy?" Lee asked, searching the faces before mistakenly scooping up one of young Rob's playmates. The shock of being unrecognized would be the boy's first memory of his father.

The senior Lee could have been forgiven had he forgotten something else when reaching Arlington: that he was no longer in the District of Columbia. Save for the excavations taking place at the edge of the opposite bank—George Washington Parke Custis had recently joined a procession to deposit the giant white-marble block that would serve as the Washington Monument's cornerstone—the Potomac panorama looked much the same. The broad river still ran between Arlington and the city of Washington. But the two sides were no longer one entity. During Lee's absence, Virginia had reannexed the land it had ceded for the District of Columbia. The city of Alexandria and its namesake county, which included Arlington, once again belonged to the Old Dominion.

Alexandrians had cast the final votes in favor of retrocession on September 2, 1846, the same day Lee left Arlington for Mexico. Packing up his gear, he heard his father-in-law share the early polling results. "The polls are to be kept open tomorrow," Lee wrote on the eve of his departure, but Custis "says nearly all the votes are cast & there will be about 500 majority for retrocession." Custis had emerged as a leading supporter of retrocession despite previously opposing it out of respect for his adoptive father, who had purposely included Alexandria within the diamond-shaped District of Columbia. The arrangement, though initially popular among Alexandrians eager to bind their future to the nation's capital, had proven less so as residents found themselves at the mercy of a meddlesome Congress in which they had no representation. Like his neighbors, the first president's adopted son could not vote for president.

Another issue underlay the drive for retrocession: the future of slavery in the District of Columbia. As the Potomac's most prominent port, Alexandria had grown into a hub for the domestic slave trade. Tidy brick fronts lining the city's streets concealed interior pens where black slaves sleeping behind iron gates awaited shipment to the cotton states. The bustling trade offended some Northerners, who sent petitions demanding Congress outlaw it. Even if Congress could do little to regulate slavery in the Southern states, Alexandria's merchants worried that the federal government might flex its muscles in the federal district. This fear, mostly unspoken because of its unseemliness, cast a shadow over the retrocession debate. While Custis and the other commissioners overseeing the referendum tallied the votes, blacks standing outside the courthouse greeted the results with "suppressed wailings and lamentations."

Soon after, Custis delivered a speech celebrating the outcome. So it was that the aging-but-still-acknowledged guardian of Washington's legacy found himself rejoicing in the ruin of the perfect ten-mile-square diamond that had sprung from Washington's hopes for the Union. And so it would be that when Custis died a decade later, Robert E. Lee inherited a confounding and complicated legacy: how to reconcile union and slavery.

That Alexandria's retrocession vote coincided with Lee's departure for Mexico was more than a coincidence. To many Northern eyes, the war, like retrocession, had an ulterior purpose: the spread of slavery. As much as President James K. Polk insisted that the fighting had begun over a dispute concerning Texas's borders, he could not deny his ambition to acquire vast swaths of what would become Arizona, California, Colorado, Nevada, New Mexico, Utah, and Wyoming. Though Lee questioned "the justice of our cause," he believed that wars, once begun, must be won. "We now cannot stop short of the capital of Mexico, where we must dictate the terms of peace," he told Mary. The soldier in him was "anxious to join the army in Mexico." Advancing his career depended on it.

After the early years at Cockspur and Fort Monroe had come an administrative posting in Washington and then engineering assignments that had taken him to the rapidly developing west and industrializing north. There had been a posting on the Mississippi, where he had labored to correct the course of the river—an internal improvement project emblematic of an age that would become known as the transportation revolution. He had watched his impressionable boys, during a period when they joined him, build pretend steamboats out of books and chairs. Then had come a posting at Fort Hamilton, where he had overseen improvements to New York Harbor's defenses, admired how Yankee wives ran their homes without servants and slaves, and warned his own wife about the "dangerous" temptations awaiting her in the city's stores. "They shew you so many handsome things." But for all that he had seen, he lacked the experience that mattered most to a West Point graduate: battlefield experience.

Mexico would complete his training. Lee joined the staff of the military's most knowledgeable teacher: Winfield Scott, the colossal six-foot-four Virginian who served as the army's general in chief. Like George Washington before him, Scott had an eye for talent, probably because he had seen it in his own youthful exploits during the War of 1812. Now over sixty, Old Fuss and Feathers, as he was known because of his sensitivity to slights and his love of pomp, wanted to remind his detractors what all the fuss was for. Under Scott's command, close to ten thousand Americans landed at Vera Cruz on the Gulf of Mexico in March 1847, laid siege to the city, and then marched west toward Mexico City. Far from home with his troops often outnumbered, Scott could not afford heavy casualties. The flanking maneuvers he thus preferred as a way of avoiding costly frontal assaults presented opportunity for an engineer intrepid enough to explore attack routes around the enemy's main force. According to all accounts, Lee excelled. "His talent for topography was peculiar, and he seemed to receive impressions intuitively, which it cost other men much labor to acquire," said an admirer.

In April, Mexican forces fortified a position blocking the American advance through the Cerro Gordo pass. To the left, or north, of the Mexican army lay ravines that looked "impassable" to most soldiers, but not to Lee. A reconnaissance expedition around the enemy's flank brought him to a spring where he saw Mexican soldiers loitering. There he was behind enemy lines, completely undetected thanks to a hiding place he had found. More than one Mexican soldier drinking from the spring sat atop a certain "fallen tree" without noticing the American lying below it. Nightfall finally permitted Lee's escape. Two days later, he headed back up the trail he had blazed, this time with a division of reinforcements. What the Mexicans had considered a virtually unassailable position suddenly became untenable. "Seeing their whole left turned," Lee wrote Mary, "they broke and fled. . . . All their cannon, arms, ammunition, and most of their men fell into our hands. The papers can not tell you what a horrible sight a field of battle is." Even so, the papers could tell Mary what honors her husband had earned. "We see by the official dispatches that Capt. Robert E. Lee, of the Engineer Corps, has been honorably distinguished at the brilliant battle of Cerro Gordo," the *Alexandria Gazette* wrote. "This gallant officer, we knew, would show the mettle he is made of, whenever and wherever he could have an opportunity."

More opportunities followed. Crossing the Rio Frio Mountains in early August gave the Americans a glimpse of Mexico City. "Lighted by the soft, bright moon, with every village, spire, hut and mountain reflected in its silver lakes, you would think it even surpassed the descriptions we read of it," Lee would later write. Choosing to approach the city from the south, Scott found the enemy in force up the main road. To the west was an alternative road running almost parallel to the main one before merging into it above the Mexican position. Scott realized he could outflank the Mexican force if only he could find a way to send some of his men up this other road. The difficulty lay in the miles of volcanic rock separating the two roads.

Once again, Scott asked Lee to find a path through the impassable. Find a path Lee did, but he also found a large enemy force awaiting the American troops who crossed on August 19. That night, which Scott described as "exceedingly dark" with a "cold rain," Lee traversed the treacherous lava field twice more to coordinate action between the two wings of the American army. Scott would call Lee's treks "the greatest feat of physical and moral courage performed by any individual, in my knowledge, pending the campaign." When day broke, so did the enemy lines: first on the alternative road and then on the main one, as the American forces converged. "We could have entered Mexico [City] that evening or the next morning at our pleasure, so complete was the disorganization of their army," wrote Lee, who had been in the thick of battle for a day and a half straight. During the final battle for Mexico City, Lee showed he could go even longer without rest. Suffering a "slight wound," he eventually passed out, but not for so long that he missed seeing the American flag hoisted over the Halls of Montezuma on September 14, 1847. The Stars and Stripes would fly there for the next nine months, as politicians back home, still divided over how the war had begun, debated how it should end. "We hold and can continue [to] hold their country, & have a right to exact compensation for the expenses of a war continued if not provoked by the willful ignorance or vanity on the part of Mexico," Lee said, even as he admitted being "ashamed" of how America had "bullied" her "weaker" neighbor.

As it turned out, the true impediment to America realizing its manifest destiny as a continental power had not existed on the winding paths around the Mexican army but rather in the winding speeches of American politicians, who could not decide how much territory, if any, to annex. Lee considered the situation absurd. To his wife, he wrote, "It would be curious now if we should refuse to accept the territory we have forced her [Mexico] to relinquish & fight her three years more to compel her to take it back. It would be marvelously like us." The eventual peace treaty giving the United States the land Polk had originally wanted—though not as much as he had come to want—only intensified the fighting in Congress. The question over whether these new western territories should allow slavery threatened to rip the whole Union apart.

It was, to borrow Lee's word, "marvelously" like the United States. Since the country's founding, a series of rickety compromises had bridged the widening chasm between the largely free-labor North and the slave-driving South. The Constitutional Convention, which George Washington chaired, had avoided one sectional impasse by agreeing to count each slave as three-fifths of a person. Washington and the other Founding Fathers had not been blind to the inherent contradictions between a revolution dedicated to liberty and an economic system based on forced labor, but they could see no solution except the naïve hope that time would fix the problem. Just the opposite happened. As Northern states abolished slavery during the early years of the republic, Southern states grew more reliant on their "peculiar institution." By 1820, friction between North and South had grown so fierce that Congress decided to divide the country's remaining territories along an east-west line demarcating free soil from slave soil. This passed as compromise.

For a time after the Mexican War, it seemed that crafty politicians would once again deliver. A compromise brokered in 1850 succeeded in building slight majorities for each measure in a series of bills that could never have passed as one. One provision banned the slave trade in the nation's capital. Kentucky senator Henry Clay insisted there was "less ground for objection now that a large portion of the District has been retroceded to Virginia." But in 1854, a new debate over Kansas and Nebraska divided Congress along the same old lines. The relentless western expansion that Thomas Lee and George Washington had foreseen locked North and South into a vicious cycle of conflict.

Meanwhile, for all the fighting over Texas's borders, the state still could not defend its frontier against Comanche Indian raiding parties. In 1855, Congress accepted Secretary of War Jefferson Davis's recommendation to form two new cavalry regiments. The discussion then turned to personnel. Davis wanted elite officers, and no officer had proven more elite during the late war than Lee. Lee, Davis recalled, "came from Mexico crowned with honors, covered by brevets, and recognized, young as he was, as one of the ablest of his country's soldiers." As a tribute to Lee's distinguished service, the army had assigned him to the West Point superintendent's office, a prized post reserved for engineers. The awed cadets he supervised there had taken to calling him the "Marble Model" because of "his reticence and faultless figure." The news that Davis had appointed Lee as a lieutenant colonel of cavalry represented a sudden and sharp change. It meant that Lee the engineer would command, as his father had, in the saddle. It also meant exchanging the superintendent's scenic house on the Hudson River for the parched plains of Texas. First to San Antonio and then far west of Fort Worth to the five rows of tents called Camp Cooper, Lee traveled. Never, not even in Mexico, had he been somewhere that felt more distant from Arlington.

Futile searches for hostile Indians subjected Lee and his men to temperatures that vacillated as wildly as the grasses in the wind. Hot days could end with nights so frigid that every blanket in Lee's tent could not keep him warm. Lee encountered few Comanches and found those he did "uninteresting." Feeling isolated and "in the dark" about current events back east, he begged his wife to send newspapers. He pressed to learn who had won the 1856 presidential election, and praised the results when news arrived. "Mr. Buchanan," he wrote, "is to be our next President. I hope he will be able to extinguish fanaticism North & South, & cultivate love for the Country & Union, & restore harmony between the different sections."

The distance between Lee and Mary imposed a different but familiar set of trials on their own union. At times, Mary had accompanied him to his posts; always she preferred Arlington. She gave birth to all but the first of her seven children in the house. It remained her home and, in some sense, his too, for whenever Lee received leave, there he returned. He never managed to establish any other permanent home. "I unfortunately belong to a profession, that debars all hope of domestic enjoyment, the duties of which cannot be performed, without a sacrifice of personal & private relations," he explained.

Though Lee imagined Mary joining him on the Texas frontier, he knew it could not be. Her health had deteriorated in a fashion reminiscent of his mother's. Mary traveled to springs in search of a cure for the "pain" and "stiffness" that left her an invalid. "I walk very unsteadily & not often without a crutch," she reported. Lee proposed the remedies he had administered to his mother. "Suppose you get a single one horse carriage that can shut up close, & a quiet horse for yourself, &

ride regularly." At one point, Lee sent Mary a prescription for opium and quinine pills that he had sampled for her. He also acknowledged the obvious: Mary Custis Lee was not the frontier sort. "The more I see of Army life in Texas, the less probability do I see of your ever being able to join me here." One of his letters nostalgically described a newlywed army wife. "It is a beautiful thing to see the young so hopeful. It is sad to think how soon the clouds of disappointment darken the prospect of life's horizon."

Stricken from Lee's letters was the old playfulness except when occasionally writing to his younger children about fanciful scenes, such as a spoiled Texas house cat dying after an overdose of "coffee & cream for breakfast," "pound cake for lunch," "turtle & oysters for dinner," and "buttered toast for tea." Instead, his letters succumbed to what he called his "old habit of giving advice," even though his two oldest sons had ignored his advice against joining the army. Lee's oldest son, who went by Custis Lee, had graduated first in his class from West Point. More concerning was Lee's second son, the impulsive yet affectionate William Henry Fitzhugh Lee, who had wept upon hearing the "insuperable difficulties" to his obtaining admission to the military academy. Forced to attend Harvard for a time, Rooney, as he was known, convinced his classmate Henry Adams, the grandson and great-grandson of presidents, to draft his acceptance letter after finally procuring an infantry commission in 1857. Lee worried about the debts that Rooney had accumulated in Cambridge. "I doubt whether he knows his indebtedness," Lee wrote. "He inherits much of that disposition from both branches of his family, & does not seem to strive to overcome it."

As Lee well knew, neither of Rooney's grandfathers had overcome their disposition toward debt. Custis never developed the bookkeeping habits that his adoptive father had encouraged. "Keep an account-book, and enter therein every farthing of your receipts and expenditures. The doing of which would initiate you into a habit, from which considerable advantages would result," Washington had preached to no avail. Old age had made Custis all the more neglectful. Before leaving for Texas, Lee discovered that his father-in-law had exposed himself to the kind of bookkeeping scam that would have sickened George Washington. The overseer of Custis's White House plantation on the Pamunkey River had overcharged Custis by thousands of dollars. "Many of his debits, or charges against Mr. C. are not supported by vouchers at all," Lee noted, as he tried to clean up the accounting books.

The problems followed Lee to Texas. From Mary, he learned that Custis would "take no step without consulting you & trusting to your better judgment." Lee concurred that Custis needed help. "At his age & present state of life, persons prefer their matters being accomplished by others." But there was only so much Lee could do from so far away. Letters took weeks to arrive if they arrived at all. "What I most regret is that I may not be able to relieve your father of the trouble incident to a change of manager at the White House," Lee wrote. "I am utterly at a loss what to do at this distance." On October 21, 1857, a telegram arrived bearing the answer. Lee would have to come home not because he missed Arlington's comforts, not because his wife was sick, not because his sons needed his guidance; he would have to come home because Custis had died.

Whether he would ever return to his regiment, Lee could not say. What he could say was that responsibility for closing an estate as large and messy as Custis's would be all consuming. To his commanding officer, Lee wrote:

> I am very sorry to be compelled to leave the Regt. at this time. I can make no calculations for the future, but I can see that I have at last to decide the question, which I have staved off for 20 years, whether I am to continue in the Army all my life, or to leave it now. My preferences which have clung to me from boyhood impel me to adopt the former course, but yet I feel that a man's family has its claims too.

Since childhood, Lee had defined duty as deferring his own desires, but never had the claims for his services been less compatible. Lee, it seemed, would have to choose between the demands of the army and the demands of Arlington.

* * *

On the way home, Lee must have read the obituaries running in newspapers across the country. "To the day of his death," one said of Custis, "all the recollections of his life centered around or radiated from, the time when he was one of Washington's family." Another newspaper remembered how Custis had opened Arlington to thousands eager to "look upon the touching memorials there treasured up with care of him who was first in the hearts of his countrymen." Lee had known this hospitality since childhood. He would mourn the old man's passing. "I miss every moment, him that always received me with the kindness & affection of a father," he wrote.

By the time Lee reached Arlington on November 11, 1857, grass had already grown over his father-in-law's grave. Influenza had forced the seventy-six-year-old to bed and constricted his breathing. Before losing consciousness, Custis had asked his family to bury him beside his wife, who had died four years earlier. Nearly a thousand mourners, including the secretary of war, military officers, and veterans of the War of 1812, attended Custis's funeral. The hordes of Washingtonians crossing the river clogged the bridge and filled the ferries. White families sitting in carriages rode past black families making the trip on foot. According to one account, the most "affecting incident of the day" was "the sorrow evinced by the colored people, who, at the expense of a long and painful walk, have started in numbers to be present at the funeral." Lee's daughter Agnes noted how the "so-called great" stood with the "servants" to pay their respects beneath the "dark autumn leaves." A slave named Jim Parks remembered the scene slightly differently. "We were standing with the other black folks apart from the white folks, when they laid Mr. Custis beneath his own trees," he said.

Mary had waited to open her father's will. "I will do my best," she had written Lee after Custis's death, "but you can do so much better & it is time now you were with your family." From earlier conversations with her father, she understood that matters would require her husband's attention. Just how much of his attention Lee discovered when he unsealed the will and saw himself listed as executor. Custis had left Arlington, including "every article . . . relating to Washington," to Mary for the rest of her life and then to her oldest son, George Washington Custis Lee. The White House plantation east of Richmond would go to Rooney, and a neighboring plantation called Romancoke would go to Rob Jr. To Lee's four daughters—Mary, Annie, Agnes, and Mildred—Custis left ten thousand dollars each. Short as always on cash, Custis assumed that these wondrous sums could be raised by working the plantations left to his younger two grandsons. In effect, he placed liens on their lands.

If the will had stopped there, Lee would have faced an arduous task but one achievable in time. But the document did not stop there. At the bottom appeared a long, grammatically tortured sentence so open to different interpretations that Lee needed to file suit asking the Alexandria County Circuit Court to clarify its meaning. It read:

> *And upon the legacies to my four granddaughters being paid, and my estates that are required to pay the said legacies being clear of debt, then I give freedom to my slaves, the said slaves to be emancipated by my executors in such manner as to my executors may seem most expedient and proper, the said emancipation to be accomplished in not exceeding five years from the time of my decease.*

Had Custis intended to emancipate the slaves only after the estate paid the legacies and debts, or had he intended to free the slaves regardless within five years? If the latter, Custis had demanded the impossible. How could the plantations raise sums that would take many years if the slaves who raised the crops were emancipated within five years? There was also a larger concern. For generations, the Custis estates had depended on slave labor. How could the Lees afford to maintain them without it? Custis himself surely did not know.

It was not that Custis had given no previous thought to liberating his slaves. To the contrary, the subject had occupied his mind for decades. His late wife saw to that. Mary Fitzhugh Custis had brought religious fervor to Arlington and, though not an abolitionist, believed in educating slaves for a day when they would receive their freedom. Probably at her urging, Custis had joined a society dedicated to resettling freed slaves in what would become the African state of Liberia. In 1825, Custis brought Lafayette to one of the society's meetings. On the way, the Frenchman recalled how he had once proposed a similar plan for liberating slaves. He had tried to convince his friend George Washington to join the venture. "Such an example as yours might render it a general practice," Lafayette had told Washington. Inspired by the story, Custis soon published his own scheme for manumission. He would pay his slaves one day a week until they could purchase their freedom and sail for Africa. Nothing came of the idea.

Custis might also have viewed emancipating his slaves as finishing a task his adoptive father had begun. Seeing the inefficiency and inhumanity of slavery had slowly convinced Washington that the institution was economically and morally backward. Preoccupied with his place in history, he could not rest easy on the wrong side. As a statesman, he contented himself with privately expressing his preference for eventual abolition while officially abdicating responsibility. "I can only say that there is not a man living who wishes more sincerely than I do, to see a plan adopted for the abolition . . . but there is only one proper and effectual mode by which it can be accomplished, & that is by Legislative authority," Washington wrote in 1786, after Quaker abolitionists had angered him by abetting a runaway Virginia slave. But then five years later when other Quakers followed his advice by petitioning Congress for gradual emancipation, Washington refused to help. He stayed silent, except to note that he hoped the issue would not "awake" for another two decades. In Washington's view, future generations would have to solve the problem of a union half slave and half free.

At Mount Vernon, however, Washington hoped to leave a tidier personal legacy. How to emancipate the farm's slaves consumed more of his time during his later years. The question was not an easy one, because just 123 of the property's slaves were his outright. Many more, 153 to be exact, were dower slaves belonging to the Custis estate. They had come to Mount Vernon because of Martha and would leave when she died. Their future belonged to either George Washington Parke Custis or his siblings. If Washington wanted to free every Mount Vernon slave, he would need the consent of every Custis heir, and that consent would not come cheap. In 1796, Washington proposed a plan. By contracting out the dower slaves, he could use the income to purchase their freedom from the Custises. Both sides must have realized the plan was unworkable, for negotiations ceased. When Washington died, he left a will ensuring the eventual freedom of his own slaves but not the dower slaves. "It not being in my power," Washington wrote, "under the tenure by which the dower Negros are held, to manumit them." Like his legacy on the national stage, Washington's legacy at Mount Vernon was half slave and half free.

Among the 153 dower slaves that Washington could not free, about a quarter of them became the property of George Washington Parke Custis. Records suggest that all the heirs drafted their shares of the slaves, and sentiment seems to have guided Custis's selections. The four slaves who had last seen Washington alive all appeared on his list. Housemaid Caroline Branham was number one. Like her new master, Caroline learned to use her Mount Vernon connections to her advantage. According to one account, she agreed to share her recollections of Washington's death in exchange for her grandson's emancipation. Another slave liked to speak about the "good old times" at Mount Vernon. "The general," she once exclaimed, "was only a man!"

In some cases, the attachments between Arlington and Mount Vernon slaves proved painful. A large percentage of slaves belonging to Washington had married slaves belonging to the Custis estate. While Washington had avoided splitting up these families during his life, his inability to emancipate the dower slaves along with his own slaves guaranteed this "most painful" scenario would come to pass. One victim would be a slave named Frank Lee, the brother of the legendary Billy Lee, who served as Washington's manservant during the Revolution. The brothers, both mulattoes, took their surname from their former master, who was Harry Lee's uncle and whose widow had sold them to Washington. At Mount Vernon, Frank Lee married a dower slave and had a son named Philip. Because slave children belonged to their mothers' owners, Philip could not claim his freedom when his father did. For decades afterward, Philip Lee labored at Arlington as Custis's "favorite body servant." Custis described him as "highly intelligent" and promised his bondage would not last "much longer."

When Custis died in 1857, his estate still included a small number of original Mount Vernon slaves and a much larger number of slaves whose ancestors had come from the old house. Altogether, Arlington had sixty-three slaves, the White House ninety, and Romancoke forty-three. Custis had been a master true to his own personality: negligent enough to invite complaints about the shabbiness of the White House slave quarters; depraved enough to expose himself to gossip about impregnating slaves; warmhearted enough to allow Lee's children to conduct reading and writing classes for blacks in defiance of Virginia law; and lazy enough to create a culture of indolence that infected Arlington's every acre. "The servants here have been so long accustomed to do little or nothing," said Mary.

Lee would have to change more than the culture. Time and neglect had reduced Arlington to a shadow of its former splendor. For all his father-in-law's interest in sheep shearing, the estate had lost all its lambs. Lee also found that Custis had between eleven and twelve thousand dollars of unpaid bills. "Debts are pouring in on me, not in large amounts, but sufficient to absorb my available funds," Lee wrote. He estimated that Arlington would require ten thousand dollars in repairs. "What am I [to] do," he wrote. "Everything is in ruins & will have to be rebuilt." Still undecided about his own future, he confided that he did not see himself as a farmer. "I feel more familiar with the military operations of a campaign than the details of a farm."

At the same time, with his two oldest sons assigned to posts far from home and his youngest son still in school, Lee realized his leave from the army would have to last until at least the end of 1858. Custis Lee sent a letter from San Francisco offering to give his interest in Arlington to his father. "Since I first became aware of the requirement of my dear Grandfather's will, I have been convinced that it was not only right and proper, but in accordance with the best interests of all of us, that Pa should have unlimited control over the whole property." "Touched" as Lee was, he refused. It was as close as he ever came to owning Arlington. He told his son, "If you could pick up in California some bags of gold, or marry some nice woman with enough for both, you might then resign if you felt disposed, & live the life of a country gentleman." Short of striking gold, Lee could see "little prospect" of liberating the slaves within five years. His only hope was that the courts would construe the will in a way that allowed him to delay emancipating the slaves as long as needed to pay the debts and his daughters' legacies.

While awaiting the court's decision, Lee made his presence known to Arlington's slaves. He had previous experience as a slaveholder. He had spent his early years on a plantation, and his mother had left him several slaves in her will. For most of his adult life, however, Lee had gone out of his way to avoid dealing with slavery by either hiring out his blacks or stashing them away on Custis's far-flung plantations. "Do not trouble yourself about them, as they are not worth it," he had told Mary. In his own will, which he drafted before leaving for the Mexican War, Lee provided for "Nancy and her children at the White House" to be "liberated so soon as it can be done to their advantage & that of others." As the wording suggests, Lee believed immediate emancipation would benefit neither blacks nor whites, even as he wished for slavery's eventual demise. To his wife shortly before Custis's death, he had written:

> In this enlightened age, there are few I believe, but what will acknowledge, that slavery as an institution, is a moral & political evil in any country. It is useless to expatiate on its disadvantages. I think it however a greater evil to the white than to the black race, & while my feelings are strongly enlisted in behalf of the latter, my sympathies are more strong for the former. The blacks are immeasurably better off here than in Africa, morally, socially & physically. The painful discipline they are undergoing, is necessary for their instruction as a race, & I hope will

prepare & lead them to better things. How long their subjugation may be necessary is known & ordered by a wise & merciful Providence.

Deferring to providence, of course, conveniently excused Lee from any personal responsibility for ending slavery, never mind that he wanted a court to extend it in the case of the Custis slaves. As long as slavery lasted, he expected blacks to do their duty, just as he had always done his own. Searching for an overseer for Arlington, he described the ideal candidate as "an energetic honest farmer, who while he will be considerate & kind to the negroes, will be firm & make them do their duty." That, he thought, should not be too much to ask of the people living off his family's land.

Lee asked for more than he realized. The slaves, Mary reported, "cannot be convinced of the necessity now of exerting themselves to accomplish the conditions of the will," even though "the sooner they do the sooner will they be entitled to their freedom." One reason the slaves were "accustomed to do little" may have been that there was little for them to do; Custis had kept far more slaves than Arlington's limited operations required. Lee considered many of the slaves "a charge" on the estate rather than an asset because their "advanced" age rendered them "incapable of labor."

Complicating matters was the confusion over when the slaves could expect their freedom. The controversy stirred passions far beyond the Virginia countryside because the blacks in question had not just belonged to anyone. They had belonged to Washington's adopted son. With the facts few and fuzzy, stories spread. According to one rumor, Custis had summoned his slaves to his deathbed and granted them immediate emancipation. His heirs, the story went, had then conspired to dash these hopes. The whispers attracted attention. Mary observed strangers "lurking about" Arlington. She heard them telling the slaves "they had a right to their freedom immediately & that if they would unite & demand it they would obtain it." Previously Mary had described fulfilling her deceased mother's ambition of relocating the family's slaves overseas as a "sacred duty." Now she prayed that God would cure her servants of their "ingratitude." They had become an "immense burden."

On December 30, 1857, the *New York Times* republished an anonymous letter accusing Custis's heirs of violating his will. "It would be awful if the last remaining member of the household of Washington should not be allowed, should be prevented by fraud, from carrying out those precepts which he had learned, standing by the knee, and hearing from the lips, of that immortal Sage!" Although Lee published a letter denying the charges, the stories did not disappear. Arlington's slaves began believing them.

When Lee tried to hire out slaves for jobs outside the estate, several "thwarted" his plans by telling employers they "were illegally held in slavery." Mary described the slaves as "discontented & impertinent" and her husband as "harassed," a condition common among border-state slaveholders. As much as "enlightened" masters claimed to dislike slavery, they considered the abolitionists to their north the greater evil. Lee worried that the agitators would pit slaves and masters against each other. His prediction almost came to pass in the spring of 1858, when three Arlington slaves revolted. The rebels, Lee wrote, "refused to obey my orders, & said they were as free as I was." Lee jailed the perpetrators but could not lock away the thought.

By the summer of 1859, Lee had delayed his return to Texas multiple times. Every time one extension expired, the soldier normally known as "the most punctual man" found himself explaining to commanding officers why his personal affairs necessitated another. The legal questions surrounding the will remained unresolved. An unfavorable ruling from the circuit court in May prompted Lee to appeal the case to the Virginia Supreme Court. Meanwhile, Mary's health declined again. "I really begin to despond of her recovery and fear she will never be entirely relieved," Lee wrote his oldest son in July. Between his wife's rheumatism and his father-in-law's "unsettled business," Lee could see no hope of rejoining his regiment until at least the fall.

"God knows whether I have done right, or whether my stay will be an advantage."

Whether Lee had done right depended on one's perspective. From his own perspective, Lee believed that fulfilling Custis's will required the kind of strenuous exertion his father-in-law had spent a lifetime avoiding. When Rooney returned to Virginia to marry his sweetheart in the spring of 1859, he could not believe Arlington's physical transformation. Lee had cleaned up the hill and dramatically increased the acreage under cultivation. Plus, with his second son soon to be in position to manage the White House on a permanent basis, Lee could focus even more of his energies on Arlington. Among other improvements, Lee fixed the leak in the roof over the house Custis had erected to keep the first president's relics dry. "I hope to prevent the decay of what has been previously constructed & transmit the Estate to its future possessor in tolerable preservation," Lee wrote.

Even fierce critics conceded that Lee had succeeded in keeping Arlington's laborers "harder at work than ever." While that work held up Arlington's roof, it provoked a national debate over whether Lee had degraded the estate's foundations. On June 24, 1859, the *New York Tribune* published a pair of letters resurrecting the allegation that Custis's heirs had deprived his slaves of their freedom. Previous articles had not attacked Lee by name; these two did. According to the letters, an officer had recently apprehended three black runaways belonging to the estate. When brought back to Arlington, the slaves faced their master's fury. One letter writer using the pseudonym "citizen" described Lee's reaction this way: "Col. Lee ordered them whipped. They were two men and one woman. The officer whipped the two men and said he would not whip the woman, and Col. Lee stripped her and whipped her himself. These are facts as I learn from near relatives of the men whipped." The other letter writer, also using a pseudonym, rebuked his countrymen for their silence as Lee's injustice stained a site sacred by its associations with George Washington. "Next to Mount Vernon, we associate 'the Custis place' with the 'Father of this free country.' Shall

'Washington's body guard' be thus tampered with, and never a voice raised for such utter helplessness?"

Whatever the truth—Mary claimed to be "only astonished" at her husband's "forbearance"—Lee declined to respond. "The N.Y. Tribune has attacked me for my treatment of your grandfather's slaves, but I shall not reply," he told his oldest son. Since returning from Texas, Lee had viewed his times and trials through a slaveholder's eye. To save Arlington and to emancipate the slaves Washington could not free, Custis had willed it so. "He has left me an unpleasant legacy," Lee wrote, still unaware of the troubles brewing upriver.

CHAPTER FIVE

Washington's Sword

About sixty miles up the Potomac from George Washington Parke Custis's troubled estate lay the town of Harpers Ferry and, near there, a country house called Beallair, belonging to another gentleman proud of his connections to George Washington. His name was Lewis Washington, and he was the first president's great-grandnephew. A balding, burly man with a bushy beard and a high opinion of himself, Lewis Washington had recently accepted the honorary title of colonel. Choosing to live behind the Blue Ridge Mountains, which seal eastern Virginia off from the Shenandoah Valley and the western Appalachians beyond, Lewis Washington donated his famous relative's birthplace downriver to the state. He also claimed he could resolve a long-standing controversy over the authorship of the farewell address George Washington had issued at the end of his presidency. Documents in his possession, Lewis said, proved that the president had written the address himself, even though the president had not.

Such was Lewis Washington's reputation that it did not faze him when a blue-eyed man whom he had met only once before paid a visit to his house in September 1859 and requested to see his family relics. Lewis supposed the visitor was one of the hundreds of workers at the federal armory at Harpers Ferry. "Almost all of [them]," Lewis explained, "know me, though I do not know them." Happy to oblige, Lewis welcomed the man and let him handle a pistol that Lafayette had given General Washington. "It would never be shot again," Lewis

Washington said when asked how well it fired. He also showed off a dress sword, one of five that George Washington had left to his nephews. In his will, George Washington had given specific instructions regarding their use. "These Swords are accompanied with an injunction not to unsheath them for the purpose of shedding blood, except it be for self defence, or in defence of their Country and its rights; and in the latter case, to keep them unsheathed, and prefer falling with them in their hands, to the relinquishment thereof." What exactly those words meant would mean a great deal in the coming months.

Shortly after midnight on October 17, 1859, Lewis heard his name summoned. Except for his slaves, there should have been no one else on the estate. Drowsy, disoriented, and dressed in a nightshirt and slippers, he opened his bedroom door. Several men carrying rifles and revolvers barged in. "Is your name Washington?" their leader, a man named Stevens, asked.

"That is my name," Lewis responded. There was no point pretending otherwise; one of the other assailants had already confirmed it. The voice sounded familiar. Had they met before? Through the smoky torchlight, Lewis Washington saw blue eyes. It was the stranger who only a few weeks earlier had asked to see his relics. That visit had been a ruse, a covert scouting operation for what would become known as John Brown's Raid.

"You are our prisoner," said Stevens, instructing Lewis to dress himself appropriately for a ride into the cold autumn night. At this point, Lewis Washington had many questions. First among them: Why? "We have come here for the purpose of liberating all the slaves of the South," came the answer.

Accounts diverge over how the conversation went. Lewis recalled mocking his captors' manhood. "I should doubt your courage; you have too many arms to take one man. . . . I believe with a pop-gun I could take either of you in your shirt tail." One intruder recalled Lewis begging for his life and saying, "You can have my slaves, if you will let me remain." The men refused to bargain. They had come to seize the master of Beallair, and that was not all. They wanted his weapons, especially the famous sword. It was a black member of the raiding party, Osborne Anderson, who stepped forward to take the sword from Lewis. The symbolism was more than George Washington's great-grandnephew could bear. "The Colonel," Anderson later claimed, "cried heartily when he found he must submit, and appeared taken aback." After the sword had changed hands, the kidnappers loaded Lewis and a few of his slaves into a caravan bound for Harpers Ferry, where John Brown himself waited. Lewis Washington did not recognize the name. Soon enough the whole world would know it. America's most violent abolitionist had stolen George Washington's sword. The task of retrieving it would fall to Lieutenant Colonel Robert E. Lee.

Lee understood the symbolism of a sword touched by Washington because he owned one himself. On Washington's Birthday in 1848, Custis announced he would present the relic to his son-in-law, then in Mexico. Washington had originally given the sword to Custis in 1799 with the same injunction he later gave his nephews: to never unsheathe it save in defense of the country. By presenting the sword to Lee, Custis probably hoped to draw attention to his son-in-law's impressive military record. Newspapers across the country swallowed the bait. "When this interesting relic of a past age shall arrive in Mexico, will not many a martial spirit of our gallant army delight to grasp a hilt that once was grasped by the Father of his Country?" the *Daily National Intelligencer* asked. Lee already knew the answer. He had seen how Washington's relics dazzled his fellow soldiers. For a Christmas dinner in Mexico, he had the table set with Revolutionary-era knives and forks that Custis had lent. "They were passed around the table with much veneration & excited universal attention," Lee reported back to Arlington.

Evidently Lee also felt personal responsibility for protecting Washington's legacy, especially the farewell address, which had warned Americans to prize the Union over party and sectional loyalties. The controversy over the authorship of the address touched a chord. That Alexander Hamilton's son would claim his father had ghostwritten the words angered Lee. He would have known about Lewis Washington's supposed evidence to the contrary because Lewis's father had told Lee's brother Carter about it. At one point, Lee asked his father-in-law to settle the debate. "You have doubtless seen the injudicious claim (not to speak of it in harsher terms) set up by a son of Gen. Hamilton. If he could prove what he desires, it would take from this matchless paper its greatest value." Custis, Lee said, must straighten the record. "Not that I think Washington's fame will ever need defense. But I fear that the influence of his glorious acts & paternal advice may be attempted to be weakened by the miserably selfish who ignorant of virtue & patriotism are unable to appreciate unfailing wisdom & spotless integrity."

On the morning of October 17, 1859, as if to fulfill that prophecy, came word of Harpers Ferry. The first telegrams reporting the insurrection caused a flurry at the War Department in Washington. "Telegraphic advices present a serious affair at Harper's Ferry, where United States Armory, and our bridges are in full possession of large bands of armed men, said to be abolitionists. . . . The guns from Armory have been taken for offensive use," read a message begging the War Department to send troops. Secretary of War John B. Floyd needed an officer to command. Fortunately, one of the finest had taken leave across the Potomac. Floyd sent Lieutenant J. E. B. Stuart, a flamboyant twenty-six-year-old West Point graduate, to fetch Lee.

Across the bridge to Arlington rode Stuart. He found Lee standing in a field, supervising the Custis slaves. The harvest would have to wait. If the story Stuart shared checked out, a mob of three thousand had seized the federal armory. Lee must report at once to Washington. No less than the president of the United States waited. In a meeting at the executive mansion, James Buchanan ordered Lee to take command of all federal forces converging at Harpers Ferry. With Stuart as his aide, Lee would go west, as his father and Washington had during the Whiskey Rebellion, to reassert federal control.

It had been President Washington who insisted on placing a federal armory at Harpers Ferry. Advisers had scoffed at the idea. Building a military installation the republic could little afford in a western backwoods made little sense unless one believed, as Washington did, that the Potomac represented the pathway to the west. The scenery surrounding Harpers Ferry fed Washington's fantasy. At the base of three towering bluffs in the Blue Ridge, the town claims the slice of land where the Shenandoah River, flowing north, meets the Potomac, flowing east. "In the moment of their junction," Thomas Jefferson had said, "they rush together against the mountain, rend it asunder, and pass off to the sea." That waterpower could turn the wheels needed to manufacture arms while the mountains provided protection, or so Washington thought. "This spot affords every advantage that could be wished for water works to any extent; and that no place is more capable of complete defence at a small expense," he wrote in 1795. The government would have to buy the land, but that should not stand in the way. Washington already knew one landowner in the area who desperately needed cash—Harry Lee. Washington had "no doubt" his friend would "dispose of his right on very reasonable terms."

By the time Harry Lee's youngest son set out for Harpers Ferry in 1859, the armory manufactured about fifteen thousand guns a year. That the town had prospered, however, did not mean Washington's vision for the Potomac had prevailed. In fact, the route Lee traveled to Harpers Ferry suggested the opposite. Washington wanted the wealth from the west floating down the Potomac to port in the District of Columbia, but other towns had their own plans for diverting this trade. The rivalry between Washington, DC, and Baltimore escalated on July 4, 1828, when the two cities broke ground on competing transportation projects intended to stake their place as the gateway to the west. The nation's capital, still under its namesake's influence, started another canal; Baltimore began a railroad. So decisive was the Baltimore & Ohio Railroad's victory that by the 1850s the river could not even offer the best route between two towns on its own banks. To go from Washington to Harpers Ferry, Lee took one train north to Baltimore and then transferred to another heading west.

Late on the night of October 17, Lee and Stuart met up with ninety marines at Sandy Hook, the B&O's last stop on the Maryland side of the Potomac before a covered bridge carried the tracks into Harpers Ferry. They would cross the river together.

One night earlier, John Brown and eighteen followers had also crossed the Potomac. In Brown's mind, there would be no going back. He had plotted this moment for months at the Maryland farmhouse he rented. God had chosen him to take the crusade against slavery south of the river. Visions of "Old Testament justice" blinded the fifty-nine-year-old to the cycle of wild expectations and spectacular failures that had marked his business career. His megalomania also blinded the Northern patrons who funded his plans so long as he promised to spare them the gory details. Behind Brown's long white beard and gray eyes, Boston's leading thinkers saw a man willing to act, and act he would. Already he had massacred proslavery settlers in the disputed Kansas territory. Now he would seize the arsenal at Harpers Ferry, liberate the area's slaves, and lead an army snowballing in size southward. The constitution he planned to impose on the conquered territories declared slavery a "violation of those eternal and self-evident truths set forth in our Declaration of Independence." The Founding Fathers had proclaimed all men held the right to life and liberty, and John Brown intended to make it so. Perhaps that was why Brown wanted George Washington's sword.

It had taken only minutes for the raiders to subdue the watchman guarding the armory and take control of the chain of riverside buildings constituting the complex. A smaller contingent had then headed into the countryside to capture Lewis Washington, his neighbors, and their slaves. When the kidnappers returned, Brown welcomed his famous hostage. "I presume you are Mr. Washington," he said. "I wanted you particularly for the moral effect it would give our cause, having one of your name as a prisoner." Brown, however, was not without courtesy. When he heard how pained Lewis had been to part with the famous sword, he pledged to return it once he had achieved his end. "I will take especial care of it." For the next day, Brown himself would hold the sword.

While the element of surprise had given Brown an advantage during the night, his situation deteriorated when the sun rose. Across the countryside, enraged citizens toting guns headed for Harpers Ferry. Looking for high ground around the armory, they found it everywhere, for Brown had chosen to make his stand on the lowest point in all of western Virginia. Months before, he had debated whether George Washington was history's greatest general. Now he made the same miscalculation that Washington had made: The mountains did not protect the armory. They encircled it. Short on ammunition but not content to wait for forces from Washington, DC, the locals melted down pewter plates and utensils into bullets, loaded their rifles, and took positions overlooking the armory. "Brown and those of his party who were with him in the armory buildings were completely hemmed in," said one local. "The bridges over both rivers, north and east, together with the western or upper end of the armory grounds, were in possession of the citizens, who occupied every 'coign of vantage' from which they could get a fair shot at the insurgents." By noon, bullets rained down on the raiders from every direction.

With casualties mounting and more militiamen arriving, Brown led his force inside a small engine house near the armory gate. Its sturdy brick walls offered protection against the storm of fire, but the single room could not accommodate the more than thirty hostages Brown had accumulated. He would have to choose whom to keep. Ten men, including Lewis Washington, each felt a tap on the shoulder. "I want you," Brown said. A few at a time, they filed into the engine house, where they crouched on the cold brick floor, away from the slits and holes through which the insurgents returned fire. At nightfall, Brown locked the wooden doors. Even in the darkness, he could see the day's fighting had reduced his force to five combat-ready men. Two of his sons lay wounded; his vision of slaves rising en masse against their masters lay in tatters. Still, Brown stayed calm. To one son, he said, "If you must die, die like a man." That was what Brown planned for himself. Lewis overheard the man carrying his family sword say as much.

Sometime around midnight, under a light rain, Lee led the marines across the Potomac into the armory. He arranged his forces around the engine house. Brown and his cohorts would have no escape. Lee would have ordered an immediate assault against the raiders but, as he put it, "for the fear of sacrificing the lives of some of the gentlemen held by them as prisoners." It had become widely known that Lewis Washington was among the hostages, and no doubt Lee had him in mind when he telegraphed the secretary of war that Brown held "some of our best citizens." "Their safety," Lee recalled, "was the subject of painful consideration." If the marines charged into the engine house in the darkness, they would have no way of telling friends from foes. Operations would have to wait until the morning. Even so there would be no sleep. With J. E. B. Stuart standing over his shoulder, Lee agonized over his plan. He also sent word back to Washington that additional reinforcements would be "unnecessary." The earlier reports had vastly overstated the size of the rebellion.

At dawn, two thousand "spectators" gathered around the armory to see what Lieutenant Colonel Lee had planned. They would not have to wait long. Lee stationed himself about a dozen yards from the engine house—close enough to give orders, far enough away to survey the entire scene. In his haste to leave Arlington the previous day, he had forgotten his military uniform and still wore civilian clothes. The concern he felt for the hostages did not show on his face. The lips below the dark mustache never quivered. "He had no arms upon his person, and treated the affair as one of no very great consequence, which would be speedily settled," said a marine. At about seven o'clock in the morning, Lee sent Stuart to the engine house under a flag of truce. Brown cracked the door just enough so Stuart could see his weathered face and read him the note Lee had drafted.

Colonel Lee, United States army, commanding the troops sent by the President of the United States to suppress the insurrection at this place, demands the surrender of the persons in the armory buildings. If they will peaceably surrender themselves and restore the pillaged property, they shall be kept in safety to await the orders of the President. Colonel

Lee represents to them, in all frankness, that it is impossible for them to escape; that the armory is surrounded on all sides by troops; and that if he is compelled to take them by force he cannot answer for their safety.

As soon as Stuart finished presenting Lee's terms, Brown tried to negotiate better ones. Stuart explained that Lee had authorized him only to give terms, not to receive them. In that case, Brown declared he would fight on. "I choose to sell my life as dearly as possible." Less welcome words the hostages could not have heard. Several cried out for Lee to negotiate until a booming voice from the back of the engine house silenced them all. "Never mind us, fire!" Lewis Washington yelled. Familiar with the voice, Lee supposedly muttered, "The old revolutionary blood does tell."

Fearing what desperate act Brown might commit in his last moments, Lee wanted to keep the time between the parley and the assault as short as possible. For that reason, he had already ordered Lieutenant Israel Green to prepare his storming party. As soon as the conversation with Brown ended, Stuart waved his cap. It was the signal for the marines. Twelve of them wearing bright blue charged the doors, which Brown had tied shut. Though their sledgehammers bounced off the wood, a ladder they wielded as a battering ram broke through. The marines could have fired into the opening, but Lee worried the bullets might strike the hostages. So through the doors, with bayonets and swords drawn, the marines went. A bullet whizzing past Lieutenant Green struck one marine in the stomach. Smoke filled the room. In the confusion, Green saw a figure kneeling to reload. "This is Osawatomie," shouted Lewis Washington, using Brown's nickname from Kansas. That was all Green needed to know. Raising his dress sword, he whacked Brown's head and then thrust at his breast, but the blade crumpled. Unlike most of the insurgents, Brown would live to face trial.

Minutes after beginning, the operation ended. Lee had reestablished federal control over the armory. The crowd cheered for the hostages, all of whom immediately exited the engine house save one who lingered. Lewis Washington had suffered enough indignities already. He would not let two thousand gawkers see how he had soiled his hands in captivity. Only after pausing to put on a pair of kid gloves did he walk out with his great-granduncle's sword in hand. Brown had kept at least one promise: the sword was safe. Brown had set it down moments before Lee ordered the assault.

That afternoon, Lee allowed a group of distinguished citizens, including Virginia senator James Mason, Lewis Washington, and a few newspapermen, to come see Brown recuperating on the floor of the paymaster's office. The blood gushing from his head wound had matted down his hair and stained his face. He did not appear to be in any condition to answer questions. If Brown did not feel up to an interview, Lee would force the visitors to come back another time. Brown asked them to stay. They were eager to ask questions, and he was eager to answer them. "He was glad to be able to make himself and his motives clearly understood," a reporter wrote. Lee had given Brown exactly what he wanted: the opportunity to make himself heard.

The question-and-answer session, which newspapers published verbatim, started Brown on his march to martyrdom. His plot to free the slaves, he explained, had been part of God's plan. "It is, in my opinion, the greatest service a man can render to God." When asked why he refused to surrender despite the impossible odds, he said, "I did not think it was my duty." Others would pick up the sword he had held. "You had better—all you people at the South—prepare yourselves for a settlement of that question that must come up for settlement sooner than you are prepared for it," he said. "I am nearly disposed of now; but this question is still to be settled—this negro question."

The search Lee had ordered of Brown's Maryland farmhouse had by this time uncovered thousands of additional weapons along with correspondence linking the insurgents to Northern intellectuals. What Senator Mason and the other Virginians interrogating Brown most wanted to know was how far the conspiracy extended. Was Brown just the first wave of violence preparing to pour across the Potomac? Given the trouble that abolitionists had brought to Arlington, one might expect Lee to have thought so. But the official report he filed on the incident concluded otherwise. Brown's scheme, he said, had stood no chance. "Its temporary success was owing to the panic and confusion he succeeded in creating by magnifying his numbers." Nothing better demonstrated the plan's absurdity, in Lee's opinion, than the aversion the slaves belonging to Lewis Washington had shown for Brown. "The blacks whom he forced from their homes in this neighborhood, as far as I could learn, gave him no voluntary assistance." Indeed, Lewis Washington later testified that he had not lost any of his own slaves, though one he had hired from another master mysteriously drowned. "If anything," Lewis Washington said, the experience made his slaves "much more tractable." That loyalty, so far as Lee cared to look, said it all. "The result proves that the plan was the attempt of a fanatic or madman, which could only end in failure."

There was a corollary to Lee's conclusion: Brown may have been deluded, but then so was every Virginian petrified his plan might prevail. At nine o'clock in the evening on October 19, a refugee from a neighboring town brought an alarming tale to Harpers Ferry. He had fled his home after hearing "cries of murder and the screams of the women and children." While Lee gave the story "no credence," he nonetheless led the marines on a night march of four and a half miles to make sure. "I was happy to find it a false alarm," he wrote. It was one of the first of many false alarms that would sweep across Virginia and contribute to a "panic mentality." Three decades earlier, Lee had criticized whites for overreacting to Nat Turner's rebellion. Now, as before, his opinion on the actual danger dissented from the majority. A committee, which the state legislature appointed to investigate Harpers Ferry, concluded, "The evidence before your committee is sufficient to show the existence, in a number of northern states, of a widespread conspiracy, not merely against Virginia, but against the peace and security of all the southern states."

Virginia's pugnacious governor, Henry A. Wise, delivered an

address warning Virginians not to underestimate the danger. The speech refuted Lee's characterization of Brown as a madman. "You must not imagine that this invasion was so insignificant, or that Commander Brown was mad, because his force was so small." While praising Lee as "worthy of any service on earth," Wise proclaimed his embarrassment that the state militia had declined the honor of leading the storming party against the engine house. Curiously, Lee had given the militia this option before tapping the marines, even though the armory belonged to the federal government. That the militia officers had worried their inexperience could cost Lewis Washington his life did not excuse their dereliction of duty, at least not in Wise's eyes. "I chided them for their mistake," the governor said, "and told them that if Gen. George Washington had been one of the prisoners and even his life had been imperiled by the attack, it should not have been delayed five minutes." Shortly afterward, state officials asked Lee for advice on bolstering the militia.

Even if John Brown had accomplished as little as Lee suspected, the raid had given Lee the opportunity to accomplish something himself. On October 20, 1859—one day shy of two years since learning about Custis's death—Lee returned to Washington. The credit he earned during his short stint at Harpers Ferry more than compensated for whatever opportunities he had lost during his long leave from Texas. Stuart said Lee deserved a gold medal. Secretary of War Floyd asked Lee for "quite a long" briefing. President Buchanan asked Lee to dinner. And when Governor Wise said he feared Northern radicals would attempt to rescue Brown from the gallows, there could be no doubt whom the War Department would dispatch.

At the end of November, Lee led four companies back to Harpers Ferry. Whatever else happened during Brown's execution, the federal government would not risk letting Brown's allies seize the armory again. Lee wrote Mary that he had kept busy "posting sentinels & picquets to ensure timely notice of the approach of the enemy." While

Lee underlined "enemy" in jest—the threat struck him as hysteria—Brown had proven a more formidable opponent when locked in prison than when locked in the engine house. Several miles to the west in a jail in Charlestown, Virginia, Brown awaited death. "Now, if it is deemed necessary that I should forfeit my life for the furtherance of the ends of justice, and mingle my blood with the blood of millions in this slave country whose rights are disregarded by wicked, cruel, and unjust enactments, I say let it be done," Brown had told a courtroom. Happy to comply, the judge scheduled the hanging for December 2. As the date approached, the second wave of Northern invaders, which Governor Wise feared, did not flood across the Potomac, but prayers and letters praising Brown's courage did.

The day before the hanging, Lee did receive a visit from one Northerner: Brown's wife. She had taken the train to Harpers Ferry in the hope of seeing her husband one last time. Governor Wise had imposed such stringent security that she needed permission to travel the rest of the way to Charlestown. Lee could not help because as a federal officer he had no say over who visited a prisoner in Virginia's custody. "It is a matter over which I have no control & wish to take none," he wrote. Despite his disinterest, he showed his customary courtesy, which Brown's wife reportedly appreciated.

Standing guard at Harpers Ferry the next day, Lee could not hear the church bells ringing across the North, nor could he see Brown flailing above a field outside Charlestown. One who did witness the hanging was an eccentric brown-bearded Virginia Military Institute professor named Thomas Jackson. His blue eyes admired Brown's "unflinching firmness." Jackson confided to his wife, "I was much impressed with the thought that before me stood a man, in the full vigor of health, who must in a few minutes be in eternity." John Brown's body dangled in the wind. But as best his executioners could tell, not a doubt stirred in his mind. He knew he had fulfilled his destiny.

The strength of Brown's convictions, it seemed, impressed nearly everyone except Lee. Even Lewis Washington described Brown as "the coolest and firmest man I ever saw." To conclude likewise, of course, would have been antithetical to Lee's personality. A soldier schooled to deny himself could not admire a fanatic egotistic enough to conflate his own wishes with God's will. It was not that Lee lacked faith. He had come a long way since calling himself "sinful Robert." In 1853, he had knelt for confirmation in the Alexandria church that George Washington had attended. The religious views Lee adopted, however, differed from the self-denial he had practiced since childhood only in one sense: where before he resigned himself to never having his own way, he now accepted the forces confining his options as God's way. And so it was with slavery. "While we see the course of the final abolition of human slavery is onward, & we give it the aid of our prayers & all justifiable means in our power, we must leave the progress as well as the result in his hands who sees the end; who chooses to work by slow influences; & with whom two thousand years are but as a single day," Lee wrote. "The abolitionist must know this, and must see that he has neither the right or power of operating except by moral means & suasion."

That George Washington's sword might cut a new direction never dawned on Lee. So unrevolutionary was his thinking that he would be unable to rebel against rebellion in the next chapter of his life. Within less than a year and a half's time, he would order Thomas Jackson to lead troops back to Harpers Ferry not to protect the federal armory but to seize the machinery of war. Already the gears had begun turning. Soon so would Lee.

CHAPTER SIX

The Decision

Before the sun rose on February 10, 1860, Robert E. Lee left Arlington for San Antonio. Orders had arrived instructing him to assume temporary command of the Department of Texas. Although sad to leave Arlington, he comforted himself by considering what would have happened to the estate had he not come home at all. "When I compare the present state of things, with what they would have been, had I left no representative behind, I have so much cause for gratitude, & take so much comfort, that my mind is comparatively easy." His stay had made a difference; now his absence would make little. The army had transferred his oldest son to the capital. From that position, Custis Lee could assume control of Arlington.

The house was back in the news thanks to the posthumous publication of George Washington Parke Custis's memoirs. For years, the *Daily National Intelligencer* had published articles that Custis had written about his adoptive father and life at Mount Vernon. "Friends in all parts of the Union," Mary Lee said, had urged her father to publish these recollections "in the more durable form of a volume, as a legacy to his countrymen." In typical fashion, Custis died without finishing the project. "It is my purpose as soon as I can command the time and make a minute investigation of all his papers to see what materials were collected for his memories of Washington," Mary told Benson J. Lossing, a noted historian whom she asked to edit the volume. For the introduction, Mary composed a brief biography that said more about her father's ancestry than about his life. More interesting was how the correspondence she included between her father and George Washington revealed the tensions between the two.

Lee supported these editorial decisions. "It would have been very easy to have said more in your memoir of your father, but it is difficult to draw the line between what would be pleasing & interesting to friends [and the] public," he told Mary. "A man engaged in public affairs, the events in which he participates, lends interest to his history. But one who has passed his days in retirement, & shone in domestic scenes, is without the means of eliciting general interest." Little doubt Lee's harsh assessment reflected two years of resentment against his father-in-law's legacy. Less Custis, Lee thought, made for a better book; hence the title *Recollections and Private Memoirs of Washington*.

Reading the book's reviews—mixed as they were—amused Lee during his travels. "I have been much pleased that your publication of your fathers memoirs has been so well received & has been so highly mentioned by the press," he wrote Mary. "I hope the sale will be extensive, & encourage the publisher to issue another edition. You might then I think make some improvement in the text." Already Mary had worried about how "our northern readers" would respond to mention of slaves. Lee now recommended omitting a letter she had included detailing a business partnership that gave Washington a financial stake in a privateer vessel during the Revolution. Some readers, Lee worried, might view Washington's involvement as war profiteering. "It may suit the mercantile taste of the East more than it does mine." By "East," Lee almost certainly meant northeast. How Americans viewed Washington's legacy increasingly depended on where they lived. Even the Father of His Country had become sectional.

Despite the divisions in the country, the railroad continued its conquest of the continent. The trip from Arlington to New Orleans took Lee a mere three and a half days. Ever the engineer, Lee insisted it should have been shorter. "When the route becomes properly organized and operated, the time will be reduced to 3 days. In fact, 12 hours were unnecessarily consumed at various points as I came along." On February 19, Lee reached the department headquarters in San Antonio. New buildings had sprung up since his last visit, but the still largely treeless skyline depressed his spirits. "I know it is useless to indulge these feelings, yet they arise unbidden, & will not stay repressed. They start in me in the business hours of the day & the waking hours of night, & seem to hover around me working or sleeping," he wrote to his daughter Annie on February 22.

By the start of spring, rumors about a Mexican outlaw named Juan Cortina had grown numerous enough that Lee headed to the Rio Grande to investigate. Accounts of the outlaw's whereabouts conflicted, and Lee considered even "the most reliable sources" unreliable. Riding along the river—sometimes covering forty miles in a day—exhausted his body. The temperature swings aggravated the rheumatism in his right arm. "I am sure I [am] not getting young," he told Mary. Thirteen years had passed since he outflanked the Mexican army. Now, at age fifty-three, he could not even overtake a Mexican bandit.

Lee warned his oldest son to cherish time while young because it became a rare commodity when old. "You are a young man, & a steady progressive pace, regulated with prudence, will carry you a long way. It was the reverse with me. I knew if I wished to accomplish anything, I had no time to spare." A letter announcing his first grandson's birth made Lee contemplate the legacy he would leave. Rooney, whose "infant cheek" still glowed in Lee's memory, had married the previous year and now had his own infant. Lee discouraged, but did not dissuade, the young couple from naming the child Robert. "I wish I could offer him a more worthy name & a better example. He must elevate the first & make use of the latter to avoid the errors I have committed."

First among those errors, Lee believed, was not resolving the conflict between the army and his family. "A divided heart I have too long had, and a divided life too long led. That may be one cause of the small progress I have made on either hand." Professionally, his career had stalled at lieutenant colonel, while political connections had lifted his friend Joseph Johnston, who had graduated just thirteenth in the West Point class of 1829, to quartermaster general. Lee discounted the prestige of his own title as head of the Department of Texas because he knew the posting would last only as long as the regular commander, General David Twiggs, remained on leave. On the personal side of the ledger, Lee had played the absent father so often that he wondered whether his family would miss him. "It is better too I hope for all that I am here," he told his daughter Annie. "You know I was much in the way of every body, & my tastes & pursuits did not coincide with the rest of the household. Now I hope everybody is happier."

Still, his children could not escape his advice. Either because he worried his letters would not get to his sons or because he worried their contents would not get through their heads, he repeated over and over his instructions for managing the Custis estate. He badgered Rooney to buy fire insurance for the White House plantation in case the spirit of rebellion ever inflamed "your people," by which, of course, Lee meant the property's slaves. Better safe than sorry, the hero of Harpers Ferry reasoned.

John Brown had hanged at the end of 1859, but his soul hung over the presidential election of 1860. In Charleston that spring, the Democratic Party, which had long dominated American politics, deadlocked after Southern delegates demanded more safeguards for slavery than their Northern counterparts could accept. Trying again soon after in Baltimore, the party split in two: Northern Democrats nominated Senator Stephen Douglas of Illinois; Southern Democrats nominated US Vice President John Breckinridge of Kentucky. Meanwhile, a new party called the Republicans, commandeering the old Jeffersonian name, united a diverse coalition of Northerners intent on stopping slavery's spread into new territories. Convening in Chicago, the Republicans nominated a former one-term congressman. The name Abraham Lincoln had once appeared alongside Lee's in a newspaper article listing 230 honorary managers for President Zachary Taylor's inaugural ball. Whatever Lee may have remembered about the name eleven years later did not dispose him to the Rail Splitter's candidacy. While Lee generally subscribed to a pox-on-both-houses view of politics—his military career had cemented a cynicism about career politicians who pursued popularity instead of patriotism—he understood the game and knew that the divisions among the Democrats would assure victory for the Republican. "If Judge Douglas would now withdraw & join himself & party to aid in the election of Breckinridge, he might retrieve himself before the country & Lincoln be defeated," Lee wrote in July. "Politicians I fear are too selfish to become martyrs."

That Lee said little else about the campaign preceding the most consequential election in American history might seem strange until one remembers that elections reveal their consequences only in hindsight. True, Lee heard the Southern threats to secede rather than submit to Republican rule, but he had also heard those threats in 1856 when the Republican Party ran its first presidential candidate. Back then, Lee said he preferred a Democratic victory but did "not fear" a Republican one. He probably felt the same way in 1860. The Union had always stood half slave and half free; somehow that way it would remain. In fact, just months before the election, Lee considered doing something he abhorred: buying a slave. He needed a servant in Texas. Much as he preferred to hire a white man, he struggled to find one willing to work.

On November 6, 1860, Lincoln won the presidency. Of the 180 electoral votes he secured, all came from the free states. Of the more than 1.8 million popular votes cast in his favor, not one came from a total of ten Southern states. "The Union of the present day is not the Union of our fathers," a San Antonio newspaper editorialized on November 17. "It has been utterly perverted from its original design, and it has become an engine of oppression, wrong and tyranny, which those fathers never contemplated." By late November, every state in the lower South had either called a convention to consider secession or taken steps toward doing so, with the exception of Texas, which hesitated because pro-Union governor Sam Houston, who had once wooed Mary Custis, stood against the storm. Nevertheless, Lee could now tell which way the Texas winds were blowing. Wherever he looked, he saw the state's iconic Lone Star flag flapping. A postelection meeting at the Alamo nearly ended in bloodshed after a Unionist named Charles Anderson, whose brother Robert had recently taken command of federal forts in Charleston, South Carolina, assailed secession. "The Southern States seem to be in a convulsion," Lee wrote. "It is difficult to see what will be the result."

If Texas seceded, the department's more than two thousand soldiers—representing more than one-tenth of the United States Army—would suddenly occupy hostile soil. Soldiers wondering what would happen talked of little else. One clue came in December, when General Twiggs finally returned to San Antonio. Twiggs, an old veteran of the War of 1812, announced that within six weeks, the Union would be no more. He expected the people of Texas would secede and seize the federal forts. Sympathetic to their cause, he did not plan to resist. His fellow officers would then have to decide for themselves where their loyalties lay: to the Union or to their respective states. Lee thought some compromise still possible. Otherwise, he would have accepted one of the invitations Twiggs freely granted officers wishing to return home. Instead, Lee accepted orders to head to Fort Mason on the Texas frontier.

Before leaving, Lee received a visit from Charles Anderson. Despite the near riot he had caused at the Alamo, Anderson had continued his pro-Union activities. He appeared now as a messenger bearing a confidential memo that General in Chief Winfield Scott had prepared outlining his opposition to secession. Scott had asked Anderson to share it first with Twiggs and then separately with Lee, even though the latter officer was under the former's command. The breach of protocol had insulted Twiggs. "I know General Scott fully believes that God Almighty had to spit on his hands to make Bob Lee," he had huffed. Lee proved more polite. After reading Scott's memo and listening to Anderson denounce the South, Lee responded that he faulted extremists on both sides. Moderate voices, he hoped, would prevail. But if forced to choose between the Union and Virginia, he would support his state. "He said that he was educated to believe, and he did believe, that his first obligations were due to Virginia," Anderson recalled. The reply stunned Anderson and not because it was the first time he had heard such sentiments. Other Southern officers in Texas had concluded likewise, but no other officer had married the daughter of George Washington's adopted son. Anderson had expected Lee to endorse words from Washington's farewell address: "The name of American, which belongs to you, in your national capacity, must always exalt the just pride of Patriotism, more than any appellation derived from local discriminations." How could the son of Harry Lee have been raised to think anything else? "Here was Washington's heir-at-law almost, and much like him too," Anderson later said. "I sadly asked myself: 'whence was this education?'"

The question Anderson feared to ask aloud was more complicated than he allowed. The farewell address offered fodder for both the North and the South. Though Washington had urged Americans to view their union and liberty as one and the same, he had also warned against sectional political parties. Even Lincoln could not deny that the Northern-based Republican Party fit that description. Early in the election cycle, Lincoln acknowledged that geographic lines had fractured the parties but pinned the blame south of the Mason-Dixon line. George Washington, after all, like the Republicans, had wished to place slavery on a path to extinction, not expansion. Lincoln asked the South, "Could Washington himself speak, would he cast the blame of that sectionalism upon us, who sustain his policy, or upon you, who repudiate it? We respect that warning of Washington, and we commend it to you." More to the point, after his election, Lincoln argued that dividing the country would dishonor the patriots who fought for its independence. "I am exceedingly anxious that this Union, the Constitution, and the liberties of the people shall be perpetuated in accordance with the original idea for which that struggle was made," the president-elect said.

Secessionists did not cede Washington's memory without a fight. More than one counterargument originated with the late John C. Calhoun. A quarter century after approving Robert E. Lee's West Point application, the South Carolina statesman had died "with disunion on his lips." In his final days, he warned Northerners that Washington worship would not save the Union. Washington, Calhoun declared, "was one of us—a slaveholder and a planter. We have studied his history, and find nothing in it to justify submission to wrong. . . . On the contrary, we find much in his example to encourage us, should we be forced to the extremity of deciding between submission and disunion." The Revolution itself had been a rebellion against a union, albeit one with Britain. Just as Washington had not hesitated to sever those bonds, Southerners would not now hesitate to cut their cords with the North. If that made them rebels in Northern eyes, then rebels they would be, a Texas newspaper declared. "The Abolitionists and their allies . . . call the Secessionists, 'rebels.' That is exactly what the tories called our revolutionary fathers."

What Washington himself would have done at the start of the Civil War remains a hypothetical question that historians cannot answer, though a member of Washington's cabinet once heard the president say that, in the event the Union split in half, "he had made up his mind to remove and be of the Northern." More important than which side Washington would have chosen is that both sides believed these arguments worth making. Both sides understood that Washington still commanded the allegiance of his countrymen. It was thus fitting that one of the foremost experts on Washington's life had appeared on the ballot that November as a vice-presidential candidate. Considered America's finest orator, Massachusetts statesman Edward Everett had released *The Life of George Washington* around the same time he joined Tennessee's John Bell on a desperate third-party ticket. The so-called Constitutional Union party hoped to unite moderates in the North and South but ultimately carried only three border states. That Virginia was among the three indicated just how strong Union sentiment remained in Washington's home state.

By the end of January, six states—South Carolina, Mississippi, Florida, Alabama, Georgia, and Louisiana—had seceded. Would the Old Dominion follow suit or cleave to the country its statesmen had done so much to create? A soldier waiting to learn could not have chosen a more poorly suited spot than Fort Mason. On the same line of western defenses as Fort Cooper, the post marked the edge of civilization. Mary Lee called it "one of the last places on the face of the earth." Only dated newspapers from New Orleans ever came. "I am so remote from the scene of events & receive such excited & exaggerated accounts of the opinions & acts of our statesmen, that I am at a loss what to think," Lee wrote. Cut off from current events, he turned, as Anderson had hoped, to history. Mary had mailed a copy of Edward Everett's new book; she knew her husband admired the author. Now, amid the crisis, Lee began reading *The Life of George Washington*. "I recd . . . Everetts life of Washington you sent me, & enjoyed its perusal very much. How his spirit would be grieved could he see the wreck of his mighty labours," Lee wrote Mary on January 23. "I will not however permit myself to believe till all ground for hope is gone that the work of his noble deeds will be destroyed, & that his precious advice & virtuous example will so soon be forgotten by his countrymen."

The Washington who emerged from Everett's pages had taken an expansive view of federal power, favored Hamilton's policies over Jefferson's, distanced himself from the French Revolution, and crushed the Whiskey Rebellion. This Washington, Lee concluded, would condemn secession. To his son Rooney, he wrote:

> *The framers of our Constitution never exhausted so much labour, wisdom & forbearance in its formation, surrounded it with so many guards & securities, if it was intended to be broken by every member of the Confederacy at will. It was intended for perpetual union, so expressed in the preamble, & for the establishment of a government, not a compact, which can only be dissolved by revolution or the consent of all the people in the convention assembled. It is idle to talk of secession. Anarchy would have been established, not a government, by Washington, Hamilton, Jefferson, Madison & the other patriots of the Revolution. In 1808, secession was termed treason by Virginia statesmen. What can it be now?*

Lee's analysis reflected an imperfect grasp of the document his father had endorsed. The phrase "perpetual union" appeared in the Articles of Confederation adopted during the Revolution, not in the subsequent Constitution. Still, the sentiment placed Lee in good company. Lincoln, among others, reasoned that since the Constitution promised "a more perfect union," the perpetuity pledged in the previous charter remained in effect.

Lee may have misread the opening lines of the Constitution, but no one could misread his own line on secession. The Founding Fathers had not sanctioned it, and he opposed it. That did not mean he supported the new administration. He agreed when Rooney wrote that the North had "aggrieved" the South. Lee had seen firsthand how Northern abolitionists had insulted slaveholders, inflamed slaves, and tried to incite rebellion on Southern soil. "I feel the aggression," he responded. "But I can anticipate no greater calamity for the country than a dissolution of the Union. It would be an accumulation of all the evils we complain of, & I am willing to sacrifice every thing but honour for its preservation." What Lee would not sacrifice, as it turned out, was his loyalty to his home, Virginia. He added:

> *A Union that can only be maintained by swords & bayonets, & in which strife & civil war are to take the place of brotherly love & kindness, has no charm for me. I shall mourn for my country, & for the welfare & progress of mankind. If the Union is dissolved & the government disrupted, I shall return to my native state & share the miseries of my people & save in her defence will draw my sword no more.*

That last line echoed the injunction Washington had placed on his swords. But something had changed, something crucial. Where Washington had instructed his heirs never to raise their swords save in "defence of their Country," Lee said he would raise his sword only for Virginia. "Country" had somehow mutated into "state." That was the mystery Anderson and others could not solve. Whence was this education?

The Decision

* * *

Governor Houston argued in vain to keep Texas in the Union. A state convention assembled toward the end of January and on the first of February voted to secede. Three days later, Lee received new orders. General Scott wanted to have a talk face-to-face in Washington. The journey home took Lee back through San Antonio. He arrived in that town on February 16 at three o'clock in the afternoon. The timing could not have been worse. Texas Rangers circled like vultures as Lee entered the plaza. "Who are those men?" he demanded. An army wife explained that early that morning a thousand Texans under the command of former ranger Ben McCulloch had entered town, seized the arsenal, and demanded the surrender of all federal forces and forts in the state. General Twiggs had complied. Lee could not believe his eyes. Had he still been in charge, he would have resisted. "He was determined to defend his post at all hazards," a fellow officer recalled. Now loyal Union men wept in the street. Everywhere there was disorder: militia members gallivanting on horses and mules; defiant federal regiments still playing patriotic tunes; the Stars and Stripes flapping over the Alamo one moment, the Lone Star flying the next. "Has it come so soon as this?" Lee whispered through quivering lips.

With federal forces vacating the town, Lee checked into a hotel, changed into civilian clothes, and braced for a confrontation with the commissioners representing the state convention. They threatened to hinder his passage across the state unless he resigned from the Union army and swore allegiance to something called the Confederate States of America. Lee refused. Texas had not even officially joined this new Southern confederacy. More important, Virginia remained a member of the Union. The insult was more than Lee could bear. Tempers flared. "I was even surprised, not at his emotions, but at this exhibition of them," said a witness, who contrasted Lee's outburst with his usual "cold dignity of bearing and the prudential reserve of his manners." A woman staying a floor below Lee in the hotel heard him pacing through the night. Eventually Lee arranged his transportation and departed in peace.

The Man Who Would Not Be Washington

When Lee arrived at Arlington on March 1, a rare pleasant surprise awaited: his grandson. The baby slept in Mary's bed. In his diary, Lee recorded, "Found all well." But all was not well across the river in Washington. The old Southern statesmen who had long sat atop the city's social scene had begun vacating their houses. New arrivals from the North heard conspiracy and treason in every Southern drawl. A desperate peace conference held under a portrait of George Washington at Willard's Hotel could barely keep the peace among its own decrepit delegates. A few blocks from the hotel, the man still occupying the White House believed that states had no right to secede but that his office gave him no power to stop them. On the morning of February 22, President James Buchanan canceled the military parade in honor of Washington's Birthday. Federal troops marching down the streets, he worried, might send the wrong signal. Only a last-minute intervention convinced him to let the show go on. "There was such a disappointment that he countermanded the order," wrote Mary, who had followed her father's tradition of crossing the river for such occasions. The morning after, Abraham Lincoln arrived in secret so as to avoid the assassins who, according to rumor, lined the train tracks. Around the time Lincoln took the oath of office, Lee gazed across the river at the city of Washington, where the Capitol had shed its old wooden dome in favor of an iron one still under construction, and said, "That beautiful feature in our landscape has ceased to charm me as much as formerly. I fear the mischief that is brewing there."

The first decision awaiting President Lincoln was whether to resupply the federal troops at Fort Sumter in Charleston Harbor or to surrender the post to the Confederate batteries preparing to blow its brick walls to pieces. Robert Anderson, the fort's commander and Charles Anderson's brother, warned Lincoln that he could not hold the position much longer. Lincoln had few options, none good. Trying to reinforce the position could spark civil war, stick Lincoln with the aggressor label, and drive Virginia and other border states still clinging to the Union into the Confederate column. Withdrawing federal forces without a fight would depress Northern morale and make a mockery of the pledge Lincoln had issued in his inaugural address: "to hold, occupy, and possess the property, and places belonging to the government." That pledge had not pleased Lee. Based on his engineering expertise, he believed "military necessity" would eventually force the Union to surrender Sumter but hoped Lincoln would back down before the situation became so dire. "I fear all the good that might be expected by the withdrawal of troops will be lost by the tardiness & grounds of the act."

The day after Lincoln's inauguration, Lee visited General Scott in Washington and discussed the bleak "prospects" with other officers. It was probably on this same visit that General Scott's military secretary, Erasmus Keyes, insinuated that Lee had "concurred in Twiggs' surrender in Texas." Deeply insulted, Lee "assumed an air of great seriousness" and demanded to see General Scott alone. The two men spoke behind closed doors for the next three hours. Like Lee, Scott hailed from Virginia. Unlike Lee, Scott had declared his first allegiance to the Union. Now the general in chief hoped Lee would do the same. A show of solidarity among army officers, Scott thought, might deter disunion. If Scott was pleased to hear that his protégé opposed secession, he was pained to hear what else Lee had to say: that he did not want to again be in a position, as in Texas, where duty might necessitate coercive action against a state seceding from the Union; that he would follow his own state and his own state alone; and that if allegiance to Virginia prohibited service in the federal army, then so be it. Lee would resign. That was exactly what Scott hoped to avoid. He assured Lee that the situation did not demand such a drastic step. Sure, Lincoln had blustered in his inaugural, but behind the scenes the administration wanted peace. Lee left relieved.

With new faith in the prairie lawyer, Lee joined the military brass at a White House reception on March 12. As one biographer notes, it may have been the only face-to-face encounter Lee and Lincoln ever had. Waiting to pay their respects to the new commander in chief, the army officers arranged themselves according to rank. When fully formed, the receiving line snaked around three sides of the executive mansion's East

Room. Then, on the fourth side, a door opened. In walked, as one officer put it, "a dignified, though an extremely awkward looking person; tall and gaunt to ungainliness, with a face of extreme homeliness." Scott greeted Lincoln and then, stopping to introduce every officer, directed the line to proceed past him. An officer standing somewhere behind Lee recalled, "The President was thoughtful and almost silent, occasionally a faint smile lighted up his homely countenance, but immediately he would relapse into the appearance of sadness."

When Lee's turn came, Lincoln probably paid special attention. This was the officer whose "military genius" Scott fancied "above that of any other officer of the army." In the event of war, Scott had joked, "It would be cheap for the United States to insure Lee's life for $5,000,000 a year!" Lincoln must have wondered whether Lee was as indispensable as Scott claimed. A look at Scott himself would have suggested so. After nearly seventy-five years, the general's waistline had caught up with his enormous appetite. He had ballooned to more than three hundred pounds. Only ice buckets relieved his gout-ridden feet. That he could not climb into the saddle without aid raised concerns about how he could lead an army into battle. At the very least, he would need to delegate field command to a younger officer. Lee presented the obvious choice. Though standing beside Lincoln and Scott would have made Lee seem relatively short, his wide shoulders, squat neck, and "dignified carriage" made him appear "every inch a soldier." By month's end, Lincoln had offered—and Lee had accepted—a promotion to colonel.

Why Lincoln wanted to retain Lee's services for the Union requires less explanation than why Lee accepted a new commission given the reservations he had already expressed. Lee later said that the conversation with Scott had convinced him that the country would avoid war altogether. There was also, of course, ambition. Lee believed soldiers should accept promotion when offered. Surely he had earned this one. At the same time, there were limits. That March, he received a letter offering him an even higher-ranking command: brigadier general. It came from the new Confederate government. That offer, as far as is known, went unanswered. Lee's loyalty was not for sale. It belonged to Virginia, and Virginia still belonged to the Union. So long as that remained the case, Lee could remain in Union blue. From the outset of the crisis, he had said, "I wish for no other flag than the 'Star Spangled banner,' & no other air than 'Hail Columbia.'" Evidently, at this stage, he thought he still might get his way.

Living at Arlington indulged this fantasy. "We were traditionally, my mother especially, a conservative, or 'Union' family," Lee's oldest daughter recalled. The house built as a shrine to the first president continued to welcome prominent Northerners, including relatives of the second president. Rooney's classmate Henry Adams and his father, Charles Francis Adams, attended a party at Arlington as late as February. Lee's wife later claimed her "unsuspecting mind" did not realize "the possibility of the dissolution" until late in the crisis because the Union had been for "so long our boast & pride." When she finally awoke to the danger, she lashed out against not only uncompromising Northerners but also secessionists in her own state. "I pray the Almighty may listen to the prayers of the faithful in the land & direct their counsels for good & that the designs of ambitious & selfish politicians who would dismember our glorious country may be frustrated, especially that our own state may act right." The beginning of spring brought hope. In Washington, rumors buttressed Scott's prediction that Lincoln would surrender Fort Sumter rather than risk war. Meanwhile, in Richmond, where delegates from across Virginia had assembled to debate secession, a moderate faction maintained control. On April 4, a motion to secede mustered only forty-five votes, half as many as the ninety opposed.

Events rendered the vote meaningless. Lincoln had found an option between being an appeaser and an aggressor. He notified the South Carolina governor he would resupply Sumter for humanitarian reasons but not reinforce it for military ones. If the Confederates wanted war, their guns would have to fire first. The Confederacy's new president, Jefferson Davis, obliged. On Sunday, April 14, Lee attended services in Alexandria. Leaving the old church where George Washington had prayed, Lee heard the news: after a thirty-three-hour bombardment,

Major Robert Anderson had surrendered Fort Sumter. Lee's oldest daughter recalled how a crowd formed around her father. "The excitement & confusion were intense & every one flocked around Papa." Lee feigned calm. Poor Major Anderson, he remarked. "He was a determined man, & I know held out to the last." The war had begun, and Lee's first feelings were for the Union.

Lincoln immediately called for seventy-five thousand troops to quell the rebellion. Every state would have to fill its quota. Everyone wondered whether Virginia would secede rather than submit to the demand. The president, according to his personal secretaries, was particularly interested in what one Virginian would do: Robert E. Lee. To learn once and for all, Lincoln enlisted Francis Preston Blair, an old Washington power broker whose son Montgomery served in the cabinet. On April 18, inside the house belonging to his family on Pennsylvania Avenue, Blair welcomed Lee for a "long interview." Lee found his host "very wily and keen." Blair explained that the government had begun raising an army to crush the insurrection. Scott's age rendered him unsuitable for field command. Lincoln had chosen Lee. The country looked to Lee, Blair said, "as the representative of the Washington family." Would he lead the fight to save Washington's Union?

Only one word now separated Lee from the pinnacle of his profession, from command of what would be the largest American army ever assembled, from glory that no American since Washington had known. Blair, in Lee's telling, "tried in every way to persuade" him to say yes. The conversation moved from secession to slavery. Lee agreed the former was "folly" and the latter provided no justification for war. "Mr. Blair, I look upon secession as anarchy. If I owned the four millions of slaves in the South I would sacrifice them all to the Union but how can I draw my sword upon Virginia, my native State?" Here, Blair family tradition says Lee hesitated, as if searching for an answer. If Lee did so, it was only because he did not yet know that Virginia had voted to secede the previous day. For his part, Lee denied showing any ambivalence. As he told the story, he gave his answer once and at once. Saving the Union might require conquering Virginia. That he could not do. "After listening to his remarks, I declined the offer he made me, to take command of the army that was to be brought into the field; stating, as candidly and as courteously as I could, that, though opposed to secession and deprecating war, I could take no part in an invasion of the Southern States."

There was nothing left to do now but go see Winfield Scott. The old general deserved that courtesy. Lee's answer disappointed Scott but did not surprise him. "Lee," Scott said, "you have made the greatest mistake of your life, but I feared it would be so." The time for a decision had arrived, Scott added. If Lee could not serve the Union, he should resign his commission. On the way back to Arlington, Lee consulted his brother Smith, who faced his own decision as a naval officer. The brothers discussed their dilemma until dark, when an exhausted Lee returned to Arlington. Rumors of Virginia's secession had by then reached the house. "I presume the poor old State will go out," he said. "I don't think she need do so, yet at least, but so many are trying to push her out that she will have to go." Out walking by Arlington the next day, daughter Agnes learned her father's prediction had come to pass. "I cannot yet realize it," she wrote. "It seemed so dreadful. But she [Virginia] had to take one side or the other." Now Lee realized he must do the same.

A young relative staying at Arlington on April 19 remembered "commotion" as the sun set behind the house. Through a window, the boy saw Lee "pacing up and down among the trees." Mary Lee described that night as "the severest struggle of his life." Lee already knew the course he would take. Only one remained. An army officer reluctant to obey any order he might receive could not retain his commission without risking dishonor. Knowing that he must resign, however, made the act no less painful. As Lee walked along Arlington Heights, he believed his duty lay south of the Potomac, even though he could plainly see Washington standing on the other side. If Lee believed, as he said, that George Washington would condemn secession, then whence was this education?

The answer, in some measure, must return to Washington himself.

Though, unlike other Confederates, Lee saw the Union as Washington's bequest to the nation, Washington's personal bequest to Lee had been altogether different. From Washington, Lee had received a duo of disappointments: a father-in-law still the child of Mount Vernon, and the Custis slaves still slaves. The estate tangling the two tied Lee to the taskmaster's whip, bound his family's fortune to plantations, sullied his name in Northern newspapers, and spoiled the river view he had once cherished. All this tilted Lee's sympathies to the South but would not have been enough to turn his loyalties from the Union but for his first inheritance: self-control. That quality—the trait separating Washington from Harry Lee—now gave Robert E. Lee the strength to deny himself. Much as he treasured the Union and much as he deplored secession, he ignored his own wishes. That many thought his example could sway others mattered not. Willing, as he was, to sacrifice everything but honor for the Union, Lee was unwilling to believe his actions could influence anything. "I must try & be patient & await the end for I can do nothing to hasten or retard it," he said. At this critical juncture, Lee surrendered to events. He could not have his own way. So he would have Virginia's way.

Here, the pacing stopped. There would be no more shuffling from side to side. The next morning, Lee sat down in his study and dispatched a slave to deliver two letters: one to Secretary of War Simon Cameron and the other to General Scott. Lee then summoned family members and read aloud what he had written to the old general.

> *Since my interview with you on the 18th Inst: I have felt that I ought not longer to retain my Commission in the Army. I therefore tender my resignation, which I request you will recommend for acceptance. It would have been presented at once, but for the struggle it has cost me to separate myself from a service to which I have devoted all the best years of my life, & all the ability I possessed.*

When Lee finished reading, a hush fell over the room. "None of us could speak," his daughter remembered. Finally, breaking the silence,

Lee said, "I suppose you all think I have done very wrong, but it had come to this." To his brother Smith, who had expected one last consultation, Lee wrote that circumstances had forced his hand. "After the most anxious inquiry as to the correct course for me to pursue, I concluded to resign, and sent in my resignation this morning. . . . I am now a private citizen, and have no other ambition than to remain at home." Perhaps giving up the army, he thought, would permit his settling down at Arlington permanently.

After unsealing Lee's letter, General Scott "mourned as for the loss of a son." Sprawled out on a sofa, he banned any mention of his protégé's name. Such was the gossip that Orton Williams, a relative on Scott's staff, brought to Arlington. "Now that 'Cousin Robert' had resigned every one seemed to be doing so," Williams reported.

The excitement spilled into Alexandria, where Lee came for church the next day. On streets he had strolled as a boy, crowds celebrating secession and cheering the Confederate colors half expected ships sporting the old Stars and Stripes to sail down from Washington and bombard the town. A woman who saw Lee in his pew sighed with relief; she had heard that the federal authorities had arrested him. In hindsight, Lincoln would wish he had. Already newspapers floated Lee's name for command of Virginia's armed forces. "There is no man who would command more of the confidence of the people of Virginia, than this distinguished officer," the *Alexandria Gazette* stated. "His reputation, his acknowledged ability, his chivalric character, his probity, honor, and—may we add, to his eternal praise—his Christian life and conduct—make his very name a 'tower of strength.' It is a name surrounded by revolutionary and patriotic associations." Influential men in Richmond agreed. That evening, back at Arlington, Lee received a summons. He agreed to depart for the state capital the next morning. He had promised to follow Virginia; now, as he would learn, Virginia wanted to follow him.

On the morning of April 22—for the last time—Lee passed

through the columns crowning Arlington Heights. He had a train to catch. The track led south, away from Washington. Lee claimed it was the only way, yet he never seemed certain it was the right way. He advised his son Custis Lee to chart his own course. "Tell Custis he must consult his own judgment, reason, and conscience as to the course he may take. I do not wish him to be guided by my wishes or example. If I have done wrong, let him do better." Though Custis Lee ultimately left Arlington, he waited more than a month and, at least, considered his options before accepting a commission in the Virginia army. He was heard to say that "were he able to dictate proceedings," he would resist secession by "fortifying" his own home. Union officers adopted that advice. By the end of May, the commander of what would become the Union Army of the Potomac had established his headquarters at Arlington. Had Lee taken the job, Arlington and the army would have been his, together at last. Now he would have neither.

PART III

★

Bellum

CHAPTER SEVEN

The Battle for Arlington

The house Robert E. Lee left loomed over the capital. The sight troubled Colonel Joseph Mansfield, who had briefly served as Lee's commanding officer at Cockspur. Now, with a long white beard, Mansfield commanded the city of Washington's defenses. On the evening of May 2, he brought his concerns to General Scott. "I must remark that the President's House and Department buildings in its vicinity are but two and a half miles across the river from Arlington high ground, where a battery of bombs and heavy guns, if established, could destroy the city with comparatively a small force after destroying the bridges." Scott agreed. There was only one thing to do: seize Arlington.

Engineers went to work on a plan. Execution might have to wait until Virginia voters officially ratified their state's secession in a referendum scheduled for May 23. Then again, waiting might pose unacceptable risks. Already newspapers carried stories about Virginians lugging artillery up the heights. "It is quite probable that our troops assembled at Arlington would create much excitement in Virginia, yet, at the same time, if the enemy were to occupy the ground there a greater excitement would take place on our side," Mansfield argued. Lee had gone south, but the battle for his father-in-law's treasury had just begun. Whoever controlled Arlington controlled Washington.

* * *

The first responsibility awaiting the new commander in chief of Virginia's armed forces was among the most terrifying: delivering a formal reply to the convention that had confirmed his nomination. Lee opened by describing himself as "not prepared" for "the solemnity of the occasion." Probably he was unprepared for how directly the convention president, John Janney, compared him to George Washington. "I would have much preferred had your choice fallen on an abler man," Lee said before closing with his old standby echoing but ever so slightly distorting Washington's will. "Trusting in Almighty God, an approving conscience, and the aid of my fellow-citizens, I devote myself to the service of my native State, in whose behalf alone will I ever again draw my sword."

Outside the state capitol, crowds crying "On to Washington!" wanted more than words. They wanted to take the fight to the other side of the Potomac. Two street orators argued over whether the federal city would fall in sixty days or thirty. Both were wrong, according to the calculations of the Confederate secretary of war. The Confederate flag would wave above Washington by month's end. Lee knew better than the "bravado and boasting" he heard around town. He knew that affections for the Union ran stronger than blood; his own sister Anne, a Unionist living in Maryland, broke with him over his decision. He also knew many Northerners from his years in the federal army, and, contrary to the Southern taunts, he believed they could and would fight. They also had General Scott, who, for all his infirmities, remained America's foremost military mind. New aides arriving at the headquarters Lee opened in the Virginia Mechanics Institute heard him predict a "prolonged and bloody" struggle. "The war may last 10 years," he wrote; that is, if Virginia itself could last ten weeks.

Virginia needed at least fifty-one thousand volunteers. The militia started with fewer than twenty thousand. Recruiting men proved easier than turning them into soldiers. While Lee admired the "zeal" the recruits brought, they needed training and supplies, the shortage of which "very much embarrassed" him. For now, many soldiers would have to make do with "old flint-lock muskets" akin to what Virginians had carried during the last foreign invasion in 1814. For now also, these deficiencies led to an inescapable conclusion: Virginia must play defense. And there was much to defend.

To the east along the Chesapeake, four parallel rivers—the Potomac on top, the Rappahannock and York in the middle, and the James on the bottom—divided the Virginia Tidewater into a series of peninsulas and provided pathways to the state's interior for an enemy, like the Union, possessing unquestioned naval superiority. While Virginia had captured the Norfolk shipping yards, including a frigate named the USS *Merrimack*, federal troops had retained Lee's first married home at Fort Monroe on the tip of the Virginia Peninsula between the York and James Rivers.

To the northwest, where the B&O railroad passed through the mountains, economic ties to the North held fast. When a report reached Lee's office that "this section is verging on a state of actual rebellion," it meant rebellion against Richmond. On the back side of the Blue Ridge, at the doorstep of this region, was a bright spot. Former governor Wise had arranged for militia to storm Harpers Ferry immediately after the state convention had approved secession. Retreating federal forces had torched the arsenal, but the machinery for producing muskets and the newer rifle models, whose accuracy would make the war deadlier than anyone expected, had survived. Any hope of employing these factories for the duration of the conflict depended on relocating them to a safer location. As John Brown had discovered, Harpers Ferry was difficult to hold. But so long as the Virginians did hold it, the Potomac current spinning the factory wheels could power arms production. To carry out this balancing act, Lee assigned Colonel Thomas Jackson to Harpers Ferry. "Every rifle that you can finish will be of advantage, but it will be necessary to send off that machinery as soon as the musket factory is removed," Lee instructed. The canal connecting Harpers Ferry to Washington, Lee added, offered federal troops "a means of carrying ordnance and munitions . . . against you." If that happened, Jackson might have to destroy Washington's waterway to the west.

THE DISTRICT OF COLUMBIA.

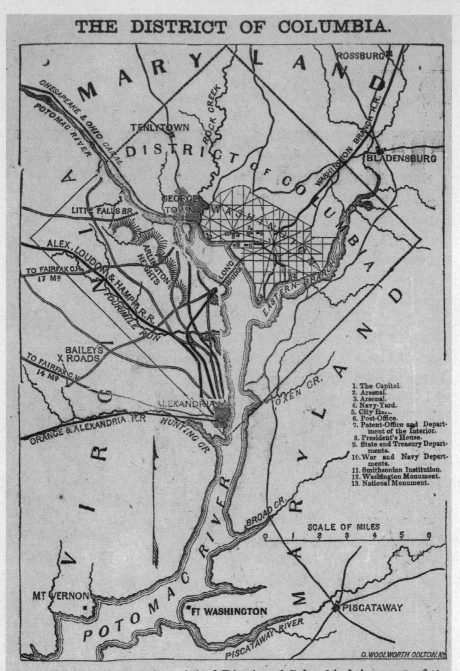

The portion of the original District of Columbia lying west of the Potomac River was retroceded to the State of Virginia in 1846, and now forms the County of Alexandria.

The Battle for Arlington

North of Richmond, a massive Union army assembled at Washington. The officer commanding Virginia's Potomac Department, Philip St. George Cocke, a wealthy West Point graduate whose long face by year's end would take a bullet courtesy of his own hand, estimated that Lincoln had fifty thousand troops along the Potomac. Intelligence indicated that any day now the hordes might cross the bridges from Washington and seize Alexandria. Cocke issued a dramatic appeal for reinforcements: "Should Virginia soil or the grave of Washington be polluted by the tread of a single man in arms from north of the Potomac, it will cause open war. Men of the Potomac border, men of the Potomac Military Department, to arms! Your country calls you to her defense." Virginia should defend Alexandria block by block if necessary, Cocke added. Lee dismissed the idea. Fighting for Alexandria against overwhelming odds, he said, "would, in my opinion, have had no other effect than to hazard the destruction of the city." He instead planned to make a stand west of Alexandria at a railroad junction, where a line to the Shenandoah Valley met a line connecting to Richmond. That junction was called Manassas.

As Lee weighed troop allocations, he recognized the personal price: Arlington would fall as soon as the first Union soldiers crossed the Potomac. Despite the rumors in Washington, he gave no thought to defending the house. He presumed Arlington lost. All he could do was buy time by avoiding antagonizing the federal forces across the river. Lee warned his wife to pack up their belongings, especially the Mount Vernon relics. The events at Fort Sumter had whipped the North into such a frenzy that Lincoln probably could not restrain looters even were he so inclined. "Among such a mass of all characters it might be considered a good smart thing to cross into Virginia & rob, plunder, & c., especially when it is known to be the residence of one of the Rebels

◀ This map of the District of Columbia appeared in the *New York Tribune* in 1861 as part of a series illustrating the different theaters of war. The city of Washington was only one part of the original diamond-shaped District of Columbia, which included Arlington and Alexandria until their retrocession to Virginia.

leaders," Lee wrote Mary. "I think therefore you had better prepare all things for removal, that is the plate, pictures, & c., & be prepared at any moment." At the very least, Lee wanted his wife out of harm's way. "I want you to be in a place of safety. To spare me that anxiety."

As Lee had learned early in married life, asking Mary to leave Arlington was not the same as making her leave. On April 26, he sent a warning to evacuate. For at least a week, Mary ignored it. She went about her usual routine: praying, painting pictures, and tending her gardens. "I never saw the country more beautiful, perfectly radiant, the yellow jasmine in full bloom & perfuming all the air," she wrote.

Then, shortly after Colonel Mansfield made his recommendation, Mary's relative Orton Williams barged into her chamber. Despite his conflicted loyalties, he had not yet resigned from General Scott's staff and, as a result, had overheard the plans. "You must pack up all you value immediately," Williams warned. The Union army would cross the bridge the next day. "There was little time to deliberate," Mary recalled. Packing through the night, she started with the silver her father had inherited from Mount Vernon. By the time the sun rose, Mary had boxed up the family plate along with original copies of George Washington's letters, her husband's correspondence, and other irreplaceable items. She sent four chests and two trunks to Richmond. Once there, her husband would send them across the Blue Ridge to a town called Lexington. After a sleepless night, Williams returned with an update. Scott had delayed the attack. "My sanguine spirit hoped the evil day would never come," Mary wrote. But deep down, she knew it would. "My beautiful home," she wrote, "may become a field of carnage." The reprieve offered nothing more than more time to pack. The most cherished portraits and antiques, including Washington's deathbed, went to Ravensworth, a relative's home west of Alexandria. Mary stashed other relics, including the Society of the Cincinnati china, in the closets, the garret, and the cellar and left her father's paintings hanging on the walls. "The rest of our effects must take their chance," she said.

Daughter Agnes worried what would happen to the slaves. "The servants distress at our leaving them." One slave, Agnes claimed, described the army massing across the river as filled with "low vulgar sort of white people." Another slave allegedly called the Northern boys "vipers," who would steal and plunder. "They all agree in wishing they would stay on their own side of the river," Agnes wrote. One can only assume that "all" did not include those slaves who had earlier tried to escape across the Potomac.

With the carpets rolled up, most of the paintings taken down, and the most valuable relics either removed or hidden, the house seemed empty. Rob Jr. was at the University of Virginia, Mildred at boarding school. Annie had joined Rooney at the White House. There were no more visits from Orton Williams; his duplicity had earned him a stay in a Union prison. Then, on May 8, after entrusting their pet cat to a slave, Agnes and her older sister Mary left for Ravensworth. Lee assumed his wife had gone, too. When he learned otherwise, he sent another warning. The war, he wrote, "may burst upon you at any time. It is sad to think of the devastation, if not ruin it may bring upon a spot so endeared to us. But God's will be done. We must be resigned." Mary, of course, was not the only straggler. Custis Lee still had not left for Richmond. He had inherited his father's "piercing eye," as well as his fatalism. "Custis astonishes me with his calmness with a probability of having his early & beautiful home destroyed," Mary wrote. "He never indulges in invective or a word of reflection on the cruel course of the administration. He leaves all that to his Mamma and sisters."

Though Mary had once opposed secession, she now wanted to oppose the Northern aggressors. She proudly sent General Scott an article recounting the reception her husband had received in Richmond. "Were it not that I would not add one feather to his load of care, nothing would induce me to abandon my home," she added. To her daughter Mildred, she fantasized about resisting Arlington's occupation.

I would not stir from this house even if the whole Northern Army were to surround it. The zealous patriots who are risking their lives to pre-

serve the Union founded by Washington might come & take the grand-daughter of his wife from her home, & desecrate it, for whatever I have thought & even now think of the commencement of this horrible conflict now our duty is plain, to resist unto death.

On May 11, one of Philip St. George Cocke's aides asked Mary for permission to look around her property. Though, per Lee's orders, Cocke had focused on protecting Manassas, he still hoped to muster enough force to prevent the Union from occupying Arlington Heights. All too happy to help, Mary offered suggestions for where the Virginians could post guards. Custis Lee laughed at her wishful thinking.

At last, Mary agreed to join her daughters at Ravensworth. An age, she said, "must be commencing when Satan is to be let loose upon earth to blacken & mar its fair surface & while we must feel that our sins both personal and national merit the chastisement of the Almighty we may still implore him to spare us." She spoke of returning soon if for no other reason than to collect the rest of the family relics. In the meantime, the keys to the house, including the hiding places, would go to a beloved slave named Selina Gray. As Mary said her final farewells, she recalled the slaves weeping. Some already sensed her departure might be final indeed.

On May 23, a beautiful spring day, Virginians ratified secession in a landslide. That night, as they slept, thousands of Union soldiers prepared to cross the river. Fresh rumors had circulated that Lee planned to fortify Arlington Heights. According to one report, General Lee had sold Arlington to the Virginia government in recognition of its strategic position. "Perhaps they've only purchased a graveyard, which was very provident in them, for that's a sort of estate that they will need," a Boston newspaper editorialized. The invasion could wait no longer. At two o'clock in the morning on May 24, Colonel Daniel Butterfield led the first forces over the Long Bridge. A year later, he would partner with a musician in his camp to arrange taps, the bugle call destined to be associated with the graveyard the Union, in fact, had just purchased.

At the Washington Navy Yard, meanwhile, soldiers boarded steamers for Alexandria. As the USS *Pawnee* pulled alongside the town, an officer aboard carried a flag of truce ashore. "It would be madness to resist," he told the Virginians. There had been no battle for Alexandria in 1814, and there would be none now. The Virginia sentries guarding the shore fired their muskets once, then fell back, and retreated toward Manassas. Into the undefended town a regiment of New Yorkers followed their young colonel, Elmer Ellsworth, who had clerked in Lincoln's law office before the war. Residents peering out windows hissed at the invaders rushing through the streets, but what caught Ellsworth's eye was the Confederate flag flying over a hotel. He barged in and up the stairs and seized the flag. On the way back down, he met the proprietor's double-barreled shotgun. The shot struck his heart. Blood gushing from the wound stained the flag in his hand. The first Union officer to fall in the war would die in George Washington's hometown. His corpse would lie in state at the White House.

Despite the casualty, the operation had succeeded. For the first time in more than a decade, the federal government controlled the entire diamond-shaped district. Later that day, Major General Charles Sandford of the New York militia hiked up Arlington Heights. There, he found the Custis slaves but, contrary to the rumors, no artillery and no defenses. "I stated to some of the servants left there that had the family remained I would have established a guard for their security from annoyance; but, in consequence of their absence, that I would, by occupying it myself, be responsible for the perfect care and security of the house and everything in it," Sandford wrote. Soon after, the shoveling began. The heights needed earthworks for defense. Soldiers set up camp in a grove behind the house. "The place on which we are now encamped is most beautiful—on the top of a hill, sloping gradually back, from the Potomac to the height of about two hundred feet, overlooking Washington and Georgetown," wrote a New York soldier.

Given the house's associations with the Father of His Country, the soldier joked about relic hunting. "There is an orchard just here, it may contain a tree grown from a sprout, or even from the seed of the fruit, that grew upon the identical apple-tree that little George cut down. . . . If I succeed in finding the aforementioned tree, I will send you a twig."

Such stories did not amuse Arlington's owner in exile. Lafayette himself had admired those trees. Her husband may have ceded the ground, but Mary Lee had not. On May 30, she fired off a note to General Sandford. "It never occurred to me Gen'l Sandford that I could be forced to sue for permission to enter my own house and that such an outrage as its military occupation to the exclusion of me and my children could ever have been perpetrated." Realizing that berating Northern officers might not serve her interests, Mary shifted her tone halfway through the letter. "I forget that I am a suppliant and cannot trust my pen to write what I feel. You have a beautiful home and people that you love & can sympathize perhaps even with the wife of a 'traitor & a rebel!'" She asked the general, if nothing else, to allow her slaves to go about their normal routines and to send one, "my boy Billy," through the lines. She could not get by without him.

Sandford, it turned out, was no longer in command at Arlington. Irvin McDowell, a forty-two-year-old bearded brigadier general who had been but a brevet major weeks before, had taken charge of the new Department of Northeastern Virginia. In essence, he received the job that Lee had refused. But unlike Lee, McDowell did not possess Scott's trust. His precipitous promotion resulted from political interference. Lincoln expected McDowell to advance against Richmond at once. No sooner had McDowell set up his headquarters at Arlington than he received the letter from Mary Custis Lee. He responded immediately with a series of jarring exclamation points in an otherwise courteous note. "With respect to the occupation of Arlington House by the United States troops I beg to say it has been done by my predecessor with every regard to the preservation of the place!" Given how the war had strained ties between former brothers in arms, McDowell promised to sleep in a tent rather than occupy General Lee's bedrooms. Only one officer would sleep in the house and he just for its protection. McDowell also pledged to honor Mary's requests regarding the slaves and invited her to return whenever she pleased. "You will find things as little disturbed as possible."

Mary soon heard otherwise. Orton Williams's sister Markie, who had stayed loyal to the Union, received a pass to visit Arlington and wrote Mary about the changes. "There is a large encampment just below the cedar park & tents & soldiers along the road side & interspersed everywhere. I was blinded with tears & choked with sorrow as I tried to gaze on scenes once so familiar, now so strangely distorted."

Lee urged his wife to learn to live with Arlington's loss. "I do not think it prudent or right for you to return there, while the U.S. troops occupy that country." It was not that he failed to sympathize. He shared her attachments to the house and feelings of grief. "I have experienced them myself & they are constantly revived." Losing Arlington seemed like divine punishment for his sins. "I fear we have not been grateful enough for the happiness there within our reach, & our heavenly father has found it necessary to deprive us of what He had given us. I acknowledge my ingratitude, my transgressions & my unworthiness, & submit with resignation to what He thinks proper to inflict upon me."

To his detractors, Lee had inflicted the punishment on himself. The governor of South Carolina said Lee would have saved the South "much blood and insult" had he immediately blown up the bridge from Washington and fortified his wife's property. "If Lee had been the man his reputation makes him, he never would have allowed them to cross the long bridge without a fight," said the governor. "Lee is not with us at heart, or he is a common man, with good looks, and too cautious for practical Revolution."

Northern newspapermen inspecting Arlington Heights agreed that Lee could have inflicted a fearful fire upon the federal city. A *New York Times* correspondent wondered why Congress "stupidly" retroceded land so critical to the capital's security in the first place. "These Heights," the reporter concluded, "should never again be surrendered by the Government under any circumstances."

* * *

On June 8, the governor of South Carolina and the other snipers from the Southern sideline got their wish: Lee lost his army. Nominally, he remained the commander in chief of Virginia's armed forces, but those forces now belonged to the Confederate States of America. President Jefferson Davis and his government had recently set up shop in the commonwealth's capital, which would henceforth double as the Confederacy's capital. Although the new administration awarded Lee one of the Confederacy's highest ranks, it gave him no army to lead. The spotlight shifted to two other West Pointers. At Manassas, the Louisiana-born Creole commander P. G. T. Beauregard, who had overseen the siege of Fort Sumter and styled himself the hero of that place, had taken charge. At Harpers Ferry, Lee's ambitious old classmate Joseph E. Johnston, jealous as ever of rank, had superseded Jackson and quickly determined to withdraw his forces to a stronger position in the Shenandoah Valley.

It was left to Lee to draft a report summarizing what Virginia had accomplished in the weeks between seceding from the Union and ceding military command to the Confederacy. Altogether, Lee had managed the mobilization of about forty thousand soldiers. "When it is remembered that this body of men was called from a state of profound peace to one of unexpected war, you will have reason to commend the alacrity with which they left their homes and families, and prepared themselves for the defence of the State," Lee told Virginia's governor. "The assembling of the men, however, was not the most difficult operation. Provision for their instruction, subsistence, equipment, clothing, shelter, and transportation in the field, required more time and labor."

Correspondence had claimed the most time. The issues crossing Lee's desk ranged from the pettiest personnel problems to the most momentous decisions regarding where to mass troops on land and where to place batteries on the previously defenseless rivers. The writing taxed Lee's patience, but he paid his due to the details. Lieutenant Walter Taylor, a former Virginia Military Institute student who joined

126

Lee's staff during this period, remembered his chief being "early at his office, punctual in meeting all engagements, methodical to an extreme in his way of despatching business." After office hours, Lee would ride out to examine the preparations. "The city is full of military," a fellow rider observed. "The drum & fife are constantly sounding and soldiers marching up and down the streets." As the general inspected the men, he indulged his old fondness for chatting with girls and young ladies, who admired his bright brown eyes.

Now Lee indulged another old fantasy: retreating from public life. "I do not know what my position will be," he wrote his wife after transferring his command. "I should like to retire to private life, if I could be with you & the children, but if I can be of any service to the State or her cause, I must continue." Mary annoyed him by asking why he could not go from being Virginia's commander in chief to the Confederacy's commander in chief. "I have never heard of the appointment, to which you allude . . . nor have I any expectation or wish for it," he wrote back. "President Davis holds that position." There was no doubt about that. As a West Point graduate, a Mexican War hero, and a former secretary of war, Davis would have preferred a command in the field to being commander in chief. With sunken eyes, protruding cheekbones, and a jaw described as "too hollow to be handsome," Davis had little patience for officers who considered their judgment superior to his, but he liked Lee. Here was a general who knew how to subordinate his wishes. "Where I shall go I do not know," Lee said, "as that will depend upon [the] President." For now, Davis kept Lee in Richmond as an adviser.

According to the strategy Lee had coordinated, Beauregard's army at Manassas and Johnston's army in the Shenandoah Valley could reinforce each other on short notice by using the east-west Manassas Gap Railroad. A junction between the two offered the best hope for stopping the juggernaut in Washington. The question was how soon the armies should unite. On June 12, Beauregard announced his support for an immediate concentration in Manassas. The hero of Fort Sumter wanted to seize the offensive in Virginia. "We could, by a bold and rapid movement forward, retake Arlington Heights and Alexandria."

Davis rejected the scheme. Like Lee, he believed that until the enemy disclosed more of its plans, the undersupplied Confederate armies must take a wait-and-see defensive approach. "Concurring fully with you in the effect which would be produced by possession of Arlington Heights and Alexandria," Davis told Beauregard, "possession, if acquired, would be both brief and fruitless." Thus, rejecting an attack on Arlington, Davis and Lee waited for the advance that would surely come from Arlington.

The advance came in mid-July, when McDowell's army marched out of the Arlington fortifications and sauntered west. If Mary Lee had not already moved to another refuge farther west, she would have fallen behind enemy lines. The movement set Union forces on a collision course with Confederate forces at Manassas. Lee hoped to take the field if not at Manassas then deep in the mountains, where the Confederacy had suffered setbacks. But as the battle drew near, President Davis did not want to leave Richmond understaffed, lest disaster strike. He ordered Lee to stay. As for Davis himself, he headed to the front on the morning of July 21. The battle would begin at any moment. He could not stand the suspense. No one in Richmond could. The first dispatches indicated a draw. Then that night came word from the president: victory. Beauregard had arranged his troops behind a stream called Bull Run. The Union army had crossed farther upstream and nearly folded the Confederate left flank before hitting what became known as the stonewall. It was Thomas Jackson's brigade, which had arrived just in time with Johnston's force from the Shenandoah, as Lee had hoped, via the railroad.

Bull Run spilled into a rout. The Federals fled back to Arlington. A couple of days later, President Lincoln crossed the Potomac. The troops at Arlington, he heard, needed their spirits lifted. Going from camp to camp, he gave the same heartfelt speech. Would they keep fighting, he asked? As long as needed, the boys at Arlington answered.

Lee never doubted the Union's resolve. The enemy would regroup, reinforce, and return. "The battle will be repeated there in greater force," he predicted. "I wished to partake in the former struggle & am mortified at my absence but the President thought it more important I should be here." Finally, Davis agreed to let Lee take the field. He would go, as planned, to western Virginia. Two aides would join him. One was Walter Taylor. The other was Colonel John Augustine Washington III, known as Augustine. During the first American Revolution, the owner of Mount Vernon had invited a Lee onto his staff. Now, more than eighty years later, the heir to Mount Vernon would serve on Lee's staff. It would be a short tenure.

CHAPTER EIGHT

The Last Heir

They would have to share a tent. Not that Robert E. Lee, Walter Taylor, and John Augustine Washington III minded. The tent was spacious, the nights cool, and their clothes wet. It had rained "some portion of every day" since their arrival in the mountains at the end of July. Only by miracle had they not caught cold. "Have become so used to being wet and damp that I hardly think of drying," forty-year-old Augustine Washington wrote. To come to this wilderness they had taken a train through the Blue Ridge and ridden across the Shenandoah Valley and up the Allegheny Mountains. The experience was unlike anything Augustine had known. "Sometimes we were threading by the course of a Mountain torrent, some long Valley or narrow defile between the rocks & hills, which a hundred men might hold against a thousand, and then climbing by a slow, tortuous road cut out of its side some long lonely Mountain & every now & then through some opening catching glimpses of the thousand Mountains piled and thrown together in apparently endless confusion."

Lee had traveled this way once before, in 1840. "If any one had then told me that the next time I travelled that road would have been on my present errand, I should have supposed him insane," he told Mary. The other side of Virginia now seemed like the other side of the world. From the Allegheny Mountains west to the Ohio River, the land belonged to the Old Dominion in name alone, for sympathies in these valleys and mountains belonged to the Union. A convention in Wheeling, near the Ohio border, had declared the secessionist regime in Richmond illegal and elected its own governor. Then, as if to reinforce these political developments, a thirty-four-year-old Union general named George McClellan had chased a Confederate army out of the region and back to the eastern edge of the Allegheny Mountains. His success had caused two presidents to shuffle personnel. Lincoln summoned America's Young Napoleon, as the papers now proclaimed the precocious McClellan, to command Union forces in northeastern Virginia. Davis dispatched Lee to salvage the wreck in western Virginia.

Even if Lee could not reclaim the territory on the other side of the Alleghenies, he needed to stop the Union from penetrating through the mountains into the Shenandoah Valley, the so-called breadbasket of the Confederacy. Which side prevailed would depend on who controlled a handful of mountain passes, the most important being the Staunton-Parkersburg turnpike connecting the Shenandoah Valley to the Ohio River. As Lee ascended into the Alleghenies, a defeated Confederate army awaited him on the turnpike. It could not proceed farther west because up the road was Cheat Mountain, whose imposing summit Union forces had fortified. A frontal assault against the position would meet certain doom. More promising was a road that wound behind Cheat Mountain. It started to the south and ran through a place called Huntersville; already a second Confederate army had begun gathering there. Here was an opportunity to get in the enemy's rear. The problem was that President Davis, while wishing "to strike a decisive blow," had denied Lee decisive authority. Lee arrived on August 3 at Huntersville less to take command than to supervise the commanders already in the field.

Lee knew who commanded the army at Huntersville because he had personally assigned Brigadier General William Loring to the job the previous month and apparently had neglected to tell him to expect company. Loring, a fellow officer remembered, "could not suppress a feeling of jealousy." Lee, meanwhile, could not suppress a feeling of disgust at the conditions in camp. "The soldiers everywhere are sick. The measles are prevalent throughout the whole army, & you know that disease leaves unpleasant results . . . especially in camp where accommodation for the sick is poor," Lee wrote. Despite his concerns about the situation, Lee sidestepped a power struggle with his subordinate by moving his own tent north along the Huntersville road to Valley Mountain, an advanced position closer to the rear of Cheat Mountain. Loring would follow with the rest of the army when ready. And though Loring showed no signs of soon being so, Lee chose to wait rather than demand his own way. "I think that in a few days the general will strike a blow at the Yankees," Augustine Washington wrote wishfully.

On August 6, Lee reached Valley Mountain. "The mountains are beautiful, fertile to the tops, covered with the richest sward of blue grass & white clover. The inclosed fields waving with the natural growth of timothy. The habitations are few & population sparse," he wrote Mary. "This is a magnificent grazing country, & all it wants is labour to clear the mountain-sides of its great growth of timber." While camped in the tall grass, Lee camouflaged his rank. Few would have guessed his quarters housed the Confederacy's soon-to-be-confirmed third-ranking general. "Gen. Lee told us to take as little baggage as possible, and leave some of the servants—and have every thing light for quick motion—so the Gen., Mr. Taylor & I put clothes into one valise for the three, left our beds, trunks and supplies . . . [and] struck one tent and packed it in the lightest wagon," Augustine wrote. Lee shared with his aides not only his tent but also his wash basin and meals. Breakfast was at six o'clock in the morning, dinner at six o'clock in the evening. Tin dishes substituted for porcelain. In the eyes of Lee's men, the simplicity of his camp manifested his self-denial, the trait they already most associated with him. "He always seemed anxious to keep himself in the background, to suppress all consideration of himself, to prevent any notice of himself," said Taylor.

Augustine slept on the ground and, through Lee's example, discovered he needed little else besides a Bible in his hand and a tent above his head. Happiness, he wrote a friend, could be found far from worldly comforts. It was exactly the epiphany that many thought the heir to Mount Vernon needed.

The Last Heir

The heir to Mount Vernon, as it turned out, no longer owned Mount Vernon. The house had passed down from his great-granduncle George Washington to his granduncle Justice Bushrod Washington and then to his father, John Augustine Washington II. By 1841, when John Augustine Washington III began his stewardship, the house had fallen into disrepair. The new heir dreamed of restoring its greatness and, indeed, looked like the man for the job. Like George Washington, he had reddish-brown hair, large eye sockets, and a graceful bearing. But despite Augustine Washington's best efforts, fame had assured the house's fall. Much as he might increase the acres under cultivation, he could not stop the swarms of tourists trampling the fields. They had plagued the property since George Washington's return from the Revolutionary War. In the opinion of a family physician, the nervous strain of watching strangers "pulling down his fences," "trampling his crops," "breaking his shrubbery," "lounging on the lawn," "peering through the windows," and "forcing their way into every room in the house" had killed Augustine Washington's father. By the 1850s, tourists exceeded ten thousand a year.

Unable to keep visitors out, the business-minded heir decided to cash in. He struck a deal with a steamboat company that brought tourists in boatloads. Souvenir searchers, who in the past had peeled the bark from the trees, now snatched up the wooden canes Augustine had contracted to manufacture from authentic Mount Vernon wood. Some customers left less than pleased. "[The] Mecca of Freemen," a critic exclaimed, "has become a temple of Mammon!" What outraged some Northerners more was the sight of slaves. Had not George Washington freed his? But no clause in the famous will prevented bringing new slaves to work the fields, and the heirs did exactly that. More and more was there talk of saving the house by buying it from the degenerate Washington family. One plan called for establishing a national cemetery on the grounds. The winning formula came from a sickly South Carolinian spinster named Ann Pamela Cunningham.

Under her plan, the ladies of America would purchase and preserve the house as a national shrine. The shocking sum Augustine Washington demanded—two hundred thousand dollars—did not deter her. She united women in every state in the Union under the banner of the Mount Vernon Ladies' Association. Edward Everett, the great orator, lent his voice to the cause. Hitting the speaking circuit, he raised almost seventy thousand dollars.

Augustine did not relish the idea of doing business with women. He hoped the state of Virginia or the federal government would step in as the buyer. Alas, when both disappointed, he consented and signed a contract in 1858. Not long after, he made the worst publicity mistake of his life: advertising seven of his slaves for hire. "Here we have Mount Vernon transmogrified into a regular slave shamble where human beings are sold out to the highest bidder—the proprietor living on their wages," the *New York Tribune* editorialized. "Let us pay off the $200,000, relieve the necessities of Mr. Washington, and protect the memory of his revolutionary ancestor." Augustine brushed off the attacks. In fact, instead of divesting from slavery, as the *Tribune* suggested, he used the proceeds from selling Mount Vernon to purchase eight new slaves along with a new plantation for his family.

In 1860, just months after the Mount Vernon Ladies' Association officially took possession of the house, a personal loss caused Augustine to question his priorities. His dear wife, Nelly, died. Mary Custis Lee, who had visited Nelly earlier that year, learned that she had looked "perfectly well" when suddenly a choking sensation seized her. By the time Augustine brought water, her face had turned "dark purple." Her pulse then faded away. A family friend told Augustine to consider the tragedy a wake-up call. God wanted the heir to Mount Vernon to mend his ways. "He has seen how the things of earth were engrossing your time & thoughts, that there was great danger you would become so entirely satisfied with your earthly portion, as to desire nothing better."

Then came the war. For Augustine Washington, the outbreak must have seemed like salvation, the fife and drum sounding from Richmond like heavenly harps. Though neighbors would have understood had he stayed home—his seven children had lost their mother—he arrived at the capital in May to volunteer and validate his birthright. "I am sure you will feel, my dear daughter, that I am performing a sacred duty," he wrote.

> *When yet a boy, I learned at my mother's knee that after my duty to God, my first and great obligations were to my country; and I then resolved, and it has been the determination of my life, that when my country was attacked I would go out to defend her. The occasion has arrived to test my principle, and though the sacrifice is like the tearing of the very heart-strings, I should be recreant to my conviction and undeserving my name, were I to shrink from the performance of duty.*

Lee hated seeing highbred men in low positions, so he invited Augustine Washington to serve as his aide. "No greater compliment could have been paid him as a man of ability and as a gentleman than that by General Lee," a friend said. Like Lee, Augustine yearned for combat. Stories of Yankees desecrating homes like Arlington angered him. "The Yankees are for the most part a set of plundering fellows, who will steal and bully. . . . I hope the time is not far distant when by the blessing of Heaven on our arms, we shall drive them back whipped and disgraced to their own country."

All that saved Mount Vernon from Arlington's fate, as one historian of the house points out, was Augustine Washington's decision to sell. Like Arlington, Mount Vernon fell behind Union lines early in the war. Unlike Arlington, Mount Vernon went unoccupied by the army. Sarah Tracy, a Mount Vernon Ladies' Association secretary who stayed at the house during the war, begged officials in Washington to treat it as neutral ground "belonging alike to North and South." General Winfield Scott agreed despite incorrect but incessant reports that the Mount Vernon Ladies' Association had allowed Augustine to carry off George Washington's bones to the mountains.

* * *

By the time General Loring brought the rest of his army to Valley Mountain on August 11, the opening for an advance had closed. A strong Union force now blocked the road leading to the rear of Cheat Mountain. Only three miles separated the opposing picket lines. Lee would have to find a different path through the mountains. Not long after this realization, a Confederate officer noticed three men examining the ground between the two armies. Sure that these scouts must have come from the Union side, the Confederate formed a posse to give chase. Only at the last moment, when "dashing through the brushwood," did he realize his mistake. He had caught his own general. High command had not lifted Lee's sights too high to study the ground. "There was not a day," an officer wrote, "when it was possible for him to be out that the general, with either Colonel Washington or Captain Taylor, might not be seen crossing the mountains, climbing over rocks and crags, to get a view of the Federal position." Impenetrable mists would often limit visibility to fewer than fifty yards. Then, without warning, the clouds would part, and every peak and valley within thirty miles would come into view.

Looking north from Lee's position on Valley Mountain revealed that the Federals had entrenched themselves about ten miles down the Huntersville road at a place called Elkwater. Seven miles east of Elkwater was Cheat Mountain, where the Federals retained their position blocking the other Confederate force still stuck on the Staunton turnpike. Thus, with the Union controlling the two key roads, any maneuver would require whacking through trees and undergrowth, an unpalatable prospect given that the rain had turned even the roads themselves into mush. Wagons supplying the camp sank so deep their axles ground against the road. "It rains here all the time, literally. There has not been sunshine enough since my arrival to dry my clothes," Lee wrote his daughters toward the end of August. "I have on all my winter clothes & am writing in my overcoat. All the clouds seem to concentrate over this ridge of mountains."

The situation had degenerated into a stalemate. Lee believed his army strong enough to stop the enemy from breaking into the

Shenandoah Valley but not strong enough to break through the mountain passes. Measles and other illnesses had reduced some regiments by more than half. "Those on the sick list would form an army," Lee remarked. Ignorance among the volunteers about sanitation frustrated officers accustomed to professional soldiers. "They are worse than children," Lee said of the volunteers, while doing what he could to relieve their suffering. A thirsty private returning from picket duty had just bent before a spring when he heard Lee's voice. "Don't drink out of that spring; my horse uses it. Come and drink out of this spring near my tent." Lee concealed his army's misery from the press. To fill the vacuum, Southern newspapers fabricated stories of fantastic maneuvers, which raised hopes back home unreasonably high. "Do not believe anything you see about me. There has been no battle, only skirmishing with the outposts, & nothing done [of] any movement," Lee wrote Mary. If the weather did not change soon, he would dispatch Augustine Washington to Richmond. President Davis needed to hear the truth.

Then, at the start of September, the sun shone. Under the clear skies, Cheat Mountain suddenly looked vulnerable from two directions. From the east on the Staunton turnpike, where the Confederates had hopelessly gazed at the mountain, came word that a scout had discovered an off-road route around the side of the summit. Soldiers who forded freezing waters, scrambled up jagged rocks, and brushed through undergrowth would find the Union's flank unprotected. From the southwest, the weeks of scouting at Valley Mountain revealed a second off-road route by which a column could advance up and behind Cheat Mountain. As the Confederates coming from the east flanked the Union force, the Confederates arriving to the west could block any retreat.

The two discoveries coinciding with the improving weather meant the moment had arrived. For more than a month, factors beyond Lee's control had checked his army. There had been skirmishes but not the battle Richmond expected. The public had waited. He had waited. Now he would exert his will. "The enemy . . . cannot have everything his own way," he wrote. "Now to drive him farther a battle must come off, and I am anxious to begin it." It would commence on September 12. In the days before, while the columns sneaked around Cheat Mountain, Lee and Loring would lead the rest of the army from Valley Mountain northward for an attack on Elkwater. If Cheat Mountain fell, so eventually would Elkwater; the layout of the roads assured it. The Confederate troops carrying Cheat Mountain could immediately advance up the Staunton turnpike to the intersection with the Huntersville road, at a point north of Elkwater. With these troops in their rear and Lee and Loring in their front, the Union forces at Elkwater would find themselves surrounded. The plan, which required detached columns of untrained soldiers to synchronize maneuvers over unwieldy territory, bordered on grandiose, but Lee had confidence. "The eyes of the country are upon you," he told the men. "The safety of your homes and the lives of all you hold dear depend upon your courage and exertions."

The safety of his lands was much on the mind of Augustine Washington. Though he had sold Mount Vernon, he still owned other farmlands that had fallen under Union control. Now he considered those properties as lost as his old manor house. Even the proceeds from the Mount Vernon sale had not escaped the attention of Union officials, who would attempt to confiscate his deposits from an Alexandria bank. "I want my children to understand at once that they are poor and instead of living as we have done, that they will have to work," he wrote. "I don't believe this will do us any harm, probably will be of service to us." Everything he had experienced since joining Lee's military family had reinforced his friend's prayer: his desires had shifted from the physical to the spiritual. Physically, he had shed thirty pounds—"superfluous beef," as he called it—which left him a sporty one hundred fifty pounds and "in better condition for service than I have been for many years." Spiritually, he led prayers twice a day and, when not reading his Bible, pressed flowers into the pages for his daughters. From him, they also received lectures about the "blessing" of "self-denial."

As Augustine prepared for his first battle, he welcomed the prospect of it being his last. "I know that I am perfectly willing, if need be, to die for this cause, and sooner than see it fail, had rather that myself and children, and all I hold, were swept from existence," he wrote. "For myself, I have no fear, for should my life be lost, it is only anticipating by a few years what must happen at any rate. The whole matter is in the hands of God, who will do with me, as seems best to him." The heir to Mount Vernon had remade himself in Lee's service. Augustine Washington had denied himself.

"The rain came as though the windows of heaven were opened." That was how one Confederate remembered the storm on the night of September 11. Nonetheless, Lee's plan proceeded. "All the projected movements had been successfully made, & each brigade was in position at the appropriate time, notwithstanding the difficulties they encountered," Lee wrote afterward. "So well regulated had been the march of the surprise columns, that the enemy's pickets were captured by each." That Lee had maneuvered such raw soldiers through such raw weather over such raw terrain represented a tremendous feat. The question now shifted to whether he could complete the surprise. Lee needed a signal that would carry over the mountains and rivers separating his army. Since every part of the plan depended on the column from the east flanking Cheat Mountain, Lee instructed his other troops to attack only after they heard gunfire from there.

Drenched and drained from the march, the soldiers waited. Men dared not sleep for fear of drowning in the downpour. "They had to stand up till daylight," Lee remembered. When the sun rose, the clouds cleared over Elkwater. The Union camp lay as vulnerable as Lee had hoped. "I could see the enemy's tents on Valley River, at the point on the Huttonsville [Huntersville] road just below me," he wrote. "It was a tempting sight. We waited for the attack on Cheat Mountain, which was to be the signal." Midmorning approached. No gun from the flank fired. The more time passed, the more restless the men grew. Everyone wondered what had happened. Not until a day later did Lee learn the truth: an eager officer who had petitioned and procured Lee's permission to lead the movement around Cheat Mountain had lost his nerve, and Lee had thus lost his offensive. Even if he wished to execute the rest of the operation, how could he coordinate the columns? "All chance for surprise was gone," he concluded. For more than a month he had waited for a moment that would now never be.

The next day, Lee and Loring pondered their options. Though the attack on Cheat Mountain had failed, perhaps the Confederates in front of Elkwater could still turn the Union right, or western, flank. Augustine Washington delivered orders requesting reconnaissance to the closest cavalry commander: Rooney Lee. Both of General Lee's older sons by this time had attained high rank: twenty-eight-year-old Custis as a colonel and aide to President Davis and twenty-four-year-old Rooney as a major of cavalry. Naturally, the old nepotism charges that had dogged the family since Harry Lee's time resurfaced. Lee paid no attention. Having his second son nearby lifted his spirits. "I have enjoyed the company of Fitzhugh since I have been here," he told Mary. "As yet the war has not reduced him much." Hardly at all, in fact. A hulk on horseback, Rooney weighed 220 pounds and stood six foot three.

Now, as Rooney read his new orders, he noticed Augustine grinning. The heir to Mount Vernon had often asked permission to accompany the cavalry on expeditions. This time, for some reason, Rooney's father had acquiesced. The party set off at once. "We had to lead our horses up and down the mountains," Rooney remembered. "Notwithstanding the difficulties of the march, Colonel Washington seemed to enjoy it, and frequently expressed himself as delighted."

After reaching the edge of a narrow ravine close to the Union camp, Rooney Lee decided his troopers had ventured close enough. He ordered them back to base. "Oh no," Augustine exclaimed. About a half mile away in the ravine stood a seemingly solitary Union soldier on horseback. "Let us ride down and capture that fellow on the gray horse," said Augustine. Rooney hesitated. They had already encountered Union cavalry once during the day. More, he realized, might be on the way. Still, the daring proposal appealed to a rashness in Rooney, a quality that had always concerned his father. Leaving most of their fellow horsemen behind, Rooney Lee and Augustine Washington charged down the side of the ravine. Rooney assumed their target would fire once and then flee. They had covered only a few hundred yards when bullets tore through the undergrowth lining the bluffs. It was an ambush. In later years, Rooney would struggle to explain how exactly he had escaped. His own horse had collapsed; somehow he had managed to ride away on Augustine Washington's.

Augustine had fallen to the ground. He attempted to lift himself but could only prop up his back on his elbows. Lying down hurt. Three bullets had pierced his backside. The ambushers emerging from the brush gathered around the bearded stranger. He begged for water and then died. Who was this casualty? At first, no one could say. The fancy uniform and shoulder straps indicated an officer of some rank. The identity remained a mystery until someone saw a name on the gauntlets. Here lay the heir to Mount Vernon. The Federals scoured his body for souvenirs. The sergeant credited with the kill received one of the two pistols Augustine Washington carried. The other went to Secretary of War Simon Cameron. "I shall always prize it as a memorable relic of the present glorious struggle for freedom and the Union," Cameron wrote.

Back behind Confederate lines, the tale Rooney shared upset his father. It all had been so unnecessary. "I fear they were carried away by their zeal," Lee said. Though Augustine had still been alive when Rooney retreated, Lee realized the gravity of the wounds. On September 14, under a flag of truce, he sent a message requesting information. "Lieutenant Colonel John A. Washington, my Aide-de Camp, whilst riding yesterday with a small escort was fired upon by your pickets and I fear killed. Should such be the case, I request that you will deliver to me his body." Union commanders quickly complied. It would be Rooney who retrieved the body.

General Lee knew others who had already perished in the war. None of their deaths affected him as much as Augustine Washington's. "I saw him," remembered one soldier, "when he had just learned of the death of Colonel Washington. He was standing with his right arm thrown over the neck of his horse . . . and I was impressed first of all by the man's splendid physique, and then by the look of extreme sadness that pervaded his countenance." Lee sent his condolences to the family. He told Augustine's daughter Louisa how much he had admired her father. "My intimate association with him for some months has more fully disclosed to me his great worth, than double so many years of ordinary intercourse would have been sufficient to reveal. We have shared the same tent, and morning and evening has his earnest devotion to Almighty God elicited my grateful admiration." That Augustine Washington's death orphaned his already motherless children saddened Lee; that it deprived the country of Mount Vernon's last heir embittered him. To a friend, Lee suggested that it discredited the entire Union cause. "Our enemies have stamped their attack upon our rights with additional infamy by killing the lineal descendant and representative" of George Washington.

Mary Custis Lee predicted that those who had reproached Augustine Washington in the past—no doubt including the Yankees who had savaged him during the Mount Vernon controversy—would now regret their "hasty" words. She misread the mood of her Northern neighbors. In their minds, the death completed the storyline of the ingrate who had sold one inheritance and sold out another. "He justly met with a traitor's deserts," the *Daily Cleveland Herald* declared. "My wish is that the memory of the great immortal Washington will not be insulted by laying the bones of the wretched namesake upon any portion of Mt. Vernon. The distance between the burial places should be continents," wrote a correspondent for the *Cincinnati Daily Enquirer*. "While referring to the untimely end of Col. Washington," the *Daily National Intelligencer* editorialized, "we cannot refrain from signalizing the melancholy circumstance that he should have fallen in arms against the Government which the great man whose name he bore did so much to establish and adorn." That irony eluded Lee.

* * *

While the Northern press danced on Augustine Washington's grave, Southern papers doled out blame. Lee took his share. In Richmond, the venerable *Daily Dispatch* said that the days Lee had spent "weaving ingenious webs of strategy about Cheat Mountain" had only given the Union more time to tighten its grip on the region. "Every day's delay to reconquer Western Virginia adds to the strength of the enemy, by converting true men among its population over to the side of the North." The crisis called for a warrior, not an engineer. The *Dispatch* doubted whether Lee could fix the mess. "Legs and powder and ball do much better in the mountains than even the science of . . . a Lee." Events bolstered the argument. A few weeks later, seventy-five miles to the southwest, uncooperative officers and weather once again frustrated Lee's hopes of striking a blow against the enemy. General Scott's protégé had disappointed.

On October 31, Lee returned to Richmond. The mountains had changed his appearance. Hair now covered his cheeks and chin. The rough-looking result disappointed one woman, who missed the more manicured marble model. "Why, you would not have a soldier in the field not to look rough, would you? There is little time there for shaving and personal adornment," Lee told her. "I have a beautiful white beard," he informed his daughter Mildred. "It is much admired. At least, much remarked on." An officer more concerned with public relations would have shaved, for the "wiry" beard reinforced an unflattering nickname Lee had earned—"Granny Lee." The attacks upset Mary more than her husband. He accepted them as an inevitable consequence of public life. "I am sorry," he wrote, "that the movements of the armies cannot keep pace with the expectations of the editors of papers. I know they can regulate matters satisfactorily to themselves on paper. I wish they could do so in the field."

Lee's refusal to defend himself impressed the person whose opinion counted most. President Davis had enough quarrelsome generals. He had banished Beauregard to the west for leaking reports insinuating that the administration had thwarted him from destroying the federal army. Meanwhile, Johnston, who had taken over the army at

Manassas, fumed that Lee's commission as a general outranked his own. The self-restraint that defined Lee's character contrasted with the self-promotion preoccupying his peers. "Though subjected to depreciatory criticism by the carpet-knights who make campaigns on assumed hypotheses, he with characteristic self-abnegation made no defense of himself," Davis wrote. Since Lee would not defend himself, Davis did. He placed Lee in charge of coastal fortifications in South Carolina, Georgia, and eastern Florida, and penned a letter defending his choice to South Carolina's governor. When Lee reached the lower South, he named a new aide: Thornton A. Washington, another of the first president's relatives. T. A. Washington did not serve long on Lee's staff before transitioning to other assignments. There was no replacing the heir to Mount Vernon. The last in the line had perished. And the bloodshed was just beginning.

CHAPTER NINE

White House Burning

If he wished to see Cumberland Island, Georgia, now was the time. Events would soon force Lee to order Confederate forces to abandon the place to the Union. Defending every island off the coast against the Union navy would require spreading Confederate forces thinner than Robert E. Lee would allow. Better to concentrate troops, he thought, at key points farther inland. Touring the coast in January 1862 took Lee through the channel separating Cumberland from the mainland. Without stating his purpose, Lee asked his artillery chief and soon-to-be military secretary, Armistead Lindsay Long, "to accompany him on a sacred mission." The two landed at a wharf on the island. Oaks and magnolias lined the road that led Lee and Long to a large but unfinished mansion. The property had belonged to the Revolutionary War general Nathanael Greene. After admiring the portraits in the parlor, Lee and Long headed to the garden. "Passing on, we came to a dilapidated wall enclosing a neglected cemetery," Long recalled. "The general then, in a voice of emotion, informed me that he was visiting the grave of his father."

So rarely had Lee mentioned his father that when recounting the visit for his wife, he felt the need to remind her how Harry Lee had ended his days in Georgia. "He died there you may recollect on his way from the West Indies, & was interred in one corner of the family cemetery," Lee wrote. Lee himself did not know all the details: how his father had disembarked there en route home from the Caribbean, demanded to see the descendants of his old deceased commander, and then ranted and raged until dying in a third-floor bedroom. Now his ravaged body lay below a marble slab. Lee approached alone. Despite his years at Cockspur, he had never before come here. Why he chose this moment to visit the man who had abandoned him can only be guessed.

Certainly the pilgrimage his daughters had recently made to Stratford Hall, his father's old house in Westmoreland County, had turned his thoughts to the past. "I am much pleased at your description of Stratford & your visit," Lee wrote. "It is endeared to me by many recollections & it has always been a great desire of my life to be able to purchase it. Now that we have no other home, & the one we so loved has been so foully polluted, the desire is stronger with me than ever." Arlington, he added, "has been so desecrated that I cannot bear to think of it. I should have preferred it to have been wiped from the earth, its beautiful hill sunk, and its sacred trees buried, rather than to have been degraded." Newspaper reports confirmed Lee's worst fears. The Washington heirlooms his wife had stashed away at Arlington had begun disappearing. General McDowell had been completely unaware of their presence until housekeeper Selina Gray alerted him to the theft. "This place is not a safe one for the preservation of anything," said McDowell, who decided to ship the remaining relics to a more secure location: the Patent Office in Washington. "Nor is it surprising that, after all her protestations to the contrary, the wife of the Confederate general should have left behind some of the choicest and most valuable mementoes of the home life of him whose wise teachings both she and her husband have so thoroughly ignored," a Northern newspaper gloated.

In leaving Arlington the previous spring, Lee had also, of course, bid farewell to his most precious relic: the daughter of Washington's adopted son. He had not seen Mary since. Moving from house to house had worsened her health. "I suffer so much. Nothing I have taken here seems to afford me the slightest relief," she wrote. "I cannot walk a single step without crutches & very few with them." By Christmas, Mary had migrated to the White House plantation, the profitable estate Rooney had inherited on the Pamunkey River. She celebrated the holiday there with Rooney, his wife, Charlotte, and his son, Robert E. Lee III. Rob Jr., Annie, and Agnes also joined them. "I am very glad to find that you had a pleasant family meeting Xmas & that it was so large," Lee wrote. "I am truly grateful for all the mercies we enjoy, notwithstanding the miseries of war."

At the White House, Mary Custis Lee also could have celebrated the anniversary of the marriage that united her family with George Washington. Probably at the White House itself but possibly at nearby St. Peter's Church, Washington had wed Martha Custis on Twelfth Night 1759. The original house had burned. But the smaller two-story dwelling standing in its place retained the original name and charm, though observers noted it looked more brown than white. Mary called it Washington's first married home. "The farm is lovely, the land lying level near the river & breaking into beautiful hills as you go back inland," Rob Jr. wrote. Beyond its historical value, the property also possessed military significance. Just to the east, the Pamunkey River turned into the York River and hence marked the northern edge of the Virginia Peninsula. Twenty-three miles to the west, a railroad running past the house reached Richmond. Thus, from White House Landing, an army invading the Peninsula could transfer cargo coming up the York and Pamunkey Rivers onto trains bound for the Confederate capital. The old Custis farm would provide the perfect supply base for a siege of Richmond.

West of the White House on the Pamunkey, clouds gathered over the so-called White House of the Confederacy in Richmond. On Washington's Birthday in 1862, when President Davis delivered his inaugural address—his powers had to that moment been provisional—rain poured. Standing near an equestrian statue of Washington on the Capitol Square, Davis admitted, "The tide for the moment is against us." West Virginia had all but achieved its independence from the Old Dominion. A Union general named Ulysses S. Grant had conquered Forts Henry and Donelson in Tennessee. Lincoln had ordered a blockade; the Union navy had started seizing ports. New Orleans, the Confederacy's largest city, would fall that spring. As Lee noted, "Wherever his fleet can be brought no opposition can be made to his landing." Nowhere did the Union's advantage in manpower and supplies seem clearer than in the more than 160,000 troops George McClellan had amassed, trained, and equipped around Washington. McClellan had turned the amateurish army that had marched to Manassas into the proud and professional Army of the Potomac. Though McClellan proved cautious to commit his army to battle—he defied Lincoln's order to time his advance around Washington's Birthday—no one doubted the advance would come soon. In March, Joseph Johnston retreated to the Rappahannock River.

Lee viewed the South's problems as fatalistically as he viewed his own. God wanted to teach his countrymen the self-denial his mother had taught him. The times, he wrote, "look dark at present, & it is plain we have not suffered enough, laboured enough, repented enough, to deserve success." In South Carolina, where secession had started, the spirit of the volunteers disappointed him. "They have all of a sudden realized the asperities of war, in what they must encounter, & do not seem to be prepared for it." Lee had not wanted this war. He had predicted these problems. Now he reveled in being right.

> *Our people have not been earnest enough, have thought too much of themselves & their ease, & instead of turning out to a man, have been content to nurse themselves & their dimes, & leave the protection of themselves & families to others. To satisfy their consciences, they have been clamorous in criticising what others have done, & endeavoured to prove that they ought to do nothing. This is not the way to accomplish our independence. I have been doing all I can, with our small means & slow workmen, to defend the cities & coast here.*

Trouble recruiting and retaining soldiers convinced Lee that the Confederacy needed a universal draft law. "He thought," an aide recalled, "that since the whole duty of the nation would be war until independence should be secured, the whole nation should for the time be converted into an army."

On March 2, under fire from critics for micromanaging the war, President Davis recalled Lee to Richmond. The order indicated that Lee would oversee "the armies of the Confederacy." In truth, Lee would oversee nothing. He would serve as Davis's adviser, a glorified assistant secretary of war. While the new office did allow Lee to help enact America's first conscription law, he did not relish a desk job, especially one that included occasionally handling the president's personal correspondence. "I do not see either advantage or pleasure in my duties," he wrote Mary. "But I will not complain, but do my best."

Later that month came alarming reports that thousands—tens of thousands—of Union soldiers had begun landing at the tip of the Virginia Peninsula. "The re-enforcements of the enemy," one source said, "extend as far as the eye can observe. . . . The force is immense—entirely out of my power to estimate." The troops had come from Alexandria. After months of delays and disappointments, which had squandered the goodwill McClellan had acquired in western Virginia, the Young Napoleon had finally loaded his army onto ships. One after another the vessels headed past Mount Vernon, through the mouth of the Potomac, and down the Chesapeake. As a historian of the campaign puts it, "Nothing comparable to the movement of the Army of the Potomac to the Virginia Peninsula had ever before been seen in America." Within weeks, more than 120,000 troops would land on the Virginia Peninsula. Instead of marching his army south, McClellan had decided to march west up the Peninsula to Richmond.

The Army of the Potomac would first have to cross a defensive line that the flamboyant Confederate Major General John Magruder had drawn across the width of the Peninsula from the James to the York. It should have been a nuisance and nothing more. To guard a line spanning fourteen miles, Magruder initially counted fewer than ten thousand men. If Union boats succeeded in ascending either the James or the York, they could outflank Magruder's line and supply McClellan's army en route to Richmond. The approach up the York River seemed probable to Lee because the South had its most intimidating weapon defending the James: the *Merrimack*. The Confederates had transformed the old wooden frigate seized from the Norfolk shipyards into an ironclad monster called the CSS *Virginia*, which had already sunk two Union wooden ships and battled the new Union ironclad, the *Monitor*, to a draw. The need to avoid the Confederate ironclad would steer McClellan to the York, and that, in turn, would steer him to the Pamunkey and the White House. "Should they select that, their whole army & c. will land at the White House," Lee warned Mary on April 4. "To be enveloped in it [the advance] would be extremely annoying & embarrassing, as I believe hundreds would delight in persecuting you."

On the Peninsula, Magruder had placed the far left of his line at Yorktown, where George Washington had laid siege to the British. Rather than digging fresh trenches in certain spots, the Confederates simply commandeered the old British defenses. "These frowning battlements on the heights of York are turned in this second war of liberty against the enemies of our country," Magruder told his soldiers. The Army of the Potomac could have quickly breached the under-manned line, but, as if bound by the past, McClellan opted for a more time-consuming option: a second siege of Yorktown. "Gen. McClellan obviously means to repeat the brilliant strategy of Washington," exclaimed the *New York Times*. In what would emerge as a pattern, the paranoid McClellan dithered because he believed his army outnumbered. And while that was not the case—and never would be—the delay allowed reinforcements from Johnston's army to reach the Peninsula. When Johnston himself arrived to inspect the position, he concluded, "No one but McClellan could have hesitated to attack."

Nonetheless, Johnston wanted out of Yorktown. That was the message he and his generals brought to Richmond for a remarkable meeting in mid-April with Davis, Lee, and Secretary of War George Randolph, who happened to be Thomas Jefferson's grandson. Johnston insisted that all Confederate forces should fall back on Richmond. The time had come for a united stand against McClellan. If the troops at Yorktown did not withdraw soon, Union boats fighting their way up the York River would outflank the position. Though Lee in his letter to Mary had also anticipated this possibility, he did not accept its inevitability. He argued that the Peninsula offered advantages for a smaller army battling a larger one. The secretary of war agreed with Lee. Abandoning the Yorktown line would cost the Confederacy Norfolk and maybe the *Virginia*. The debate raged from eleven o'clock in the morning to six o'clock in the evening and again from seven o'clock at night until past midnight. Finally, at one o'clock in the morning, Davis made a decision that underscored his growing trust in Lee. The troops, he said, must hold the line. Johnston would bring more of his army and command in person. "Though General J. E. Johnston did not agree with this decision, he did not ask to be relieved," Davis recalled. That, as it turned out, was only because Johnston had decided to humor the president for the time being.

On May 2, readers of the *New York Times* awoke to another history lesson. "The army commanded by Gen. McClellan has now been before Yorktown precisely the period it took Washington to reduce that stronghold," an article using questionable math explained. "It only remains that the same result should follow the operations." Little did the paper know that Johnston had planned a retreat for that night. The order stunned Lee and Davis. "It is not known under what necessity you are acting or how far you can delay the movements of the enemy, who it is presumed will move up York River as soon as opened to him," Lee wrote. Perhaps the *Virginia* could still escape from Norfolk, swing around the Peninsula, and stop the Union boats coming up the York and Pamunkey Rivers. It was wishful thinking. Yorktown and Norfolk would fall, and so would Washington's first married home. Johnston would get his last stand before Richmond.

The first Union soldiers to reach the White House belonged to a regiment under the command of Lawrence Williams, whose brother Orton had betrayed General Scott's trust a year earlier. Lawrence's loyalties also aroused suspicion, especially when fellow officers noted his "great interest in the protection of the property of his cousin, General

Lee." On a door to the White House, the bluecoats found a note reading, "Northern soldiers, who profess to reverence Washington, forbear to desecrate the house of his first married life, the property of his wife, now owned by her descendants." The letter writer, who identified herself only as "a granddaughter of Mrs. Washington" but was obviously Mary Lee, had chosen not to greet the Union troops in person. Her husband, it seemed, had convinced her that she could ill afford to fall behind enemy lines. "How are you to live?" he had asked. "The Confederate money would be valueless & the Virginia money perhaps not very current if I could get it to you." Given Richmond's uncertain fate, he advised she flee to the Carolinas or even Georgia, though to avoid panic, he asked her to keep that opinion secret.

Shortly before noon on May 16, General McClellan himself arrived at the White House. Like McDowell at Arlington, he initially honored Mary's request. "I have taken every precaution to secure from injury this house, where Washington passed the first portion of his married life. I neither occupy it myself nor permit others to occupy it," he wrote new Union secretary of war Edwin Stanton. A guard whom McClellan assigned to the house penned a response under Mary's note. "Lady—A Northern officer has protected your property in sight of the enemy, and at the request of your overseer."

While protecting the actual house, Union soldiers transformed the rest of the property into a massive supply base capable of handling the six hundred tons of daily provisions the Army of the Potomac required. Working parties erected wharves along the Pamunkey and repaired the railroad to Richmond. As the supplies headed to the front lines, the White House prepared to receive the wounded in return. Medics setting up a hospital pitched 170 tents. As many people saw it, the White House would serve as the staging ground for the last battle of the war. Union officers confidently called it "our final depot." "I cannot number the vessels lying off White House. To say there are a thousand of all descriptions would not be saying too much," a correspondent for the *Daily National Intelligencer* wrote. "The stars and stripes are gaily flying; hundreds of soldiers meet you at the landing, and all combined gives White House landing a picturesque aspect." The news-papermen touring the plantation learned about its history from an old slave named Diana. In turn, they told her that the "Yankees would be very likely to kill Massa Lee." According to one account, she replied, "De Lord will must be done unto him."

Soldiers scouring the neighborhood on May 23 discovered a surprise. Mary Custis Lee had not taken her husband's advice to move south of the James; she had merely moved up the Pamunkey River to a different house. "The wife & two grown daughters of Gen. Lee . . . are living in a place commanded by the enemy, & almost within their lines, & on a farm on which & throughout the whole neighborhood the slaves are in general rebellion," wrote a Virginian monitoring the situation. Eventually Union officers assigned Mary guards not for her safety but for their own. Being so close to the capital, they worried she would slip messages to her husband. They need not have worried. Lee had heard reports of his wife's detention but, as he explained, "nothing since" and felt "very anxious."

First Martha Washington's house and now her great-granddaughter had fallen into McClellan's control. At least, Lee knew McClellan. They had served together as engineers in Mexico and, though many years apart at the academy, could relate to each other's West Point training. Curiously they used the same adjective—"timid"—to describe each other. Either because of this relationship or because the guards tired of Mary's tirades, McClellan in early June sent word that he would happily return his captive whenever Lee pleased. On June 10, a carriage transporting Mary Custis Lee and two of her daughters crossed the Confederate picket lines. "Cheer after cheer went down the long line of soldiers," an escort remembered. For the first time in more than a year, Mary had the opportunity to see her husband. He now wore a gray coat with dark blue pants tucked into his boots. The insignia on his collar indicated only a colonel—the rank he had held in the Union army when Mary had last seen him—but he was now a general and not just in name. Davis had shuffled personnel again. Lee had replaced Johnston.

* * *

"Johnston is a great soldier," Winfield Scott once observed, "but he has an unfortunate knack of getting himself shot in nearly every engagement." At the Battle of Seven Pines on May 31, Joseph Johnston lived up to only half his reputation. He failed to demonstrate the qualities of a great soldier, but he did get himself shot. Johnston had chosen to strike McClellan after part of the Union army crossed the Chickahominy River, a marshy James River tributary that starts above and behind Richmond, flows down in front of it, and ends southeast of it. Because of this diagonal path, the southern half of an army approaching Richmond from the east crosses the river before the northern half. McClellan's army was thus divided on May 31. Only two of the Union's five corps lay south of the Chickahominy. Johnston planned to concentrate his own army against these isolated Federals. From the beginning, the plan misfired. Late in the day, Johnston rode to the front to see what had gone wrong. No sooner had he lectured a young soldier about the futility of trying to dodge gunfire than a bullet hit his shoulder and an explosion threw him to the ground. Around the same time, Davis and Lee also set off to the front in search of answers. Johnston had neglected to consult either man about his plans. What Davis and Lee found now was confusion, carnage, and casualties, Johnston among the wounded. At nightfall, Davis and Lee rode back to Richmond. The president had been kept in the dark long enough. He reassigned Lee to the field.

On the first of June, Lee assumed command of what he optimistically titled "the Army of Northern Virginia." The Southern soldiers who had once threatened the Potomac now cowered below the Pamunkey and behind the Chickahominy. The battle a day earlier had cost them dearly—more than six thousand killed, wounded, and missing—and purchased not a yard. The enemy before them could see the "spires of Richmond"; the nervous civilians behind them had begun evacuating. The sound of artillery shook Richmond's streets and windows. The Confederate government prepared its essential papers for removal. A couple of miles outside town, Lee set up his headquarters at a house belonging to the Widow Dabbs. Near there, he convened his army's top generals in council. Should the army hold its ground or retreat even closer into the city? Many of the generals advocated for the latter course. The current position exposed their soldiers to Union artillery. Their argument struck Lee as self-defeating. "If we leave this line because they can shell us, we shall have to leave the next for the same reason, and I don't see how we can stop this side of Richmond," he reasoned. Having consulted his generals, Lee now faced the awkward prospect of disregarding their advice. As of yet, he commanded neither their loyalty nor their trust. Cheat Mountain still clouded his reputation. He adjourned the council without announcing the decision he had already made. He would stand his ground, and so would his army. The order went out to dig in.

As often as he could, Lee rode up and down the line on Traveller, his new gray horse. While watching the earthworks go up, he heard soldiers carping that digging was beneath their dignity. They wanted to lift muskets, not spades. The latter belonged in the hands of black slaves. For these complaints, Lee had no patience. The industrious Yankees did not hold these prejudices. "Our people are opposed to work. . . . All ridicule & resist it. It is the very means by which McClellan has & is advancing. Why should we leave to him the whole advantage of labour," Lee wrote. Indeed, his fellow engineer McClellan had not planned a battle of arms but "a battle of posts," as Lee termed it. McClellan would bring up his heavy guns, force the Confederates back, inch his army forward, fortify the new ground, and repeat as many times as needed until his cannons could bombard Richmond. Then the siege would start. "It will require 100,000 men to resist the regular siege of Richmond, which perhaps would only prolong not save it," Lee wrote. To avoid this nightmare, Lee needed to go on the offensive. The soldiers who resented digging defenses misread their general's aggressive mind-set. As he explained to President Davis, "I am preparing a line that I can hold with part of our forces in front, while with the rest I will endeavour to make a diversion to bring McClellan out."

The idea maturing in Lee's mind called for a maneuver larger than a diversion. Lee had noted during his own reconnaissance that McClellan's right flank, north of the Chickahominy, did not extend as far as it should. To confirm his suspicions, Lee asked his audacious cavalry commander, Brigadier General J. E. B. Stuart, who had served him so ably at Harpers Ferry, to gather intelligence about the Union position. Stuart delivered. With twelve hundred horsemen following the plume in his hat, he raced around the Union right flank, deeper and deeper into the strip of land between the Pamunkey and Chickahominy Rivers. Rooney Lee, who now headed one of Stuart's regiments, could nearly see the White House plantation before the cavalry turned south and completed a circuit around the entire Union army. Besides embarrassing McClellan, Stuart's ride had confirmed the Union's weakness. As McClellan had approached Richmond and transferred more troops below the Chickahominy, he had exposed his supply lines back to the White House above the river. Of the Union's five corps, only Brigadier General Fitz John Porter's remained on the north side.

It was a dangerous position, not entirely of McClellan's making. Lincoln had worried from the start of the Peninsula Campaign that McClellan's decision to approach Richmond from the Chesapeake would leave the Union capital open to an overland attack. He had thus detained one corps of the army closer to Washington. McClellan had anticipated that this sixth corps would eventually link up with Porter's corps. What McClellan had not anticipated was how his commander in chief would react after Thomas Jackson, who had earned the epithet Stonewall at Manassas and then returned to the Shenandoah as a major general, chased the main federal army in the valley across the Potomac in late May. Lee had orchestrated the diversion in the hope that a Confederate victory in the valley, followed by a feint against the Potomac, would keep federal reinforcements from Richmond. "An attack," he had told Jackson back in April, "will prove a great relief to the pressure." Lincoln played into Lee's hands. Instead of sending the missing corps to McClellan, the Union commander in chief sent it after Jackson, who escaped south back up the valley. On the next hand,

Lee raised the wager. He reinforced Jackson and let word of it reach Washington. Lincoln suspected a bluff but would not take the bet, not when Jackson had already threatened the Potomac. On June 20, the president informed McClellan not to expect additional reinforcements.

By that time, Lee had won the trick, or rather Lincoln had fallen for it. With federal reinforcements frozen, Lee summoned his own. He ordered Jackson's army to leave the valley, descend on the Pamunkey, and turn McClellan's vulnerable right flank. The addition of Jackson's troops and others would give the Army of Northern Virginia an unprecedented and afterward unequaled 92,400 soldiers. "The sooner you unite with this army the better," Lee told Jackson on June 16. "I should like to have the advantage of your views and be able to confer with you." So secret did Lee keep the plan that seven days later when a "dusty" and "travel-worn" Jackson showed up at the Dabbs house for a meeting, his appearance astonished the headquarters staff. Lee had also invited three other major generals: James Longstreet, D. H. Hill, and the unrelated A. P. Hill. Their three divisions, Lee explained, would cross the Chickahominy once Jackson flanked McClellan's right. A. P. Hill would cross first, drive the enemy back, and clear another bridge downriver for D. H. Hill and Longstreet. "The four divisions keeping in communication with each other and moving in echelon," Lee added, "will sweep down the Chickahominy, and endeavor to drive the enemy from his positions."

President Davis had already raised the obvious objection. Throwing the bulk of the army against one Union corps north of the Chickahominy would leave only a small force to fend off four Union corps south of the river. McClellan could charge through the undermanned trenches and seize Richmond. The plan would succeed only if McClellan, as Davis put it, "should behave like an engineer officer, and deem it his first duty to protect his line of communication." Lee did not appreciate the dig at engineers. But in essence, his plan did rely on that reading of McClellan. The idea, as Lee told a sharp new aide named Charles Marshall, "was to compel General McClellan to come out of his works and give battle for the defence of his communications with the White House." Just how much McClellan valued his base at the White House would soon be revealed.

In the eyes of McClellan's Northern detractors—and there were a growing number of them—the answer to how much the Union commander valued the White House was clear: too much. Critics accused McClellan of striking a deal with the Lee family to protect the home. There had been little fuss when McDowell first promised to protect Arlington, but that had been a year ago, before the Union lost more than thirteen thousand men in the Battle of Shiloh in Tennessee and more than five thousand in the Battle of Seven Pines. The wounded from the latter piled up around the White House. "Many were confined on steamboats, which were lying in the Pamunkey River, a dirty, muddy stream, and were obliged to drink bad water; and others were in hospital tents, pitched on muddy grounds," a doctor recorded. Reports of soldiers suffering in tents scandalized Washington. Why had McClellan not converted the White House into a hospital? "Very urgent complaints are being made from various quarters respecting the protection afforded to the rebel General Lee's property, called the White House, instead of using it as a hospital for the care of wounded soldiers," Secretary of War Stanton telegraphed McClellan on June 7. "It seems to me that the necessities of our suffering soldiers require that this property should be devoted to their use rather than be protected for rebel officers by whose arms our troops have fallen."

The accusation enraged McClellan. "The White House of the rebel General Lee, referred to, is a small frame building of six rooms . . . and the medical director states that it would not accommodate more than thirty patients," he fired back. He had safeguarded the house out of respect for who had once lived there, not who currently lived there. "I have given special directions to protect the property of the White House from any unnecessary injury or destruction because it was once the property of General Washington, and I cannot believe that you will regard this as a cause for rebuke."

Congressmen decided to visit the White House to investigate. Back in Washington, on the House floor, they shared their findings: the horror of seeing wounded men suffering in "indifferent tents" while Union soldiers guarded the modern-looking house that had replaced Washington's old home. "Shall we conciliate the man Lee, who was responsible for the wounds inflicted upon the soldiers who were denied access to the accommodations of that very White House? I say that it is a burning disgrace," said one congressman. "I do not believe if Washington were alive he would object to these premises, from any sentimentality, being occupied by sick and wounded soldiers," said another. "It would be more honor to his memory if it were used for the sick and wounded soldiers who are battling in defense of the Union for which he suffered so much."

One day after the debate, a doctor upset about the conditions at the White House on the Pamunkey brought his case to the White House on the Potomac. Lincoln confessed that McClellan had given Mrs. Lee his word. "He doesn't want to break the promise he has made," Lincoln said. "I will break it for him." On June 18, Stanton informed Congress that Lincoln had issued orders appropriating the house. What he did not add—because he did not know—was that Stonewall Jackson was already en route.

The afternoon of June 26 found Lee still on the south side of the Mechanicsville Bridge. He had planned to cross the Chickahominy hours ago. So had the two divisions that Longstreet and D. H. Hill had concealed behind a hill. The soldiers had been lying on their weapons since the morning. A. P. Hill had yet to clear the bridgehead because Jackson had yet to flank the Union right. Every part of the plan depended on Jackson doing his part. The orders called for Jackson to strike early in the day. Actually, when Jackson had come to the Dabbs house three days before, he had proposed striking a full day earlier. Longstreet, the usually taciturn senior division commander who hid his lips behind an "ample" brown beard, had recommended that

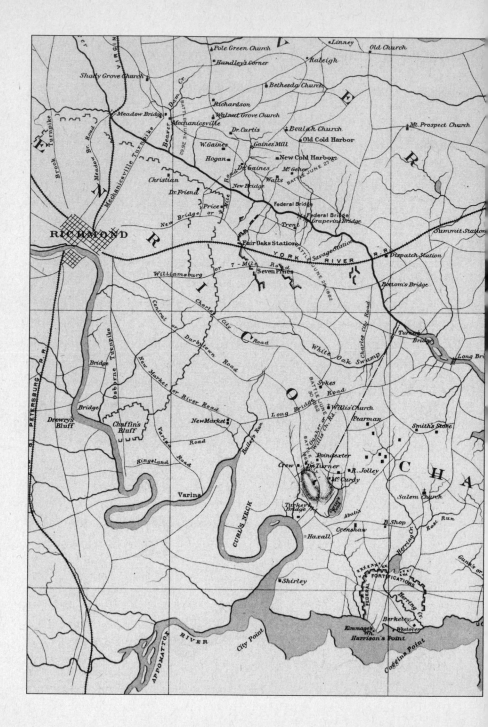

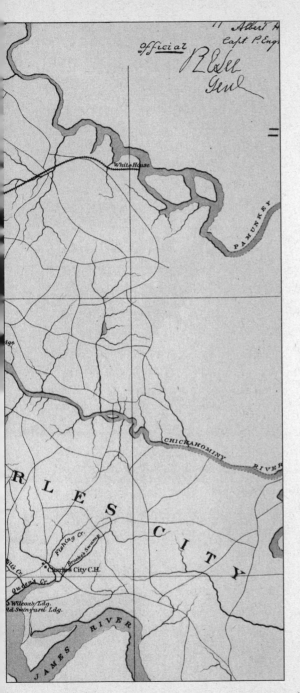

◄ A slice of the map accompanying Robert E. Lee's report on the battles of what became known as the Seven Days. The York River Railroad running past the White House on the Pamunkey River made the old Custis estate the perfect supply base for a Union siege of the Confederate capital.

Jackson give his troops the additional day; while Jackson had ridden ahead to Richmond, the rest of his valley army still had a long way to go. Evidently so. As Lee waited, an observer noted how "his eyes were restless with the look of a man with fever." Seeing the nervous strain on the face of President Davis, on hand to see the battle, must have worsened the feeling. Instead of redeeming his reputation from Cheat Mountain, Lee seemed doomed to reinforce it.

At a bridge upriver, A. P. Hill had other ideas. Just thirty-six years old, A. P. Hill commanded the Light Division, which, as the name suggested, traveled light and fast. By three o'clock in the afternoon, A. P. Hill decided he had waited long enough for Jackson. He ordered his troops over the Chickahominy. Sweeping down the left bank, the Light Division opened the Mechanicsville Bridge for D. H. Hill and Longstreet. At around five o'clock, Lee joined his men on the north side. The troops advancing east behind A. P. Hill faced scant resistance until entering the range of the guns guarding the main Union line behind a creek called Beaver Dam. Federal forces had fortified the wooded ridge behind the steep banks. "About a mile of open ground was to be gotten over, most of which was swept by three or four batteries," an officer in the Light Division recalled. The strength of the position did not surprise Lee. He knew that the Federals had fortified it. That was why he had ordered Jackson to turn the position: to avoid a direct assault. Now that Jackson had disappointed him, Lee had no other option. Suspending his offensive above the Chickahominy would invite McClellan to resume his own below it. "In order to occupy the enemy and prevent any counter movement," Lee considered himself "obliged to do something."

That something was to allow A. P. Hill, sporting the red shirt he preferred for battles, to continue his march toward the creek. "Apparently unaware, or regardless, of the great danger in their front, this force moved on with animation and confidence, as if going to parade, or engaging in a sham battle," a Union officer wrote. "Suddenly, when half-way down the bank of the [creek's] valley, our men opened upon it rapid volleys of artillery and infantry." A Confederate brigade commander described the fire as "the most destructive cannonading I have yet known." With few exceptions, the troops reaching the creek could not cross. Many ended the night, as others had started the day, lying flat on their weapons. At nine o'clock in the evening, the firing slackened. All that an aide surveying the field could see of Lee's master plan was dead Confederates. Lee's army had suffered more than fourteen hundred casualties and inflicted fewer than four hundred.

The Union guns thundered again early in the morning for an hour and then fell silent. Confederates venturing forward discovered that Union corps commander Fitz John Porter had evacuated Beaver Dam. Federal scouts overnight had located the long-lost valley army; Jackson was on the Union flank. He had actually arrived about five o'clock the previous afternoon—inexcusably behind schedule—and then inexplicably had neglected to inform Lee. Had Jackson joined the battle even at that late stage, he might have altered the outcome. That, as far as Lee could concern himself, was blood under the bridge, for his men had repaired a crossing over Beaver Dam and could now continue their sweep down the Chickahominy toward the Union supply lines. A. P. Hill and Longstreet proceeded on the right, and Jackson and D. H. Hill on the left. Lee expected the Federals to make another stand near Gaines's Mill a few miles east, but Union engineers found a stronger position on high ground a little farther downriver. Fitz John Porter arranged his men in a semicircular line tracing a swampy tributary that curved around a wooded hillside from the northeast to the southwest. Such was the state of the Confederacy that the name Boatswain's Swamp did not appear on Lee's map.

Rows of Union soldiers lining the hillside opened fire and repulsed A. P. Hill's men on the Confederate right. Lee imagined that McClellan had finally brought up "the principal part" of his army. In reality, Lee still faced a single though slightly augmented corps of thirty-five thousand. If he could bring the columns on his left into the fight, he would have a three-to-two advantage, perhaps enough to overrun the hillside. The problem was that Jackson had gone missing again. Late that afternoon, Lee found his mysterious lieutenant holding one of the lemons he often sucked. His troops had taken a wrong turn but had finally joined the battle. "I am very glad to see you. I hoped to be with you before," Lee said. "That fire is very heavy. Do you think your men can stand it?" Jackson swore they could. Lee ordered an all-out assault across his line.

Still the Union line held. A stalemate would not do. Toward the center of the line, Lee rode over to Brigadier General John Bell Hood, who had served under him in Texas. "This must be done," Lee said to Hood. "Can you break his line?" Hood offered to try. He ordered his men to keep their lines and hold their fire until told otherwise. "Onward we marched under a constantly increasing shower of shot and shell," he later wrote. "Our ranks were thinned at almost every step forward." Approaching the creek, they trampled over the mangled bodies lining the bank and then crossed through the swampy water. "Amid the fearful roar of musketry and artillery," Hood recalled, "I gave the order to fix bayonets and charge. With a ringing shout we dashed up the steep hill, through the abatis, and over the breastworks, upon the very heads of the enemy." The blue line broke here and almost simultaneously everywhere. "The enemy," Lee wrote President Davis, "after a severe contest of five hours [has been] entirely repulsed from the field." Lee had lost nearly eight thousand men but had won the day. Porter withdrew south of the Chickahominy.

Early on June 28, Lee sent his cavalry on a raid six miles down the Chickahominy to Dispatch Station, where the railroad crossed en route to the White House on the Pamunkey. Lee had bet the entire campaign that an engineer like McClellan would defend this critical supply line. Even now that the Union right had folded and exposed the railway, Lee assumed that McClellan would attempt to save his base at the White House. But that was not how the situation appeared at Dispatch Station. Tearing up the railway tracks proved suspiciously easy. J. E. B. Stuart decided to venture up the line toward the White House, twelve miles to the northeast. As the troopers approached, they saw clouds of smoke rising. Nightfall forced them into camp a few miles shy of their goal. In the darkness, they could see flames behind the trees. These were signs of retreat. The Federals must have deserted and destroyed their base. After sunrise, Rooney Lee guided Stuart the rest of the way to the house. Only the tall brick chimneys that had flanked either end remained standing. The home that once stood between these two towers had vanished. In its place lay smoldering rubble. The stench and heat from the burning stores overwhelmed the riders. "An opportunity," Stuart wrote, "was here offered for observing the deceitfulness of the enemy's pretended reverence for everything associated with the name of Washington, for the dwelling-house was burned to the ground, and not a vestige left except what told of desolation and vandalism."

In truth, the Union commanders evacuating the White House had intended to burn only the military provisions, not the private property. A Union private disregarding these orders had set fire to the house. Such things were bound to happen in the chaos of retreat. Barely a week had passed since Lincoln had ordered the house converted into a hospital. McClellan had responded by soliciting more medical opinions opposing the idea. To the last, McClellan had tried to defend the White House against Lincoln. What he had failed to defend against was Lee. Amid the ruins, Stuart's men found that much of the Union bounty had survived. "Provisions and delicacies of every description lay in heaps," Stuart wrote. That night, as the famished troopers feasted on eggs, strawberries, figs, and iced lemonade, Rooney inspected his property. A fellow rider never forgot the sight. "In the quiet of a summer evening with the enemy fled, and only a distant, random gun heard, he surveyed the widespread havoc and smoking piles."

The decision to abandon the White House meant the end of McClellan's drive toward Richmond. There would be no siege. The Army of the Potomac withdrew from the outskirts of the city and retreated south toward the James River. Lee sounded the pursuit. An army transferring its base on the run presented a ripe target. There might never be a better chance to destroy the Union army. But Lee's plans requiring detached commands to synchronize their movements once again confounded his generals and produced disjointed attacks, culminating in a bloody and futile assault at a place called Malvern Hill. When told the enemy was slipping away, Lee seethed. "Yes," he said, "because I cannot have my orders carried out!" By July 2, McClellan had reached the safety of his gunboats on the James. The battles of what became known as the Seven Days had ended. Though disappointed the federal army had escaped, Lee declared victory. One week earlier, the enemy had stood in sight of Richmond. "Today," Lee wrote, "the remains of that confident and threatening host lie upon the banks of the James River, thirty miles from Richmond, seeking to recover, under the protection of his gunboats, from the effects of a series of disastrous defeats."

In one week, Lee had flipped the Confederacy's fortunes and his own. The Northern newspapers Stuart's men found littered around the White House ruins had predicted Richmond's imminent fall. Now those headlines looked laughable, though no more so than the Southern papers that had condemned Lee after the western Virginia campaign and now sang his praises. "The rise which this officer has suddenly taken in the public confidence is without a precedent," the *Daily Dispatch* wrote. "No Captain that ever lived could have planned or executed a better campaign." Lee himself would have never claimed that distinction, and not just because of modesty. While failing to destroy his opponent, he had decimated his own ranks. Starting with the smaller army, he had suffered the larger losses. His 3,494 dead were twice as many as McClellan's. In one week, the Army of Northern Virginia had suffered more than twenty thousand casualties. Lee had saved Richmond but at a high price.

"The sorrow that surrounds us every where, the wail of the widows & orphans, drives away all the joys of our brilliant successes," Mary Lee wrote. Those sorrows visited the Lees. Their sons all survived the Peninsula Campaign; their grandson, Robert E. Lee III, did not. Forced from the White House, Rooney's wife had taken the toddler to North Carolina, where he died of a lung infection. In her grief, Mary conflated the child's passing with the White House burning. The site that had kindled the Custis-Washington connection had become a victim of Lee's attack on the Union. Mary blamed the Federals. "We left all the furniture there, not supposing such an act of vandalism could be committed on a place sacred as having been the early home of Washington in wedded life. The thievish villains, although they had military stores there to the value of millions, employed their time & transports in robbing the house of every article," she told a friend. "I trust I may live to see the day of retribution."

That day might not be far off. After the Seven Days, Lee once again divided his army, this time into two corps: one under Jackson, whose poor performance on the Peninsula had not stolen the stardom he had earned in the Shenandoah, and the other under the reliable Longstreet, who had immediately impressed his chief as a "Capital soldier." At the end of August, the two wings reunited on the old Manassas battlefield and shredded another Union army. Like the first battle at Bull Run, the second one ended with federal soldiers fleeing back toward Washington. Though Lee lacked the strength to besiege the heavily fortified capital, the Maryland countryside west of the city lay open. A year of fighting and foraging had ravaged the Old Dominion. The war needed to change. The North needed to feel it. Lee would cross the Potomac.

CHAPTER TEN

Emancipation

Among the possessions Mary Custis Lee found missing from the White House were most of the slaves. The Union army had deemed them "contraband of war," a loosely defined term that made them not quite slaves but not quite free. Nevertheless, federal officers evacuating the plantation had offered the contrabands free passage down the Pamunkey on canal boats. "Old and young, all rushed on board indiscriminately," a *New York Herald* correspondent wrote. "From the happy gyrations of their facial organs they appeared to be unanimous on leaving their masters in the 'Old Dominion.'" Mary put a different spin on the story. In her telling, "the thievish villains . . . forced off all our negroes, in spite of their tears and supplications." The Union, she added, "had not even the pretext of freeing ours as by my father's will they would have been free this winter."

That last comment, at least, bore the benefit of being true. The circuit court had ruled that Custis's will "entitled" the slaves "to their freedom" within five years regardless of whether Robert E. Lee had raised the ten-thousand-dollar legacies owed to his daughters. Lee had filed an appeal. His lawyer argued that since the will required the White House and Romancoke "to be worked to raise the aforesaid legacies," prematurely emancipating their workforces would defeat its intent. In November 1861, the Virginia Supreme Court of Appeals issued its ruling in a case awkwardly listing Lee as the plaintiff and his wife and children as the defendants. "The slaves," the judges said, "if not nec-

168

essary for the payment of debts are entitled to their freedom at the expiration of five years." Technically speaking, as the *Daily Dispatch* pointed out, the decision reversed the lower court. Whether the ruling gave Lee discretion to defer emancipation was a separate matter, which depended on whether he could define the "debts" and legacies as one and the same. Lee was tempted to do so until his lawyer recommended against it. That settled it. "The decision of the court must be taken as the enunciation of your Grandfather's will. It is due to his memory therefore that it should be accomplished," Lee told Rooney.

A few lines after requiring the slaves freed from their work, the court had reminded Lee of his own. "It is the duty of the executor to work the estates." The war, of course, had complicated that task. "How I can expedite its completion during the continuance of the war I cannot see," Lee wrote. He could not manage an army and an estate at the same time. Neither could he easily dip into his own assets. "The bonds that I hold of the Northern railroads & cities will all be confiscated & those of the Southern states will be much depreciated & cannot pay interest so my revenue will be much reduced if not cut off," he told his oldest son. "You must allow me to advise that you economize your funds, for I expect to be a pauper if I get through the war." As before, Lee also worried that emancipating the slaves too soon might not benefit them in the long run. "If emancipated under present circumstances, even if I could accomplish it, I do not see what would become of them." Even so, Lee would have to act. Before the end of 1862, the Custis slaves, whom George Washington had failed to free, must be released.

In Washington, DC, President Lincoln also eyed the end of the year as a milestone in the march of freedom. Though Lincoln had long believed that the Founding Fathers had intended to put slavery on the path to extinction, he had started the war with a stated goal of only preserving the Union, not perfecting it. The fiasco on the Peninsula altered his calculations. The rebellion proved what Lincoln had famously said back in Illinois about a country half slave and half free: it could not stand. On July 22, 1862, he informed his cabinet that he intended to issue a document that would forever free all slaves in states still in rebellion as of the first day of 1863. Secretary of State William Seward worried that announcing the proclamation in the wake of a military defeat would appear desperate. Lincoln agreed to wait for a victory. Thinking McClellan too cautious to deliver one, he placed his faith in a more aggressive general named John Pope. But it was Pope whom Lee humiliated at the Battle of Second Manassas. As Lee led his army into Maryland, Lincoln restored McClellan to command. The president then swore an oath to God: if Lee were forced back across the Potomac, he, Abraham Lincoln, would free the slaves. One way or another, Lee's decision to cross the Potomac would change the war.

The Army of Northern Virginia forded the Potomac east of the Blue Ridge Mountains between September 4 and September 7. Lee had not crossed the river since turning down the Union command. Instead of leading the biggest and best-supplied army in American history, as General Scott had envisioned, Lee led soldiers who seemed as ragged and threadbare as their Revolutionary forebears. The thousands of bleeding and bare feet splashing across the shallow Potomac astonished Marylanders who had known only the tidy columns of Union blue. "Were these dirty, lank, ugly specimens of humanity, with shocks of hair sticking through holes in their hats, and dust thick on their dirty faces, the men that had coped and encountered successfully, and driven back again and again, our splendid legions?" one woman wondered. Lee looked equally unimpressive. Several days earlier, a commotion had startled Traveller. The horse had jumped and caused his master, who had been holding his bridle, to fall, sprain both wrists, and break one hand. An ambulance would have to transport Lee over the river.

Being dragged onto Union territory matched Lee's own conception of why he had come: his army had no choice. "So much depends upon circumstances beyond its control," Lee remarked. Although he had promised at the dawn of the war never to draw his sword "save in defence" of his native state, he had concluded that protecting Virginia required staying on the offensive. It would be the irony of the war that a general who privately considered himself a captive of circumstance would become publicly known for his ability to retain the initiative against enormous odds. "What was General Lee to do?" snapped an aide years later when a critic challenged the "wisdom" of the Maryland campaign. Having chased one army from the outskirts of Richmond, he could not just wait for Lincoln to dispatch another immense and, in Lee's opinion, immoral blue army. By crossing the Potomac east of the Blue Ridge, Lee would threaten both Washington and Baltimore and force Lincoln to deploy every soldier at his disposal in their defense. "As long as the army of the enemy are employed on this frontier I have no fears for the safety of Richmond," Lee told Davis in a letter proposing the plan on September 3. True, the army lacked the supplies needed for a sustained invasion. The soldiers would have to buy what provisions they could in Maryland and then live off the land, even if that meant a diarrhea-inducing diet of green corn. "Still," Lee concluded, "we cannot afford to be idle, and though weaker than our opponents in men and military equipments, must endeavor to harass, if we cannot destroy them." Certain that Davis would agree, he commenced crossing before receiving a response.

There was good reason to assume Davis would approve. Lee had impressed his commander in chief, and he knew it. "Confidence in you overcomes the view which would otherwise be taken of the exposed condition of Richmond," Davis had told Lee upon the return of the Army of Northern Virginia to its namesake region. The two men had also often discussed the idea of invading Maryland. Since the war's first days, Southerners had fantasized—and Northerners had feared—that Maryland, a slave state, would secede. The new slave confederacy would then surround the city of Washington. "If it is ever desired to give material aid to Maryland and afford her an opportunity of throwing off the oppression to which she is now subject, this would seem the most favorable," Lee told Davis. Perhaps the river that George Washington had envisioned connecting America could still unite Virginia and Maryland.

On the march to Frederick, Maryland, soldiers bellowed the pro-Confederate lyrics of "Maryland, My Maryland," including "Dear mother! burst the tyrant's chain . . . Virginia should not call in vain." Longstreet later insisted that Lee added his own voice to the chorus. In case any Marylander missed the message, Lee issued a proclamation explaining his army's intentions. "The people of the South," it read, "have long wished to aid you in throwing off this foreign yoke, to enable you again to enjoy the inalienable rights of freemen, and restore independence and sovereignty to your State. In obedience to this wish, our army has come among you." Privately, Lee doubted the likelihood of a mass uprising. Attachments to the Union in western Maryland, as in western Virginia, held firmer than in the eastern Tidewater. "About here I think the population about equally divided in sentiment," Lee's aide Walter Taylor noted. "Some appear rejoiced at our advent amongst them; others manifest either indifference or a silence which bespeaks enmity." More pleasing to Taylor's ears was how "gloomy" the Northern newspapers sounded. "Just now it does appear as if God was truly with us."

For once, Lee agreed. The course the army traveled might not be his own way, but he trusted the direction. He could see where it might lead. His army might be an instrument in God's hands. "The present posture of affairs, in my opinion, places it in the power of the Government of the Confederate States to propose with propriety to that of the United States the recognition of our independence," he wrote Davis. "Such a proposition coming from us at this time, could in no way be regarded as suing for peace, but being made when it is in our power to inflict injury upon our adversary, would show conclusively to the world that our sole object is the establishment of our independence." Though Lee had previously cautioned against looking overseas for aid, his feats in the field had lifted hopes for Southern diplomacy. British and French leaders, judging Northern war aims unachievable, might intervene to stop the bloodshed. So might Northern voters by casting ballots for peace candidates in the upcoming midterm elections. Winning a major battle on Northern soil might end the war, and that, as Lee would later say, was his chief purpose. "I went into Maryland to give battle."

To start, Lee intended to isolate Washington, DC, from the west. He would not let reinforcements from the mountains and beyond rescue the eastern cities. He would destroy the B&O Railroad and, once more, that pesky Potomac canal. Lee would also send separate columns to seize the three heights surrounding Harpers Ferry so as to capture the ten thousand federal troops reportedly occupying that hapless post. Lee's ambitions did not end there. When Brigadier General John Walker visited Lee's tent, he learned what else his chief had in mind. After the army captured Harpers Ferry and severed the lower routes to the west, the army would reunite and march on Harrisburg, Pennsylvania, and blow up the railroad bridge over the Susquehanna. "There will [then] remain to the enemy but one route of communication with the West, and that very circuitous, by way of the Lakes," Lee explained. "After that I can turn my attention to Philadelphia, Baltimore, or Washington, as may seem best for our interests."

The audacity of it all astonished Walker. The plan required the army to fall behind the Blue Ridge, or South Mountain as the range was called in Maryland, and divide into four parts: three to seize the heights around Harpers Ferry and one to hold the pass through South Mountain. Dividing the army would expose it to great danger, especially since an epidemic of straggling had already shrunk its size. Of the fifty-five thousand soldiers who had started the campaign, Lee estimated he had lost a third or even half. Once McClellan reassembled the Army of the Potomac, he could march out of Washington and overwhelm the isolated columns one at a time. The concern showed on Walker's face. "Are you acquainted with General McClellan?" Lee asked rhetorically. "He is an able general but a very cautious one. His enemies among his own people think him too much so. His army is in a very demoralized and chaotic condition, and will not be prepared for offensive operations—or he will not think it so—for three or four weeks." By then, Lee planned to have his columns consolidated and in Pennsylvania, no less.

Stonewall Jackson embraced the plan. He would circle back across the Potomac upriver, approach Harpers Ferry from the west, and then assume command of the other columns converging from the other directions. On September 9, Lee included all his instructions in Special Orders No. 191. An aide produced copies for key commanders. The fear of the calamity that would unfold if an order dividing the army fell into Union hands inspired a few officers to take unusual precautions. Longstreet, who had misgivings about the operation, chewed up his copy. Another soldier whose identity has never been proven wrapped a copy around three cigars. Evidently he misplaced them, for on September 13, after the Confederates left town, a Union soldier entering Frederick found the bundle. Soon McClellan had Lee's plan in hand. "Here is a paper," he rejoiced, "with which if I cannot whip 'Bobbie Lee,' I will be willing to go home."

Across the creek, a wall of blue filled the gaps between the trees. The Union soldiers kept coming. "The number increased," Longstreet wrote, "and larger and larger grew the field of blue until it seemed to stretch as far as the eye could see, and from the tops of the mountains down to the edges of the stream gathered the great army of McClellan." Lee could scarcely believe the sight. It seemed so unlike McClellan. So sure had Lee been that the Army of the Potomac would idle east of South Mountain that he had left even fewer troops than initially planned to guard the passes. A fifth column had detached from the fourth and joined Longstreet and Lee on an expedition thirteen miles northwest to Hagerstown. A message had reached Lee there on the evening of September 13 that a Confederate informant inside the Union camp had seen McClellan's demeanor change upon viewing a mysterious document. Events the next day had borne out the intelligence. Union soldiers had charged the mountain passes. The Confederates had fought a desperate delaying action and then, on Lee's orders, withdrawn west into the rolling farm country behind a creek named Antietam.

Emancipation

On the ridge above the creek, Lee arranged the portion of his army not at Harpers Ferry on a north-south axis. His men numbered just eighteen thousand. Their backs faced the small town of Sharpsburg and, behind that, the Potomac River, which snaked its way south for a stretch before turning east again around the Confederate right flank and meeting the Antietam. Longstreet thought Lee should have retreated across the river. There was but one ford behind him. If Lee did not lead an orderly crossing now, the blue line forming on the eastern bank of the Antietam might prevent one later. By dawn on September 16, the Federals already stood sixty thousand strong, with many more men on the way.

Lee had considered retreating. He had gone so far as to say he would. Then Stonewall Jackson sent a letter announcing, "Through God's blessing, Harper's Ferry and its garrison are to be surrendered." Leaving A. P. Hill to process the estimated eleven thousand Union prisoners, Jackson promised to rush the rest of his army to Sharpsburg. If Lee could hold out a little longer, he could unite his army and perhaps salvage a campaign whose prospects until recently had looked bright. All the factors that had forced his army into Maryland now tempted him to stay: the hope that a victory on Northern soil would change the war; the belief that withdrawing would surrender both the initiative and any hope of extending the Confederacy across the Potomac; the knowledge that his soldiers had overcome overwhelming odds before; and the insight that the federal commander—odd as his recent behavior seemed—remained a cautious man at heart.

McClellan already showed signs of returning to form. Lee's decision to arrange his troops for battle under the circumstances so stunned the Union general that he hesitated to send his men across the Antietam on September 16. Had McClellan done so at first light, he could have chased the Confederates off the ridge into the Potomac and turned the river into a bloodbath. By early afternoon, Jackson had arrived. Lee calmly shook his lieutenant's hand. "If he had had a well-equipped army of a hundred thousand veterans at his back, he could not have appeared more composed and confident," Walker noted. McClellan, for one, believed Lee did have a hundred thousand troops. In reality, even as Jackson's men extended the line leftward, the odds still favored McClellan by about three to one. Under a light rain that night, fewer than 26,500 Confederates facing eastward waited for the attack they knew would come as surely as the sunrise. On the left flank, to the north, was a cornfield; in the center, a sunken road; on the right flank, where the Antietam curved closest to the line, a stone bridge.

It commenced in the cornfield. Shortly after dawn, a federal corps that had crossed upcreek the previous day plowed south into the stalks. A Union general seeing bayonets peeking out over the corn ordered his batteries to fire. Canister shot ripped through the field. Within seconds, the general reported, "Every stalk of corn in the northern and greater part of the field was cut as closely as could have been done with a knife, and the slain lay in rows precisely as they had stood in their ranks a few moments before." When Brigadier General John Bell Hood counterattacked, it required all his skill as a horseman to avoid trampling the wounded. Hood sent an urgent message alerting Lee that the Federals had smashed the Confederate left. The frantic courier did not have to travel far to find the commanding general. Healed enough to get back in the saddle but not to hold the reins, Lee had asked an orderly to guide Traveller toward the fire. "Don't be excited," Lee told the courier. "Reinforcements are now rapidly approaching." He had ordered troops brought up from his already flimsy right flank to his beleaguered left.

No sooner had Lee plugged the hole on his left than the battle moved to the middle of his line. Union soldiers clearing the top of a ridge repeatedly charged the troops D. H. Hill had arranged in a sunken wagon road resembling a trench. Lee and Longstreet encountered D. H. Hill observing the action on horseback. The two senior officers climbed off their horses out of concern that being mounted would draw fire from the Union gunners across the Antietam. Hill brushed aside their fears and remained defiantly on his steed. "If you insist on riding up there and drawing the fire, give us a little interval so that we may not be in the line of the fire when they open upon you,"

Longstreet said. Just then, peering through his field glasses, he saw "a puff of white smoke" from across the Antietam. A few seconds passed, and then a cannonball crashed through the horse's legs. Hill emerged unharmed from beneath the mangled animal. But only the smallest interval had saved Lee and his top lieutenant. So the day would go.

As the Federals fought their way to the sunken road, the steep sides that had previously protected the Confederates from fire now penned them in range. The sunken road became a bloody lane covered in corpses. Men climbed over their fallen comrades to retreat. A wave of blue prepared to sweep Lee's army into the Potomac. One more thrust would tear the line in two. It never came. McClellan refused to risk his reserves. Meanwhile, an exhausted, grimy-faced artillery-man from Jackson's wing had worked up the courage to ask whether Lee intended to send his battery back into the battle. "Yes, my son," said Lee, recognizing his youngest son, Robert Jr., who had insisted on enlisting in the ranks. "You all must do what you can to help drive these people back."

By this time, the demands on the left had reduced Lee's right flank to three thousand soldiers facing four times their number. For three hours, their rifle fire had held the enemy on the east side of the stone bridge. But an hour past noon, the Union soldiers charged across the Antietam. If Lee's right flank folded, Union soldiers would occupy the space between his army and the sole ford back across the Potomac. There would be no escape. Just one hope remained: a fuzzy-looking column Lee saw approaching in the distance. He could not tell which flag the column flew. Unable to hold a telescope with his injured hands, he asked a lieutenant to look into a lens and identify the colors. The United States flag, the lieutenant answered. Lee ordered him to look again. The response this time came as the Virginia and Confederate flags. That was the answer Lee had anticipated. "It is A. P. Hill from Harpers Ferry," he explained. A. P. Hill had started the seventeen-mile march that morning after receiving an urgent summons from Lee. Once again wearing his red battle shirt, Hill threw his men into the fight and drove the Union soldiers back to the bridge.

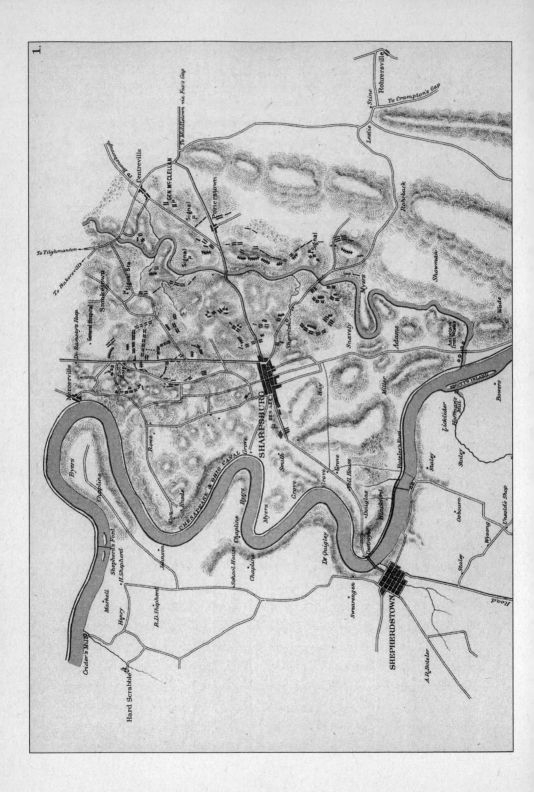

Emancipation

The sun sank with Lee in possession of the ford. Yet when it rose the next morning, he had not crossed. The Army of Northern Virginia held its ground. Lee expected the Union to attack again—reinforcements had refreshed the blue ranks—but McClellan had seen enough bloodshed. Between the two armies, the casualties for the battle approached twenty-three thousand, a total that no other day in American history before or since has equaled. Confederate losses accounted for a little less than half the total. Given the disparity between the two armies, however, losing slightly fewer men than McClellan still meant Lee had lost more as a percentage of his overall fighting force. Nearly a third of the Confederates who had fought had fallen. With them went any hope for an extended campaign in Maryland. That night, the Army of Northern Virginia returned to the Old Dominion. As Brigadier General John Walker rounded up his wounded, he saw Lee astride Traveller in the middle of the Potomac. Days earlier, Walker had heard Lee share his grandiose plans. Now he heard Lee ask how much of the army remained in Maryland. Mostly just wagons, Walker answered. "Thank God!" said Lee.

Never having more than forty thousand men on the field, the Army of Northern Virginia had fought the Army of the Potomac to a draw. From a military perspective, the Confederates could take pride in what they had accomplished. Lee summed it up in a congratulatory order. "On the field of Sharpsburg, with less than one third his numbers, you resisted from daylight until dark the whole army of the enemy, and repulsed every attack along his entire front of more than four miles in extent. The whole of the following day you stood prepared to resume the conflict on the same ground." The armchair generals in the North would aim their fire at McClellan. How could he have let the Con-

◄ A slice of the Confederate map attached to Robert E. Lee's report on the Battle of Sharpsburg shows the positions of the Army of Northern Virginia (lighter gray) and of the Army of the Potomac (darker gray). Severely outnumbered, Lee made a bloody defensive stand between Antietam Creek and the Potomac River. The only escape route for his army was the ford below town.

federates escape? By delaying and then staggering his attacks instead of deploying his full army, McClellan had squandered an opportunity to destroy Lee. That at no point in the battle did Lee have a similar opportunity to prevail raises the question, again, of why he stayed to fight. All that can be said is that he considered the political objectives worth the military risk, and based on those standards, the campaign had fallen short. A feeling of failure trailed the men back into Virginia. "One of the bands commenced the air 'My Maryland' & was prevented from proceeding by the groans & hisses of the soldiers," Walter Taylor wrote. "This will convey to you some idea of the effect of the recent invasion."

The discovery of Special Orders No. 191 had doomed the campaign, or so Lee would say once he learned the full story. "Had the Lost Dispatch not been lost, and had McClellan continued his cautious policy for two or three days longer, I would have had all my troops reconcentrated." For the rest of his life, he would consider the sequence "a great calamity." Subordinates struggled to understand how it happened. At the start of the campaign, Taylor had been sure God marched behind Lee. Afterward, he reflected, "It looks as if the good Lord had ordained that we should not succeed." Abraham Lincoln also detected a divine hand behind the bloodshed at Antietam. It was not the definitive victory that Lincoln had wanted, but it passed the test he had set. On September 22, Lincoln told his cabinet that he had sworn to emancipate the slaves if his army could drive Lee back across the Potomac. That had happened. And though there were still doubts, word would go out about the coming of Lincoln's Emancipation Proclamation. "God," Lincoln said, "had decided this question in favor of the slaves."

The hand injury nagged Lee into the fall. Not until October 19 could he handle his own correspondence. Soon after, he received a letter from his wife announcing the death of his daughter Annie. She had succumbed to typhoid. "I cannot express my dear Mary the anguish I feel at the death of our sweet Annie," he responded. "I can write no more. The rest is pent up in my troubled thoughts." The only thought that offered solace was that Annie had reunited with "her sainted grandmother" in heaven. Lee conspicuously omitted her grandfather Custis from the reference and the reunion.

Aides marveled at how Lee concealed his grief in their presence. "His army demanded his first thought and care; to his men, to their needs, he must first attend, and then he could surrender himself to his private, personal affairs," Taylor wrote. "General Lee was naturally . . . of strong passion; and it is a mistake to suppose him otherwise; but he held these in complete subjection to his will." More than any other period of Lee's life, the last months of 1862 tested this ability to compartmentalize. His thoughts shifted between two of the most oddly paired tasks: first, defeating a federal army that as of New Year's would dedicate itself to emancipating the Confederacy's slaves, and second, emancipating the Custis slaves before that deadline. "I hope you will be able to arrange for the people whom I wish to liberate the 31 December," he wrote his oldest son on November 28. "Indeed I should like to include the whole list at Arlington, White House & c., if it can be done so as to finish the business. It is possible that during the winter though hardly before Xmas I might get to R[ichmond] to attend to it." Seeing Richmond any sooner would mean that Lee had failed to thwart the newest Union advance. Lincoln had replaced McClellan with yet another general, Ambrose Burnside, who was leading yet another drive on Richmond.

On December 11, Union soldiers forced their way across the Rappahannock River into Fredericksburg. Lee's army held the heights overlooking the historic town, which George Washington's mother had called home. A thick fog concealed the Union's preparations until the morning of December 13, when the clouds lifted and sparkling columns of bayonets paraded into view. Into the Confederate fire, the Federals marched. "Our batteries poured a rapid and destructive fire into the dense lines of the enemy as they advanced," Lee recorded. Still more Federals came. Still more Federals fell. "Six times did the enemy, notwithstanding the havoc caused by our batteries, press on with great determination to within one hundred yards of the foot of the hill, but here encountering the deadly fire of our infantry, his columns were broken and fled in confusion to the town." Never would Lee achieve an easier victory. Watching the battle, he remarked, "It is well this is so terrible! We should grow too fond of it." Before the slaughter subsided, Burnside's casualties surpassed twelve thousand, twice as many as Lee's. The bluecoats, Lee wrote his wife, "suffered heavily as far as the battle went, but it did not go far enough to satisfy me." Less than two years had passed since Lee mourned the destruction of the Union. Now nothing less than total destruction of the federal army would content him. The proclamation Lincoln had promised clarified the stakes. "The savage and brutal policy he has proclaimed," Lee wrote, "leaves us no alternative but success or degradation worse than death."

Just a few sentences after bemoaning to his wife that more Federals had not fallen at Fredericksburg, Lee deployed a hopeless transition: "as regards the liberation of the [our] people." It sounded awkward because it was. Yet Lee insisted that he wished "to do what is right & best" for the Custis slaves. So on December 29—three days before Lincoln issued his Emancipation Proclamation—Lee reviewed his own draft. "Know all men by these presents, that I, Robert E. Lee, executor of the last will and testament of George W. P. Custis deceased, acting by and under the authority and direction of the provision of the said will, do hereby manumit, emancipate and forever set free from slavery the following named slaves." About two hundred names followed. A small number could call Mount Vernon their first home. Even those unfamiliar with George Washington's home had descended from a name that once appeared on his ledgers, if not as a dower slave then as a slave in trust for the Custis children. Lee noticed that the document omitted some names. He inserted the ones he could remember and then signed his own.

One stroke of a pen, according to Lee's understanding, liberated no one. Under Virginia law, emancipated blacks required individual papers attesting to their freedom. How to transmit these documents to the slaves who remained at Arlington and to those who had fled the Pamunkey plantations posed a problem. Between these slaves and Lee stood the Army of the Potomac. "Those at Arlington & Alexandria I cannot now reach," Lee concluded. "They are already free & when I can get to them I will give them their papers." What else could he do? Lee's emancipation proclamation carried no force in jurisdictions beyond his army's control. Something similar was said of Lincoln's Emancipation Proclamation. Critics accused the president of emancipating the slaves he could not free and leaving in bondage those he could. Indeed, the Emancipation Proclamation exempted the border states and even many counties in the Confederacy where Union troops had subdued the rebellion. But absent among the list of "excepted" counties was federally occupied Alexandria, Virginia. It was called "an exception" to the exceptions. For all that Lincoln's Emancipation Proclamation left undone, it completed the task that Washington and Lee had failed to finish. The Arlington slaves were forever free.

CHAPTER ELEVEN

The Indispensable Man

"Old General Scott was correct in saying that when Lee joined the Southern cause it was worth as much as the accession of 20,000 men to the 'rebels.'" So concluded a British magazine article reprinted across America in early 1863. Over and again, the Army of the Potomac had outnumbered the Army of Northern Virginia. Over and again, the Army of Northern Virginia had outwitted and outmaneuvered the Army of the Potomac. Over and again, Lee had flouted the military maxim against dividing an army in the face of a larger foe. Over and again, the Union generals were the ones who looked ignorant and incompetent. Why could the officers commanding Union armies, Abraham Lincoln asked in vain, "not do what the enemy is constantly doing?"

Perhaps Scott had been correct. America had known at least one "indispensable man" before. Harry Lee had eulogized George Washington "as the man designed by heaven to lead." Perhaps Robert E. Lee was the indispensable man of this new age. "The country should feel grateful that Heaven has raised up one in our midst so worthy of our confidence and so capable to lead. The grand-son of Washington, so to speak," read a newspaper profile stretching Lee's marital connections. Lee, the writer added, "is six feet in height; weighs about one hundred and ninety pounds; is erect, well formed, and of imposing appearance; has clear, bright, benignant black eyes, dark gray hair, and a heavy gray beard." Another correspondent described Lee's eyes as "direct and honest," his teeth as "a fine unbroken row of white," and his voice as "fine and deep." Soldiers had come to recognize and revere his stately figure. "Whenever he appeared among them," a staff officer wrote, "his approach was announced by 'Here comes Mars' Robert!' and he would be immediately saluted with the well-known Confederate yell." Said one man, "It does not seem possible to defeat this army now with General Lee at its head."

Lincoln took a different view. Whatever the merits of one man, the Union had many more men. The North had started the war with a three and a half–to–one advantage in white men of fighting age. Viewed in this context, the body count at Fredericksburg had hurt the Confederacy more than it did the Union. That arithmetic, "awful" as it seemed, consoled Lincoln. "If the same battle were to be fought over again, every day, through a week of days, with the same relative results, the army under Lee would be wiped out to its last man, the Army of the Potomac would still be a mighty host, the war would be over, the Confederacy gone." In other words, the North could bleed the South dry.

Lee the engineer intuitively grasped the problem Lincoln's arithmetic posed. The question was how to solve it. "The lives of our soldiers are too precious to be sacrificed in the attainment of successes that inflict no loss upon the enemy beyond the actual loss in battle," Lee warned James Seddon, the new Confederate secretary of war. During the Revolution, Washington had deferred his dreams of destroying the enemy's army in favor of preserving his own in the hope that time would wear away the redcoats' will to conquer a land an ocean away. Lee harbored no such hopes from the blue behemoth only a river away. The longer the war dragged on, the larger the disparity between the two armies would grow and the deeper the wounds to the Southern body politic would penetrate. More cities would fall under Union control; more houses and farms would burn; more families would suffer; more slaves would go free. A strategy of trading territory for time would yield neither. The South needed to snap the North's political will before the North shredded the South's social order.

As if bent on proving his own calculations, Lincoln signed a new conscription act in early March. "Nothing now can arrest . . . the most desolating war that was ever practiced, except a revolution among their people," Lee wrote. "Nothing can produce a revolution except systematic success on our part." And by systematic success, Lee meant obliterating the federal army. "Our salvation," he predicted, "will depend on the next few months." Although he would have rejected the term "indispensable," he had come to define his duty just that way. "I tremble for my country when I hear of confidence expressed in me," he told Mary. "I know too well my weakness."

Through the winter of 1863, the Army of Northern Virginia held the hills behind Fredericksburg. Command of the Army of the Potomac passed from Ambrose Burnside to Joseph Hooker. The Northern newspapers called the new chief "Fighting Joe." Lee showed his opinion by playfully abbreviating that to "Mr. F J Hooker." As Lee waited for his opponent to live up to his nickname, a barrage of snow and rain pelted his tent. Much to his aides' dismay, he refused to occupy a house or even a yard. "The only place I am to be found is in camp, & I am so cross now that I am not worth seeing anywhere," he wrote to his daughter Agnes. Others seconded that opinion. Between early December and late February, nearly ten thousand papers deluged Lee's headquarters. Aides presenting documents for his signature would watch his neck "twist or jerk" in frustration. "No man could see the flush come over that grand forehead and the temple veins swell on occasions of great trial of patience and doubt that Lee had the high, strong temper of a Washington, and habitually under the same strong control," an aide named Charles Venable wrote. "I never worked so hard to please any one, and with so little effect as with General Lee," Walter Taylor added. He thought his chief needed "a little stimulant," by which he meant a drink now and then. Lee almost always abstained. When Mary asked why she did not hear from him more, he erupted. "You forget how much writing, talking & thinking I have to do, when you complain."

It proved too much for the fifty-six-year-old. His health had wavered before. "As usual in getting through with a thing I have broken down a little," he had admitted in July 1861 after transferring control of Virginia's armed forces. Now, in early spring 1863, at the start of the fighting season, his constitution collapsed before he had even begun the task at hand. "I have not been so very sick, though have suffered a good deal of pain in my chest, back, & arms. It came on in paroxysms, was quite sharp," Lee reported. He called it "a bad cold." His doctors, he explained, called it "some malady which must be dreadful if it resembles its name." Modern doctors would call it "atherosclerosis." Even at this early stage, the constriction of his coronary arteries may have caused a mild heart attack. Doctors bundled his body in blankets and hustled him to a house outside camp. Slowly his pulse calmed, his cough quieted, his discomfort eased, and his impatience to return rose. His army needed him back.

Intelligence indicated that the Army of the Potomac had expanded to more than 150,000 troops. Though Lee thought that number exaggerated, he knew he could count only 65,000 soldiers on his own line. He had Stonewall Jackson's full corps but only a couple of divisions from James Longstreet's. Longstreet had taken his other divisions to gather food and supplies below the James. Shortages and scurvy had become so commonplace that Lee countenanced reducing his fighting force in favor of this foraging operation. "The troops of this portion of the army have for some time been confined to reduced rations," he informed Richmond. "The men are cheerful, and I receive but few complaints; still, I do not think it is enough to continue them in health and vigor, and I fear they will be unable to endure the hardships of the approaching campaign." Lee privately wondered whether he himself could withstand the hardships. On April 24, he confided, "I . . . feel oppressed by what I have to undergo for the first time in my life."

Five days later, a young officer carrying an urgent message found Lee once again sleeping in his tent. Federal troops had crossed the Rappahannock River right below Fredericksburg. To that news, Lee said, "I thought I heard firing, and was beginning to think it was time some of you young fellows were coming to tell me what it was all about."

Despite his ailing heart, the news barely raised his pulse. A report arriving soon after from J. E. B. Stuart about another crossing well to the west concerned Lee more. He had no infantry that far upriver to oppose it. He initially assumed that these columns on his flank intended to strike a railway junction farther west; then they began circling back around toward his rear. The fuzzy intelligence slowly came into focus: Hooker had divided his army as if to squash a bug between his palms. While the forty thousand soldiers composing the left hand held the Army of Northern Virginia in place behind Fredericksburg, the seventy thousand forming the right hand would sweep in for the kill. To Lee's aides, it seemed that Hooker had copied one of their general's old battle plans. That criticism would have pleased Hooker's boss in Washington. A Union commander had finally proven capable of doing what the enemy "constantly" did.

Being between the palms of the Union army, however, handed Lee at least one advantage: interior, and hence shorter, lines for dividing his own army. Early on May 1, leaving only 12,400 troops on the heights over Fredericksburg, Lee spun the rest of his army around to meet the threat coming from the west. For reasons lost on Union corps commanders, Fighting Joe withdrew from the challenge and fell back to Chancellorsville, ten miles west of Fredericksburg. Having done little besides build a brick tavern at a crossroads, the Chancellor family had stretched the truth by adding "ville" to the name. Only a military eye could see the spot's true value: it was the largest of the few clearings in the otherwise sprawling, opaque woodland known as the Wilderness.

As daylight faded, Lee joined Stonewall Jackson about a mile and a half southeast of the Union lines. The position placed them in easy range of a federal battery sending shrapnel through the trees. "How can we get at these people?" Lee asked. Almost certainly Jackson expected Lee to answer his own question; almost certainly Lee obliged. Neither chest pains nor sniper fire had deterred him from inspecting the Federals' new front. The Union, as he saw it, occupied "a position of great natural strength surrounded on all sides by a dense forest filled with a tangled undergrowth, in the midst of which breastworks of logs had been constructed with trees felled in front so as to form an almost impenetrable abatis." Plainly, a frontal assault would fail. From Mexico onward, Lee had made his career by maneuvering around such positions. For all his complaints that he could never have his preferred way, he had demonstrated a peculiar talent for finding alternative ways and then explaining his masterworks as if each stroke followed inexorably from the unbending laws of physics. Now, with a map in hand, he told Jackson, "General, we must get ready to attack the enemy, if we should find him here to-morrow, and you must make all arrangements to move around his right flank." His finger then traced a wide arc on the map through the Wilderness below Chancellorsville and all the way around the westernmost point in the Union line.

For the second time in two days, Lee would divide his army. Some yet-to-be-determined number of troops would break off from the main force and follow Jackson through the Wilderness. The path would take them almost 180 degrees around Chancellorsville, from a point southeast of the clearing to one due west. According to cavalry scouts, the roads to the enemy's rear lay unprotected. The discussions went deep into the night. After a few hours of sleep under pine trees, Lee rose before the sun and saw Jackson sitting beside a fire with his cap visor pulled low. Lee pulled up a cracker box beside his hard-charging lieutenant and sat. "General Jackson," he said, "what do you propose to make the movement with?" Jackson responded that he intended to take his entire corps. "What will you leave me?" exclaimed Lee, knowing full well it would leave him just two divisions: 13,915 infantrymen to stand alone against five times their number for as long as it took Jackson to complete his circuitous march. A moment of silence passed as Lee weighed the rewards that might develop later in the day against the risks required in the meantime. If Hooker attacked before Jackson reached the Union right—if catastrophe ensued—there was "no question," Lee later said, where the blame would belong. It would be his and his alone. "Well," he finally said to Jackson, "go on."

* * *

Around three o'clock the next morning, a voice talking to Walter Taylor woke Lee. It was a messenger from Jackson's corps. Immediately Lee asked for "all the news" west of Chancellorsville. The messenger reported how Jackson had marched his columns twelve miles through the Wilderness, how the Confederate battle line had charged out of the woods toward the end of the day, and how the federal retreat had turned into a stampede. Lee had already deduced much of that from the sounds emanating from the western woods. Sadly, the messenger had more to say. In the night's darkness, a group of Confederates had mistaken Stonewall for a bluecoat and shot him once in the right hand and twice in the left arm. "Any victory is dearly bought that deprives us of the services of Jackson even temporarily," said Lee. Then, without pause, he ordered the attack resumed. How quickly fortune's hand had flipped! Hooker still clung to Chancellorsville. But now it was his army between the Confederate palms: Lee to his southeast and J. E. B. Stuart, who had temporarily replaced Jackson, to his west. "It is necessary that the glorious victory thus far achieved be prosecuted with the utmost vigor, and the enemy given no time to rally," Lee wrote Stuart. By simultaneously advancing, Stuart and Lee could reunite and dislodge Hooker from Chancellorsville.

Forward, then backward, and forward again went the battle lines. Each surge of gray brought Lee's left flank and Stuart's right flank closer to a junction. A Prussian observer accompanying Lee later recalled the "frightful" scene in the present tense as if replaying the battle. "The cannon spray death and destruction. Whole ranks are mowed down by the close salvos. Still, the cold bayonet's steady courage breaks the resistance of the Unionists firing . . . and with clear, victorious yells and shouts, the attackers now fall upon the wavering lines." When the Prussian commented on the courage of the soldiers, Lee said, "War is a savage business, and one must accustom the men as well as possible to self-control." No sooner had Lee finished the thought than he handed his awestruck guest a souvenir: a minié ball that moments earlier had missed his foot.

By midmorning, Lee's line coming from the southeast and Stuart's coming from the west had clasped hands and penetrated the ring of trees surrounding Chancellorsville. In one long line, they chased the Army of the Potomac north into the woods. Dueling artillery set the brush ablaze. Wounded soldiers unable to escape screamed as fast-spreading flames burned their bodies. Confederates clearing the ash from their eyes saw an iron-gray horse carry their commander into the clearing. The flames leaping from the Chancellor tavern blazed in his brown eyes. The account of his aide Charles Marshall immortalized the moment. "One long, unbroken cheer, in which the feeble cry of those who lay helpless on the earth blended with the strong voices of those who still fought, rose high above the roar of battle, and hailed the presence of the victorious chief." Lee doffed his hat. "I thought," added Marshall, "that it must have been from such a scene that men in ancient days rose to the dignity of gods."

If, in that moment, victory seemed to herald a new birth of independence, the moment faded fast. Lee wanted to press the advantage before the Army of the Potomac escaped across the Rappahannock. But while scouting the new federal line, which proved surprisingly strong, he learned that the thin line he had left to hold the heights behind Fredericksburg had broken. The smaller eastern wing of Hooker's army had started marching west. Lee could not let this threat to his rear go unchecked. So for the third time in three days, he divided the troops he had around him. He shuttled one division and eventually another eastward, orchestrated an attack, and then grew visibly irritated not with the outcome but with how much time obtaining this small victory had wasted. Not until late on May 5 did Lee have enough troops back at Chancellorsville for a final assault against Hooker. It would have to wait until morning. And by then, the Union army had escaped across the Rappahannock. A young general had the misfortune of telling Lee. "That is the way you young men always do," Lee growled. "You allow those people to get away. I tell you what to do, but you don't do it!"

For that, Lee should have been grateful. The attack he had planned would have required repeated frontal assaults against a heavily fortified

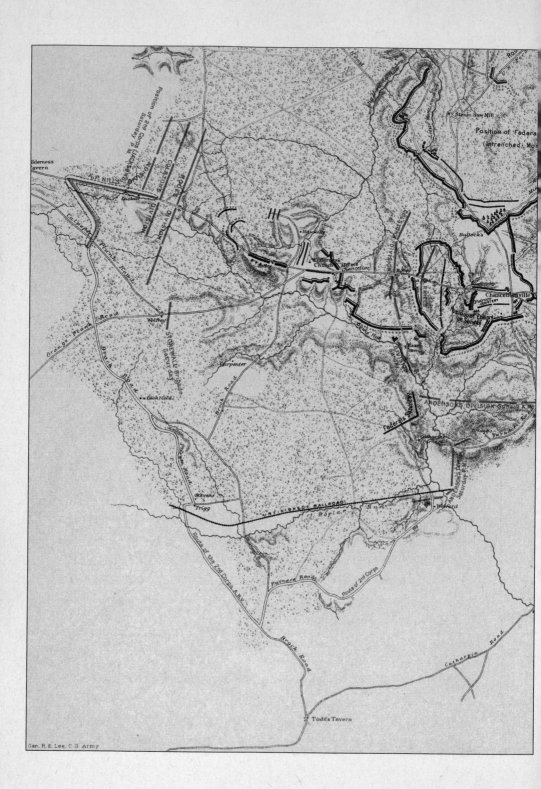

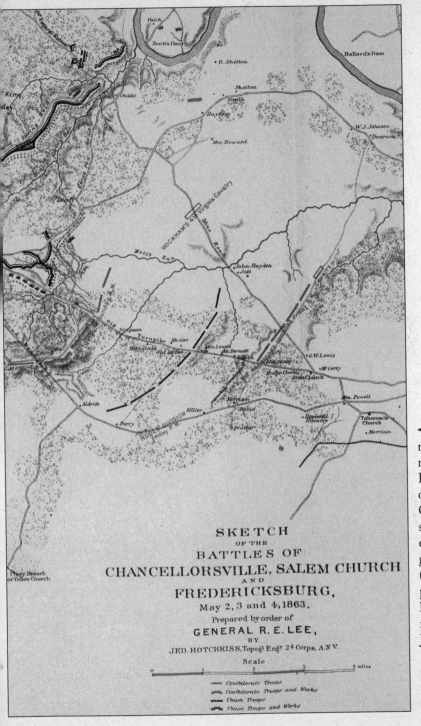

SKETCH
OF THE
BATTLES OF
CHANCELLORSVILLE, SALEM CHURCH
AND
FREDERICKSBURG,
May 2, 3 and 4, 1863.
Prepared by order of
GENERAL R. E. LEE,
BY
JED. HOTCHKISS, Topog! Engr 2ᵈ Corps, A.N.V.
Scale

Confederate Troops
Confederate Troops and Works
Union Troops
Union Troops and Works

◄ A slice of a
map accompa-
nying Robert
E. Lee's report
on the Battle of
Chancellorsville
shows Confed-
erate (lighter
gray) and Union
(darker gray)
positions. On the
left side is the
route Stonewall
Jackson and the
Second Corps
took around
the Union right
flank.

line. "The strength and completeness" of the entrenchments "amazed" the Confederate engineers who found "impenetrable" abatis shielding the entire front. Union rifles firing behind logs would have mowed down Lee's men. The able Confederate artillery officer Edward Porter Alexander called Hooker's decision to retreat "the mistake of his life" because it had spared Lee from making the greatest mistake of his life.

Lee had already lost 13,460 men, just 4,000 fewer than his enemy. Among the casualties was Stonewall Jackson; surgeons had amputated the mangled left arm. "He has lost his left arm; but I have lost my right arm," Lee famously said. When told that Jackson might lose more than an arm, Lee could scarcely believe it. The Confederacy needed Jackson. The army needed Jackson. Lee needed Jackson. But, alas, all would have to live without him. On May 10, the only officer whose present stardom rivaled Lee's died in semidelirium. Losing Jackson made Lee all the more indispensable. "Our labor [is] rendered more severe, more onerous by his departure," Lee wrote. "I do not know how to replace him." Instead of trying, he reorganized his army. Where there had been two corps before, now there would be three: the first under Longstreet, who returned from below the James; the second under Richard Ewell, who had lost a leg serving as one of Jackson's division commanders; and the third under young A. P. Hill. With two rookie corps commanders, Lee would have to rely even more on himself. No wonder, he said, he felt "more depressed" than ever after the battle. Out of victory had come death, and little else. "Our loss was severe, and again we had gained not an inch of ground and the enemy could not be pursued." The next time he had the Army of the Potomac in his sights, he would not let it escape. He would finally have his way.

How many times did he have to say it? "The enemy is there." He gestured east to the ridge running north–south, almost parallel to the one his army occupied. Cemetery Ridge, the Union position was called because the people of this previously peaceful Pennsylvania town, Gettysburg, had been burying their dead on the hill at its northern terminus. About a mile of open farmland separated the two ridges. "Not more than fourteen hundred yards," Lee's eye told him. That slender valley was the ground his army must cross, the space between war and peace. Why could no one else see it?

Persuading Confederate Secretary of War Seddon not to send part of the Army of Northern Virginia to the west had cost every coin of political capital Lee had earned. No one doubted the urgency of the situation at Vicksburg, Mississippi; if the Confederacy's last stronghold on the Mississippi River fell, the Union would reopen the Father of Waters and tear the Confederacy in two. Lee simply doubted whether a halfhearted attempt at plugging holes in the west was worth springing new leaks in the east. Already Chancellorsville had left his ranks depleted. "You can, therefore, see the odds against us, and decide whether the line of Virginia is more in danger than the line of the Mississippi," he had told Seddon.

Only one policy offered the slightest promise of relieving pressure on both fronts, and it happened to suit Lee's wishes: an offensive across the Potomac, this time into Pennsylvania, where his men could live off the land, where every move would threaten the great eastern cities, and where, if a battle occurred, a federal defeat would finally produce political consequences. "It would very likely cause the fall of Washington City and the flight of the Federal government," he had told an aide hunched over a map. That was the message a pale-looking Lee had brought to Richmond in mid-May. Davis had reluctantly consented to the invasion but had refused a few of Lee's requests for reinforcements. No more than eighty thousand men would participate.

Persuading fellow officers had proven no easier. All had set their sights on different horizons. The quiet but determined Longstreet, whom soldiers called an "old bull-dog," had longingly eyed a transfer to the west. He had grown wary of Lee's tactics. In Longstreet's opinion, the Army of Northern Virginia should always choose its ground first and then let the enemy attack, never the other way around. He had lent his support to the Pennsylvania campaign under the condition that the army would follow the defensive tactics of Fredericksburg instead of the bloody aggression of Chancellorsville. That Lee had said he also preferred the former to the latter if given the choice apparently struck Longstreet as a promise.

During the crossing of the Potomac in June, Stuart had also chosen to interpret his general's orders to flatter his own ego. Instead of deploying his cavalry between the army's right flank and the enemy as a screen, he had stretched a poorly written discretionary order into permission for a more glamorous assignment: interposing his horsemen between the enemy and Washington, DC, by circling through Rockville, Maryland. With "the eye of the army," as Lee called the cavalry, detached from its main body, Hill's and Ewell's corps had stumbled into a fight west and then north of Gettysburg on July 1. An unknown number of Federals had fallen back below town to Cemetery Ridge.

Lee had not wanted to bring on a battle, not yet, anyway. But now that it had begun, not a doubt stirred in his mind about how to proceed. His lieutenants needed to seize Cemetery Ridge. From the start, they hesitated. On the afternoon of July 1, he instructed Ewell "to press 'those people'" and to seize the hills at the north end of the ridge if "practicable." Many of Ewell's subordinates thought it plenty practicable, but the new corps commander dragged his feet until the Federals had entrenched. Hopes the next day shifted to sending Longstreet's corps on a flanking march around the Union left, which reportedly did not extend anywhere near as far south along the ridge as the rocky hills known as the Round Tops at the bottom. Longstreet protested. Had not Lee promised to fight a defensive battle? Only grudgingly did Longstreet submit. The "apathy in his movements" afterward was "apparent." Nothing then went as planned. The flanking march took longer—and, worse, the Union line stretched longer—than expected. Ferociously as the Confederates fought, they failed to roll up that ridge. As to why, there would be time enough to debate later.

Now it was July 3. Tomorrow would be July 4, four score and seven years since two Lees had approved a document declaring the colonies free and independent states. One more ridge to clear, and then Virginia might be free and independent again. "If God gives us the victory, the war will be over and we shall achieve the recognition of our independence," officers had heard Lee say. The Union newspapers he scoured for intelligence echoed the growing Northern chorus crying for conciliation. He had begged President Davis to encourage these voices of peace as a counterweight against the Northern war machine running on inexhaustible supplies of blood and treasure. "Under these circumstances we should neglect no honorable means of dividing and weakening our enemies that they may feel some of the difficulties experienced by ourselves. It seems to me that the most effectual mode of accomplishing this object, now within our reach, is to give all the encouragement we can, consistently with truth, to the rising peace party of the North." Davis agreed. This very day, July 3, Confederate Vice President Alexander Stephens would sail from Richmond down to Fort Monroe and ask permission to proceed up the Chesapeake Bay to Washington, DC, for negotiations. How much stronger his position would look—how much more expansive the talks might be—if the Army of the Potomac no longer stood between Lee and the city of Washington.

Longstreet advised maneuvering around the federal line instead of charging through it. He claimed to have found a way to swing the entire Confederate army below the Union left flank so as to take a position between the enemy and his capital. But the enemy was on that ridge. The senior corps commander might not understand, but the men in the ranks did. "There never were such men in an army before. They will go anywhere and do anything if properly led." Cocksure Major General George Pickett would lead part of the charge and was "sanguine of success." Pickett's fresh division would wait by the woods while Confederate artillery disabled the enemy's. Then the troops would march into the open, clear what remained of the fences lining the Emmitsburg Road, and ascend that ridge. Two groves of trees five hundred yards apart would serve as the goalposts, a stone wall running between as the crossbar. That was the center of the federal line. That was where the Union would break in two. A second division and part of a third forming on Pickett's left would converge with his

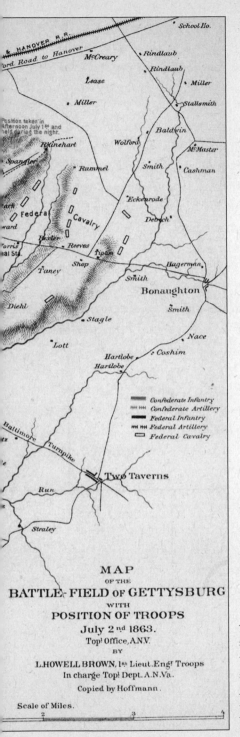

MAP
OF THE
BATTLE-FIELD OF GETTYSBURG
WITH
POSITION OF TROOPS
July 2ⁿᵈ 1863.
Topᶦ Office, A.N.V.
BY
L.HOWELL BROWN, 1ˢᵗ Lieut.Engʳ Troops
In charge Topᶦ Dept. A.N.Va.
Copied by Hoffmann.

Scale of Miles.

◄ A slice of a Confederate map attached to Robert E. Lee's report on the Battle of Gettysburg shows the attack against the Union left on July 2, 1863. The next day, Lee would order the disastrous frontal assault against the Union center on Cemetery Ridge.

men there. In all, they would be about thirteen thousand men. Looking depressed, Longstreet registered another protest for posterity. "It is my opinion that no fifteen thousand men ever arrayed for battle can take that position."

An hour and seven minutes after the sun started its descent in the clear summer sky, two cannons fired the signal. More than a hundred guns facing Cemetery Ridge responded in unison. Never on American soil had there been such a sound. Never had there been such a sight as that offered when the firing slackened and the battle flags marched out of the woods. The gray battle line when fully formed stretched more than a mile and a half. Officers hoisting their swords in the air stepped forward as if to see who would follow. In common time, the ranks did. Onward they marched despite the shells and shots and bullets enfilading their line courtesy of the gunners on the Round Tops to the right and Cemetery Hill to the left, and the blue skirmish lines closing in on both flanks. Upward, into the canister and rifle fire raining down from Cemetery Ridge, they charged. Toward the stone wall, the boldest still standing swarmed before disappearing into an impenetrable cloud of smoke. Visions of Washington falling vanished with the view. Cheers rose in the distance. For one last moment, so did hope in Lee's heart. He mounted Traveller. "See what that cheering means," he instructed an officer. Before hearing back, he knew. Those cheers were for the Union. Clumps of Confederates limping his way carried the answer on slumped shoulders. Told to prepare his division for a counterattack, Pickett said he had "no division." Fewer than half the men in that magnificent battle line had returned unwounded. Lee greeted the remnants at the edge of the woods. "All this has been my fault," he told an officer. "It is I that have lost this fight, and you must help me out of it in the best way you can."

Although that would be Lee's most famous explanation for Gettysburg, it would not be his only explanation. He faulted subordinates for failing to inform him that the cannonade preceding Pickett's charge would leave scant ammunition to support the battle line. He faulted his corps commanders for fighting the whole battle in an "imperfect, halting way." First Ewell had shown indecision; then Longstreet and Hill "could not be gotten to act in concert." He faulted Stuart for leaving his army blind in enemy territory. He even faulted Stonewall Jackson, or at least suggested his demise at Chancellorsville deprived the Confederacy of victory at Gettysburg. Mostly, Lee fell back on a familiar formulation, one that stripped him of any agency in events. "With the knowledge I then had, & in the circumstances I was then placed, I do not know what better course I could have pursued." His reports described the battle as "unavoidable" once the armies had collided. "Victory," he later said, "trembled in the balance for three days." The Confederacy had come so close. "But God willed otherwise."

Gettysburg had been God's way. Or had it? Try as he might, Lee could not shake those first feelings of responsibility. A belief in his army's invincibility had seduced him into ordering his soldiers to perform the impossible. "No blame can be attached to the army for its failure to accomplish what was projected by me," he wrote. "It has accomplished all that could have been reasonably expected. It ought not to have been expected to have performed impossibilities or to have fulfilled the anticipations of the thoughtless & unreasonable." Thoughtless and unreasonable was exactly how Lee's behavior had seemed to Longstreet. "There is no doubt that General Lee, during the crisis of that campaign, lost the matchless equipoise that usually characterized him, and that whatever mistakes were made were not so much matters of deliberate judgment as the impulses of a great mind disturbed by unparalleled conditions."

Longstreet was not alone in recalling his chief as off balance. Lee himself conceded that he had lost control over his body. His health had grown worse. "I am becoming more and more incapable of exertion, and am thus prevented from making the personal examinations and giving the personal supervision to the operations in the field which I feel to be necessary. I am so dull that in making use of the eyes of others I am frequently misled," he wrote President Davis. The Army of

Northern Virginia needed a younger and more vigorous commander. He offered Davis his resignation. "I cannot even accomplish what I myself desire. How can I fulfill the expectations of others?" A letter of advice Lee penned shortly afterward to his daughter Mildred offered an unintentional insight into why he had lost Gettysburg. "The struggle which you describe you experience between doing what you ought & what you desire, is common to all." At Gettysburg, the space between those ridges separated what Lee ought to do from what he desired to do. He had ordered the men across. It had been his way.

How then could Gettysburg be both God's way and Lee's way? Lee never answered that question because in the heat of battle, when the Confederacy's fortunes "trembled in the balance," he lost sight of the difference between the two. A lifetime of self-denial had left Lee unable to even recognize his own desires. He had made the same mistake as that megalomaniac abolitionist who had usurped Washington's sword. Like John Brown, Lee had blurred his desires with his country's destiny. As Brown had vainly sought to purify the Declaration of Independence through blood, Lee had sought, in vain, to win a new independence on the anniversary of its adoption. The day after Gettysburg would instead be, as Lincoln later proclaimed, "a new birth of freedom" for the Union.

For secessionists, July 4 brought a succession of setbacks. At Vicksburg, Confederates stacked their weapons before the master of the Mississippi, Ulysses S. Grant. At Fort Monroe, federal officers received orders from Washington to "hold no communication" with the Confederate vice president unless told otherwise. At Gettysburg, the Confederate retreat toward the Potomac started under a strong storm. Men could not hear orders over the wind; horses and mules could not see through the driving rain. "Canvas was no protection against its fury, and the wounded men lying upon the naked boards of the wagon-bodies were drenched," recalled an officer leading a wagon train. "O God! Why can't I die?" the wounded cried. Union cavalry striking like lightning pierced the long trains as they moved through the storm.

By the time the army reached the Potomac just upriver from

Sharpsburg, the water had risen too high to ford. For a week, the swollen river separated the Army of Northern Virginia from the safety of its namesake soil. "Had the river not unexpectedly risen, all would have been well with us," Lee wrote. "I trust that our merciful God, our only help & refuge, will not desert us in this our hour of need, but will deliver us by His almighty hand." Lincoln urged his cautious generals to destroy the remains of the rebel army. Lee nervously waited as the river receded. At last, on July 13 and 14, one corps waded across while the two others marched across a pontoon bridge.

Lee had escaped. To call it divine deliverance would ignore what he left behind: the dead, the wounded, the missing. "The death of our gallant officers & men throughout the army causes me to weep tears of blood & to wish that I never would hear the sound of a gun again," he said. Of the eighty thousand men Davis had agreed to supply for the invasion, a startling 27,125 became casualties. If arithmetic posed a problem before Gettysburg, it would crest toward crisis after. The battle would have claimed one last casualty in August had Davis accepted Lee's resignation. But who could supplant the savior of the Seven Days and the victor of Second Manassas, Fredericksburg, and Chancellorsville? In the minds of most, no one could. No one would. As Davis put it, "To ask me to substitute you by some one in my judgment more fit to command, or who would possess more of the confidence of the army, or of the reflecting men of the country, is to demand an impossibility." So for twenty more months, Robert E. Lee would remain a soldier. He was, in a word, indispensable.

CHAPTER TWELVE

The Cemetery

Gettysburg would be long remembered thanks, in part, to the brief remarks Abraham Lincoln made at a cemetery dedication there in November 1863. That Robert E. Lee had retreated on the anniversary of the Declaration of Independence provided an irresistible theme. Lincoln cast the Union boys now lying in the ground as defenders of the "new nation" that, as he put it, "four score and seven years ago our fathers brought forth on this continent." Had the president not cared for the symbolism, he could have waited to dedicate a cemetery closer to home. The bodies Lee's men had shot and gouged packed Washington's hospitals and then its graveyards. By late 1863, the Old Soldiers' Home cemetery north of town approached capacity and looked, in one officer's opinion, "miserable." Washington needed more land for burials.

The federal government, as it turned out, had its eye on acquiring permanent title to the hills across the Potomac, the eleven hundred acres constituting the Arlington estate. A law passed during the war assessed special taxes on properties in "insurrectionary districts." If the levies went unpaid—as vengeful sponsors in Congress fully expected would happen—the properties would head to auction. This, it seemed, would be Arlington's fate. In the fall of 1863, the federal government announced the property would "be sold for unpaid taxes." Up to this point, the Union occupation of Arlington had been temporary. Now, barring a last-minute intervention, it would be permanent.

While newspapers reported the unpaid taxes on Arlington, Lee did not hear about them until years later. His mind was more focused on the loss of his second son than the loss of his house. Rooney had been captured in June while recovering from a wound. "I hope his exchange may be soon effected," Lee said. "But nothing can be done to hasten it. The more anxiety shewn on our part, the more it will be procrastinated by our enemies, whose pleasure seems to be to injure, harass, & annoy us as much as their extensive means enable them." Not only the son of the rebels' most famous general but also now a brigadier general himself, Rooney made a prized prisoner. Union authorities dangled him as a hostage to be hanged lest the Confederacy proceed with a threat to execute two federal officers. One Lee relative had already gone to the gallows. Orton Williams, who had been arrested early in the war for betraying General Scott's confidence, had been captured again and sent to the scaffold as a spy. "I see no necessity for his death except to gratify the evil passions of those whom he offended by leaving Gen. Scott," Lee wrote, perhaps pondering his own future.

Shortly before Christmas 1863, meetings brought Lee to Richmond, where he saw how Rooney's wife, Charlotte, suffered. Waiting and worrying for her husband had shattered her health. Lee could have stayed with her for the holiday—Mary had set up a house in town—but, to no one's surprise, he refused. "It would be but natural for him to remain with his family during the week, but it will be more in accordance with his peculiar character, if he leaves for the Army just before the great anniversary to show how very self-denying he is," his aide Walter Taylor said. Back at camp, Lee received word of Charlotte's death. "Thus dear Mary is link by link of the strong chain broken that binds us to earth, & smooths our passage to another world," he wrote.

Lee had more connections on earth than he cared to admit, even a few friends above the Potomac. Around this time, Philip Fendall, a lawyer and "Union man" living in Washington, arrived at the tax office in Alexandria on a strange errand: he wished to pay the property taxes for Arlington. A number of Lee's relatives, including his brother-in-law in Baltimore, had seen the advertisements about Arlington's impending sale and had asked Fendall to pay the $92.07 tax and the $46.04 penalty on their behalf. The tax commissioners refused the payment. According to a controversial rule, owners had to pay in person. The collectors, a witness remembered, "said they were not willing to receive the taxes, because it did not belong to him, but that it belonged to Robert E. Lee." The cost of retaining Arlington under this interpretation would have been the general surrendering himself in Alexandria. Fendall tried arguing that Arlington belonged to Mary Lee, not General Lee. It mattered not. Mary's health would have prevented her from making the journey even had, as an early biographer speculated, she been willing.

The auction would proceed. President Lincoln directed the commissioners not just to sell but also to purchase, as he put it, the "estate, lately occupied by Robert E. Lee." On January 11, 1864, for a bid of just $26,800—$7,300 below value—the United States bought Arlington for "government use." A mansion built to honor George Washington would soon memorialize men who had died fighting Robert E. Lee.

That more men would die seemed the sole certainty as the campaign of 1864 commenced. For the first time since George Washington held a commission, an officer in the United States Army obtained the outright title of lieutenant general. The honor fell to Ulysses S. Grant, a tanner's son who had been middling born in what now passes as the Midwest and had graduated in the middle of his West Point class. Lincoln summoned Grant to Washington. For three years, the president had cycled through eastern generals: McDowell, McClellan, Pope, Burnside, Hooker, and more recently George Meade at Gettysburg. In that last battle, Meade had defined victory as driving "the invaders from our soil" across the Potomac. "The whole country is our soil," an exasperated Lincoln had retorted. The generals had never understood what needed to be done: the destruction of Lee's army. Nor had they understood by what means it should be done: overwhelming force.

The Cemetery

Knowing the numbers favored the North, Lincoln had told past generals, "In your next fight put in all of your men." The advice had gone unheeded. "No general yet found can face the arithmetic, but the end of the war will be at hand when he shall be discovered." In U. S. Grant, Lincoln had finally found his "man." As the new general in chief of Union forces, Grant would oversee every theater but follow Meade and the Army of the Potomac in the field. "Lee's army will be your objective point. Wherever Lee goes, there you will go also," Grant told Meade.

Lee could remember meeting Grant once during the Mexican-American War but little else about him. Grant had been a young officer then, nowhere near as important as Lee. As Lee now tried to picture his new opponent's face, he struggled to "recall a single feature." In Walter Taylor's opinion, Grant owed his success in the west more to his opponents' mistakes than to his own merit. "He will find, I trust, that General Lee is a very different man to deal with & if I mistake not will shortly come to grief if he attempts to repeat the tactics in Virginia which proved so successful in Mississippi." The aides seemed almost eager to expose Grant as a fraud, unworthy of Washington's lofty rank. So eager was Lee himself for the challenge that the thought of the coming campaign lifted his flagging health. "He had been complaining somewhat," Taylor said, "and it really seemed to do him good to look forward to the trial of strength soon to ensue between himself & the present idol of the North." While analyzing Grant's movements one April afternoon in his tent, Lee blurted out, "We have got to whip them, we must whip them and it has already made me better to think of it."

Even now, Lee wished to take the offensive. Reports suggested that Grant would advance against Richmond from two directions: the main army marching south overland and a smaller one coming west up the James River. "If Richmond could be held secure against the attack from the east, I would propose that I . . . move right against the enemy on the Rappahannock. Should God give us a crowning victory there, all their plans would be dissipated, & their troops now collecting on the waters of the Chesapeake will be recalled to the defence of Washington," Lee wrote. For the fourth year, an offensive against Richmond would end with Washington on the defensive. With the North holding a presidential election in November, voters might deny Lincoln four more years.

Trouble was Lee did not have enough provisions to maintain his army, let alone mount a campaign. An anonymous letter informed him that dwindling rations had forced his soldiers to steal for subsistence. "The commanding general considers it due to the army to state that the temporary reduction of rations has been caused by circumstances beyond the control of those charged with its support," Lee announced in general orders prodding the men to continue down "the road by which your fathers marched through suffering, privations, and blood, to independence." Privately he doubted how much more his men could bear. "The time is coming, indeed has come, when every one must put out their strength. They cannot consult their feelings or individual opinions where to serve," he told Custis Lee. Everyone, in this exigency, included his wife and daughters, who sewed socks for the troops. Not trusting Mary's inventories—bookkeeping had never come naturally to the Custis clan—Lee tallied every pair she sent. Always mindful of feet—his children when young had known to tickle his toes during story time—Lee now showed the irritability of his increasing age when his tallies deviated from hers. "I am again at a loss to know whether all the socks arrived that were sent," he moaned.

While consuming his energies counting socks, Lee severely undercounted the bluecoats in his front. Unable to replenish his own ranks from Gettysburg, Lee started May 1864 with only about 60,000 soldiers in camp west of Chancellorsville, below the Rapidan River, a tributary that intersects with the Rappahannock just north of the old battlefield. He assumed Grant had no more than 75,000 soldiers across the river. In truth, Grant had begun amassing 120,000. Lee could at least be thankful for one reinforcement: Rooney had been released. His exchange had come too late for poor Charlotte but not too late, as Lee saw it, for Rooney to fulfill his duty to the Confederacy. "We cannot indulge in grief however mournful," Lee wrote. "To resist the powerful combination now forming against us, will require every man at his place. If victorious we have everything to hope for in the future. If defeated nothing will be left us to live for." Lee meant what he said. As soon as the Army of the Potomac crossed the Rapidan in early May, he fought as if he preferred death to defeat.

Before Grant could strike Lee, Lee decided to strike Grant's flank. He caught the Army of the Potomac filing through the dark and dense thickets that had twisted Hooker's brilliant plans a year earlier. The Wilderness tangled the two armies into weeks of continual engagements, shifting successively southward. There were moments when the gray line seemed on the brink of breaking. More than once, the men saw their general ride to the front and wondered if he would lead the countercharge himself. "Go back, General Lee! For God's sake, go back!" the men yelled on May 12 during the battle of Spotsylvania. "If you will promise to drive those people from our works, I will go back," said Lee. The men kept their promise. They had already lost many of their finest officers. Longstreet had shared Jackson's fate of suffering a wound from friendly fire in the Wilderness. Then the newly better-mounted and better-armed Union cavalry led by Philip Sheridan shot J. E. B. Stuart. Longstreet would recover and return; Stuart, as Lee learned that very day, would not.

It was Grant's men who suffered the most, their bodies littering the forests and fields after charging the trenches that Lee's men, once so reluctant to dig, had made the emblem of their army. But instead of retreating, Grant reinforced. Checked one place, the Union army simply moved south around Lee's right flank to another.

After Spotsylvania, Lee saw an opening to stop the federal advance at the North Anna River, just northwest of the Pamunkey. Then Lee's health faltered again. As he lay in bed, he ranted about what the army must do. "We must strike them a blow—we must never let them pass us again—we must strike them a blow." It was no use. By the start of June, the Army of Northern Virginia had its back to the Chicka-hominy. Grant had crossed the Pamunkey. The Union had once again established a supply base and hospital amid the ruins of the White

House. Two years had passed since Lee had assumed field command, and the armies had essentially returned to where they had started.

Back in Washington, DC, seven years after the removal of the old wooden dome, the new iron cap atop the US Capitol accepted its crown: a bronze lady toting a sword. Her sculptor had originally conceived her as Armed Liberty; the public would call her the Statue of Freedom. She would have worn a "liberty cap" indicating a freed slave, but Jefferson Davis had been secretary of war during the design phase and had vetoed the proposal. As early as 1853, Davis had assigned an energetic engineer to oversee the Capitol renovations. The officer's name was Montgomery C. Meigs. Lee had served with Meigs early in his career and considered him the most "capable & qualified" officer for "works of such a national character." Meigs, for his part, had admired Lee as "the model of a soldier and the beau ideal of a Christian man"—that is, until Lee sided with the Confederacy. "No man who ever took the oath to support the Constitution as an officer of our army . . . & who has since actively engaged in rebellion in any civil or military station should escape without loss of all his goods & civil rights," Meigs had written at the start of the war. "Arlington Heights in Virginia, overlooking the Potomac and opposite the Executive Mansion," he had added, "posed special problems." It would be Meigs, now the Union's quartermaster general, who would find the solution.

In addition to supplying troops in the field, the quartermaster general had to deal with the dead piling up in Washington. And in the spring of 1864, the bodies came in unprecedented numbers. On June 3, at the Battle of Cold Harbor, near where Lee had won his first victory with the Army of Northern Virginia, Grant ordered a doomed charge against Lee's trenches and lost thousands of men in mere minutes. During just a month of fighting, Grant had suffered more than fifty thousand casualties, about twice as many as Lee. Those numbers might ultimately suit Lincoln's arithmetic, but the bloody tide of bodies washing up the Potomac and landing at Washington's wharves stunned the

1. *George Washington as Colonel in the Virginia Regiment* by Charles Willson Peale. This famous painting hung in Arlington House until Mary Custis Lee hid it from Union soldiers during the war and brought it afterward to Lexington, Virginia.

2. *The Washington Family* by Edward Savage. Young George Washington Parke Custis is to the left of his adoptive father, George Washington, whose hand lies on a map of the District of Columbia. To the right is Custis's sister, Nelly, and his adoptive mother and biological grandmother, Martha Washington.

3. *Henry Lee* by Charles Willson Peale, from life, circa 1782. Before fathering Robert E. Lee, Henry Lee III became known as "Light-Horse Harry" during the Revolutionary War. He famously eulogized his commander in chief, George Washington, as "first in war, first in peace, and first in the hearts of his countrymen."

4. *Robert E. Lee in the Dress Uniform of a Lieutenant of Engineers* by William Edward West, 1838. "Splendid-looking" was how one admirer described Lee.

5. *Portrait of Mary Anna Randolph Custis Lee* by William Edward West, 1838. Robert E. Lee's wife was heir to Arlington House and its collection of Mount Vernon relics.

6. The final moments of the standoff inside the engine house at Harpers Ferry, as depicted in *Frank Leslie's Illustrated Newspaper* on November 5, 1859. George Washington's great-grandnephew Lewis Washington (far left) was among the hostages John Brown held. Said Brown, "I wanted you particularly for the moral effect it would give our cause, having one of your name as a prisoner."

7. The marines under Robert E. Lee's command at Harpers Ferry, as depicted in *Frank Leslie's Illustrated Newspaper* on October 29, 1859. A junior officer said Lee deserved a medal for his conduct of the operation.

9. General Winfield Scott in old age. After his protégé Robert E. Lee turned down command of the Union army that was being raised to crush the rebellion, Scott said, "You have made the greatest mistake of your life, but I feared it would be so."

8. A reprint of a photograph of Robert E. Lee taken between the Mexican–American War and the Civil War. "I unfortunately belong to a profession that debars all hope of domestic enjoyment," Lee wrote.

10. "Balloon View of Washington, DC," as depicted in *Harper's Weekly* on July 27, 1861, showing the US Capitol dome under construction. Union officials feared that Virginians would fortify Arlington Heights across the river and bombard the city.

11. "The advance guard of the Grand Army of the United States crossing the Long Bridge over the Potomac, at 2 a.m. on May 24, 1861," as depicted in *Harper's Weekly* on June 8, 1861. Only reluctantly did Mary Custis Lee flee Arlington House shortly before the federal soldiers crossed.

12. Union soldiers occupying Arlington during the Civil War. Robert E. Lee would never enter the house again.

13. John Augustine Washington III. A great-grandnephew of George Washington and the heir to Mount Vernon, John Augustine died while serving as an aide to Robert E. Lee.

14. The White House on the Pamunkey River as it looked when Union forces occupied the property in 1862. Union General George McClellan claimed that he wanted to protect the house out of respect for its associations with George Washington, not because of its connections to the Lee family.

15. The remains of the White House on the Pamunkey. The house burned in June 1862, when Robert E. Lee's offensive forced the Union troops occupying the property to retreat.

16. The aftermath of Antietam, as photographed by Alexander Gardner. The bloodiest day in American history signaled the end of Robert E. Lee's first campaign across the Potomac and allowed Abraham Lincoln to announce the Emancipation Proclamation.

17. Robert E. Lee astride his favorite horse, Traveller, in the moment of victory at Chancellorsville, as illustrated for an early biography. "It must have been from such a scene that men in ancient days rose to the dignity of gods," said one of Lee's aides.

18. An Alfred R. Waud sketch capturing the dramatic moment at Appomattox on April 9, 1865, when Robert E. Lee and Charles Marshall rode away after surrendering to Ulysses S. Grant. "There is nothing left me but to go and see General Grant," Lee had said.

19. A photograph taken by Mathew Brady days after Appomattox. George Washington Custis Lee (left) and aide Walter Taylor (right) stand on either side of the defeated Confederate general in chief.

20–21. A photograph of Mary Custis Lee by Michael Miley, and a copy of Gilbert Stuart's portrait of her great-grandmother Martha Washington. The side-by-side comparison reveals the resemblance that some detected between Robert E. Lee's wife and George Washington's.

The Funeral of Gen. R. E. Lee — October 1870

22. A photograph of Robert E. Lee's funeral on the campus of what became known as Washington and Lee University, by Michael Miley. Southerners rushed to eulogize their deceased general as "first in war, first in peace, and first in the hearts of his countrymen."

23. A photograph of the building of Arlington Memorial Bridge, by Theodor Horydczak. The arches run on an axis between the Lincoln Memorial and the house that Robert E. Lee left at the start of the war.

24. The modern view from Arlington House, as photographed by Jet Lowe. Behind the headstones on the hillside is the bridge leading across the Potomac to the Lincoln Memorial; the Washington Monument and the Capitol appear in the distance.

public. The stench of the dead filled the city, and the bodies "exhausted" the last plots around the Old Soldiers' Home. Meigs cast his sights across the river for space. The first burials at Arlington took place that May. By mid-June, the quartermaster decided the time had come to ask permission for the transformation he had already begun. Secretary of War Edwin Stanton immediately approved the request. Almost exactly two years to the day that McClellan had received orders to convert the White House on the Pamunkey into a military hospital, Meigs received orders to convert Arlington into a military graveyard. "The bodies of all soldiers dying in the Hospitals of the vicinity of Washington and Alexandria will be interred in this Cemetery," Stanton wrote.

Stanton was not without care for the living residents of the property as long as they lacked the family name Lee. He instructed Meigs to arrange the cemetery so as to avoid disturbing another project the War Department had established: a freedman's village for the newly emancipated slaves pouring into the Washington area. Fortunately for Meigs, the village, which stood a half mile from the main house, posed no obstacle to his grand design for the cemetery. He wanted the graves "encircling" the mansion. When officers stationed at Arlington resisted—opting to bury bodies out of sight instead—Meigs carefully arranged graves around the flower garden beside the house.

Between the freedman's village and the cemetery, finding meaning in the changes at Arlington required little poetic license. "How appropriate," said one newspaper, "that Lee's lands should be dedicated to two such noble purposes—the free living black men whom Lee would enslave, and the bodies of the dead soldiers whom Lee has killed in a wicked cause." Visitors seeking the old Mount Vernon lantern, china, and other relics would have to look across the river, behind the glass cases of the Patent Office. Cobwebs and dust greeted anyone who bothered to pass through the portico into Arlington House. "Here Lafayette sat a guest; here sparkled jest and wine; here rose the song, died out so long ago in sighing; here woman's smile shone round the board now faded out in dying," wrote one correspondent struggling to reconcile the mansion's past and present.

Miles away, beside the bloody trenches, Lee also remembered how different the view from Arlington Heights had looked many summers ago. On June 30, 1864—his wedding anniversary—he wrote Mary, "Do you recollect what a happy day thirty three years ago this was? How many hopes & pleasures it gave birth to? God has been very merciful & kind to us & how thankless & sinful I have been."

If Lee read the newspaper articles in June about Arlington's conversion into a cemetery, he probably reacted with the same resignation he had shown earlier in the month when a Union army storming up the Shenandoah Valley approached the town of Lexington, where he had sent the Mount Vernon silver and other heirlooms at the start of the war. With Lexington in harm's way, Mary worried these relics might join the others in the Patent Office. Lee rejected her pleas to move them. The silver, he said, "will incur more danger in removal than in remaining. It must bide its fate." Fortunately for the Lees, friends buried the treasures underground before June 12, the day Union soldiers occupying the town burned the Virginia Military Institute and plundered a small school known as Washington College. That night, without yet knowing all the details of the destruction, Lee ordered Jubal Early, a notoriously crotchety general who professed undying loyalty to the Confederacy despite originally opposing secession at the Virginia convention, to lead Stonewall Jackson's old corps back to the valley. Before dawn, Early departed with eight thousand soldiers who would join two thousand others Lee had detached earlier. In total, the force accounted for a quarter of Lee's infantry.

No sooner did Early depart than President Davis wondered whether Lee might need the old valley corps back. First light on June 13 revealed that Grant's army had vanished from the trenches around Cold Harbor. Subsequent scouting showed that the Federals had once again "broken up" the White House depot. Where had Grant gone? Lee could not say, though he speculated that part of the Army of the Potomac had sailed down the Pamunkey while the rest had sneaked to the other side of the Peninsula in preparation for a crossing of the James River. The prospect of the bluecoats skipping the James had worried Lee as early as 1862. Below the river and twenty-three miles south of Richmond was the city of Petersburg, a rail hub through which key lines connecting the Confederate capital to the south passed. If Petersburg fell, then so would Richmond. And if the Confederacy lost its capital—with all the strategic and symbolic significance it had acquired—who could avoid wondering what else might be lost? Already the smaller army that Grant had sent to the James at the start of his offensive had tried to sever the rail connection between the two cities. Now, as Lee groped for Grant, the Army of the Potomac swung below the James for the assault on Petersburg. Only the fatigue of the Federals—plus a desperate but determined stand by the small Confederate army manning the city's entrenchments—denied Grant a speedy victory.

By the time Lee arrived at Petersburg on June 18, the parallel trenches running north–south in front of the city already pointed toward the protracted siege-like warfare to come. All told, the defenses spanned twenty-six miles wrapping around Petersburg to the west and then running north all the way back across the James to the outskirts of Richmond. The longer the siege lasted, the longer and deeper the trenches would run as Grant punched above and below the James, especially south and west of Petersburg where Lee's left flank could not extend far or fast enough to guard the city's supply lines. Lee needed to defend every point; Grant could strike any point. For a time, the trenches would keep Lee's undermanned army from being overrun. But Lee knew that over time his army would dig its own grave. "We must destroy this army of Grant's before he gets to James River, if he gets there, it will become a siege, and then it will be a mere question of time," Lee had told Early before his departure for the valley.

An offensive north down the valley now represented the best hope for avoiding the "battle of posts," which Lee had long dreaded. That was why he had resisted Davis's suggestion to recall Early to Petersburg. "I still think it is our policy to draw the attention of the enemy to his own territory," Lee wrote Davis. A victory over the federal forces in the valley would open, for the third consecutive summer, the path to the Potomac; the crossings looked especially inviting this year because Grant, as Lee discovered, had stripped the defenses of Washington so as to exert maximum pressure against Petersburg. Two could play the game. According to Lee's orders, once across the Potomac, Early should "threaten Washington" and, if possible, "take it." There was more to the plan than Early knew. While Early marched toward the Potomac upriver from Washington—the federal forces in the valley put up even less resistance than expected—Lee and Davis discussed an audacious scheme for springing twelve thousand Confederate soldiers imprisoned at Point Lookout, Maryland, downriver from the capital. "The prisoners [could be] liberated and organized, and marched immediately on the route to Washington," Lee wrote on June 26. "As far as I can learn, all the troops in the control of the United States are being sent to Grant, and little or no opposition could be made by those at Washington." So much depended on secrecy that when Lee decided to inform Early of the plot, he dispatched his youngest son as the messenger. On July 6, Rob Jr. caught up to the valley army, just across the Potomac, not far from Antietam.

Back by the James, Lee scoured Northern newspapers for signs of panic. One article he read in the *New York Herald* puffed up the invading force to as many as thirty thousand. "The position and strength of the enemy's forces on the Upper Potomac are still involved in great uncertainty," another article in the paper said. "There can be no question of a widespread panic and general hegira. The excitement is more intense than on any former invasion." The reports pleased Lee enough that he forwarded the newspaper to Davis. "The people in the U.S. are mystified about our forces on the Potomac," he wrote. "The expedition will have the effect I think at least of teaching them they must keep some of their troops at home & that they cannot denude their frontier with impunity." Indeed, Grant raced reinforcements back to the poorly defended capital. Properly manning the extensive fortifications encircling Washington required more than thirty-four thousand soldiers. In July 1864, Washington had about one-third that number, a combination of convalescents in no condition to fight and recruits who had no idea how. Whether reinforcements would arrive in time remained uncertain on July 11, when Early crossed the District of Columbia's northern limits. The soldiers marching toward the White House could see the Statue of Freedom atop the Capitol dome in the distance. Only Fort Stevens, about five miles from the executive mansion, halted their advance.

Fifty years had passed since an enemy army had come this close to Washington. Lee had been a child when the British burned the capital in 1814. At any point between then and 1861, if anyone had suggested that the next breach of the district's borders would be on his command, Lee would have, as he said on other occasions, "supposed" the soothsayer "insane." But more than three years after he had forsaken the home on the hill commanding Washington, here within rifle range of Fort Stevens was an invading force following his dictates. Equally unlikely were the characters on the ramparts opposing the Confederates. Among the convalescents and clerks manning the defenses was "a very conspicuous figure" wearing "a long frock coat and plug hat." There, on the walls of Washington stood Abraham Lincoln himself. Not far behind was Quartermaster Meigs, bringing up fifteen hundred armed government workers.

The sight did not impress some of Early's soldiers, who thought the city open for the taking. "Undoubtedly we could have marched into Washington," said one officer. But Early, who had boasted to his troops during their march that he "would take them into Washington that day," no longer held that opinion. Marching and skirmishing in the summer sun had tired the men. The decision whether to storm the city would have to wait till the next morning. And by then, the choice looked as clear to Early as the blue veterans he saw lining the parapets. Grant's reinforcements had arrived. Whatever might have been yesterday could not be today. The two armies facing off in front of the fort exchanged shots, including one that barely missed Lincoln, who had returned to the ramparts. That night, having learned the Point Lookout plot had been compromised, Early began the trek back toward

Virginia. "Washington can never be taken by our troops unless surprised when without a force to defend it," Early wrote Lee, perhaps to preempt critics who would say he had found Washington in exactly such a state.

If the outcome disappointed Lee, he did not say so. The raid had reopened the Shenandoah Valley and forced Grant to send some troops back to Washington. Those results alone made it a modest success. But what Lee needed at this stage was a major success, and probably nothing short of sacking Washington would have sufficed. The siege of Petersburg would go on.

The constant mortar fire reminded Lee's aide Walter Taylor of the Independence Day celebrations he had once known: shells whirring through the air, fearful noises crescendoing, and then explosions shaking the ground and illuminating the sky. "Those poor fellows in the trenches certainly do suffer many inconveniences and it fills me with dread to look forward to a winter in these fortifications," he wrote in September. Wood for fires was scarce. So was soap for bathing. Dirt and disease were everywhere. "Indeed," remarked Taylor, "an armistice would come very opportunely just now." It was wishful thinking. True, the Yankees in the opposing trenches shared in the suffering. The enormous mine they had dug and then exploded beneath the Confederate line had turned into a death trap; their own men had poured into the crater only to find it too deep to climb back out. But the Yankees could afford losses the Confederates could not. "Where are we to get sufficient troops to oppose Grant?" Lee asked. "His talent & strategy consists in accumulating overwhelming numbers."

Desperately, Lee spoke of the "natural military consequences of the enemy's numerical superiority"; doubtfully, he entertained proposals for evening the odds. Delusional talk of foreign intervention tested his patience. "As far as I have been able to judge, this war presents to the European World but two aspects. A Contest in which one party is contending for abstract slavery & the other against it. . . . As long as this lasts, we can expect neither sympathy or aid," he wrote. More encouraging to his ears was talk of enlisting slaves as soldiers in exchange for emancipation. For months, the Union had deployed black soldiers—former Custis slaves among them, according to Lee's sources—but such ideas met considerably more opposition in a confederacy dedicated to securing slavery. "We must decide whether slavery shall be extinguished by our enemies and the slaves be used against us, or use them ourselves at the risk of the effects which may be produced upon our social institutions," Lee wrote. "My own opinion is that we should employ them without delay."

The last best hope for winning the war hinged on defeating the man in charge of Washington. As early as 1863, Lee had viewed the November 1864 presidential election as a turning point. "If successful this year," he had written before the battles of Chancellorsville and Gettysburg, "next fall there will be a great change in public opinion at the North. The Republicans will be destroyed & I think the friends of peace will become so strong as that the next administration will go in on that basis." As late as August 1864, Lincoln expected the prophecy to come to pass; war-weary Northern voters would elect a Democrat who, as Lincoln put it, "will have secured his election on such ground that he can not possibly save" the Union. Then, with the beginning of fall came another chain of calamities for the Confederacy: In Georgia, the vital manufacturing center of Atlanta fell to General William Tecumseh Sherman. In the Shenandoah, Sheridan routed the remains of the army Early had led to Washington. Across a rejuvenated Union, all but three states went for Abraham Lincoln. "I think you may make up your mind that Mr. Lincoln is re-elected President," Lee told Mary. "We must therefore make up our minds for another four years of war."

So grim were the times by year's end that four more months of war seemed improbable. Richmond's most respected newspaper hinted at the necessity of a military dictator. "In the latter year of his command, Washington was, in point of fact, a Dictator," claimed the *Daily Dispatch*, leaving no doubt as to who should be "generalissimo" in the current crisis. "General Lee is, beyond all question, the greatest of living captains. . . . He possesses a weight of character, and an estimation with the multitude, such as no other man but one ever possessed in this country, and that other was Washington. The whole people look up to him with a respect amounting to reverence, and a belief in his capacity almost superstitious." Those closest to Lee were not so sure. "Our old Chief is too law abiding, too slow, too retiring for these times," Walter Taylor whispered, not that Lee would have disagreed. To Davis, Lee admitted, "The arrangement of the details of this army extended as it is, providing for its necessities & directing its operations engrosses all my time & still I am unable to accomplish what I desire & see to be necessary. I could not therefore propose to undertake more." Lee could not even feed or clothe his men. The soldiers defending the right flank, Lee wrote on February 8, "had been without meat for three days, and all were suffering from reduced rations and scant clothing, exposed to battle, cold, hail, and sleet." The next day, out of duty and without joy, he assumed the role of general in chief of all Confederate forces. It was a title not worth having; so few forces remained. Lee suggested his old classmate Joseph Johnston lead the force opposing Sherman, who had ravaged his way from Atlanta to Savannah before steering his army up the Carolinas toward a nexus with Grant. "It may be necessary to abandon all our cities, & preparation should be made for this contingency," Lee said.

As Grant wrapped his army farther around Petersburg, Lee stretched his trenches and his temper to the breaking point. Words like "calamity" and "dire" filled his correspondence. He warned Davis that the army would have to abandon the line. Talk of whether Richmond could hold out shifted to how soon it would fall. As if to rationalize failure, Lee made a point of questioning how anyone could have expected any other outcome. "While the military situation is not favorable, it is not worse than the superior numbers and resources of the enemy justified us in expecting from the beginning. Indeed, the legitimate military consequences of that superiority have been postponed longer than we had reason to anticipate," he wrote in March. During a visit to Richmond around this time, a nephew watched Lee pacing in front of a fire with his hands behind his back and a grave look on his face. "Mister Custis," Lee said to his oldest son, who had joined him, "when this war began, I was opposed to it, bitterly opposed to it, and I told these people that, unless every man should do his whole duty, they would repent it; and now . . . they will repent." Of the possibility of negotiating with Grant, Lee wrote, "My belief is that he will consent to no terms, unless coupled with the condition of our return to the Union. Whether this will be acceptable to our people yet awhile I cannot say." He could not speak for the people at the end of the war because he did not count himself among the people who had wanted independence at the start.

That spring, with the Confederacy collapsing, Lee did what he had done four years earlier when the Union had collapsed: he read a book. This time, it was Winfield Scott's recently released autobiography. "You have made the greatest mistake of your life," the older Virginian had told the younger during their last meeting. Now, with eyes admittedly "weary" and "sleepy," Lee rummaged through the memoirs of his mentor and concluded this: "He appears the bold sagacious truthful man he is."

Lee's staff picked the site: a brick house belonging to a man who had left his old home at Manassas to escape the war. Grant, once he arrived, would pick just about everything else. It had come to this as Lee waited to surrender. There was no other way, he would say. There were bluecoats before him and bluecoats behind him. A Confederate officer attempting to break through had called for reinforcements, and there were no reinforcements available. There was no going back either; Richmond and Petersburg had fallen. Of the thirty thousand infantrymen who on the night of April 2 had started the retreat west toward the promise of provisions—and then, if all went according to plan, south toward a junction with Johnston—less than half had lasted as long as this day, April 9, and as far as this place, Appomattox Court

House. With their starving horses nibbling the bark off trees, aides scrounged for breakfast, their last meal in the army. "There is nothing left me but to go and see General Grant," said Lee.

But, of course, there were alternatives; there always had been. Lee suggested one while surveying the sea of blue swallowing his army. "How easily I could get rid of this, and be at rest! I have only to ride along the line and all will be over." The artillery officer Edward Porter Alexander suggested another option: scatter the army rather than surrender it. The soldiers could fight like "rabbits and partridges in the bushes." For a second, Alexander thought his proposal for guerrilla warfare had convinced his chief. Then Lee spoke.

> If I took your advice, the men would be without rations and under no control of officers. They would be compelled to rob and steal in order to live. They would become mere bands of marauders, and the enemy's cavalry would pursue them and overrun many wide sections they may never have occasion to visit. We would bring on a state of affairs it would take the country years to recover from. And, as for myself, you young fellows might go to bushwhacking, but the only dignified course for me would be, to go to Gen. Grant and surrender myself and take the consequences of my acts.

Grant himself had proposed a way to spare Lee the embarrassment of surrendering in person: the two commanders could appoint surrogates instead. At the end of the Revolutionary War, Cornwallis had conveniently excused himself from presenting his sword in person to Washington. But if Lee remembered his father's memoirs, as an aide believed he did, then he recalled that Harry Lee, of all people, had criticized the British general for "obeying emotions which his great character ought to have stifled."

So, for half an hour, dressed in his best uniform, Lee waited, wondering what punishment the Federals might concoct. He brought just one fellow officer, his aide Charles Marshall, whose granduncle had been the famous Federalist Supreme Court justice and Washington biographer, John Marshall. From the moment Grant arrived onward, people would contrast the appearance of the two commanders: Lee's hair looking "silver gray," the younger Grant's looking "nut brown"; Lee standing erect, the shorter Grant stooping his shoulders; Lee buttoning his gray uniform to his throat, Grant leaving the blue blouse he wore over his waistcoat unbuttoned; Lee wearing "handsome spurs," Grant wearing muddy boots; the blade of Lee's sword descending from a gilt-wrapped handle, Grant carrying no sword at all. The two men talked as Union officers wishing to witness history filed into the room. While the meeting would not officially end the war, Grant hoped the surrender of this army would lead to the surrender of all the other Confederate armies. As he scribbled out the parole terms, he paused, looked down at Lee's ornate sword, and added that officers could keep their sidearms, baggage, and horses. "Each officer and man will be allowed to return to their homes, not to be disturbed by United States authority so long as they observe their paroles and the laws in force where they may reside." When Grant finished, Lee put on spectacles, examined the terms, and "was evidently touched," a Union officer recalled, by the generosity of the last lines. "This will have a very happy effect upon my army."

For most of the meeting, Lee left his conquerors to wonder what emotions swirled inside him. "As he was a man of much dignity, with an impassable face, it was impossible to say whether he felt inwardly glad that the end had finally come, or felt sad over the result, and was too manly to show it," Grant said. Once the signatures had been affixed and handshakes exchanged, Lee excused himself. His ruddy face turned a darker hue as he headed to the front porch. He smacked his hands together and called impatiently for his horse. Just as he mounted Traveller, Grant stepped down from the porch and lifted his hat. In unison, every Union man copied the gesture until, at last, Lee did, too. Then he rode off toward the army in tattered gray. The soldiers cheering his return could tell by his expression that their war for independence had ended. Tears long suppressed ran down his cheeks as the men gathered around his horse and grasped for his hand. Be "worthy citizens," he told them, and "return" home. It was the only advice he thought to give, though it was advice he could not follow. Arlington belonged to new residents: hundreds of the four million slaves who had gained their freedom, thousands of the six hundred thousand soldiers who had given their lives.

Lee had lost his family's home. He had lost his wife's inheritance, the same fortune John Adams believed made George Washington first in war and first in peace. Despite all that Lee had done differently—despite all the discipline he had demonstrated from his childhood in Alexandria through his career ending at Appomattox—he had repeated his father's fate. He was not a Washington. He was a Lee. At fifty-eight years old, he had just passed the age when his old man had eased into exile in the Caribbean. But unlike the father, the son would not sail down the river of his ruin. The Army of the Potomac had prevailed. Robert E. Lee would return to his wife.

PART IV

★

Postbellum

CHAPTER THIRTEEN

Washington and Lee

With a sword at his side, Robert E. Lee rode to Richmond. On the afternoon of April 15, crowds cheered his arrival. Even the Union soldiers occupying the blocks of charred chimneys and blackened walls saluted. The fires that had consumed the Confederate capital after the evacuation from Petersburg had approached the house his wife rented, but Mary Custis Lee had remained defiant. Lee found her seated in the same chair where she had knit while Richmond had burned. Abraham Lincoln had entered the city shortly after the flight of Jefferson Davis and the Confederate government. "I wish you could have witnessed Lincoln's triumphal entry into Richmond. He was surrounded by a crowd of blacks whooping & cheering like so many demons," Mary wrote. Lincoln had gone forever by the time her husband returned, and so had his words about "malice toward none" and "charity for all." The bullet puncturing the president's head the previous night had, by that morning, deprived the country of his generous spirit. Lee publicly condemned the assassination, which he expected Northerners to blame on the South. Brooding alone except when seeing visitors his relatives could not turn away and when stepping outside at dark, Lee wrote Davis a letter calling further bloodshed "useless." In response came news of Joseph Johnston's surrender and Davis's capture. The American Civil War was over. A little girl who knew no better asked Lee why he looked sad. "Why shouldn't I?" he said. "My cause is dead! I am homeless—I have nothing on earth."

How easy it would have been to follow the currents that had whisked his father to sea. Foreign shores called, and some Confederates answered. But they went against Lee's urging. The South, he told a newspaperman shortly after Appomattox, needed her sons to stay. That the new American president, Andrew Johnson, excluded Lee and other high-ranking officers from the general amnesty granted to other Confederates did not change his opinion. Nor did a grand jury's decision to indict him for treason, an action that, in his view, violated the assurances given at Appomattox. "Altho' the prospects may not now be cheering," he wrote, "I have entertained the opinion that unless prevented by circumstances or necessity, it would be better for them [former Confederates] and their country, to remain at their homes and share the fate of their respective States." When America had conquered Mexico, Lee had said that victors "are entitled to dictate the terms of peace." Being on the losing side now did not alter that conviction.

At Appomattox, Ulysses S. Grant had asked Lee to use his influence to urge Southerners outside the Army of Northern Virginia to accept defeat. "There was not a man in the Confederacy whose influence with the soldiery and the whole people was as great as his," Grant claimed. Lee's only hesitation then had been a soldier's reluctance to usurp political power from elected leaders like Davis. With that no longer an issue, Lee resolved to provide a model of obedience. On June 13, he applied to President Johnson for amnesty and encouraged those who asked his advice to do the same. "The questions which for years were in dispute between the State and General Government, and which unhappily were not decided by the dictates of reason, but referred to the decision of war, having been decided against us, it is the part of wisdom to acquiesce in the result, and of candor to recognize the fact. . . . All should unite in honest efforts to obliterate the effects of war, and to restore the blessings of peace."

The speed with which Lee transitioned from a leader of the rebellion to a leader for reconciliation should have surprised no one who had monitored his behavior at the war's outset. Here, after all, was a man who had resisted resigning from the United States Army but, after finally doing so, had waited scarcely three days before accepting command of a rebel army, and who had decried secession but spent four years killing in its defense. To Lee, the consistency of one's cause mattered less than submission of oneself. "I need not tell you that true patriotism sometimes requires of men to act exactly contrary, at one period, to that which it does at another, and that the motive which impels them—the desire to do right—is precisely the same. The circumstances which govern their actions change, and their conduct must conform to the new order of things," Lee famously told General Beauregard after Appomattox. As proof, Lee cited the example of George Washington: "At one time he fought against the French under Braddock, in the service of the King of Great Britain; at another, he fought with the French at Yorktown, under the orders of the Continental Congress of America, against him. He has not been branded with reproach by the world for this; but his course has been applauded." If Washington could switch sides, so could Lee. In that way, Washington's example could justify every step Lee had taken from Arlington to Appomattox and from unionist to separatist to unionist again. Never before had Lee come so close to making the case that given the same circumstances, the Father of His Country would have followed the same course—that the man who had forged the Union in the eighteenth century would have fought against it in the nineteenth.

Now Lee wanted to pursue the path that Washington had taken, for a time, after the War for Independence. He wanted to exchange his sword for a plow. He wanted to be a farmer. "I am looking for some little quiet house in the woods where I can procure shelter and my daily bread if permitted by the victor." Whether the victors would permit him to purchase land remained unknown. General Grant had voiced his opposition to charging his old adversary with treason, but the president ignored Lee's pardon request. "We may expect procrastination in measures of relief, denunciatory threats, etc. We must be patient, and let them take their course," Lee wrote. In the meantime, eager to escape Richmond, he moved his family up the James to a four-room cottage a friend offered. "We are all well & established in a comfortable but small house, in a grove of oaks," he wrote that summer. Around then and there, a traveler from the Shenandoah Valley appeared. He wore a new broadcloth suit he had borrowed specially for the errand. The men he represented had heard Lee needed a job, and had sent him to convey a bold offer: Would Lee accept the presidency of Washington College?

That the South's most famous son would consider accepting the presidency of an insignificant institution in the backlands behind the Blue Ridge stunned some of the college's friends, not to mention Lee's. A church official counseling Lee remembered feeling "chagrin" and "revulsion" when hearing about the offer. "The institution," the bishop told Lee, "was one of local interest, and comparatively unknown to our people."

Washington College would hardly have been unknown to someone like Lee, who had read Edward Everett's biography of George Washington and thus learned how the Father of His Country had once plucked the small school in the Shenandoah Valley out of obscurity. Washington's connection to the school had flowed out of his advocacy for the Potomac route to the west. In 1784, when Virginia and Maryland incorporated a company for improving the Potomac, the legislature in the former state chartered a separate company for improving the James and voted to present Washington stock in both ventures: fifty shares in the Potomac and one hundred shares in the James. "No circumstance has happened since I left the walks of public life which has so much embarrassed me," Washington said of the gifts. Accepting the stock, he worried, would prompt rumors he had promoted the projects for personal gain. But refusing it might offend the people of Virginia. From careful deliberations came a compromise. Virginia would instead appropriate the shares to a charitable cause of Washington's choosing, and Washington chose higher education. "The time is therefore come, when a plan of universal education ought to be adopted in the United States," he wrote. "Not only do the exigencies of public and private life demand it, but, if it should ever be apprehended, that prejudice would be entertained in one part of the Union against another, an efficacious remedy will be, to assemble the youth of every part under such circumstances as will, by the freedom of intercourse and collision of sentiment, give to their minds the direction of truth, philanthropy, and mutual conciliation." The stock in the Potomac Company would go toward establishing a national university in the federal city. The stock in the James company went to a school called Liberty Hall, which promptly renamed itself after its great patron.*

During the Civil War, Washington College suffered the misfortunes of being in Lexington, the same town where the Lees hid their Mount Vernon relics and where Union soldiers burned the Virginia Military Institute. Washington College fared slightly better. The distinctive colonnade of white pillars lining the campus's brick buildings had survived. The bluecoats had settled for smashing the windows and pelting the statue of George Washington staring down from the cupola. "But the damage done by the invader to the . . . external parts of the buildings is trifling, compared with what was done inside," the faculty reported. The laboratories presented "a scene of desolation and destruction"; half the books belonging to the library and literary societies had disappeared. The school had little left other than its name and the stock its namesake had bestowed. In 1865, the old James River shares accounted for more than half the school's investments. Rare amid the ruins of war were students who could afford tuition, and no more than forty-five had attended during the past year.

It was in desperation that on August 4 the trustees elected Lee president. Silence had followed the vote. "How could they announce to the world that they had elected to the presidency of a broken-down college not only the greatest man in the South, but in many respects the greatest man in the world?" wondered the board members. They

---

*This Washington College should not be confused with Washington College in Maryland or other similarly named institutions.

need not have worried. To the bishop who demeaned the offer, Lee countered, "The cause gave dignity to the institution, and not the wealth of its endowment or the renown of its scholars."

And the cause was near to Lee's heart. For four years, boys who might otherwise have enrolled in classes had enlisted in his army. Duty had required him to arm them for battle; now it demanded that he equip them for peace. "So greatly have those [educational] interests been disturbed at the South, and so much does its future condition depend upon the rising generation, that I consider the proper education of its youth one of the most important objects now to be attained," he wrote. His tenure as superintendent of West Point after the Mexican-American War had provided experience running a college, albeit a more prestigious institution. Whether this new opportunity was worthy of his stature, however, never troubled him. What troubled him was the opposite question: Was he worthy of it? On August 24, he wrote the trustees a letter listing his concerns. "The proper education of youth requires not only great ability, but I fear more strength than I now possess, for I do not feel able to undergo the labour of conducting classes in regular courses of instruction. I could not therefore undertake more than the general administration & supervision of the Institution." Of greater concern to Lee was that Northerners might censure Washington College for its association with him. "It is particularly incumbent on those charged with the instruction of the young, to set them an example of submission to authority, & I could not consent to be the cause of animadversion upon the College." Then, just when the trustees reading Lee's response might have lost hope, his letter shifted tone. "Should you however take a different view, & think that my services in the position tendered me by the Board will be advantageous to the College & Country, I will yield to your judgment & accept it."

Surely not to Lee's surprise, the board did take a different view. The advantages Lee's name brought for attracting donations and students outweighed the risks. Other ventures that had no need for Lee's services would have employed him for use of his name alone. That Lee summarily rejected those more lucrative opportunities but ultimately accepted the summons from the Shenandoah spoke to his belief that his service there might be useful. George Washington had praised higher education as an "efficacious remedy" to sectionalism. Across the Blue Ridge and south up the valley, Lee rode alone to Lexington to test that proposition.

On October 2, the president-elect took the oath of office after a ceremony that he insisted on keeping short and solemn. Among the few speakers Lee allowed was a pastor who prayed for the president of the United States. Within hours of taking office, Lee signed another oath, which unbeknownst to him earlier had been necessary for his amnesty application. "I, Robert E. Lee," it read, "do solemnly swear, in presence of Almighty God, that I will henceforth faithfully support, protect and defend the Constitution of the United States."

"And here we leave him," a *New York Herald* correspondent covering Lee's inauguration wrote, "in his home that is to be secluded and shaded and hedged about by imposing mountains, and miles away from railroads, and with never a longing thought, doubtless, for the great outer world and its more enticing and splendid prizes." Only 108 miles separated Lexington from the cottage where Lee had left his family, but the lack of rail access made the distance feel farther. Getting to the nearest train station required either an uncomfortable twenty-three-mile stagecoach ride or a fifty-mile canal trip. The Lees considered the canal "the easiest way of reaching Lexington from the outside world," though the route was far from easy given those fifty miles took twelve hours. Much as Lee cherished the mountain scenery, it walled Lexington off from the Tidewater society his family had called home. "Lexington I fear is a long way off from many old friends," Mary wrote as she contemplated joining her husband.

Where Lexington was situated hardly made any difference to impoverished Southern families desperate to enroll their sons in "General Lee's College," as they called it. From across the South came letters like the one from a Mississippi man worried about his nephew's future. "His education has been greatly neglected owing to difficulties in our schools during the first years of the war, and the fact that he was a soldier in our armies in 1864 & 1865—I scarcely now hope for him an extended, liberal education becoming a gentleman." But the writer hoped the boy could still learn proper morals. "I believe this latter main object can be best allowed by placing him in your college where I feel assured your character will emulate the students to a high, healthy moral tone." Enrollment tripled during Lee's first year. Students came from as far away as Texas and Florida.

Their families begged Lee to look after their children, and he did. He looked for them at the services he attended each morning, read their progress reports during the six hours of office time he held each day, and attended their oral exams. Boys falling short of standards would receive a summons to his office and, often with weepy eyes, would pledge to reform when reminded of how their families had sacrificed. Lee understood their parents' plight; his application to West Point had contained a note saying he could "lose no time in selecting the employment to which his future life is to be devoted." Not surprisingly then, Lee looked beyond the traditional classical curriculum to more practical offerings for "the commercial, agricultural, & mechanical classes" of society, people whose needs most colleges to date had ignored. "Such a course of instruction is requisite to meet present wants of the country; and to enable those young men . . . to enter at once upon the active duties of life," Lee told the Virginia-born but Chicago-based inventor Cyrus McCormick. "To you, who are so conversant with the necessities of the country, and its vastly underdeveloped resources, the benefit of applying scientific knowledge and research, to agriculture, mining, manufactures, architecture, and the construction of ordinary roads, rail-roads, canals, bridges &c., will be at once apparent." McCormick agreed and donated ten thousand dollars.

In exchange for his labors, Lee drew an annual base salary of fifteen hundred dollars. The job also offered a perquisite: a house. The *Herald* reporter described the portico and pillars in front of the brick house as "massive," but, of course, they looked minuscule compared with Arlington's grandeur. Still, Lee looked "bright and even gay" the December morning his youngest son escorted Mary off a canal boat and into the president's house for the first time. "We were all very grateful and happy—glad to get home—the only one we had had for four long years," Rob Jr. recalled. Lee insisted on hanging curtains and laying carpets that had adorned Arlington, even though the latter needed to be folded to fit in the smaller rooms. "It is better to use what we have than to buy others," Lee said. "Their use where originally intended is very uncertain."

Uncertain was an understatement. "All accounts agree in representing A[rlington] in an unreasonable condition for a future residence, even if it can be recovered," Lee wrote. Lee's oldest daughter went to see for herself. Without revealing her identity to the guards or stopping to speak with the former slaves, she ventured past the "Do Not Trespass" signs, past the graves, and into the "desolate" house. "It was a beautiful bright nice day and the view was lovely but the whole face of the country so utterly changed that turning my back on the house I could have scarcely recognized a feature of it," she wrote. A similar report came from Lee's older brother Smith, who also toured the property around this time. Though cemetery officials reported hearing Smith mutter "that the house could still be made a pleasant residence, by fencing off the Cemetery, and removing the officers buried around the garden," Smith told Lee that, in its current condition, the graves "are just in a place where they can't be shut out from view."

Here, talk of recovering Arlington might have ceased but for two factors that compelled Lee to continue. The first was his wife. Confined to a wheelchair, Mary obsessed over her old home. "My heart yearns for the home & scenes of my past life," she told Jefferson Davis's wife. "Much as I long to go there I dread to witness the plunder & desecration of my once cherished & beautiful home. I only wish I had set the torch to it when I left, or that it was sunk in the bottom of the Potomac than used as it now is." To another friend, she vowed never to surrender her claim. "The whole Yankee Nation could not offer a compensation meet for it." The second factor compelling Lee was his father-in-law's unfulfilled and perhaps unachievable will. After the war, Rooney and Rob Jr. resolved to restore the ruins of the White House and Roman-coke. Lee advised his younger sons to consider those plantations their own even though their sisters' legacies remained unsettled. That understanding did nothing to help Lee's oldest son, the hypothetical heir to Arlington. Custis Lee accepted a position at the nearby Virginia Military Institute while his father explored options for pressing his claims.

When Lee discovered the federal government had sold the property to itself supposedly because of unpaid taxes, he asked his lawyer to examine the legality of the sale without attracting publicity. Whatever his chances in a court of law, Lee recognized the impossibility of prevailing in the court of Northern public opinion. "I have refrained from taking any steps as to the recovery of the property, as the Executor of Mr. Custis, until I should see whether I would be restored to civil rights," Lee wrote in April 1866. Little could he know that, among other reasons the government had ignored his amnesty application, the loyalty oath he had submitted had gone missing. Not until one hundred years after his death would it resurface in a government archive.

Unable to regain Arlington, Mary fixated on recovering her father's Mount Vernon heirlooms. Her spies in Washington catalogued items on display at the Patent Office. She drafted lists of the missing relics, which included forty plates of Washington's china bearing the crest of the Society of the Cincinnati; Washington's war tent; and even a suit of Washington's clothes. Mary lost no opportunity to explain how she had left these relics behind at Arlington only because she had expected to return within weeks, how her former slave Selina Gray had tried to guard them, and how she had never imagined that Union soldiers would steal her property. "I do not suppose whatever the politics might be, that any gentleman would countenance or approve of the disgraceful plunder of a place that should have been respected for the sake of its former occupant, who for so many years gave up his life & fortune to the public & that his only child, the granddaughter of Mrs. Washington should be deprived of her house." In a bout of hyperbole, she exclaimed that the Yankees had left her only one relic: the book of her father's recollections of Mount Vernon, and only one copy at that. When her editor, the historian Benson Lossing, asked about the paintings at Arlington, Mary could provide no details because she had not seen them since stashing them at a relative's house in 1861.

Ironically, some of the worst damage came not from the "disgraceful plunder" but rather from efforts to transport the relics to Lexington. When the Lees retrieved the heirlooms that their friends in Lexington had buried for them during the war, they found that mold had tarnished the silver and that dampness had defaced—and in many cases destroyed—the original Washington letters. A similar fate awaited the portraits when Mary finally shipped them to Lexington. The canal boat transporting them sank. The water damage was a reminder of why George Washington Parke Custis had built his Washington treasury at Arlington in the first place and why the injunction in his otherwise disastrous will had ordered his executor to keep every article "relating to Washington and that came from Mt. Vernon" at Arlington.

One relic had accompanied Lee to war: a dull-looking blade that Lee cherished more than the ornate sword he had worn to Appomattox. The sword was the one Washington had given Custis and that Custis had given Lee. It, too, had carried an injunction. For the rest of Lee's life, his decision to raise his sword against the Union would hamper his wife's attempts to regain the heirlooms in the Patent Office. Even when President Johnson eventually granted her request, Congress blocked the transfer. "As the country desires them, she must give them up," Lee said of the relics. "I hope their presence at the capital will keep in the remembrance of all Americans the principles and virtues of Washington."

While plans for reclaiming Arlington stalled, Lee found himself back under its shadow in February 1866, when a joint congressional committee investigating the condition of the Southern states called him to Washington, DC. A parade of witnesses reported that no man garnered more respect in Virginia than Robert E. Lee. Reports told of

Virginians holding debates over whether Lee was a greater man than George Washington and deciding affirmatively. Not since retreating from Gettysburg had Lee crossed the Potomac. Not since resigning his Union commission had he come so close to Arlington. Never had he seen the Statue of Freedom atop the Capitol. Visiting people and places from long ago proved bittersweet. "I am considered now such a monster, that I hesitate to darken with my shadow the doors of those I love lest I should bring upon them misfortune," he said. A house he visited in Georgetown had, in old days, provided a clear view of Arlington. But Lee did not care to look. "I know very well how things are there," he wrote.

One Arlington resident hoping to see Lee was Amanda Parks, a former Custis slave. Missing him at his hotel, she sent a note asking if she had offended him. "I do not know why you should ask if I am angry with you," he responded. "I was sorry to have missed you, for I wished to know how you were, and how all the people from Arlington were getting on in the world. My interest in them is as great now as it ever was, and I sincerely wish for their happiness and prosperity."

Amanda Parks might have thought otherwise based on Lee's testimony before Congress. Asked about the future of blacks, Lee said, "I think it would be better for Virginia if she could get rid of them. That is no new opinion with me. I have always thought so, and have always been in favor of emancipation—gradual emancipation." Asked whether Confederate leaders had committed treason, Lee answered no. They had simply followed their states out of the Union. "The State was responsible for the act, not the individual." Lee was reluctant to speak on behalf of his state. He did express opposition to enfranchising blacks, and support for Andrew Johnson; the president had emerged as an unlikely conservative counterbalance to radicals in Congress who would enact laws to divide the South into military districts and to empower carpetbaggers, Southern Republicans, and freed blacks. Mostly, however, Lee tried to steer clear of the details of policy debates. He told the committee he avoided newspapers, a habit difficult to maintain in a house where his wheelchair-bound wife raged over articles about Radical Republicans such as Thaddeus Stevens and Charles Sumner. "The country that allows such scum to rule them must be fast going to destruction," Mary wrote.

For his part, Lee claimed to want nothing more than the Union that he had desired on the eve of war: the one that the Founding Fathers had intended. "All that the South has ever desired," he wrote, "was that the Union, as established by our forefathers, should be preserved; and that the Government, as originally organized, should be administered in purity and truth." What exactly the forefathers had established had been much on Lee's mind because he had agreed to contribute a biographical sketch of his own father as a preface to a revised edition of Harry Lee's memoirs. As the family's self-appointed historian, older brother Carter prepared a draft that provided most of the research and much of the prose, explaining why the haphazard final version sounds so little like the methodical Lee. To aid the process, Lee borrowed a few Washington biographies from the college library. Otherwise, he added little to the memoir except to "tone down" his brother's excess enthusiasm for their father. "I earnestly beg you will tone down, enlarge or abridge according to the dictates of your calmer judgment," Carter wrote. "I acknowledge my inability to preserve the golden mean on such a theme, & when you shall have read his [Harry's] letters to me which conclude the sketch, you will not wonder at it." Evidently the details did strike Lee as "too minute" because Carter later lobbied to limit the cuts. "It is that," Carter added of the minutiae, "which gives its chief charm to biography."

Some of the details that most troubled Lee concerned actions contrasting with his own: Harry Lee's role in quashing the Whiskey Rebellion and his opposition to resolutions James Madison and Thomas Jefferson authored allowing states to nullify federal laws. Carter sought to explain away the discrepancies by highlighting, for example, the "distressing contrast" between how Washington and Harry Lee had shown "tenderness" and "clemency" to the rebels in Pennsylvania and how "cruelly" and "ruthlessly" Union authorities had treated the Confederates in the recent war. That was not good enough for

Lee. He cut the argument entirely. "I see no similarity in the cause or course of the 'Whiskey Insurrection' with the secession of the South; & am unwilling to recognize a parallel." He retained a few choice lines declaring his father's fidelity to Virginia and opposition to Alexander Hamilton's fiscal reforms but otherwise attempted to avoid politics. "I do not wish to revive any partizan feeling or to incite party criticism against the book or to stir up sectional animosity—I would rather allay such feelings."

Lee's true struggle to reconcile his actions with the Founding Fathers' occurred outside the public eye. Back in 1861, of course, he had insisted that Washington and the other founders had not "exhausted so much labour, wisdom & forbearance" in creating a union that "was intended to be broken by every member of the Confederacy at will." But that had been before he spent four years in Confederate camps; before he urged thousands of young men to follow the road their fathers had followed "through suffering, privations, and blood, to independence"; before the bluecoats plundered Arlington, stole the Mount Vernon relics, and burned the White House; and before the South experienced the bitterness of defeat and the humiliation of military rule. When an English aristocrat in 1866 wrote asking his position on the constitutional questions at stake in the Civil War, Lee responded that "the leading men of the country for the last seventy years" had accepted the right to secession. Lee did not so much as mention that he himself had dissented from that supposed consensus. The Founding Fathers whom Lee had once cited as proponents of an unbreakable union now appeared in his argument as opponents of a strong federal government. "I need not refer one so well acquainted as you are with American history, to the State papers of Washington and Jefferson, the representatives of the federal and democratic parties, denouncing consolidation and centralization of power, as tending to the subversion of State Governments, and to despotism."

So how could Lee favor restoring the Union of old when his own constitutional theories kept changing with the times? The evidence suggests Lee wrestled with the problem to the end of his life. In a file that his oldest son parted with only on his own deathbed are a series of memoranda Lee drafted offering different and often contradictory answers. One, for example, decries Republicans for shredding the cords that connected the Union before the Civil War, but another persists in defending the South's right to secede from that very same Union. Probably the closest Lee came to a resolution was a memorandum he wrote blaming the Founding Fathers themselves for leaving their legacy open to competing interpretations that sent the country careening from crisis to compromise to crisis again and finally to civil war. Here, truth and tragedy met. On slavery and secession, the Founding Fathers had left an inconsistent and incomplete legacy. And by acknowledging that the Fathers had not predetermined history, Lee inched toward acknowledging that sons, too, had their choices. Lee never apologized for his—and maintained to the end that he could have made no other—but a professor hearing him reflect on the Fort Sumter crisis was struck that Lee did not blame his fellow Virginian Winfield Scott for making the opposite choice. "There were powerful reasons on both sides," said Lee.

In 1868, near the end of his presidency, Andrew Johnson granted amnesty to Confederates excluded from earlier proclamations. The pardon restored all Lee's rights, save the right to seek the elected offices for which admirers occasionally floated his name. Every major American war starting with the Revolution had lifted a general to the presidency, and the Civil War would be no exception. In 1869, Lee received an invitation to the White House, where he met briefly with the newest occupant, President Ulysses S. Grant.

People remembered Lee during his later years taking long rides on Traveller. Outwardly he kept his humor. A girl recovering from the mumps heard Lee feign concern that his beloved horse would catch the disease. "What shall I do if Traveller gets the mumps?" he exclaimed. He claimed that riding freed his mind. Still friends saw "sorrow" on his face and wondered where his thoughts traveled. One day, while talking with Lee, a student at the college described himself as "impatient" to compensate for time "lost" in the Confederate army. Lee snapped, "However long you live and whatever you accomplish, you will find that the time you spent in the Confederate army was the most profitably spent portion of your life." But the same young man later heard Lee say, "The great mistake of my life was taking a military education," without which, of course, he would never have become the general in chief of the Confederacy. When the cadets from the nearby Virginia Military Institute marched to a beat, Lee "consciously avoided keeping step," or so it seemed to Washington College students who found his discipline "just the opposite of what one would naturally expect from a man who had received military training and had exercised military authority for many years."

Rather than force his students "to do their duty," Lee encouraged them to do it on their own accord. Rather than worry about setting regulations, Lee emphasized just one rule at the college: "every student must be a gentleman." Rather than impose academic requirements, Lee believed that "every student should be allowed to pursue the study of his choice." Under his leadership, the college developed, as one writer puts it, "one of the first elective systems in the country." Lee expanded offerings in modern languages, applied mathematics, and practical sciences; paved the way for the annexation of a law school; called for creating schools of agriculture and commerce; and proposed scholarships for young men interested in pursuing a career he detested—journalism. At the end of the 1868 school year, enrollment surpassed four hundred and included some students from above the Mason-Dixon line. Construction finished on a new chapel that same year and a new house for the president the next. Even Mary contributed to the improvements around town. The miniature portraits she colored and sold of George and Martha Washington raised money for the local church she favored.

By early 1870, faculty members advised Lee to ease his workload. They worried about his health and recommended he travel south. Doctors described him as "habitually sad and depressed." One professor heard Lee say that, "If he did not get better, he would be obliged to resign his position as President." Just walking across campus—from the chapel to the president's house—exhausted his breath and aggravated the pain he had experienced in his chest since the attack near Fredericksburg. His back and breastbone ached. His body took cold more frequently and recovered more slowly. His pulse weakened. His heartbeat softened. His thoughts drifted ever closer to death. "My interest in time & its concerns is daily fading away & I try to keep my eyes & thoughts fixed on those eternal shores to which I am fast hastening."

Life, of course, had its lure. The southern swing he took that spring on the advice of his doctors and colleagues gave him the chance to see his daughter Annie's grave in North Carolina for the first time, his father's grave in Georgia for the last time, and adoring crowds at almost every stop. A final visit to Alexandria in July 1870 allowed for a consultation with his lawyer about the "not promising" prospect of regaining Arlington and settling the Custis will, whose terms he still wished to honor. He also wished his sons would marry. Rooney had obliged and named another baby for his father. Custis Lee gave less cause for hope. He shunned parties and showed the solemn side of his father's character. But pursuing mates for Rob Jr. exhibited another side of Lee: the old flirt. "You need not fear any one taking your place in my affections. You were firmly fixed there when you were a sweet little school girl, & will remain there forever," he wrote Rob's future fiancée. In August, Lee celebrated the news of the engagement.

Curiously, he did not encourage his daughters to marry, and they never did. "He was apt to be critical on the subject of our young men visitors and admirers," his daughter Mildred recalled. He had told her, "Experience will teach you, that not withstanding all appearances to the contrary, you will never receive such love as is felt for you by your father & mother." Almost forty years earlier, Lee had written the girl he wished to marry that her father could not "expect to have her with him always." Experience, apparently, had brought Lee around to old Custis's view.

* * *

It started to rain on the afternoon of September 28, 1870. The drops pelted Lee during his walk to the four o'clock vestry meeting. He had not wanted to go. But the other members had asked him to chair their session, so he joined them in the "cold and damp" pews. He had anticipated that the discussion might drag on, and drag on it did for three hours. The last light of the dark autumn day had faded when the treasurer said the subscription for the rector's salary had fallen short a certain sum. "I will give that sum," said Lee, looking flushed and tired. He needed to get home. He put on his hat and cloak and walked into the rain. Mary expected him for tea at seven. Not until half past the hour did he enter the house and remove his drenched outerwear.

Mary complained about his tardiness. Usually he waited for her, not the other way around. "Where have you been all this time?" she asked as he entered the dining room. There was much he could have said. In his sixty-three years, he had passed through tempests at every stage of life: as a lonely lieutenant on Cockspur, as a sheepish groom at Arlington, as an intrepid captain in Mexico, as a calm federal officer at Harpers Ferry, as an untested general on Cheat Mountain, and as an aging commander in the months before Chancellorsville and the days after Gettysburg. Mary waited for his answer. He opened his mouth, but she heard no sound. Unconcerned, she offered to pour his tea. Again he opened his mouth. This time came a noise that she could not understand but a frightful look that she did. "He essayed to answer," she remembered, "& then sat upright in his chair with an expression of resignation that was sublime. I am sure he was conscious that his last hour had come." The family fetched Lee's doctors, who arrived within ten minutes, placed cold cloths on his head and hot bottles on his feet, and laid him on his old army cot.

As Lee slept, more rain fell. "Nature seemed to grieve with convulsive throbs," Mary wrote. "Yet he lay sleeping . . . unconscious of the warring of the elements and all the next day and night the storm raged unceasingly carrying away with its fury houses, bridges, men and cattle so that for eight days we were entirely isolated from the rest of the world." A town down the valley recorded nine inches of rainfall in just twenty-four hours. The rivers rose higher and faster than anyone could remember. At the southern end of the valley, the swollen James carried the floodwaters through the Blue Ridge toward Richmond. At the other end of the valley, water and debris that had funneled down the Shenandoah River crashed into Harpers Ferry, swelled the Potomac, swallowed the canal towpath, and headed toward the unsuspecting city of Washington.

Back in the valley, the rain stopped. Lee's mind cleared as the clouds parted. He seemed "less drowsy" and "more intelligent and observant." "Has been able . . . to speak some sentences, but rarely volunteers to do so," noted his doctors. On October 10, when asked, he said, "I feel better." The doctors told him that his recovery needed to accelerate for Traveller's sake. The old horse missed his exercise. Lee "gazed earnestly at the speaker for a moment, then closed his eyes and shook his head." A couple of hours later, he insisted on trying to get out of bed but succeeded only in exhausting himself. "He never smiled," Mary recalled, "and rarely attempted to speak except in his dreams and then he wandered to those dreadful battlefields." Bedside watchers, at some point, heard him summon dead subordinates and order aides to "strike the tent." His health deteriorated. His wife no longer felt him squeeze her hand when she held his. Based on "his rapid and feeble pulse, deepening unconsciousness and accelerated breathing," the doctors declared his case "hopeless." After nine o'clock on the morning of October 12, Mary heard a "deepdrawn sigh." She was by his side even if he could no longer recognize "her almost snowy-white, fine, soft hair, in waves and curls framing her full forehead" and "her features much resembling those of her great-grandmother Martha, the wife of Washington." His body rolled over. The weary eyes that had glimpsed Lafayette and Lincoln closed, and the current carried him away.

Almost immediately—without even waiting for the funeral— the college faculty members gathered and resolved "that the name of this institution may hereafter express in fit conjunction the immortal names of Washington and Lee, whose lives were so similar in their perfect renown, and with both of whom equally by singular good fortune it is entitled to be associated in its future history." The new name, Washington and Lee, represented a step toward linking the legacies of two men whom the Potomac had divided. More work remained. The floodwaters, which had gathered in the valley and rolled down the Potomac, had destroyed the Chain Bridge above Georgetown and then swept away parts of the Long Bridge, the old causeway Lee had crossed so often between Arlington and Washington. Repairing that damage would take longer.

The Bridge

The public mourning that followed Robert E. Lee's death might have given Kentucky senator Thomas McCreery the wrong impression. Said Mary Custis Lee of the mourning for her husband, "Had he been successful instead of the Hero of a Lost Cause he could not have been more beloved and honored." In the days before and after the funeral in Lexington, Southerners wrote eulogies and resolutions proclaiming their deceased general "first in war, first in peace, and first in the hearts of his countrymen." Even newspapers north of the Potomac saluted his postwar conduct. "His unobtrusive modesty," read the obituary in the *New York Times*, "has won the respect even of those who most bitterly deplore and reprobate his course in the rebellion." To Senator McCreery, it appeared that all Americans took pride in Lee's virtues, especially his service at Washington College. "The son of 'Light-Horse Harry,' penniless as a beggar, had completed a monument to Washington!" the senator said in December after introducing a resolution that raised the possibility of disinterring the Union soldiers buried at Arlington and restoring the property to its rightful owners, the Lees.

"Radical invectives," wrote the *New York Herald*, "exploded so suddenly, and probably unexpectedly, over poor McCreery's head like a shower of aerolites." Senator after senator rose to denounce Lee as a traitor. As to the claim that he had merely stayed loyal to Virginia, one senator pointed out that Lee had lived in the District of Columbia, a fact true for much of Lee's life until Alexandria's retrocession.

Another talked about how Lee's reputation as "the immediate connection" to "the mighty Washington" made his decision to turn against the Union all the more influential and harmful. "And thus it was that thousands and thousands of young minds were lured. They were led away from the path of rectitude and patriotism and followed the flag of Lee." Even more unpopular than the thought of returning Arlington to the Lees was the thought of removing the sixteen thousand bodies that had come to rest in the cemetery by 1870. Massachusetts senator Charles Sumner claimed to know the real reason Secretary of War Stanton had signed off on burying bodies at Arlington in 1864. "He meant to bury those dead there in perpetual guard over that ground, so that no person of the family of Lee should ever dare to come upon it unless to encounter the ghosts of those patriots."

The utter failure of the resolution dashed hopes for recovering Arlington. Mary shifted to seeking the monetary compensation she had previously sworn never to accept. Despite what Senator McCreery thought, she and her children were far from destitute. The stocks and bonds Lee left totaled more than eighty thousand dollars. Among his assets were four thousand dollars of bonds that had not paid interest in many years. It was Lee's investment in the canal along the Potomac, Washington's route to the west. Mary also retained the president's house at Washington and Lee University because her oldest son, Custis Lee, had succeeded his father in office. Still Mary longed to see her old home again. While visiting Alexandria on June 2, 1873, she took a carriage ride and got her wish. "After driving around town, she took the road, and an hour's pleasant drive brought her to Arlington at eleven o'clock exactly," a newspaper reported. "Mrs. Lee did not get out of the carriage, but gazed with feelings we cannot perhaps fully appreciate, on all that she had once known." Her daughter heard her say afterward that she never wanted to see Arlington again, and she never did. Within months, she was dead, her body lying with her husband's in Lexington, the Blue Ridge shielding the view.

Mary's oldest son took the fight for his inheritance to court. He filed an "ejectment action" against the army officers in charge of Arlington.

In 1879, a jury needed just thirty minutes to rule in his favor. In 1882, a sharply divided US Supreme Court upheld the decision after Custis Lee personally assured the justices that he sought only compensation for the land, not eviction of the bodies. Congress immediately moved to purchase the title. The thorny question of how much the United States should pay Robert E. Lee's oldest son landed, by a quirk of history, on the desk of Abraham Lincoln's oldest son, Secretary of War Robert Todd Lincoln. "I have therefore directed," Lincoln wrote in January 1883, "an experienced and very discreet officer of the Quartermaster Department to investigate the subject as completely as he can, without publicity. He understands the importance of the investigation being made quietly." Before year's end, Lee's son had signed a deed for $150,000, and Lincoln's son reported "the ownership of the Arlington estate being beyond a doubt now in the United States."

More legal victories followed. In April 1901, the Justice Department advised returning the Mount Vernon relics that Union soldiers had brought to the Patent Office in 1862. William McKinley, the last of the Civil War veterans elected president, said, "It will afford me great satisfaction to give direction for the restoration to the present head of a historic family of these cherished heirlooms of the father of his country."

The city of Washington had changed since the war. The Army Corps of Engineers had dredged the Potomac and deposited the earth that had lain beneath the water on the swampy tidal flats bordering the finally completed Washington Monument. In 1902, a commission overseeing improvements to the city proposed anchoring the reclaimed land with another monument, one that would extend the line running between the Statue of Freedom atop the Capitol and the Washington Monument. In Chicago that same year, Union veteran Charles Francis Adams gave a speech asking, "Who is to have a statue . . . whom shall we consecrate and set apart as one of our sacred men?" This Harvard-educated great-grandson of John Adams gave a shocking answer: Robert E. Lee. Adams recalled how Senator McCreery's resolution had prompted tirades against Lee the traitor.

"If Lee was a traitor, Washington was also," said Adams, praising Lee as the "brave, chivalrous, self-sacrificing, sincere, and patriotic" soldier who defended Virginia despite opposing secession. Adams looked to a day when "the bronze effigy of Robert E. Lee, mounted on his charger, and with the insignia of his Confederate rank, will from its pedestal in the nation's capital gaze across the Potomac at his old home at Arlington." It was not to be. The commission had recommended the memorial across from Arlington honor someone else. On the land reclaimed from the Potomac, the commission resolved, "should stand a memorial erected to the memory of that one man in our history as a nation who is worthy to be named with George Washington—Abraham Lincoln." There, the memorial to the man who saved the Union would go.

Americans, however, did not forget what Adams had said. By the 1920s, Northern attitudes had softened enough to embolden a congressman to propose rededicating Arlington House as a tribute to Robert E. Lee amid the graves of men who died fighting him. There was opposition to the bill but not enough to prevent passage. The legislation called for restoring what it styled "the Lee Mansion" to its appearance on the eve of the Civil War so that, as an officer supervising the restoration put it, tourists would believe Lee "had gone out for the afternoon and would soon return." The house built as a shrine to Washington would soon become a memorial to Lee.

There had long been talk of binding the banks of the Potomac with a sturdier bridge. George Washington Parke Custis had favored a span between Arlington and Washington. So had President Andrew Jackson, according to a speech Custis had heard the great orator Daniel Webster give at the US Capitol. "Before us is the broad and beautiful river, separating two of the original thirteen States, and which a late President, a man of determined purpose and inflexible will, but patriotic heart, desired to span with arches of ever-enduring granite, symbolical of the firmly cemented union of the North and the South." Webster said those words on July 4, 1851, the seventy-fifth anniversary of the Declaration of Independence. Another seventy-five years passed until construction began on a granite bridge resting on nine arches, pivoting off the Lincoln Memorial, and running on a new axis toward the Lee Mansion up on the hill.

As the Arlington Memorial Bridge neared completion, the question of what exactly it memorialized arose. There was the stated purpose of bridging the river that had divided North and South during the Civil War. But the timing and placement encouraged alternative interpretations. Plans for opening the bridge around the bicentennial of George Washington's birth in 1932 suggested a memorial to the Father of His Country. The *Washington Post* favored calling the span the Bridge of Lincoln and Lee because it "connects the everlasting memorial to one with the quaint Virginia homestead of the other." A Senate resolution pushed for memorializing Grant and Lee by placing a statue of the Union general on one end and a statue of the Confederate general on the other. That proposal met opposition from the Arlington Memorial Bridge Commission's executive officer, who happened to be Lieutenant Colonel Ulysses S. Grant III. His grandfather already had a statue outside the Capitol. And the younger Grant, according to newspapers, wished to keep "the impersonal character of the span."

But removing the personalities from the places is easier said than done. Between Lee on one bank and Lincoln, Washington, and the Statue of Freedom on the other rushes the broad river carrying water from the great western expanses, past the sites of America's bloodiest day and John Brown's raid, over the Great Falls, through the original diamond-shaped federal district and the archways of the Memorial Bridge, and onward to Mount Vernon, Stratford Hall, and the Chesapeake Bay, where the English-speaking history of America really began. The dream of dominating the river's coils and currents drove the country toward the Constitution; the desperate battle to protect its banks cleared the way for the Emancipation Proclamation. If all this makes the Potomac the river of American history, then its verdict is clear: Lee stands on the wrong side. The soldier whom both sides of a civil war courted as the representative of the Washington family no longer stands closest to Washington. That place belongs to Lincoln, the prairie lawyer who grew up without any connections to the Father of His Country save for a book by Parson Weems holding out the promise that "every youth may become a Washington."

Washington himself understood the power of that promise. A discarded draft of his first inaugural address argued that his childlessness should ease any fears that the man who would not be king sought a dynasty. "I have no child for whom I could wish to make a provision—no family to build in greatness upon my Country's ruins." He could not have imagined how history would twist and toy with those words: that the greatness of his country would ultimately be built over the corpse of Mount Vernon's heir, the ashes of the White House plantation, and the captured relics and denuded heights of Arlington. All were casualties of the war Lee waged against a union he cherished and, until revising his views after the fact, considered inviolable and indivisible.

If Lee had followed those beliefs instead of his state; if he had aligned himself, his wife, and the Custis fortune with the Union; if he had commanded the federal army as skillfully as Winfield Scott had imagined, the shores of Washington might have stretched out to welcome his memorial instead of Lincoln's on that sacred spot. Much as that place in history might have suited Lee's true preferences, it would have deprived the world of a story that has defined the American identity by fulfilling the old Washington fable that passed down from Parson Weems through the generations. Because Lee was the man who would not be Washington—because the decision he made tore his ties to Washington—every child born as lowly as Lincoln can dream of being a Washington. Because Lee could not have his own way, we might all have ours.

Acknowledgments

The inspiration for this book flowed out of years spent near the river Robert E. Lee and George Washington called home. So did much of the research. Libraries and archives on both sides of the Potomac—in Virginia and Washington, DC—welcomed my visits. None proved more indispensable than the Library of Congress and its Manuscript Reading Room. At the Virginia Historical Society, Frances S. Pollard, Katherine Wilkins, and others shared their incomparable knowledge and collections. At Mount Vernon and its beautiful new Fred W. Smith National Library for the Study of George Washington, Michele Lee, Mary V. Thompson, and Dawn Bonner aided my research, answered my questions, and steered me toward newly obtained documents. At Washington and Lee University, Seth McCormick-Goodhart, Lisa S. McCown, Patricia A. Hobbs, and Cassie Ivey guided me to papers and portraits that otherwise would have escaped my attention. At the Virginia State Law Library, Gail Warren and Catherine G. OBrion went above and beyond in tracking down cases. At Tudor Place—one of the gems of Georgetown— Wendy Kail welcomed my research. The Library of Virginia, the Museum of the Confederacy (especially Cathy Wright), the University of Virginia, the Alexandria Library, the Alexandria Circuit Court Clerk's Office, and the National Archives all also opened their collections to me.

Farther from home, my research took me to the Georgia Historical Society in Savannah and Duke University's David M. Rubenstein Rare Book and Manuscript Library, where Elizabeth Dunn ensured my visit's success. Jan Perone at the Abraham Lincoln Presidential Library also assisted my research from afar.

Studying Lee's life took me beyond archives and libraries to the places where the events described in these pages occurred. The countless guides and park rangers who walked me through historic homes and over old battlefields left me in awe. Dennis Frye at Harpers Ferry was especially generous and

Acknowledgments

introduced me to William DeRoche, who shared his vast knowledge of Beal-lair. Mark Greenough gave me a memorable private tour of the Virginia State Capitol rooms where this book begins.

Every author who writes about the Civil War owes a debt to the historians whose prose and research have illuminated the defining chapter of American history. One of the great pleasures of writing my book was reading theirs. My own writing has benefited from many influences, especially from mentors at the White House, where I learned about history from a president unafraid of making it. For early encouragement and advice on this project, I am indebted to William McGurn, Ted Smyth, Philip Ruppel, Kenneth Vittor, Danny Stern, and Elizabeth N. Saunders. The generous Marc Thiessen gave me guidance I am grateful I followed. Matthew Karp and Christopher Michel, two of the smartest people I know, reviewed drafts and suggested improvements. Responsibility for any improvements still required is mine alone.

My wise and indefatigable agent, Glen Hartley, believed in this project and found the perfect publisher. At every stage, the manuscript benefited from the influence of my masterly editor, Colin Harrison. My thanks also go to the talented Katrina Diaz, Kyle Radler, Valerie Pulver, and the rest of the outstanding team at Scribner. Without their trust and support, this book would exist only in the hopes and wishes of the friends and family members who encouraged it.

I am grateful to all the Horns, Shaskans, Luses, and Nathans. My wife's parents, John and Catherine, went so far as to move a desk upstairs in their house so I could write when there. My brother Steven lent his brilliant legal mind to helping me research court cases and locate hard-to-find documents. My brother Michael, an author himself, advised me about the publishing process and inspired me with his own work. My grandparents taught me to revere the past. To my parents, I owe everything. My father taught me to think and to write what I thought. My mother taught me to care and to love what I care about.

These acknowledgments must conclude with my wife, Caroline, because this project began with three words from her: "Just go write." Caroline has been my trusted partner, my reader, and my navigator. She alone knows how true the dedication to this book is.

Custis-Lee Family Tree

Custis-Lee Family Tree*

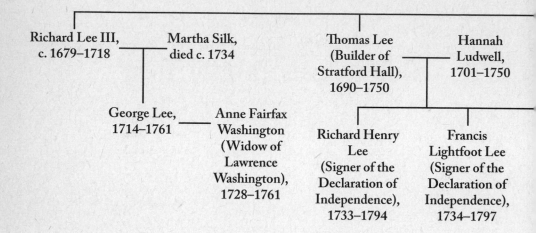

Richard Lee III, c. 1679–1718 —— Martha Silk, died c. 1734

Thomas Lee (Builder of Stratford Hall), 1690–1750 —— Hannah Ludwell, 1701–1750

George Lee, 1714–1761 —— Anne Fairfax Washington (Widow of Lawrence Washington), 1728–1761

Richard Henry Lee (Signer of the Declaration of Independence), 1733–1794

Francis Lightfoot Lee (Signer of the Declaration of Independence), 1734–1797

Henry "Black-Horse Harry" Lee IV, 1787–1837

Only select marriages and children shown.

Charles Carter Lee, 1798–1871

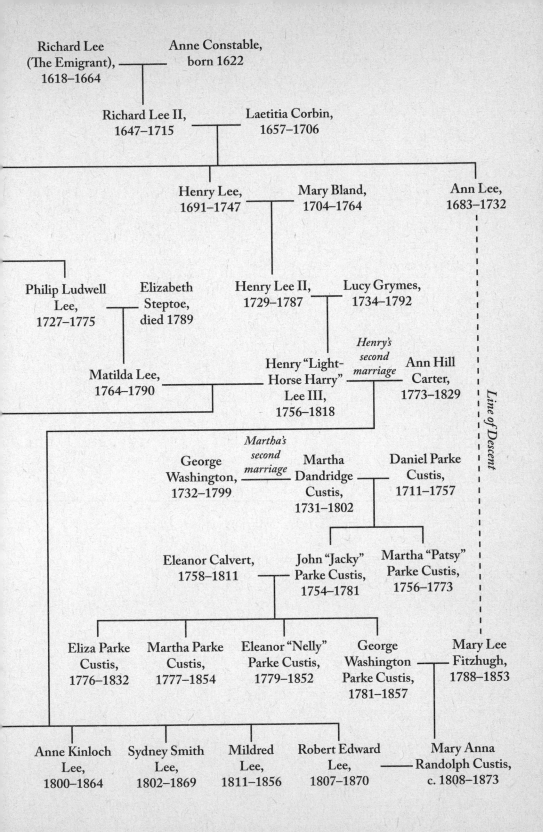

Richard Lee
(The Emigrant),
1618–1664
— Anne Constable,
born 1622

Richard Lee II,
1647–1715
— Laetitia Corbin,
1657–1706

Henry Lee,
1691–1747
— Mary Bland,
1704–1764

Ann Lee,
1683–1732

Philip Ludwell
Lee,
1727–1775
— Elizabeth
Steptoe,
died 1789

Henry Lee II,
1729–1787
— Lucy Grymes,
1734–1792

Matilda Lee,
1764–1790
— Henry "Light-
Horse Harry"
Lee III,
1756–1818
Henry's second marriage
— Ann Hill
Carter,
1773–1829

George
Washington,
1732–1799
Martha's second marriage
Martha
Dandridge
Custis,
1731–1802
— Daniel Parke
Custis,
1711–1757

Eleanor Calvert,
1758–1811
— John "Jacky"
Parke Custis,
1754–1781

Martha "Patsy"
Parke Custis,
1756–1773

Eliza Parke
Custis,
1776–1832

Martha Parke
Custis,
1777–1854

Eleanor "Nelly"
Parke Custis,
1779–1852

George
Washington
Parke Custis,
1781–1857
— Mary Lee
Fitzhugh,
1788–1853

Anne Kinloch
Lee,
1800–1864

Sydney Smith
Lee,
1802–1869

Mildred
Lee,
1811–1856

Robert Edward
Lee,
1807–1870
— Mary Anna
Randolph Custis,
c. 1808–1873

Line of Descent

Notes

*Citations containing incomplete dateline information
for letters reflect omissions in the originals.*

Prologue: The View

1 "Marble Model": Walter A. Watson, *Notes on Southside Virginia*, ed. Constance
 T. Watson (Richmond, 1925; Baltimore: Genealogical Publishing, 1977), 245;
 Elizabeth Lindsay Lomax, *Leaves from an Old Washington Diary, 1854–1863*, ed.
 Lindsay Lomax Wood (New York: E. P. Dutton, 1943), 29.
1 looked up: John S. Mosby, *The Memoirs of Colonel John S. Mosby*, ed. Charles
 Wells Russell (Boston: Little, Brown, 1917), 379.
1 same age: George Washington, Diary, October 2, 1785, in Theodore J. Crackel,
 et al., eds., *The Papers of George Washington Digital Edition* (Charlottesville: University of Virginia Press, Rotunda, 2007).
1 requested: Seventh Day of Secret Session, *Proceedings of the Virginia State Convention of 1861*, in *Secession: Virginia and the Crisis of Union, 1861*, University of
 Richmond, online.
1 "Will the": John Critcher, "Secession Convention," *Virginia Magazine of History
 and Biography* 5, no. 2 (October 1897): 220–21.
1 the Potomac view: Benson J. Lossing, "Arlington House: The Seat of G. W.
 P. Custis, Esq.," *Harper's New Monthly Magazine* 7, no. 40 (September 1853):
 433–54; Thomas B. Bryan, "War Memories," in *Military Essays and Recollections*
 (Chicago: The Dial Press, 1899), vol. 3, 14.
2 the Long Bridge: Douglas Southall Freeman, *R. E. Lee* (New York: Charles
 Scribner's Sons, 1934–1935; Safety Harbor, FL: Simon Publications, 2001), vol.
 1, 438.
2 lantern: Lossing, "Arlington House."
2 reached his decision: Mary Custis Lee to Charles Marshall, [1871], in Elizabeth
 Brown Pryor, "Thou Knowest Not the Time of Thy Visitation," *Virginia Magazine of History and Biography* 119, no. 3 (2011): 277–96.
2 "Lee, Lee,": W. W. Scott, "Some Personal Memories of General Robert E. Lee,"
 William and Mary Quarterly 6, no. 4 (October 1926): 277–88.
2 Strands of silver: J. William Jones, *Life and Letters of Robert Edward Lee: Soldier
 and Man* (New York: Neale Publishing, 1906), 137.
2 stood as Lee: Eighth Day of Secret Session, *Proceedings of the Virginia State Convention of 1861*.
2 "manly bearing": Jubal A. Early, *The Campaigns of Gen. Robert E. Lee* (Baltimore:

257

Notes

John Murphy, 1872), 5; Alexander H. Stephens, *A Constitutional View of the Late War Between the States; Its Causes, Character, Conduct and Results* (Philadelphia: National Publishing, 1870), vol. 2, 384.

2 halfway down the aisle: "Reception of Major General Robert E. Lee," *Charleston Mercury*, April 27, 1861; Freeman, *R. E. Lee*, vol. 1, 465–66. Based on oral tradition, Freeman concludes that Lee took "three short paces" into the chamber even though contemporary accounts suggest that Lee walked halfway down the aisle. Given the aisle's shallowness, Virginia State Capitol historian Mark Greenough explains that the difference between the two versions is very small. The author has gratefully accepted a suggestion to split the difference.

2 "In the eyes": Edward Lee Childe, *The Life and Campaigns of General Lee*, trans. George Litting (London: Chatto and Windus, Piccadilly, 1875), 24.

3 Washington connections: William Allan, "Memoranda of Conversations with General Robert E. Lee," in Gary W. Gallagher, ed., *Lee: The Soldier* (Lincoln: University of Nebraska Press, 1996), 10.

3 as momentous: Seventh Day of Secret Session, *Proceedings of the Virginia State Convention of 1861.*

3 white-haired: "Letter from Leesburgh," *New York Times*, November 1, 1862.

3 "soldiers and sages": Eighth Day of Secret Session, *Proceedings of the Virginia State Convention of 1861.*

3 third cousin twice removed: Frank Grizzard, cited in Crackel, ed., *The Papers of George Washington Digital Edition*; Anthony R. Wagner, "The Queen of England's American Ancestry and Cousinship to Washington and Lee," *New York Genealogical and Biographical Record* 70, no. 3 (July 1939): 201–6.

3 "When the necessity": Eighth Day of Secret Session, *Proceedings of the Virginia State Convention of 1861.*

3 "very best": Winfield Scott to J. B. Floyd, Headquarters of the Army, May 8, 1857, in Jones, *Life and Letters of Robert Edward Lee*, 127.

3 "Virginia having": Eighth Day of Secret Session, *Proceedings of the Virginia State Convention of 1861.*

3 "the Mt. Vernon": Robert E. Lee to Mary Custis Lee, Richmond, April 26, 1861, in Clifford Dowdey and Louis H. Manarin, eds., *The Wartime Papers of Robert E. Lee* (Boston: Da Capo Press, 1961), 13.

4 "we have": Eighth Day of Secret Session, *Proceedings of the Virginia State Convention of 1861.*

4 could have missed: Robert E. Lee Memorandum Book, DeButts-Ely Collection of Lee Family Papers, Library of Congress.

4 "first in war": Henry Lee, *Funeral Oration* (Philadelphia, 1800), 16.

4 "The fact": "Communications," *Alexandria Gazette*, April 29, 1861.

4 "Methinks": Lee, *Funeral Oration*, 17.

5 "like Washington": A. L. Long, *Memoirs of Robert E. Lee: His Military and Personal History*, ed. Marcus J. Wright (London: Sampson Low, Marston, Searle, and Rivington, 1886), 487.

5 "Washington without": B. H. Hill, quoted in J. William Jones, *Personal Reminiscences, Anecdotes, and Letters of Gen. Robert E. Lee* (New York: D. Appleton, 1874), 223.

Notes

5 "two splendid": Fitzhugh Lee, *General Lee* (New York: The University Society, 1905), 415.

5 "modesty": Freeman, *R. E. Lee*, vol. 1, 453. For a twenty-first-century example, see Richard B. McCaslin, *Lee in the Shadow of Washington* (Baton Rouge: Louisiana State University Press, 2001).

6 "Follow the": "Mr. Russell's Letters," *New York Times*, August 15, 1861.

6 "minutiae": Thomas L. Connelly, *The Marble Man: Robert E. Lee and His Image in American Society* (Baton Rouge: Louisiana State University Press, 1977), 96 and 125.

6 "envision": Elizabeth Brown Pryor, *Reading the Man: A Portrait of Robert E. Lee Through His Private Letters* (New York: Viking, 2007), 52–53.

Chapter 1: Foundering Father

11 "a very agreeable": George Washington to Robin, [1749–1750], in John C. Fitzpatrick, ed., *The Writings of George Washington from the Original Manuscript Sources, 1745–1799* (Charlottesville: University of Virginia Library, 2001), online.

11 blue-eyed: Ethel Armes, *Stratford Hall: The Great House of the Lees* (Richmond: Garrett and Massie, 1936), 227.

11 "I believe": McCaslin, *Lee in the Shadow of Washington*, 15.

11 married: Marriage certificate, in Edmund Jennings Lee, *Lee of Virginia, 1642–1892* (Philadelphia, 1895; Westminster, MD: Heritage Books, 2008), 297–98.

12 leased: Paul C. Nagel, *The Lees of Virginia: Seven Generations of an American Family* (New York: Oxford University Press, 1992), 30; Lease of Mount Vernon, December 17, 1754, in Crackel, ed., *The Papers of George Washington Digital Edition*.

12 fifteen thousand: Nagel, *The Lees of Virginia*, 9–14.

12 backlands: Edmund S. Morgan, *American Slavery, American Freedom* (New York: W. W. Norton, 2003), 244–45; Frederick Gutheim, *The Potomac* (Baltimore: The Johns Hopkins University Press, 1986), 44–45.

12 Thomas Lee: Nagel, *The Lees of Virginia*, 33–48.

13 "mother's womb": Lee, *Lee of Virginia, 1642–1892*, 335.

13 "Aunt Martha": McCaslin, *Lee in the Shadow of Washington*, 15.

13 quiet any talk: Undelivered First Inaugural Address, in Crackel, ed., *The Papers of George Washington Digital Edition*.

13 military family: Ron Chernow, *Washington: A Life* (New York: Penguin Books, 2010), 39–45, 217, and 291–96.

14 translations: Thomas E. Templin, *Henry "Light Horse Harry" Lee: A Biography* (University of Kentucky Dissertation, 1975), 30.

14 "first fellows": Lee, *Lee of Virginia, 1642–1892*, 329.

14 shelved plans: Ibid.

14 "That these": David McCullough, *John Adams* (New York: Simon & Schuster, 2001), 118.

14 "band of brothers": John Adams to Richard Bland Lee, Quincy, August 11, 1819, in Lee, *Lee of Virginia, 1642–1892*, 112.

Notes

14   a commission: Lee, *Lee of Virginia, 1642–1892*, 330.

14   these horsemen: Templin, *Henry "Light Horse Harry" Lee*, 46–47.

14   double agents: Henry Lee III to George Washington, October 15 and 18, 1777, in Crackel, ed., *The Papers of George Washington Digital Edition*.

14   "The contest": Henry Lee III to George Washington, January 20, 1778, in ibid.

14   "Fire away": Robert E. Lee, "Life of General Henry Lee," in Henry Lee III, *The Revolutionary Memoirs of General Henry Lee*, ed. Robert E. Lee (New York, 1869; New York: Da Capo Press, 1998), 17.

15   "I needed": George Washington to Henry Lee III, Valley Forge, January 20, 1778, in Crackel, ed., *The Papers of George Washington Digital Edition*.

15   "To have": Henry Lee III to George Washington, Valley Forge, March 31, 1778, in ibid.

15   "exemplary zeal": George Washington to Henry Laurens, Head Quarters, Valley Forge, April 3, 1778, in ibid.

15   hundred horsemen: Templin, *Henry "Light Horse Harry" Lee*, 54.

15   "extremely jealous": Charles Royster, *Light-Horse Harry Lee and the Legacy of the American Revolution* (Baton Rouge: Louisiana State University Press, 1994), 40–42.

15   "Capt. Lees": George Washington to Henry Laurens, Head Quarters, Valley Forge, April 3, 1778, in Crackel, ed., *The Papers of George Washington Digital Edition*.

15   "as fair": Charles Carter Lee, "Recollections of Stratford," Ethel Armes Collection of Lee Family Papers, Library of Congress.

15   "little hero": Royster, *Light-Horse Harry Lee and the Legacy of the American Revolution*, 17–21.

16   "may violate": Lee, "Life of General Henry Lee," 22.

16   "inhumanity": George Washington to Henry Lee III, Head Quarters, New Windsor, July 9, 1779, in Fitzpatrick, ed., *The Writings of George Washington from the Original Manuscript Sources, 1745–1799*, vol. 15.

16   150 prisoners: Templin, *Henry "Light Horse Harry" Lee*, 65–66.

16   "brilliant transaction": George Washington to John Parke Custis, West Point, August 24, 1779, in Fitzpatrick, ed., *The Writings of George Washington from the Original Manuscript Sources, 1745–1799*, vol. 16.

16   Enraged: Templin, *Henry "Light Horse Harry" Lee*, 70–72.

16   "I should be": George Washington to Henry Lee III, Head Quarters, West Point, September 3, 1779, in Fitzpatrick, ed., *The Writings of George Washington from the Original Manuscript Sources, 1745–1799*, vol. 16.

16   "private": Templin, *Henry "Light Horse Harry" Lee*, 73–74.

16   Washington sent: Ibid., 95–97.

16   turning point: Thomas Boyd, *Light-Horse Harry Lee* (New York: Charles Scribner's Sons, 1931), 88–90 and 104.

16   "The British army": Henry Lee III, *Memoirs of the War in the Southern Department of the United States*, in Lee, *The Revolutionary Memoirs of General Henry Lee*, 512.

17   "broken health": Lee, "Life of General Henry Lee," 39.

Notes

17 deflecting: Templin, *Henry "Light Horse Harry" Lee*, 145.

17 family connections: Royster, *Light-Horse Harry Lee and the Legacy of the American Revolution*, 40–42.

17 "the indifference": Henry Lee III to Nathanael Greene, January 26, 1782, quoted in Templin, *Henry "Light Horse Harry" Lee*, 198.

17 "I believe": Nathanael Greene to Henry Lee III, Head-Quarters, January 27, 1782, in Lee, "Life of General Henry Lee," 39.

17 "Envy": Nathanael Greene to Henry Lee III, March 12, 1782, quoted in ibid., 40.

17 "I am candid": Henry Lee III to Nathanael Greene, 1782, quoted in ibid.

18 "the worst road": George Washington, "Diary of Journey over the Mountains," March and April 1748, in Fitzpatrick, ed., *The Writings of George Washington from the Original Manuscript Sources, 1745–1799*, vol. 1.

18 resisted change: John C. Reed Jr., Robert S. Sigafoos, and George W. Fisher, *The River and the Rocks: The Geologic Story of Great Falls and the Potomac River Gorge* (Washington, DC: Government Printing Office, 1980), 1 and 9.

18 named president: Joel Achenbach, *The Grand Idea: George Washington's Potomac and the Race to the West* (New York: Simon & Schuster, 2004), 129.

18 "no doubt": George Washington to Marquis de Lafayette, Mount Vernon, July 25, 1785, in Crackel, ed., *The Papers of George Washington Digital Edition.*

19 "hearing little": Elkanah Watson, "Two of the Richest Days of My Life," in Jean B. Lee, ed., *Experiencing Mount Vernon: Eyewitness Accounts, 1784–1865* (Charlottesville: University of Virginia Press, 2006), 25.

19 "This business": George Washington to Henry Lee III, Mount Vernon, April 5, 1786, in Crackel, ed., *The Papers of George Washington Digital Edition.*

19 five hundred: Royster, *Light-Horse Harry Lee and the Legacy of the American Revolution*, 73 and 75.

19 "The advantages": Henry Lee III to James Madison, Alexandria, October 29, 1788, in Robert A. Rutland and Charles F. Hobson, eds., *The Papers of James Madison* (Charlottesville: University Press of Virginia, 1977), vol. 11, 321–22.

19 "No man": Henry Lee III to James Madison, Alexandria, November 19, 1788, in ibid., 356.

19 "opens a field": George Washington to James Madison, Mount Vernon, November 17, 1788, in Crackel, ed., *The Papers of George Washington Digital Edition.*

19 handful: Royster, *Light-Horse Harry Lee and the Legacy of the American Revolution*, 77.

20 6,595 acres: Nagel, *The Lees of Virginia*, 165.

20 "Nothing but": Henry Lee III to George Washington, Shirley, February 2, 1798, in Crackel, ed., *The Papers of George Washington Digital Edition.*

20 "I shall": Henry Lee III to George Washington, Alexandria, May 22, 1799, in ibid.

20 still in his debt: Eugene E. Prussing, *The Estate of George Washington, Deceased* (Boston: Little, Brown, 1927), 124.

20 "The period": Henry Lee III to George Washington, New York, September 8, 1786, in Crackel, ed., *The Papers of George Washington Digital Edition.*

Notes

20 pressed for news: George Washington to John Fitzgerald, Mount Vernon, September 9, 1786, in ibid.

21 follow-up meeting: Achenbach, *The Grand Idea*, 152–53.

21 "is now submitted": The Virginia Convention Debates, Richmond, June 5, 1788, in John P. Kaminski, Gaspare J. Saladino, Richard Leffler, Charles H. Schoenleber, and Margaret A. Hogan, eds., *The Documentary History of Ratification of the Constitution Digital Edition* (Charlottesville: University of Virginia Press, 2009).

21 "The people of America": The Virginia Convention Debates, Richmond, June 9, 1788, in ibid.

21 "Without you": Henry Lee III to George Washington, New York, September 13, 1788, in Crackel, ed., *The Papers of George Washington Digital Edition*.

21 "one of the number": David Stuart to George Washington, March 15, 1790, quoted in Royster, *Light-Horse Harry Lee and the Legacy of the American Revolution*, 108.

22 tensions surfaced: Gordon S. Wood, *Empire of Liberty: A History of the Early Republic, 1789–1815* (New York: Oxford University Press, 2009), 140–41.

22 opposing the assumption: Henry Lee III to James Madison, Stratford, March 4, 1790, Ethel Armes Collection of Lee Family Papers, Library of Congress.

22 the request: Boyd, *Light-Horse Harry Lee*, 190.

22 "be improper": Henry Lee III to Alexander Hamilton, November 16, 1789, quoted in ibid., 189–90.

22 transition: Royster, *Light-Horse Harry Lee and the Legacy of the American Revolution*, 108 and 204–5.

22 "diabolical": George Washington to Henry Lee III, German Town, August 26, 1794, in Fitzpatrick, ed., *The Writings of George Washington from the Original Manuscript Sources, 1745–1799*, vol. 33.

22 "no economy": Royster, *Light-Horse Harry Lee and the Legacy of the American Revolution*, 77.

23 "paroxysm": George Washington to Henry Lee III, Philadelphia, May 6, 1793, in Crackel, ed., *The Papers of George Washington Digital Edition*.

23 "The awful occasion": Henry Lee III to George Washington, Richmond, August 17, 1794, in ibid.

23 command: Boyd, *Light-Horse Harry Lee*, 224.

23 "an object": Templin, *Henry "Light Horse Harry" Lee*, 420–21.

23 German Lutheran: Resolution of Congress, December 23, 1799, quoted in Lee, *Funeral Oration*.

23 "exchanged": George Washington to Henry Lee III, Philadelphia, July 21, 1793, in Crackel, ed., *The Papers of George Washington Digital Edition*.

24 dark-haired: Armes, *Stratford Hall*, 271–77.

24 "Stop, stop": Samuel Storrow to Dear Sister, September 6, 1821, Ethel Armes Collection of Lee Family Letters, Library of Congress.

24 no carriage: Armes, *Stratford Hall*, 307–8.

24 prison: Boyd, *Light-Horse Harry Lee*, 297–98.

24 "Colonel Lee": "Review," *The Monthly Recorder*, April 1, 1813.

24 majority: Freeman, *R. E. Lee*, vol. 1, 1–2 and 13.

24 live out: Ann Lee to Carter Berkeley, Stratford, November 26, 1809, Ethel Armes Collection of Lee Family Papers, Library of Congress.

Notes

25   holed up: Antony S. Pitch, *The Burning of Washington: The British Invasion of 1814* (Annapolis: Naval Institute Press, 1998), 1–4.

25   knives: "An Exact and Authentic Narrative of the Events Which Took Place in Baltimore, on the 27th & 28th of July Last," *Federal Republican, and Commercial Gazette*, August 14, 1812.

25   slowly recovered: Templin, *Henry "Light Horse Harry" Lee*, 519–20.

25   sad sight: Pryor, *Reading the Man*, 29.

25   sailed down: Freeman, *R. E. Lee*, vol. 1, 15–17.

Chapter 2: A Potomac Son

26   reasons no one: Elers Napier, *The Life and Correspondence of Admiral Sir Charles Napier, K.C.B., From Personal Recollections, Letters, and Official Documents* (London: Hurst and Blackett, 1862), vol. 1, 79–80; *Alexandria Gazette*, September 8, 1814.

26   "laid in": *Alexandria Gazette*, September 8, 1814.

26   illuminated: Napier, *The Life and Correspondence of Admiral Sir Charles Napier*, vol. 1, 78.

26   humiliating terms: *Alexandria Gazette*, September 8, 1814.

26   seven thousand: U.S. Bureau of the Census, Population of the 46 Urban Places: 1810 (1998).

27   lots: Mary G. Powell, *The History of Old Alexandria, Virginia* (Richmond: William Byrd Press, 1928; Westminster, MD: Willow Bend Books, 2000), 33.

27   bottom corner: Proclamation, January 24, 1791, in Crackel, ed., *The Papers of George Washington Digital Edition*.

27   wheat: Gutheim, *The Potomac*, 146–47.

27   "Thanks be": "Capitulation of Fort Warburton and Alexandria," *Richmond Enquirer*, August 31, 1814.

27   "If General": Pitch, *The Burning of Washington*, 133.

27   perhaps they huddled: Freeman, *R. E. Lee*, vol. 1, 29–30; Worth Bailey, *Historic American Buildings Survey: Potts-Fitzhugh House*, ed. Antoinette J. Lee (Washington, DC, 1975), 4.

27   "I have read": Armes, *Stratford Hall*, 315.

28   "If he is": Letter from Henry Lee III, Barbados, September 3, 1813, Ethel Armes Collection of Lee Family Papers, Library of Congress.

28   disappeared at sea: Pryor, *Reading the Man*, 32.

28   "Dwell on": Henry Lee III to Charles Carter Lee, Turk's Island, August 8, 1816, in Lee, "Life of General Henry Lee," 58.

28   "Read therefore": Henry Lee III to Charles Carter Lee, Caicos, September 30, 1816, in ibid., 60.

28   no cost: Boyd, *Light-Horse Harry Lee*, 260–61.

28   "will impress": *Annals of the Congress of the United States*, House, 6th Cong., 2nd session, 802.

28   "Washington's official letters": Letter from Henry Lee III, Barbados, September 3, 1813, Ethel Armes Collection of Lee Family Papers, Library of Congress.

Notes

29 "Avoid debt": Henry Lee III to Charles Carter Lee, Nassau, September 3, 1817, in Lee, "Life of General Henry Lee," 73.

29 "ardent": Royster, *Light-Horse Harry Lee*, 201–2.

29 "The rocks": Charles Carter Lee to Ann Lee, Cambridge, January 31, 1819, Lee Family Digital Archive, Washington and Lee University.

29 "As there is": Ann Lee to Charles Carter Lee, Alexandria, July 17, 1816, Ethel Armes Collection of Lee Family Papers, Library of Congress.

30 "wages of": Charles Carter Lee, "Recollections of Stratford," Ethel Armes Collection of Lee Family Papers, Library of Congress.

30 "You must repel": Ann Lee to Sydney Smith Lee, Georgetown, April 10, 1827, Ethel Armes Collection of Lee Family Papers, Library of Congress.

30 "Whip": Freeman, *R. E. Lee*, vol. 1, 30–31.

30 letters arrived: Henry Lee IV to Ann Lee, April 7, 1818, George Bolling Lee Papers, Virginia Historical Society; James Causten to Ann Lee, Baltimore, April 11, 1818, George Bolling Lee Papers, Virginia Historical Society.

30 "outdoor agent": Robert E. Lee to Mary Custis Lee, Camp Cooper, Texas, June 15, 1857, DeButts-Ely Collection of Lee Family Papers, Library of Congress.

30 pleasure: Edward V. Valentine, "Reminiscences of General Lee," in Franklin L. Riley, ed., *General Robert E. Lee After Appomattox* (New York: MacMillan, 1922), 150; Emily V. Mason, *Popular Life of Gen. Robert Edward Lee* (Baltimore: John Murphy, 1872), 23–24.

30 "devoted daughter": Marietta Fauntleroy Turner Powell to My Dear Nannie, Oakley, July 17, 1886, in Marietta Minnigerode Andrews, *Scraps of Paper* (New York: E. P. Dutton, 1929), 198.

30 "housekeeper": Mason, *Popular Life of Gen. Robert Edward Lee*, 22–23.

30 "At the hour": Ibid.

31 "I have been": Robert E. Lee to Mary Custis, Baltimore, October 30, 1830, in Robert E. L. deButts Jr., "Lee in Love: Courtship and Correspondence in Antebellum Virginia," *Virginia Magazine of History and Biography* 115, no. 4 (2007): 486–575.

31 Robert studied: Powell, *The History of Old Alexandria, Virginia*, 153–54.

31 "poor": The Will of George Washington, Mount Vernon, in Prussing, *The Estate of George Washington, Deceased*, 45–46.

31 trained troops: Freeman, *R. E. Lee,* vol. 1, 21 and 29.

31 supposedly visited: Gay Montague Moore, *Seaport in Virginia: George Washington's Alexandria* (Richmond: Garrett and Massie, 1949), 202.

31 locket: "A Lee Miscellany," *Virginia Magazine of History and Biography* 33, no. 4 (October 1925): 371; Armes, *Stratford Hall*, 277.

31 divided biographers: Freeman, *R. E. Lee*, vol. 1, 22 and 453; Pryor, *Reading the Man*, 51–53.

31 "The name": "Washington's Birthday," February 22, 1858, in Walt Whitman, *I Sit and Look Out: Editorials from the Brooklyn Daily Times*, ed. Emory Holloway and Vernolian Schwarz (New York: Columbia University Press, 1932), 59.

32 "Every thing": "Tomb of Washington," *National Intelligencer*, December 19, 1818, in Lee, ed., *Experiencing Mount Vernon*, 105.

32 Washington's Birthday: Barry Schwartz, *George Washington: The Making of an American Symbol* (New York: Free Press, 1987), 33.

Notes

32 "The sculptor": *Annals of the Congress of the United States*, House, 6th Cong., 2nd session, 862–63.

32 sixty: Wood, *Empire of Liberty*, 555.

32 Robert's mother: Freeman, *R. E. Lee*, vol. 1, 23.

32 tavern walls: Charles Dickens, *American Notes for General Circulation* (London: Chapman and Hall, 1842), vol. 1, 212.

32 "magical power": Richard W. Van Alstyne, *Genesis of American Nationalism* (Waltham, MA: Blaisdell Publishing, 1970), 161–62.

32 follow in: George B. Forgie, *Patricide in the House Divided: A Psychological Interpretation of Lincoln and His Age* (New York: W. W. Norton, 1979), 28–29.

32 "Especially should": Kate Berry, "How Can An American Woman Serve Her Country," *Godey's Lady's Book* 43 (1851): 362–65.

32 Hundreds: Schwartz, *George Washington*, 194.

32 "Washington, you know": Edward G. Lengel, *Inventing George Washington: America's Founder, in Myth and Memory* (New York: Harper, 2011), 19–22.

33 "every youth": M. L. Weems, *The Life of George Washington; With Curious Anecdotes, Equally Honourable to Himself and Exemplary to His Young Countrymen*, 10th ed. (Philadelphia: Mathew Carey, 1810), 7.

33 "the earliest": Address to the New Jersey Senate at Trenton, NJ, February 21, 1861, in Don E. Fehrenbacher, ed., *Abraham Lincoln: Speeches and Writings, 1859–1865* (New York: Library of America, 1989), 209.

33 "The author": Weems, *The Life of George Washington*, title page.

33 "speaks greatly": Robert E. Lee and Mary Custis Lee to George Washington Parke Custis, August 25, 1837, Robert E. Lee Papers, University of Virginia.

33 being a surrogate son: Chernow, *Washington*, 296.

33 "Treat him": Harlow Giles Unger, *Lafayette* (New York: John Wiley & Sons, 2002), 45–46 and 194.

33 six-thousand-mile: Ibid., 354.

34 "The citizens": "Reception of Gen. La Fayette in Alexandria," *Alexandria Gazette*, October 19, 1824.

34 visit Ann Lee: *Alexandria Gazette*, December 16, 1824; Benjamin Hallowell, *Autobiography of Benjamin Hallowell* (Philadelphia: Friends' Book Association, 1883), 100.

34 "enterprising": Marquis de Lafayette to Henry Lee III, Light Camp, August 27, 1780, in Lee, "Life of General Henry Lee," 27.

34 Long Bridge: A. Levasseur, *Lafayette in America in 1824 and 1825; or, Journal of a Voyage to the United States*, trans. John D. Godman (Philadelphia: Carey and Lea, 1829), vol. 1, 180.

34 honorary marshal: Rose Mortimer Ellzey MacDonald, *Mrs. Robert E. Lee* (Boston: Ginn, 1939), 23.

34 impressive figure: Lee, *General Lee*, 26.

34 blue sash: "Gen. La Fayette in Virginia," *Richmond Enquirer*, October 26, 1824.

34 trim waist: Edward Clifford Gordon, "Recollections of General Robert E. Lee's Administration as President of Washington College, Virginia," in Riley, ed., *General Robert E. Lee After Appomattox*, 78.

34 deepening chest: Long, *Memoirs of Robert E. Lee*, 19.

34 ruddy face: John Esten Cooke, *A Life of Gen. Robert E. Lee* (New York: D. Appleton, 1871), 37.

34 Fifteen hundred: "Reception of Gen. La Fayette in Alexandria," *Alexandria Gazette*, October 19, 1824.

34 "the multitude": *Daily National Intelligencer*, October 18, 1824.

34 young heiress: MacDonald, *Mrs. Robert E. Lee*, 23.

34 short: Marietta Fauntleroy Turner Powell to My Dear Nannie, Oakley, July 17, 1886, in Andrews, *Scraps of Paper*, 202.

34 red-faced: Mary Custis Lee, "Memoir of George Washington Parke Custis," in George Washington Parke Custis, *Recollections and Private Memoirs of Washington* (New York: Derby & Jackson, 1860; Bridgewater, VA: American Foundation Publications, 1999), 72.

34 carriage behind: "Reception of Gen. La Fayette in Alexandria," *Alexandria Gazette*, October 19, 1824.

34 distant cousin: Nagel, *The Lees of Virginia*, 235.

34 owned: Bailey, *Historic American Buildings Survey*, 2–4.

34 "all a father": Robert E. Lee to Markie Williams, West Point, January 2, 1854, in Avery Craven, ed., *"To Markie": The Letters of Robert E. Lee to Martha Custis Williams* (Cambridge: Harvard University Press, 1933), 39.

35 cannons: Levasseur, *Lafayette in America in 1824 and 1825*, vol. 1, 181.

35 "pleasantly situated": Achenbach, *The Grand Idea*, 5.

35 knees: Levasseur, *Lafayette in America in 1824 and 1825*, vol. 1, 181.

35 dilapidated: "Tomb of Washington," *National Intelligencer*, December 19, 1818, in Lee, ed., *Experiencing Mount Vernon*, 104.

35 "At this awful": Custis, *Recollections and Private Memoirs of Washington*, 592.

35 blue-eyed: Chernow, *Washington*, 421.

35 "It was in": Custis, *Recollections and Private Memoirs of Washington*, 484.

35 Custis estate: Patricia Brady, *Martha Washington: An American Life* (New York: Viking, 2005), 54; Helen Bryan, *Martha Washington: First Lady of Liberty* (New York: John Wiley & Sons, 2002), 77.

36 financial freedom: Chernow, *Washington*, 98–100.

36 epilepsy: Ibid., 161.

36 indolence: Murray H. Nelligan, *Old Arlington: The Story of the Lee Mansion National Memorial* (Columbia University Dissertation, 1953), 9–15.

36 "Nothing": John Parke Custis to George Washington, New Kent, July 15, 1778, in Crackel, ed., *The Papers of George Washington Digital Edition*.

36 family lore: Eliza Parke Custis to David Baillie Warden, April 20, 1808, in William D. Hoyt Jr., "Self-Portrait: Eliza Custis, 1808," *Virginia Magazine of History and Biography* 53, no. 2 (April 1945): 89–100.

36 Catching a fatal: Nelligan, *Old Arlington*, 29–30.

36 "From this": Custis, *Recollections and Private Memoirs of Washington*, 255.

36 "domestic habits": Ibid., 121–22.

36 woke early: Ibid., 162–71.

37 white horses: Ibid., 397.

37 cornerstone: Nelligan, *Old Arlington*, 39.

37 "indulgent": Augusta Blanche Berard to Mother and Sisters, Pelham Priory,

Notes

April 18, 1856, in Clayton Torrence, "Arlington and Mount Vernon, 1856," *Virginia Magazine of History and Biography* 57, no. 2 (April 1949): 140–75.

37 "Grandmamma": Lee, "Memoir of George Washington Parke Custis," 38.

37 "You are now": George Washington to George Washington Parke Custis, Philadelphia, November 28, 1796, in Custis, *Recollections and Private Memoirs of Washington*, 75.

37 Desperate: George Washington Parke Custis to George Washington, Nassau Hall, May 29, 1797, in ibid., 84–85.

37 expulsion: Nelligan, *Old Arlington*, 43.

37 "Mr. Custis": George Washington to Mr. McDowell, Mount Vernon, March 5, 1798, in Custis, *Recollections and Private Memoirs of Washington*, 98.

37 experiment: Nelligan, *Old Arlington*, 47.

37 own finances: George Washington to Mr. McDowell, Mount Vernon, September 2, 1798, in Custis, *Recollections and Private Memoirs of Washington*, 111–13.

37 "What is best": George Washington to David Stuart, Mount Vernon, January 22, 1799, in ibid., 115.

37 Bushrod Washington: The Will of George Washington, in Prussing, *The Estate of George Washington, Deceased*, 60–62.

37 tree-covered: Nelligan, *Old Arlington*, 1–2.

37 attempt to buy: Rosalie S. Calvert to Jean Charles Stier, Mont Alban, July 3, 1802, in William D. Hoyt Jr., ed., "The Calvert-Stier Correspondence: Letters from America to the Low Countries, 1797–1828," *Maryland Historical Magazine* 38, no. 2 (June 1943): 123–40.

38 "every thing": Levasseur, *Lafayette in America in 1824 and 1825*, vol. 1, 182.

38 these treasures: The Will of Martha Washington of Mount Vernon, in Prussing, *The Estate of George Washington, Deceased*, 389–90.

38 carriage: Public Sales, in ibid., 451 and 453.

38 debt: Nelligan, *Old Arlington*, 58–59.

38 dampness: Mary Custis Lee to Laura C. Holloway, quoted in Charles W. Snell, "Construction of Arlington House, 1802–1818," *Arlington House: Historic Structures Report*, ed. Harlan D. Unrau (Denver: National Park Service, 1985), vol. 1, online.

38 new home: Nelligan, *Old Arlington*, 70–76 and 144–49.

38 amateur: Lee, "Memoir of George Washington Parke Custis," 68; Lossing, "Arlington House: The Seat of G. W. P. Custis, Esq."

38 "in precisely": Lossing, "Arlington House."

38 sheep-shearing festival: Lee, "Memoir of George Washington Parke Custis," 64–65; Nelligan, *Old Arlington*, 67, 86, and 93.

39 "melodious": Lee, "Memoir of George Washington Parke Custis," 72.

39 tedious: Pryor, *Reading the Man*, 51.

39 "the finest": Jonathan Elliot, *Historical Sketches of the Ten Miles Square Forming the District of Columbia; With a Picture of Washington, Describing Objects of General Interest or Curiosity at the Metropolis of the Union* (Washington, DC: J. Elliot Jr., 1830), 292.

39 met him: Pryor, *Reading the Man*, 48.

39 "My affections": Robert E. Lee to Markie Williams, West Point, March 15, 1854, in Craven, ed., *"To Markie,"* 43.

39 reaffirmed: Stephen E. Ambrose, *Duty, Honor, Country: A History of West Point* (Baltimore: Johns Hopkins University Press, 1999), 13–14.

39 250 cadets: Freeman, *R. E. Lee*, vol. 1, 37–38.

39 "drew each": Letter from Benjamin Hallowell, in Mason, *Popular Life of Gen. Robert Edward Lee*, 25.

39 opposed: Robert E. Lee to Mary Custis, May 13, 1831, in deButts, "Lee in Love."

39 could not imagine: Mason, *Popular Life of Gen. Robert Edward Lee*, 23.

39 Applications poured in: Freeman, *R. E. Lee*, vol. 1, 43–44.

39 the staunch: Merrill D. Peterson, *The Great Triumvirate: Webster, Clay, and Calhoun* (New York: Oxford University Press, 1987), 84–95.

40 "lose no time": William H. Fitzhugh to John C. Calhoun, Ravensworth, February 7, 1824, in Freeman, *R. E. Lee*, vol. 1, 38–39.

40 "gentlemanly deportment": Letter from W. B. Leary, in ibid., vol. 1, 40.

40 "excellent disposition": R. S. Garnett to John C. Calhoun, Washington, DC, February 16, 1824, in ibid., vol. 1, 40–41.

40 "interested herself": Sally Lee to Mary Custis Lee, Gordonsville, November 10, 1870, DeButts-Ely Collection of Lee Family Papers, Library of Congress; Long, *Memoirs of Robert E. Lee*, 28.

Chapter 3: Lee's Union

41 "engrossed": Marietta Fauntleroy Turner Powell to My Dear Nannie, Oakley, July 17, 1886, in Andrews, *Scraps of Paper*, 198.

41 saplings: Sally Nelson Robins, "Mrs. Lee During the War," in R. A. Brock, ed., *Gen. Robert Edward Lee: Soldier, Citizen and Christian Patriot* (Richmond: B. F. Johnson, 1897), 323.

41 Christmas kiss: deButts, "Lee in Love."

41 imitated: Mary Tyler Freeman Cheek, "A Brief Historical Note," in Mary Custis Lee deButts, ed., *Growing Up in the 1850s: The Journal of Agnes Lee* (Chapel Hill: University of North Carolina Press, 1984).

41 "rather irregular": Nelligan, *Old Arlington*, 80.

41 "striking resemblance": Henry S. Foote, *Casket of Reminiscences* (Washington, DC: Chronicle Publishing, 1874), 16–17.

41 grew stronger: Lee, *General Lee*, 415.

41 high marks: Chernow, *Washington*, 410.

41 shocked stares: Robins, "Mrs. Lee During the War," 328–29.

41 "rank and bringing up": Foote, *Casket of Reminiscences*, 16.

41 "addicted to": Freeman, *R. E. Lee*, vol. 1, 108.

42 her pen pals: Pryor, *Reading the Man*, 73–76.

42 letters actually arrived: Mildred Lee to Mary Custis, West River, December 23, 1829, George Bolling Lee Papers, Virginia Historical Society.

42 tardiness: Robert E. Lee Jr., *Recollections and Letters of General Robert E. Lee* (New York: Doubleday, Page, 1904), 12.

Notes

42 anxious suitors: Robert E. Lee to Charles Carter Lee, Cockspur, May 8, 1830, Robert E. Lee Papers, University of Virginia.

42 "Would Washington": Chernow, *Washington*, 98.

42 "the representative": Childe, *The Life and Campaigns of General Lee*, 24.

42 "novel situation": Robert E. Lee to Charles Carter Lee, Old Point, June 15, 1831, Robert E. Lee Papers, University of Virginia.

42 Sam Houston: Marquis James, *The Raven: A Biography of Sam Houston* (Indianapolis: Bobbs-Merrill, 1929; Norwalk, CT: Easton Press, 1988), 55–56.

42 "impregnable fortress": Mildred Lee to Mary Custis, West River, November 4, 1829, George Bolling Lee Papers, Virginia Historical Society; Pryor, *Reading the Man*, 74.

42 adjusted better: Freeman, *R. E. Lee*, vol. 1, 48–85; Ann Lee to Smith Lee, Georgetown, April 10, 1827, Ethel Armes Collection of Lee Family Papers, Library of Congress.

42 "Though firm": Freeman, *R. E. Lee*, vol. 1, 68.

43 "attractive manners": Marietta Fauntleroy Turner Powell to My Dear Nannie, Oakley, July 17, 1886, in Andrews, *Scraps of Paper*, 199.

43 graduated: Register of the Officers and Cadets of the US Military Academy, June 1829.

43 "splendid-looking": Marietta Fauntleroy Turner Powell to My Dear Nannie, Oakley, July 17, 1886, in Andrews, *Scraps of Paper*, 199.

43 he theirs: Robert E. Lee to John Mackay, St. Louis, October 22, 1837, Mackay-McQueen Family Papers, National Society Colonial Dames of America, Georgia Historical Society.

43 "wretched" or "miserable": Robert E. Lee to Mary Custis, Cockspur, November 11, 1830, in deButts, "Lee in Love"; Robert E. Lee to Mary Custis, May 13, 1831, in ibid.

43 "naturally inclined": Robert E. Lee to Mary Custis, Fortress Monroe, May 24, 1831, Mary Custis Lee Papers, Virginia Historical Society.

43 "my gravity": Robert E. Lee to Markie Williams, Lexington, January 1, 1868, in Craven, ed., *"To Markie,"* 79.

43 "vent": Robert E. Lee to Mary Custis, Baltimore, October 30, 1830, in deButts, "Lee in Love."

43 "I am not very": Robert E. Lee to Mary Custis, Cockspur, March 8, 1831, in ibid.

43 "own way": Robert E. Lee to Mary Custis, June 3, 1831, Mary Custis Lee Papers, Virginia Historical Society; Robert E. Lee to Mary Custis, June 12, 1831, in deButts, "Lee in Love."

43 "owed every thing": Jones, *Personal Reminiscences, Anecdotes, and Letters of Gen. Robert E. Lee*, 366.

43 "If R[obert]": Sally Lee to Mary Custis Lee, Gordonsville, November 10, 1870, DeButts-Ely Collection of Lee Family Papers, Library of Congress; Long, *Memoirs of Robert E. Lee*, 26.

44 July 1829: *National Intelligencer*, July 29, 1829, in Armes, *Stratford Hall*, 390–92.

44 paced: Edmund Jennings Lee, "The Character of General Lee," in Brock, ed., *Gen. Robert Edward Lee*, 383.

44 yesterday: Lee, *Recollections and Letters of General Robert E. Lee*, 363.

44   playful: Marietta Fauntleroy Turner Powell to My Dear Nannie, Oakley, July 17, 1886, in Andrews, *Scraps of Paper*, 199.

44   "I remember his": Mildred Lee to Mary Custis, West River, August 22, 1829, George Bolling Lee Papers, Virginia Historical Society.

44   ordered Lee: Freeman, *R. E. Lee*, vol. 1, 94.

44   "acute pangs": Mildred Lee to Mary Custis, West River, December 23, 1829, George Bolling Lee Papers, Virginia Historical Society.

44   "Beware": Mildred Lee to Mary Custis, West River, November 4, 1829, George Bolling Lee Papers, Virginia Historical Society.

44   between the tides: Robert E. Lee to Mary Custis, Cockspur, December 1, 1830, in deButts, "Lee in Love." In giving these descriptions, the author has assumed that Lee's first year at Cockspur was similar to his second.

44   backbreaking: Emory M. Thomas, *Robert E. Lee* (New York: W. W. Norton, 1997), 58; Robert E. Lee to Charles Carter Lee, Cockspur, May 8, 1830, Robert E. Lee Papers, University of Virginia; Robert E. Lee to Mary Custis, Cockspur, November 11, 1830, in deButts, "Lee in Love."

44   "Tell Cousin": Robert E. Lee to Charles Carter Lee, Cockspur, May 8, 1830, Robert E. Lee Papers, University of Virginia.

45   "flower of": "Death of WM. H. Fitzhugh," *Washington Daily National Journal*, May 26, 1830.

45   "the vanity of earthly": Mary Custis Lee Diary, July 22, 1830, Lee Family Papers, Virginia Historical Society.

45   rededicate her life: Mary Custis Lee Diary, July 4, 1830, Lee Family Papers, Virginia Historical Society.

45   "wept": Mary Custis Lee Diary, July 8, 1830, Lee Family Papers, Virginia Historical Society.

45   sheltered: Robert E. Lee to Mary Custis, May 24, 1831, Mary Custis Lee Papers, Virginia Historical Society; Robert E. Lee to Mary Custis, Old Point, January 10, 1831, in deButts, "Lee in Love."

45   "sinful Robert": Robert E. Lee to Mary Custis, Cockspur, January 10, 1830, in ibid.

45   "expect miracles": Robert E. Lee to Mary Custis, Cockspur, November 19, 1830, in ibid.

45   "Oh draw him": Mary Custis Lee Diary, July 10, 1830, Lee Family Papers, Virginia Historical Society.

46   "Mary, Robert": Robins, "Mrs. Lee During the War," 323.

46   "I am engaged": Robert E. Lee to Charles Carter Lee, Arlington, September 22, 1830, Robert E. Lee Papers, University of Virginia.

46   "good enough": Pryor, *Reading the Man*, 79; Henry Lee IV to Charles Carter Lee, Paris, February 16, 1831, Charles Carter Lee Papers, University of Virginia.

46   national political scandal: *Alexandria Gazette*, June 7, 1830.

46   "Black-Horse": Nagel, *The Lees of Virginia*, 203–18.

46   views on marriage: Chernow, *Washington*, 86.

47   "This is not": George Washington to George Washington Parke Custis, Mount Vernon, June 13, 1798, in Custis, *Recollections and Private Memoirs of Washington*, 106.

Notes

47 "revel in": George Washington to Elizabeth Parke Custis, German Town, September 14, 1794, in Crackel, ed., *The Papers of George Washington Digital Edition.*

47 "long years": Robert E. Lee to Mary Custis, June 3, 1831, Mary Custis Lee Papers, Virginia Historical Society.

47 "I thought": Robert E. Lee to Mary Custis, May 13, 1831, in deButts, "Lee in Love."

47 ancestors: Robert E. Lee to George Washington Custis Lee, Coosawhatchie, South Carolina, January 19, 1862, in Dowdey and Manarin, eds., *The Wartime Papers of Robert E. Lee*, 105.

47 "Never marry": J. B. Hood, *Advance and Retreat: Personal Experiences in the United States and Confederate States Armies* (New Orleans: G. T. Beauregard, 1880), 8.

47 "merit-discerning": "Memoir of the Late Major General Henry Lee, Commandant of the Partisan Legion, in the War of the Revolution," *Daily National Intelligencer*, August 26, 1828.

48 "Whenever I think": Robert E. Lee to Mary Custis, Cockspur, February 1, 1831, Mary Custis Lee Papers, Virginia Historical Society.

48 "mind was": Robert E. Lee to Mary Custis, Cockspur, November 11, 1830, in deButts, "Lee in Love."

48 "Nearly all": Robert E. Lee to Charles Carter Lee, Savannah, November 16, 1830, Robert E. Lee Papers, University of Virginia.

48 "I can scarcely": Robert E. Lee to Mary Custis, Cockspur, January 10, 1831, in deButts, "Lee in Love."

48 "I have not seen": Ibid.

49 kisses: Robert E. Lee to Mary Custis, Cockspur, December 28, 1830, in ibid.

49 "If you choose": Robert E. Lee to Mary Custis, Cockspur, March 8, 1831, in ibid.

49 "felt so grateful": Robert E. Lee to Mary Custis, Cockspur, April 3, 1831, in ibid.

49 "as soon as": Robert E. Lee to Mary Custis, Cockspur, April 11, 1831, Mary Custis Lee Papers, Virginia Historical Society.

49 "gentlemanly": Robert E. Lee to Mary Custis, Old Point, May 13, 1831, in deButts, "Lee in Love."

49 Talcott's sister: Robert E. Lee to Mary Custis, June 3, 1831, Mary Custis Lee Papers, Virginia Historical Society.

49 questions: Robert E. Lee to Mary Custis, Fortress Monroe, May 24, 1831, Mary Custis Lee Papers, Virginia Historical Society.

49 "a closet": Robert E. Lee to Mary Custis, June 12, 1831, in deButts, "Lee in Love."

49 "hand at housekeeping": Robert E. Lee to Mary Custis, Fortress Monroe, May 24, 1831, Mary Custis Lee Papers, Virginia Historical Society.

49 "We will have": Robert E. Lee to Mary Custis, June 3, 1831, Mary Custis Lee Papers, Virginia Historical Society.

50 "Fortune has never": Mildred Lee to Mary Custis, West River, December 23, 1829, George Bolling Lee Papers, Virginia Historical Society.

50 "The change": Robert E. Lee to Mary Custis, Old Point, June 21, 1831, in deButts, "Lee in Love."

50 cloudless: Margaret Sanborn, *Robert E. Lee: A Portrait, 1807–1861* (Philadelphia: J. B. Lippincott, 1966), 84.

50 told Mary: Robert E. Lee to Mary Custis, Old Point, June 21, 1831, in deButts, "Lee in Love."

50 rain: Marietta Fauntleroy Turner Powell to My Dear Nannie, Oakley, July 17, 1886, in Andrews, *Scraps of Paper*, 203; Joseph Packard, *Recollections of a Long Life*, ed. Thomas J. Packard (Washington, DC: Byron S. Adams, 1902), 157.

50 offered to send: Robert E. Lee to Mary Custis, June 12, 1831, in deButts, "Lee in Love."

50 wobbling: MacDonald, *Mrs. Robert E. Lee*, 39–40.

50 horseback: Packard, *Recollections of a Long Life*, 157.

50 "far as inches": Marietta Fauntleroy Turner Powell to My Dear Nannie, Oakley, July 17, 1886, in Andrews, *Scraps of Paper*, 202.

50 "woebegone": Packard, *Recollections of a Long Life*, 157; Note on General Lee's Wedding, January 28, 1901, Papers of Armistead Peter Jr., Tudor Place.

51 playing the piano: Sanborn, *Robert E. Lee*, 85.

51 "bold as a sheep": Robert E. Lee to Andrew Talcott, Ravensworth, July 13, 1831, Robert E. Lee Papers, Virginia Historical Society.

51 "well-behaved": Marietta Minnigerode Andrews, *Memoirs of a Poor Relation: Being the Story of a Post-War Southern Girl and Her Battle with Destiny* (New York: E. P. Dutton, 1927), 89–91.

51 "bounteously dispensed": Long, *Memoirs of Robert E. Lee*, 38.

51 "hell-fire": Andrews, *Memoirs of a Poor Relation*, 91.

51 "What can I say": Mary Custis Lee Diary, July 3, 1831, Lee Family Papers, Virginia Historical Society.

51 "I would tell": Robert E. Lee to Andrew Talcott, Ravensworth, July 13, 1831, Robert E. Lee Papers, Virginia Historical Society.

51 "I have dictated": Mary Fitzhugh Custis to Mary Custis Lee, Arlington, August 10, 1831, Custis-Lee-Mason Papers, Library of Virginia.

52 strange haze: Stephen B. Oates, *The Fires of Jubilee: Nat Turner's Fierce Rebellion* (New York: Harper & Row, 1975), 54–55.

52 axes and hatchets: Ibid., 69–97.

52 By the time: Mary Custis Lee and Robert E. Lee to Mary Fitzhugh Custis, Old Point, Sunday, Lee Family Papers, Virginia Historical Society.

52 Sixty: Oates, *The Fires of Jubilee*, 126.

52 "the whites": Mary Custis Lee and Robert E. Lee to Mary Fitzhugh Custis, Old Point, Sunday, Lee Family Papers, Virginia Historical Society.

52 Virginia lawmakers: Oates, *The Fires of Jubilee*, 135–41.

52 "but little time": Mary Custis Lee and Robert E. Lee to Mary Fitzhugh Custis, Old Point, Sunday, Lee Family Papers, Virginia Historical Society.

52 "I took": Mary Fitzhugh Custis to Mary Custis Lee, October 13, Mary Custis Lee Papers, Virginia Historical Society.

52 what she could: Mary Custis Lee to Mary Fitzhugh Custis, Old Point, Saturday, Lee Family Papers, Virginia Historical Society; Mary Custis Lee and Robert E. Lee to Mary Fitzhugh Custis, Old Point, Sunday, Lee Family Papers, Virginia Historical Society; Mary Fitzhugh Custis to Mary Custis Lee, Wednesday Night, Mary Custis Lee Papers, Virginia Historical Society.

53 "We ought not": Robert E. Lee to Mary Custis Lee, Old Point, April 24, 1832, Lee Family Papers, Virginia Historical Society.

53 "profit by example": Mary Fitzhugh Custis to Mary Custis Lee, Arlington, August 10, 1831, Custis-Lee-Mason Papers, Library of Virginia.

53 "He does scold": Mary Custis Lee to Mary Fitzhugh Custis, Old Point, Saturday, Lee Family Papers, Virginia Historical Society.

53 "experience": Mary Fitzhugh Custis to Mary Custis Lee, Wednesday Night, Mary Custis Lee Papers, Virginia Historical Society; Pryor, *Reading the Man*, 86.

53 "affection": Robert E. Lee to Markie Williams, West Point, January 2, 1854, in Craven, ed., *"To Markie,"* 39.

53 neglected: Robert E. Lee to Charles Carter Lee, Washington, May 2, 1836, Robert E. Lee Papers, University of Virginia.

53 "often in want": Nelligan, *Old Arlington*, 188.

53 "As I knew": Robert E. Lee to George Washington Parke Custis, Old Point, May 22, 1832, Robert E. Lee Papers, Duke University.

53 "withdraw Robert": Mary Fitzhugh Custis to Mary Custis Lee, Arlington, October 6, 1831, Mary Lee Fitzhugh Custis Papers, Virginia Historical Society.

54 preparations: Nelligan, *Old Arlington*, 213–14.

54 sister Eliza: "Died," *Alexandria Gazette*, January 9, 1832; Eliza Parke Custis to David Baille Warden, April 20, 1808, in Hoyt, "Self-Portrait: Eliza Custis, 1808."

54 new vault: John A. Washington to George C. Washington, March 4, 1831 and Harrison H. Dodge to L. B. Cox, December 12, 1898, compiled for the author by Mary V. Thompson, Fred W. Smith National Library for the Study of George Washington at Mount Vernon (hereafter called Mount Vernon).

54 same time: Robert E. Lee to Mary Custis, Cockspur, April 20, 1831, Mary Custis Lee Papers, Virginia Historical Society.

54 "There was a melancholy": Robert E. Lee and Mary Custis Lee to E. A. Stiles, Arlington, January 4, 1832, Mackay-McQueen Family Papers, National Society Colonial Dames of America, Georgia Historical Society.

54 planned to stay: Robert E. Lee to Mary Custis Lee, Fortress Monroe, March 28, 1832, Lee Family Papers, Virginia Historical Society.

54 shorter: Robert E. Lee to Mary Custis Lee, Old Point, June 2, 1832, Lee Family Papers, Virginia Historical Society.

54 Steamboat delays: Robert E. Lee to Mary Custis Lee, Old Point, June 6, 1832, in Norma B. Cuthbert, "To Molly: Five Early Letters from Robert E. Lee to His Wife, 1832–1835," *Huntington Library Quarterly* 15, no. 3 (May 1952): 257–276.

54 "This will never": Robert E. Lee to Mary Custis Lee, Old Point, May 19, 1832, Lee Family Papers, Virginia Historical Society.

55 "Hasten down": Robert E. Lee to Mary Custis Lee, April 24, 1832, Lee Family Papers, Virginia Historical Society.

55 comfort: Robert E. Lee to Mary Custis Lee, April 17, 1832, in Cuthbert, "To Molly: Five Early Letters from Robert E. Lee to His Wife, 1832–1835."

55 "I cannot consent": Robert E. Lee to Mary Custis Lee, May 19, 1832, Lee Family Papers, Virginia Historical Society.

55 finally arrive: Robert E. Lee to Mary Custis Lee, Old Point, June 6, 1832, in Cuthbert, "To Molly: Five Early Letters from Robert E. Lee to His Wife, 1832–1835"; Mary Fitzhugh Custis to George Washington Parke Custis, Old Point, June, Custis-Lee-Mason Papers, Library of Virginia.

55 "I do not": Robert E. Lee to Mary Fitzhugh Custis, Old Point, September 17, 1832, Custis-Lee Family Papers, Library of Congress.

55 George Washington Custis Lee: Custis Family Bible, Custis-Lee Family Papers, Library of Congress.

Chapter 4: Half Slave, Half Free

59 rode over: Lee, *Recollections and Letters of General Robert E. Lee*, 3–4.

59 two years earlier: Robert E. Lee to Charles Carter Lee, Arlington, September 1, 1846, Robert E. Lee Papers, University of Virginia.

59 furrows: Robert E. Lee to Sydney Smith Lee, Arlington, June 30, 1848, in Lee, *General Lee*, 49–50.

59 majestic stature: Marietta Fauntleroy Turner Powell to My Dear Nannie, Oakley, July 17, 1886, in Andrews, *Scraps of Paper*, 199.

59 Spec: Lee, *Recollections and Letters of General Robert E. Lee*, 6–8.

59 astonishment: Robert E. Lee to Sydney Smith Lee, Arlington, June 30, 1848, in Lee, *General Lee*, 49–50.

59 swim: Robert E. Lee to George Washington Custis Lee, Fort Hamilton, New York, June 1, 1844, DeButts-Ely Collection of Lee Family Papers, Library of Congress.

59 injured: Robert E. Lee to George Washington Custis Lee, Fort Hamilton, New York, November 30, 1845, DeButts-Ely Collection of Lee Family Papers, Library of Congress.

59 "Upon you": Robert E. Lee to My Dear Boys, Ship Massachusetts, Off Lobos, February 27, 1847, DeButts-Ely Collection of Lee Family Papers, Library of Congress.

59 "Where is": Lee, *Recollections and Letters of General Robert E. Lee*, 3–4.

60 excavations: *Daily National Intelligencer*, April 17, 1848; "The Corner-Stone of the Washington National Monument," *Daily National Intelligencer*, June 10, 1848.

60 once again belonged: "Celebration of Retrocession," *Alexandria Gazette*, March 23, 1847.

60 final votes: Mark David Richards, "The Debates Over the Retrocession of the District of Columbia, 1801–2004," *Washington History* 16 (Spring/Summer 2004): 55–82.

60 "The polls": Robert E. Lee to Charles Carter Lee, Arlington, September 1, 1846, Robert E. Lee Papers, University of Virginia.

60 despite previously opposing: Nelligan, *Old Arlington*, 84–85 and 302.

60 initially popular: A. Glenn Crothers, "The 1846 Retrocession of Alexandria: Protecting Slavery and the Slave Trade in the District of Columbia," in Paul Finkelman and Donald R. Kennon, eds., *In the Shadow of Freedom: The Politics*

of Slavery in the National Capital (Athens, OH: Ohio University Press, 2011), 144–55.

60   future of slavery: Crothers, "The 1846 Retrocession of Alexandria," 155–62.

60   concealed: Janice G. Artemel, Elizabeth A. Crowell, and Jeff Parker, *The Alexandria Slave Pen: The Archaeology of Urban Captivity* (Washington, DC: Engineering-Science, 1987), 21–41.

61   unspoken: Crothers, "The 1846 Retrocession of Alexandria," 161–68.

61   tallied: Robert E. Lee to Charles Carter Lee, Arlington, September 1, 1846, Robert E. Lee Papers, University of Virginia.

61   "suppressed wailings": Crothers, "The 1846 Retrocession of Alexandria," 166–67.

61   speech: "Celebration of Retrocession," *Alexandria Gazette*, March 23, 1847.

61   vast swaths: David M. Potter, *The Impending Crisis: America Before the Civil War, 1848–1861*, ed. Don E. Fehrenbacher (New York: Harper & Row, 1976; New York: Harper Perennial, 2011), 1–4.

61   "the justice": Robert E. Lee to Mary Custis Lee, Fort Hamilton, New York, May 12, 1846, DeButts-Ely Collection of Lee Family Papers, Library of Congress.

61   "anxious": Robert E. Lee to John Mackay, Fort Hamilton, New York, June 21, 1846, Mackay-McQueen Family Papers, National Society Colonial Dames of America, Georgia Historical Society.

62   chairs: Robert E. Lee and Mary Custis Lee to George Washington Parke Custis, August 25, 1837, Robert E. Lee Papers, University of Virginia. For the transportation revolution, see Daniel Walker Howe, *What Hath God Wrought: The Transformation of America, 1815–1848* (New York: Oxford University Press, 2007).

62   "They shew": Robert E. Lee to Mary Custis Lee, Fort Hamilton, April 18, 1841, Robert E. Lee Papers, University of Virginia.

62   six-foot-four: E. D. Keyes, *Fifty Years' Observation of Men and Events Civil and Military* (New York: Charles Scribner's Sons, 1884), 7.

62   Old Fuss and Feathers: For background on Scott, see Timothy D. Johnson, *Winfield Scott: The Quest for Military Glory* (Lawrence: University Press of Kansas, 1998).

62   "His talent": Freeman, *R. E. Lee*, vol. 1, 258.

62   "impassable": Robert E. Lee to Mary Custis Lee, Perote, April 25, 1847, quoted in Lee, *General Lee*, 38.

63   "fallen tree": Long, *Memoirs of Robert E. Lee*, 53; Freeman, *R. E. Lee*, vol. 1, 239–40.

63   "Seeing their": Robert E. Lee to Mary Custis Lee, Perote, April 25, 1847, quoted in Lee, *General Lee*, 38–39.

63   "We see": *Alexandria Gazette*, May 20, 1847.

63   Rio Frio: Freeman, *R. E. Lee*, vol. 1, 252.

63   "Lighted by": Captain R. E. Lee's Letter, Tacubaya, August 22, 1847, in *Inquiry in the Case of Major General Pillow*, 30th Cong., 1st session, 1848, Senate Executive Doc. 65, 461.

63   Find a path Lee did: Freeman, *R. E. Lee*, vol. 1, 255–67; Report of Winfield Scott, Head-Quarters of the Army, San Augustin, Acapulco Road, August 19, 1847, in *Message from the President of the United States*, 30th Cong., 1st session,

1847, Executive Doc. 1, 304–6; Robert E. Lee to J. L. Smith, Tacubaya, August 21, 1847, Letterbook No. 2, DeButts-Ely Collection of Lee Family Letters, Library of Congress.

63 "exceedingly dark": Testimony of Winfield Scott, in *Inquiry in the Case of Major General Pillow*, 73.

64 "We could have": Captain R. E. Lee's Letter, Tacubaya, August 22, 1847, in *Inquiry in the Case of Major General Pillow*, 463–65.

64 day and a half: Freeman, *R. E. Lee*, vol. 1, 271.

64 "slight wound": Ibid., 280–84.

64 "We hold": Robert E. Lee to Mary Custis Lee, City of Mexico, February 13, 1848, DeButts-Ely Collections of Lee Family Papers, Library of Congress.

64 "It would be": Ibid.

64 peace treaty: Potter, *The Impending Crisis*, 1–6.

65 naïve hope: Wood, *Empire of Liberty*, 517–31; Joseph J. Ellis, *Founding Brothers: The Revolutionary Generation* (New York: Vintage Books, 2002), 81–119.

65 compromise: For an overview of how slavery plunged Congress into turmoil, see Potter, *The Impending Crisis* and James M. McPherson, *Battle Cry of Freedom: The Civil War Era* (New York: Ballantine Books, 1989).

65 "less ground": *Appendix to the Congressional Globe*, 31st Cong., 1st session, 122.

65 new cavalry regiments: Freeman, *R. E. Lee*, vol. 1, 349.

65 "came from Mexico": Speech at Richmond, in Lynda L. Crist, Suzanne Scott Gibbs, Brady L. Hutchison, and Elizabeth Henson Smith, eds., *The Papers of Jefferson Davis* (Baton Rouge: Louisiana State University Press, 2008), vol. 12, 502–6.

65 prized post: Freeman, *R. E. Lee*, vol. 1, 317.

65 "Marble Model": Lomax, *Leaves from an Old Washington Diary, 1854–1863*, 29; Watson, *Notes on Southside Virginia*, 245.

66 change: Robert E. Lee to Markie Williams, West Point, March 14, 1855, in Craven, ed., *"To Markie,"* 52–53.

66 five rows: Robert E. Lee to Agnes Lee, Camp Cooper, Texas, August 4, 1856, in deButts, ed., *Growing Up in the 1850s*, 125.

66 every blanket: Robert E. Lee to Mary Custis Lee, Fort Brown, Texas, December 20, 1856, DeButts-Ely Collection of Lee Family Papers, Library of Congress.

66 few Comanches: Robert E. Lee to Mary Custis Lee, Camp Cooper, Texas, July 28, 1856, DeButts-Ely Collection of Lee Family Papers, Library of Congress.

66 "uninteresting": Robert E. Lee to Mary Custis Lee, Camp Cooper, April 12, 1856, DeButts-Ely Collection of Lee Family Papers, Library of Congress. For a description of the scene in Texas, see S. C. Gwynne, *Empire of the Summer Moon: Quanah Parker and the Rise and Fall of the Comanches, the Most Powerful Indian Tribe in American History* (New York: Scribner, 2011).

66 "in the dark": Robert E. Lee to Mary Custis Lee, Fort Brown, Texas, November 19, 1856, DeButts-Ely Collection of Lee Family Papers, Library of Congress.

66 "Mr. Buchanan": Robert E. Lee to Mary Custis Lee, Fort Brown, Texas, December 13, 1856, DeButts-Ely Collection of Lee Family Papers, Library of Congress.

66 birth: Custis Family Bible, Custis-Lee Family Papers, Library of Congress.

66 remained her home: Connelly, *The Marble Man*, 165–68; Thomas, *Robert E. Lee*, 17.

Notes

66 "I unfortunately": Robert E. Lee to Mary Custis Lee, San Antonio, Texas, March 7, 1857, in Francis Raymond Adams Jr., *An Annotated Edition of the Personal Letters of Robert E. Lee, April, 1855–April, 1861* (University of Maryland Dissertation, 1955), 295.

66 "pain": Mary Custis Lee to Robert E. Lee, Arlington, September 2, 1856, DeButts-Ely Collection of Lee Family Papers, Library of Congress.

66 "I walk very": Mary Custis Lee to Robert E. Lee, September 6, DeButts-Ely Collection of Lee Family Papers, Library of Congress.

66 "Suppose you get": Robert E. Lee to Mary Custis Lee, Fort Brown, Texas, January 7, 1857, DeButts-Ely Collection of Lee Family Papers, Library of Congress.

67 opium: Robert E. Lee to Mary Custis Lee, Indianola, Texas, March 20, 1857, in Adams, *An Annotated Edition of the Personal Letters of Robert E. Lee*, 306–7.

67 "The more I": Robert E. Lee to Mary Custis Lee, Fort Brown, Texas, November 19, 1856, DeButts-Ely Collection of Lee Family Papers, Library of Congress.

67 "coffee & cream": Robert E. Lee to Mildred Lee, Indianola, Texas, March 22, 1857, DeButts-Ely Collection of Lee Family Papers, Library of Congress.

67 "old habit": Robert E. Lee to William Fitzhugh Lee, Arlington, May 30, 1858, George Bolling Lee Papers, Virginia Historical Society.

67 against joining: Robert E. Lee to Markie Williams, West Point, September 16, 1853, in Craven, ed., *"To Markie,"* 37.

67 "insuperable difficulties": Robert E. Lee to Markie Williams, West Point, September 16, 1853, in ibid.

67 acceptance: Henry Adams, *The Education of Henry Adams* (New York: Modern Library, 1918; Boston: First Mariner Books, 2000), 57–59; Mary Custis Lee to Robert E. Lee, May 22, 1857, DeButts-Ely Collection of Lee Family Papers, Library of Congress.

67 debts: Mary Custis Lee to Robert E. Lee, Arlington, September 6, DeButts-Ely Collection of Lee Family Papers, Library of Congress.

67 "I doubt": Robert E. Lee to Mary Custis Lee, Camp Cooper, Texas, May 18, 1857, DeButts-Ely Collection of Lee Family Papers, Library of Congress.

67 "Keep an": George Washington to George Washington Parke Custis, Philadelphia, January 11, 1797, in Custis, *Recollections and Private Memoirs of Washington*, 80.

68 overcharged: Nelligan, *Old Arlington*, 385.

68 "Many of his": Robert E. Lee to William Wickham, Arlington, January 2, 1856, Letterbook No. 1, DeButts-Ely Collection of Lee Family Papers, Library of Congress.

68 "take no step": Mary Custis Lee to Robert E. Lee, Arlington, August 19, 1856, DeButts-Ely Collection of Lee Family Papers, Library of Congress.

68 "At his age": Robert E. Lee to Mary Custis Lee, Fort Mason, March 28, 1856, DeButts-Ely Collection of Lee Family Papers, Library of Congress.

68 "What I most": Robert E. Lee to Mary Custis Lee, Camp Cooper, Texas, August 18, 1856, DeButts-Ely Collection of Lee Family Papers, Library of Congress.

68 "I am utterly": Robert E. Lee to Mary Custis Lee, San Antonio, Texas, April 7, 1857, DeButts-Ely Collection of Lee Family Papers, Library of Congress.

68 telegram: Diary of Robert E. Lee, October 21, 1857, Lee Family Papers, Virginia Historical Society.

68 "I am very sorry": Robert E. Lee to A. S. Johnston, San Antonio, Texas, Octo-

ber 25, 1857, in Marilyn McAdams Sibley, ed., "Robert E. Lee to Albert Sidney Johnston, 1857," *Journal of Southern History* 29, no. 1 (February 1963): 100–107.

69 "To the day": *Alexandria Gazette*, October 12, 1857.

69 "look upon": "Death of Mr. Custis," *Daily National Intelligencer*, October 12, 1857.

69 "I miss every": Robert E. Lee to Anna Fitzhugh, Arlington, November 22, 1857, Robert E. Lee Papers, Duke University.

69 grass: Ibid.

69 Influenza: Mary Custis Lee to Robert E. Lee, Arlington, October 2, 1857, DeButts-Ely Collection of Lee Family Papers, Library of Congress.

69 Custis had asked: Agnes Lee, Tuesday Night the 13th, in deButts, ed., *Growing Up in the 1850s*, 100.

69 Nearly a thousand: "Washington Items," *Richmond Whig*, October 16, 1857.

69 "affecting incident": "The Funeral of G. W. P. Custis," *Washington Evening Star*, October 13, 1857.

69 "so-called": Agnes Lee, Tuesday Night the 13th, in deButts, ed., *Growing Up in the 1850s*, 100–101.

69 "We were standing": *Sunday Star*, 1928, quoted by National Park Service, Arlington House, online.

69 "I will do my best": Mary Custis Lee to Robert E. Lee, Arlington, October 11, 1857, DeButts-Ely Collection of Lee Family Papers, Library of Congress.

70 "every article": The Will of G. W. P. Custis, in Prussing, *The Estate of George Washington, Deceased*, 476–77.

70 clarify its meaning: Francis Smith to John W. Tyler, in Exr. of George Washington Parke Custis vs. Mary Anna Randolph Custis Lee and Others, Arlington Chancery Records, Library of Virginia.

70 "And upon": The Will of G. W. P. Custis, in Prussing, *The Estate of George Washington, Deceased*, 476–77.

71 religious fervor: Pryor, *Reading the Man*, 131–37.

71 proposed a similar: "Conversations of General La Fayette," *Alexandria Gazette*, May 12, 1825.

71 "Such an example": Henry Wiencek, *An Imperfect God: George Washington, His Slaves, and the Creation of America* (New York: Farrar, Straus and Giroux, 2003), 260.

71 his own scheme: "Conversations of La Fayette," *Alexandria Gazette*, October 29, 1825; Nelligan, *Old Arlington*, 169–70.

71 backward: For Washington's views on slavery, see Chernow, *Washington*; Joseph J. Ellis, *His Excellency: George Washington* (New York: Alfred A. Knopf, 2004); Philip D. Morgan, " 'To Get Quit of Negroes': George Washington and Slavery," *Journal of American Studies* 39, no. 3 (December 2005): 403–29; Wiencek, *An Imperfect God*.

71 "I can only say": George Washington to Robert Morris, Mount Vernon, April 12, 1786, in Crackel, ed., *The Papers of George Washington Digital Edition*.

71 "awake": George Washington to David Stuart, New York, March 28, 1790, in ibid.

72 proposed a plan: Morgan, " 'To Get Quit of Negroes' "; Wiencek, *An Imperfect*

God, 339–43; Fritz Hirschfeld, *George Washington and Slavery: A Documentary Portrayal* (Columbia: University of Missouri Press, 1988), 222.

72 "It not being": The Will of George Washington, in Prussing, *The Estate of George Washington, Deceased*, 43.

72 Custis's selections: List of the Different Drafts of Negroes, Letterbook F, Martha Parke Custis Peter Collection, Mount Vernon; Chernow, *Washington*, 806–9; Washington's Slave List, June 1799, in Crackel, ed., *The Papers of George Washington Digital Edition*.

72 in exchange: Powell, *The History of Old Alexandria, Virginia*, 243–44.

72 "good old": Agnes Lee, Sunday Morning the 23rd, in deButts, ed., *Growing Up in the 1850s*, 80–81.

72 large percentage: Morgan, " 'To Get Quit of Negroes.'"

72 "most painful": The Will of George Washington, in Prussing, *The Estate of George Washington, Deceased*, 43.

72 mulattoes: Chernow, *Washington*, 118; Lee, *Lee of Virginia*, 285–86.

73 son named Philip: Washington's Slave List, June 1799, in Crackel, ed., *The Papers of George Washington Digital Edition*.

73 "favorite body": George Washington Parke Custis to S. E. Burrows, Arlington House, February 17, 1832, in *Alexandria Gazette*, February 27, 1832.

73 still included: Agnes Lee, Sunday Morning the 23rd, in deButts, ed., *Growing Up in the 1850s*, 80; Inventory of the Estate of George Washington Parke Custis, January 1, 1858, Alexandria Circuit Court Clerk's Office, Will Book 7, 369–71; Enoch Aquila Chase, "The Restoration of Arlington House," *Records of the Columbia Historical Society* 33/34 (1932): 239–65; Anne Carter Zimmer, *The Robert E. Lee Family Cooking and Housekeeping Book* (Chapel Hill: University of North Carolina Press, 1997), 7 and 17; List of the Different Drafts of Negroes, Letterbook F, Martha Parke Custis Peter Collection, Mount Vernon. For an example, see George Clark, who appears on the 1858 inventory and who, though not on Custis's dower draft list, was said to have been a Mount Vernon slave.

73 own personality: Nelligan, *Old Arlington*, 395; Robert E. Lee to George Washington Custis Lee, Arlington, February 15, 1858, Robert E. Lee Papers, Duke University; Pryor, *Reading the Man*, 132–39; Levasseur, *Lafayette in America in 1824 and 1825*, vol. 2, 12.

73 "The servants": Mary Custis Lee to Dear Abby, Arlington, February 10, 1858, Robert E. Lee Family Collection, Museum of the Confederacy.

73 lambs: Joseph C. Robert, "Lee the Farmer," *Journal of Southern History* 3, no. 3 (November 1937): 422–40.

73 eleven and twelve thousand: Francis Smith to John W. Tyler, in Exr. of George Washington Parke Custis vs. Mary Anna Randolph Custis Lee and Others, Arlington Chancery Records, Library of Virginia.

73 "Debts are": Robert E. Lee to George Washington Custis Lee, Baltimore, January 17, 1858, Robert E. Lee Papers, Duke University.

73 ten thousand dollars: Robert E. Lee to George Washington Custis Lee, Arlington, February 15, 1858, Robert E. Lee Papers, Duke University.

73 "What am I": Robert E. Lee to Anna Fitzhugh, Arlington, November 22, 1857, Robert E. Lee Papers, Duke University.

73 end of 1858: Robert E. Lee to George Washington Custis Lee, Arlington, February 15, 1858, Robert E. Lee Papers, Duke University.

73 "Since I first": George Washington Custis Lee to Mary Custis Lee, Fort Point San Francisco, February 16, 1858, DeButts-Ely Collection of Lee Family Papers, Library of Congress.

74 "Touched": Robert E. Lee to George Washington Custis Lee, Arlington, March 17, 1858, Robert E. Lee Papers, Duke University.

74 "If you could": Robert E. Lee to George Washington Custis Lee, Arlington, February 15, 1858, Robert E. Lee Papers, Duke University.

74 courts would construe: Francis Smith to John W. Tyler, in Exr. of George Washington Parke Custis vs. Mary Anna Randolph Custis Lee and Others, Arlington Chancery Records, Library of Virginia.

74 avoid dealing: Thomas, *Robert E. Lee*, 108; Pryor, *Reading the Man*, 148–49.

74 "Do not trouble": Robert E. Lee to Mary Custis Lee, April 17, 1832, in Cuthbert, "To Molly: Five Early Letters from Robert E. Lee to His Wife, 1832–1835."

74 "Nancy and her children": The Will of Robert E. Lee, Rockbridge County Will Book 19, 362, Library of Virginia.

74 "In this enlightened": Robert E. Lee to Mary Custis Lee, Fort Brown, Texas, December 27, 1856, DeButts-Ely Collection of Lee Family Papers, Library of Congress.

75 "an energetic": Robert E. Lee to Edward C. Turner, Arlington, February 13, 1858, Robert E. Lee Papers, University of Virginia.

75 "cannot be convinced": Mary Custis Lee to Dear Abby, Arlington, February 10, 1858, Robert E. Lee Family Collection, Museum of the Confederacy.

75 little for them: Thomas, *Robert E. Lee*, 144.

75 "a charge": Francis Smith to John W. Tyler, in Exr. of George Washington Parke Custis vs. Mary Anna Randolph Custis Lee and Others, Arlington Chancery Records, Library of Virginia.

75 one rumor: "The Slaves of Mr. Custis," *New York Times*, December 30, 1857.

75 "lurking about": Thomas, *Robert E. Lee*, 177.

75 "sacred duty": Mary Custis Lee Diary, June 9, 1853, Lee Family Papers, Virginia Historical Society.

76 "ingratitude": Mary Custis Lee Diary, May 1, 1858, Lee Family Papers, Virginia Historical Society.

76 "immense burden": Mary Custis Lee to Dear Abby, Arlington, February 10, 1858, Robert E. Lee Family Collection, Museum of the Confederacy.

76 "It would be awful": "The Slaves of Mr. Custis," *New York Times*, December 30, 1857.

76 letter denying: Robert E. Lee, Arlington, January 4, 1858, in *Alexandria Gazette*, January 5, 1858.

76 "thwarted": Francis Smith to John W. Tyler, in Exr. of George Washington Parke Custis vs. Mary Anna Randolph Custis Lee and Others, Arlington Chancery Records, Library of Virginia.

76 "discontented": Mary Custis Lee to Dear Sir, Arlington, July 20, Robert E. Lee Papers, Washington and Lee University.

76 "harassed": Mary Custis Lee to Dear Abby, Arlington, May 7, 1858, Robert

Notes

E. Lee Family Collection, Museum of the Confederacy. For more information about conditions in Virginia during the 1850s, see William A. Link, *Roots of Secession: Slavery and Politics in Antebellum Virginia*, ed. Gary W. Gallagher (Chapel Hill: University of North Carolina Press, 2003).

76 pit slaves: Robert E. Lee to Mary Custis Lee, Fort Brown, Texas, December 27, 1856, DeButts-Ely Collection of Lee Family Papers, Library of Congress.

76 "refused to": Robert E. Lee to William Fitzhugh Lee, Arlington, May 30, 1858, George Bolling Lee Papers, Virginia Historical Society.

76 "most punctual": Lee, *Recollections and Letters of General Robert E. Lee*, 12.

76 unfavorable ruling: Circuit Court Ruling, May 25, 1859, in Exr. of George Washington Parke Custis vs. Mary Anna Randolph Custis Lee and Others, Arlington Chancery Records, Library of Virginia; Note of Argument for Appellant, Custis's Exr. v. Lee and Others, Supreme Court of Appeals of Virginia, Alexandria Library.

76 "I really begin": Robert E. Lee to George Washington Custis Lee, Arlington, July 2, 1859, in Jones, *Life and Letters of Robert Edward Lee*, 100–102.

77 transformation: Ibid., 102; Robert, "Lee the Farmer"; Nelligan, *Old Arlington*, 424; Robert E. Lee to George Washington Custis Lee, Arlington, May 30, 1859, Robert E. Lee Papers, Duke University.

77 leak: Robert E. Lee to George Washington Custis Lee, Arlington, January 2, 1859, Robert E. Lee Papers, Duke University.

77 "I hope to prevent": Robert E. Lee to Anna Fitzhugh, Arlington, November 20, 1858, Robert E. Lee Papers, Duke University.

77 "harder at work": A. to the Editor, Washington, DC, June 21, 1859, *New York Tribune*, June 24, 1859.

77 "Col. Lee ordered": A Citizen to the Editor, Washington, DC, June 19, 1859, ibid.

77 "Next to": A. to the Editor, Washington, DC, June 21, 1859, ibid.

78 "only astonished": Mary Custis Lee to Reverdy Johnson, Mary Custis Lee Papers, Virginia Historical Society.

78 "The N.Y. Tribune": Robert E. Lee to George Washington Custis Lee, Arlington, July 2, 1859, in Jones, *Life and Letters of Robert Edward Lee*, 102.

Chapter 5: Washington's Sword

79 bushy beard: Lewis Washington Sketch, *Harper's Weekly*, November 12, 1859, West Virginia Archive and History, online.

79 honorary title: "Col. Lewis W. Washington," *Daily National Intelligencer*, May 4, 1857.

79 donated: "The Birth-Place of Washington," *Daily National Intelligencer*, February 14, 1856.

79 resolve: *Alexandria Gazette*, September 9, 1857; Chernow, *Washington*, 754–57.

79 blue-eyed: Stephen B. Oates, *To Purge This Land with Blood: A Biography of John Brown*, 2nd ed. (Amherst: University of Massachusetts Press, 1984), 219.

79 hundreds: Chester G. Hearn, *Six Years of Hell: Harpers Ferry During the Civil War* (Baton Rouge: Louisiana State University Press, 1996), 5.

79 "Almost all": Testimony of Lewis W. Washington, in *Report of the Select Committee on the Harper's Ferry Invasion*, 36th Cong., 1st session, 1860, S. Rep. 278, 29–31.

80 "These Swords": The Will of George Washington, in Prussing, *The Estate of George Washington, Deceased*, 59–60.

80 dressed: Testimony of Lewis W. Washington, in *Report of the Select Committee on the Harper's Ferry Invasion*, 30–31.

80 "Is your name": "Col. Lewis W. Washington's Statement," *Alexandria Gazette*, October 26, 1859.

80 "You are": Testimony of Lewis W. Washington, in *Report of the Select Committee on the Harper's Ferry Invasion*, 30–32.

80 "I should doubt": Ibid., 32.

80 "You can have": Osborne P. Anderson, *A Voice from Harper's Ferry: A Narrative of Events at Harper's Ferry* (Boston, 1861), 34–35.

81 did not recognize: Testimony of Lewis W. Washington, in *Report of the Select Committee on the Harper's Ferry Invasion*, 32–33.

81 "When this interesting": "A Venerable Present," *Daily National Intelligencer*, March 20, 1848.

81 "They were passed": Robert E. Lee to Mary Custis Lee, Camp near Satillo, December 25, 1846, DeButts-Ely Collection of Lee Family Papers, Library of Congress.

82 told Lee's brother: George C. Washington to Charles Carter Lee, Georgetown, April 24, 1852, Ethel Armes Collection of Lee Family Papers, Library of Congress.

82 "You have doubtless": Robert E. Lee to Mary Fitzhugh Custis, Baltimore, March 17, 1852, DeButts-Ely Collection of Lee Family Papers, Library of Congress.

82 flurry: J. E. B. Stuart to My Dear Mama, Fort Riley, Kansas, January 31, 1860, in Emory M. Thomas, " 'The Greatest Service I Rendered the State': J. E. B. Stuart's Account of the Capture of John Brown," *Virginia Magazine of History and Biography* 94, no. 3 (July 1986): 345–57.

82 "Telegraphic advices": John W. Garrett to J. B. Floyd, October 17, 1859, in *Correspondence Relating to the Insurrection at Harper's Ferry, October 17, 1859* (Annapolis, 1860), 7–8.

82 fetch Lee: Freeman, *R. E. Lee*, vol. 1, 394–95.

82 found Lee standing: Pryor, *Reading the Man*, 278.

82 three thousand: J. E. B. Stuart to My Dear Mama, Fort Riley, Kansas, January 31, 1860, in Thomas, " 'The Greatest Service I Rendered the State.' "

82 Buchanan ordered: Freeman, *R. E. Lee*, vol. 1, 394–95.

82 It had been President: Merritt Roe Smith, "George Washington and the Establishment of the Harpers Ferry Armory," *Virginia Magazine of History and Biography* 81, no. 4 (October 1973): 415–36.

83 "In the moment": Gutheim, *The Potomac*, 167–69.

83 waterpower: Tony Horwitz, *Midnight Rising: John Brown and the Raid That Sparked the Civil War* (New York: Henry Holt, 2011), 69–70.

83 "This spot": George Washington to the Secretary of War, Mount Vernon, September 16, 1795, in Fitzpatrick, ed., *The Writings of George Washington from the Original Manuscript Sources, 1745–1799*, vol. 34.

83 fifteen thousand: Hearn, *Six Years of Hell*, 5.

Notes

83 rivalry: Achenbach, *The Grand Idea*, 249–62; Freeman, *R. E. Lee*, vol. 1, 395.

83 met up: Israel Green, "The Capture of John Brown," *North American Review* 141, no. 349 (December 1885): 564–69; Diary of Robert E. Lee, October 17, 1859, Lee Family Papers, Virginia Historical Society.

84 eighteen: Horwitz, *Midnight Rising*, 131.

84 Brown's mind: For background on Brown, see Oates, *To Purge This Land with Blood*.

84 "violation": "Provisional Constitution and Ordinances for the People of the United States," in *Report of the Select Committee on the Harper's Ferry Invasion*, 48.

84 then headed: Oates, *To Purge This Land with Blood*, 291.

84 "I presume": Testimony of Lewis W. Washington, in *Report of the Select Committee on the Harper's Ferry Invasion*, 34–35.

84 "I will take": "Col. Lewis W. Washington's Statement," *Alexandria Gazette*, October 26, 1859.

85 miscalculation: Horwitz, *Midnight Rising*, 73 and 154.

85 "Brown and those": Alexander R. Boteler, "Recollections of the John Brown Raid by a Virginian Who Witnessed the Fight," *Century Magazine* 26, no. 3 (July 1883): 399–411.

85 Ten: Testimony of Lewis W. Washington, in *Report of the Select Committee on the Harper's Ferry Invasion*, 35–36.

85 "I want you": Testimony of John H. Allstadt, in ibid., 43 and 45.

85 "If you must": Oates, *To Purge This Land with Blood*, 298–99.

85 planned for himself: Horwitz, *Midnight Rising*, 172.

85 light rain: J. E. B. Stuart to My Dear Mama, Fort Riley, Kansas, January 31, 1860, in Thomas, " 'The Greatest Service I Rendered the State.' "

86 "for the fear": Robert E. Lee to S. Cooper, Headquarters, Harper's Ferry, October 19, 1859, in *Report of the Select Committee on the Harper's Ferry Invasion*, 40–41.

86 widely known: Message from Fulton, Midnight, October 18, 1859, in *Correspondence Relating to the Insurrection at Harper's Ferry, October 17, 1859*, 17–18.

86 "some of our best": Robert E. Lee to J. B. Floyd, in ibid., 20.

86 "Their safety": Robert E. Lee to S. Cooper, Headquarters, Harpers Ferry, October 19, 1859, in *Report of the Select Committee on the Harper's Ferry Invasion*, 41.

86 no sleep: J. E. B. Stuart to My Dear Mama, Fort Riley, Kansas, January 31, 1860, in Thomas, " 'The Greatest Service I Rendered the State.' "

86 "unnecessary": Robert E. Lee to J. B. Floyd, in *Correspondence Relating to the Insurrection at Harper's Ferry, October 17, 1859*, 20.

86 "spectators": J. E. B. Stuart to My Dear Mama, Fort Riley, Kansas, January 31, 1860, in Thomas, " 'The Greatest Service I Rendered the State.' "

86 "He had no": Green, "The Capture of John Brown."

86 cracked: J. E. B. Stuart to My Dear Mama, Fort Riley, Kansas, January 31, 1860, in Thomas, " 'The Greatest Service I Rendered the State.' "

86 "Colonel Lee": Robert E. Lee to S. Cooper, Headquarters, Harpers Ferry, October 19, 1859, in *Report of the Select Committee on the Harper's Ferry Invasion*, 43–44.

87 negotiate: J. E. B. Stuart to My Dear Mama, Fort Riley, Kansas, January 31, 1860, in Thomas, " 'The Greatest Service I Rendered the State.' "

87 "I choose": "Mr. Washington's Capture," *Daily National Intelligencer*, November 4, 1859.

Notes

87   cried out: J. E. B. Stuart to My Dear Mama, Fort Riley, Kansas, January 31, 1860, in Thomas, " 'The Greatest Service I Rendered the State.' "

87   "Never mind": Freeman, *R. E. Lee*, vol. 1, 399.

87   time between: Robert E. Lee to S. Cooper, October 19, 1859, in *Report of the Select Committee on the Harper's Ferry Invasion*, 41–42.

87   battering ram: Green, "The Capture of John Brown."

87   strike the hostages: Robert E. Lee to S. Cooper, October 19, 1859, in *Report of the Select Committee on the Harper's Ferry Invasion*, 41.

87   "This is Osawatomie": Green, "The Capture of John Brown."

87   cheered: Boteler, "Recollections of the John Brown Raid by a Virginian Who Witnessed the Fight"; Green, "The Capture of John Brown," 567.

88   sword was safe: Testimony of Lewis W. Washington, in *Report of the Select Committee on the Harper's Ferry Invasion*, 40.

88   Lee allowed: Oates, *To Purge This Land with Blood*, 302–3.

88   "He was glad": *New York Herald*, October 21, 1859.

88   "It is": Ibid.

88   uncovered: J. E. B. Stuart to My Dear Mama, Fort Riley, Kansas, January 31, 1860, in Thomas, " 'The Greatest Service I Rendered the State' "; Oates, *To Purge This Land with Blood*, 301.

89   "Its temporary success": Robert E. Lee to S. Cooper, Headquarters, Harpers Ferry, October 19, 1859, in *Report of the Select Committee on the Harper's Ferry Invasion*, 42.

89   "If anything": Testimony of Lewis W. Washington, in ibid., 40.

89   "The result proves": Robert E. Lee to S. Cooper, Headquarters, Harpers Ferry, October 19, 1859, in ibid., 42.

89   "cries of murder": Ibid., 43.

89   "panic mentality": Link, *Roots of Secession*, 179–85.

89   "The evidence": *Report of the Joint Committee on the Harpers Ferry Outrages*, Virginia General Assembly, 1860, no. 57, 7.

90   "You must not": "Gov. Wise's Speech at Richmond on the Subject of the Harper's Ferry Rebellion," *Alexandria Gazette*, October 27, 1859.

90   advice: Robert E. Lee to Colonel August, Arlington, Washington City, December 20, 1859, Letterbook No. 1, DeButts-Ely Collection of Lee Family Papers, Library of Congress.

90   medal: J. E. B. Stuart to My Dear Mama, Fort Riley, Kansas, January 31, 1860, in Thomas, " 'The Greatest Service I Rendered the State.' "

90   "quite a long": *Alexandria Gazette*, October 21, 1859.

90   dinner: Pryor, *Reading the Man*, 280–81.

90   attempt to rescue: Horwitz, *Midnight Rising*, 244–45.

90   "posting sentinels": Robert E. Lee to Mary Custis Lee, Harpers Ferry, December 1, 1859, DeButts-Ely Collection of Lee Family Papers, Library of Congress.

91   "Now, if": Oates, *To Purge This Land with Blood*, 327 and 339.

91   "It is a matter": Robert E. Lee to Mary Custis Lee, Harpers Ferry, December 1, 1859, DeButts-Ely Collection of Lee Family Papers, Library of Congress.

91   wife reportedly appreciated: "The Burial of John Brown," *New York Tribune*, December 12, 1859.

Notes

91 church bells: Oates, *To Purge This Land with Blood*, 354; Diary of Robert E. Lee, December 2, 1859, Lee Family Papers, Virginia Historical Society.

91 brown-bearded: James I. Robertson Jr., *Stonewall Jackson: The Man, the Soldier, the Legend* (New York: Macmillan, 1997), 191.

91 "unflinching firmness": Thomas Jackson to Mary Anna Jackson, December 2, 1859, in Virginia Military Institute Archives, online.

91 "the coolest": Oswald Garrison Villard, *John Brown, 1800–1859: A Biography Fifty Years After* (Boston: Houghton Mifflin, 1911), 453.

92 knelt: Thomas, *Robert E. Lee*, 160; Pryor, *Reading the Man*, 230–34.

92 "While we see": Robert E. Lee to Mary Custis Lee, Fort Brown, Texas, December 27, 1856, DeButts-Ely Collection of Lee Family Papers, Library of Congress.

92 order Thomas Jackson: Robert E. Lee to Thomas Jackson, Headquarters Virginia Forces, Richmond, April 27, 1861, in Dowdey and Manarin, eds., *The Wartime Papers of Robert E. Lee*, 13.

Chapter 6: The Decision

93 command: Diary of Robert E. Lee, February 9 and 10, 1860, Lee Family Papers, Virginia Historical Society.

93 "When I": Robert E. Lee to Anna Fitzhugh, Arlington, February 9, 1860, Robert E. Lee Papers, Duke University.

93 "Friends": Lee, "Memoir of George Washington Parke Custis," 9–10.

93 "It is my purpose": Mary Custis Lee to Benson Lossing, November 25, 1857, Arlington House, Virtual Museum Exhibit, online.

94 "It would have": Robert E. Lee to Mary Custis Lee, San Antonio, Texas, March 3, 1860, in Adams, *An Annotated Edition of the Personal Letters of Robert E. Lee, April, 1855–April, 1861*, 580.

94 reviews: Nelligan, *Old Arlington*, 431 and 438.

94 "I have been much": Robert E. Lee to Mary Custis Lee, Ringgold Barracks, April 4, 1860, DeButts-Ely Collection of Lee Family Papers, Library of Congress.

94 "our northern readers": Mary Custis Lee to Benson Lossing, Arlington, December 13, 1858, Mount Vernon.

94 "It may suit": Robert E. Lee to Mary Custis Lee, San Antonio, Texas, July 15, 1860, in Adams, *An Annotated Edition of the Personal Letters of Robert E. Lee, April, 1855–April, 1861*, 675 and 679.

94 "When the route": Robert E. Lee to George Washington Custis Lee, New Orleans, February 14, 1860, in Jones, *Life and Letters of Robert Edward Lee*, 109.

95 reached the department: Diary of Robert E. Lee, February 19, 1860, Lee Family Papers, Virginia Historical Society.

95 treeless: Robert E. Lee to Mary Custis Lee, San Antonio, Texas, March 3, 1860, in Adams, *An Annotated Edition of the Personal Letters of Robert E. Lee, April, 1855–April, 1861*, 579.

95 "I know it": Robert E. Lee to Annie Lee, San Antonio, Texas, February 22, 1860, DeButts-Ely Collection of Lee Family Papers, Library of Congress.

Notes

95 "most reliable": Robert E. Lee to William Fitzhugh Lee, Ringgold Barracks, April 2, 1860, George Bolling Lee Papers, Virginia Historical Society.

95 forty miles: Robert E. Lee to Mary Custis Lee, Laredo, March 24, 1860, DeButts-Ely Collection of Lee Family Papers, Library of Congress.

95 "I am sure": Robert E. Lee to Mary Custis Lee, Fort Brown, Texas, May 2, 1860, DeButts-Ely Collection of Lee Family Papers, Library of Congress.

95 "You are a young": Robert E. Lee to George Washington Custis Lee, Fort Brown, Texas, April 16, 1860, Robert E. Lee Papers, Duke University.

95 "infant cheek": Robert E. Lee to William Fitzhugh Lee, Ringgold Barracks, Texas, November 1, 1856, in Adams, *An Annotated Edition of the Personal Letters of Robert E. Lee, April, 1855–April, 1861*, 198.

95 "I wish": Robert E. Lee to William Fitzhugh Lee, San Antonio, Texas, June 21, 1860, George Bolling Lee Papers, Virginia Historical Society.

95 "A divided heart": Robert E. Lee to Anna Fitzhugh, June 6, 1860, quoted in Freeman, *R. E. Lee*, vol. 1, 410.

95 political connections: Freeman, *R. E. Lee*, vol. 1, 411–12; Register of the Officers and Cadets of the US Military Academy, June 1829.

96 "It is better": Robert E. Lee to Annie Lee, San Antonio, Texas, August 27, 1860, DeButts-Ely Collection of Lee Family Papers, Library of Congress.

96 "your people": Robert E. Lee to William Fitzhugh Lee, San Antonio, Texas, March 12, 1860, George Bolling Lee Papers, Virginia Historical Society.

96 election of 1860: McPherson, *Battle Cry of Freedom*, 213–21.

96 appeared alongside: Freeman, *R. E. Lee*, vol. 1, 304–5.

97 pox-on-both-houses: Robert E. Lee to Charles Carter Lee, City of Mexico, February 13, 1848, Robert E. Lee Papers, University of Virginia; Robert E. Lee to John Mackay, St. Louis, June 27, 1838, Gilder Lehrman Collection, online.

97 "If Judge": Robert E. Lee to Earl Van Dorn, San Antonio, Texas, July 3, 1860, in Adams, *An Annotated Edition of the Personal Letters of Robert E. Lee, April, 1855–April, 1861*, 671.

97 "not fear": Robert E. Lee to Mary Custis Lee, Fort Brown, Texas, November 19, 1856, DeButts-Ely Collection of Lee Family Papers, Library of Congress.

97 buying a slave: Robert E. Lee to William Fitzhugh Lee, San Antonio, Texas, July 9, 1860, George Bolling Lee Papers, Virginia Historical Society.

97 not one came: David Herbert Donald, *Lincoln* (New York: Simon & Schuster, 1995), 256.

97 "The Union": "The Election and its Results," *San Antonio Ledger and Texan*, November 17, 1860.

97 late November: Potter, *The Impending Crisis*, 491–92.

98 Lone Star: Robert E. Lee to George Washington Custis Lee, San Antonio, Texas, November 24, 1860, Robert E. Lee Papers, Duke University.

98 bloodshed: Charles Anderson, *Texas, Before, and on the Eve of the Rebellion* (Cincinnati: Peter G. Thomson, 1884), 14–17.

98 "The Southern States": Robert E. Lee to George Washington Custis Lee, San Antonio, Texas, November 24, 1860, Robert E. Lee Papers, Duke University.

98 two thousand: J. J. Bowden, *The Exodus of Federal Forces from Texas* (Austin: Eakin Press, 1986), 2–3.

Notes

98　six weeks: Robert E. Lee to George Washington Custis Lee, San Antonio, Texas, December 14, 1860, Robert E. Lee Papers, Duke University.

98　freely granted: Anderson, *Texas, Before, and on the Eve of the Rebellion*, 26.

98　"I know": Ibid., 27–31.

99　"The name": Farewell Address, United States, September 19, 1796, in John Rhodehamel, ed., *George Washington: Writings* (New York: Library of America, 1997), 965.

99　"Here was": Anderson, *Texas, Before, and on the Eve of the Rebellion*, 31.

99　"Could Washington himself": William A. Bryan, "George Washington: Symbolic Guardian of the Republic, 1850–1861," *William and Mary Quarterly* 7, no. 1 (January 1950): 53–63.

99　"I am exceedingly": Address to the New Jersey Senate at Trenton, NJ, February 21, 1861, in Fehrenbacher, ed., *Abraham Lincoln: Speeches and Writings, 1859–1865*, 209.

100　"disunion on his": Peterson, *The Great Triumvirate*, 461.

100　"was one of us": Bryan, "George Washington."

100　"The Abolitionists": Adam Goodheart, "The War for (George) Washington," Disunion, *New York Times*, February 21, 2011, online.

100　"he had made": Wiencek, *An Imperfect God*, 362.

100　released: "New Publications," *New York Tribune*, September 15, 1860.

100　three border states: Potter, *The Impending Crisis*, 416–17 and 442.

100　Union sentiment: Link, *Roots of Secession*, 209.

100　six states: McPherson, *Battle Cry of Freedom*, 235.

101　"one of the last": Mary Custis Lee to Mildred Lee, DeButts-Ely Collection of Lee Family Papers, Library of Congress.

101　dated newspapers: Robert E. Lee to Agnes Lee, Fort Mason, Texas, January 29, 1861, DeButts-Ely Collection of Lee Family Papers, Library of Congress.

101　"I am so remote": Robert E. Lee to Markie Williams, Fort Mason, Texas, January 22, 1861, in Craven, ed., *"To Markie,"* 58–59.

101　admired: Robert E. Lee to Mary Custis Lee, San Antonio, Texas, June 3, 1860, DeButts-Ely Collection of Lee Family Papers, Library of Congress.

101　"I recd": Robert E. Lee to Mary Custis Lee, Fort Mason, January 23, 1861, in Adams, *An Annotated Edition of the Personal Letters of Robert E. Lee, April, 1855–April, 1861*, 723.

101　emerged from: Edward Everett, *The Life of George Washington* (New York: Sheldon, 1860).

101　"The framers": Robert E. Lee to William Fitzhugh Lee, Fort Mason, January 29, 1861, George Bolling Lee Papers, Virginia Historical Society.

102　"a more perfect union": First Inaugural Address, March 4, 1861, in Fehrenbacher, ed., *Abraham Lincoln: Speeches and Writings, 1859–1865*, 217–18.

102　"aggrieved": Robert E. Lee to William Fitzhugh Lee, January 29, 1861, George Bolling Lee Papers, Virginia Historical Society.

103　in vain: James, *The Raven*, 404–8.

103　new orders: Freeman, *R. E. Lee*, vol. 1, 424–25.

103　arrived in that town: Diary of Robert E. Lee, February 16, 1861, Lee Family Papers, Virginia Historical Society.

103　"Who are": Caroline Baldwin Darrow, "Recollections of the Twiggs Surrender," in Robert Underwood Johnson and Clarence Clough Buel, eds., *Battles and Leaders of the Civil War* (New York: The Century, 1887), vol. 1, 36.

103 seized the arsenal: Report of William Hoffman, Headquarters, San Antonio Barracks, March 1, 1861, in the United States War Department, *The War of the Rebellion: A Compilation of the Official Records of the Union and Confederate Armies*, hereafter called *O.R.* (Washington, DC: Government Printing Office, 1880–1901), series 1, vol. 1, 517–18.

103 "He was determined": R. W. Johnson, *A Soldier's Reminiscences in Peace and War* (Philadelphia: J. B. Lippincott, 1886), 132–33.

103 "Has it come": Darrow, "Recollections of the Twiggs Surrender," 34–36.

103 "I was even": Anderson, *Texas, Before, and on the Eve of the Rebellion*, 24 and 32.

103 pacing: Darrow, "Recollections of the Twiggs Surrender," 36.

103 arranged: Diary of Robert E. Lee, February 18 and 19, 1861, Lee Family Papers, Virginia Historical Society; Anderson, *Texas, Before, and on the Eve of the Rebellion*, 32.

104 his grandson: Robert E. Lee to Mildred Lee, Arlington, March 15, 1861, DeButts-Ely Collection of Lee Family Papers, Library of Congress; Mary Custis Lee to Mildred Lee, Arlington, February 24, 1861, DeButts-Ely Collection of Lee Family Papers, Library of Congress.

104 "Found all well": Diary of Robert E. Lee, March 1, 1861, Lee Family Papers, Virginia Historical Society.

104 not well: Margaret Leech, *Reveille in Washington, 1860–1865* (New York: New York Review of Books, 1941), 36–38; Gary May, *John Tyler* (New York: Times Books, 2008), 141.

104 no power: Potter, *The Impending Crisis*, 520.

104 last-minute intervention: Leech, *Reveille in Washington, 1860–1865*, 42–43.

104 "There was": Mary Custis Lee to Mildred Lee, Arlington, February 24, 1861, DeButts-Ely Collection of Lee Family Papers, Library of Congress.

104 arrived in secret: Leech, *Reveille in Washington, 1860–1865*, 43–44.

104 "That beautiful feature": Bryan, "War Memories," 14.

104 whether to resupply: McPherson, *Battle Cry of Freedom*, 267; Potter, *The Impending Crisis*, 570–71.

105 "to hold": First Inaugural Address, March 4, 1861, in Fehrenbacher, ed., *Abraham Lincoln: Speeches and Writings, 1859–1865*, 218.

105 "military necessity": Robert E. Lee to William Fitzhugh Lee, Arlington, March 27, 1861, George Bolling Lee Papers, Virginia Historical Society.

105 "prospects": Diary of Samuel P. Heintzelman, March 5, 1861, Samuel P. Heintzelman Papers, Library of Congress.

105 "concurred": Keyes, *Fifty Years' Observation of Men and Events Civil and Military*, 205–7.

105 solidarity: Johnson, *Winfield Scott*, 223.

105 pained: Keyes, *Fifty Years' Observation of Men and Events Civil and Military*, 205–6.

105 assured Lee: Allan, "Memoranda of Conversations with General Robert E. Lee," 9–10.

105 White House reception: "A Military Visit," *Washington Evening Star*, March 12, 1861.

Notes

105 face-to-face: Pryor, *Reading the Man*, 288.

106 "a dignified": John C. Tidball, "War Period," Library of Congress.

106 "military genius": Keyes, *Fifty Years' Observation of Men and Events Civil and Military*, 206.

106 Scott claimed: John G. Nicolay and John Hay, *Abraham Lincoln: A History* (New York: The Century, 1890), vol. 4, 97–98.

106 ballooned: Johnson, *Winfield Scott*, 222.

106 squat neck: Gordon, "Recollections of General Robert E. Lee's Administration as President of Washington College," 78.

106 "dignified carriage": Walter H. Taylor, *General Lee: His Campaigns in Virginia, 1861–1865* (Norfolk, VA: Nusbaum Book and News, 1906), 21–22.

106 promotion to colonel: Freeman, *R. E. Lee*, vol. 1, 433.

106 avoid war: Allan, "Memoranda of Conversations with General Robert E. Lee," 9–10.

106 accept promotion: Robert E. Lee to George Washington Custis Lee, Arlington, February 15, 1858, Robert E. Lee Papers, Duke University; Lee, *Recollections and Letters of General Robert E. Lee*, 81.

106 far as known: Freeman, *R. E. Lee*, vol. 1, 433–34.

107 "I wish": Robert E. Lee to Markie Williams, Fort Mason, Texas, January 22, 1861, in Craven, ed., *"To Markie,"* 58.

107 "We were traditionally": Mary Custis Lee to Charles Marshall, [1871], in Pryor, "Thou Knowest Not the Time of Thy Visitation."

107 attended a party: Charles Francis Adams, *Charles Francis Adams, 1835–1915: An Autobiography* (Boston: Houghton Mifflin, 1916), 90–91.

107 "unsuspecting mind": Mary Custis Lee, "My Reminiscences of the War," in Robert E. L. deButts Jr., "Mary Custis Lee's 'Reminiscences of the War,'" *Virginia Magazine of History and Biography* 109, no. 3 (2001): 301–25.

107 "I pray": Mary Custis Lee to Mildred Lee, Arlington, February 24, DeButts-Ely Collection of Lee Family Papers, Library of Congress.

107 Lincoln would surrender: Robert E. Lee to William Fitzhugh Lee, Arlington, March 27, 1861, George Bolling Lee Papers, Virginia Historical Society.

107 mustered only forty-five: Link, *Roots of Secession*, 235.

107 option between: McPherson, *Battle Cry of Freedom*, 271–73.

108 "The excitement": Mary Custis Lee to Charles Marshall, [1871], in Pryor, "Thou Knowest Not the Time of Thy Visitation."

108 seventy-five thousand: "Proclamation Calling Militia and Convening Congress," in Fehrenbacher, ed., *Abraham Lincoln: Speeches and Writings, 1859–1865*, 232.

108 wondered whether: *Alexandria Gazette*, April 17, 1861.

108 particularly interested: Nicolay and Hay, *Abraham Lincoln*, vol. 4, 98.

108 "long interview": Allan, "Memoranda of Conversations with General Robert E. Lee," 10.

108 "tried in every": Ibid.

108 "Mr. Blair": *National Intelligencer*, August 9, 1866, quoted in Freeman, *R. E. Lee*, vol. 1, 635.

109 "After listening": Robert E. Lee to Reverdy Johnson, Lexington, Virginia, February 25, 1868, in Lee, *Recollections and Letters of General Robert E. Lee*, 27.

Notes

109 not surprise: Allan, "Memoranda of Conversations with General Robert E. Lee," 10.

109 "You have made": Wade Hampton, *Address on the Life and Character of Gen. Robert E. Lee* (Baltimore: John Murphy, 1871), 16; Mason, *Popular Life of Gen. Robert Edward Lee*, 73.

109 resign his commission: Freeman, *R. E. Lee*, vol. 1, 437.

109 consulted: Robert E. Lee to Sydney Smith Lee, Arlington, Virginia, April 20, 1861, in Lee, *Recollections and Letters of General Robert E. Lee*, 26.

109 "I presume": Mary Custis Lee to Charles Marshall, [1871], in Pryor, "Thou Knowest Not the Time of Thy Visitation."

109 "I cannot yet": Agnes Lee to Mildred Lee, Arlington, April 19, DeButts-Ely Collection of Lee Family Papers, Library of Congress.

109 "commotion": George Lyttleton Upshur, *As I Recall Them; Memories of Crowded Years* (New York: Wilson-Erickson, 1936), 16–17.

109 "severest struggle": Mary Custis Lee, "My Reminiscences of the War," in deButts, "Mary Custis Lee's 'Reminiscences of the War.'"

110 his example: For examples of people testifying to Lee's influence, see Pryor, "Thou Knowest Not the Time of Thy Visitation."

110 "I must try": Robert E. Lee to Mary Custis Lee, Fort Mason, January 23, 1861, in Adams, *An Annotated Edition of the Personal Letters of Robert E. Lee, April, 1855–April, 1861*, 723–24.

110 read aloud: Mary Custis Lee to Charles Marshall, [1871], in Pryor, "Thou Knowest Not the Time of Thy Visitation."

110 "Since my interview": Robert E. Lee to Winfield Scott, Arlington, April 20, 1861, Custis-Lee Family Papers, Library of Congress.

110 "None of us": Mary Custis Lee to Charles Marshall, [1871], in Pryor, "Thou Knowest Not the Time of Thy Visitation."

111 "After the most": Robert E. Lee to Sydney Smith Lee, Arlington, Virginia, April 20, 1861, Lee, *Recollections and Letters of General Robert E. Lee*, 26–27.

111 "mourned": Mary Custis Lee to Charles Marshall, [1871], in Pryor, "Thou Knowest Not the Time of Thy Visitation."

111 Confederate colors: S. L. Lee, "War Time in Alexandria, Virginia," *South Atlantic Quarterly* 4, no. 3 (July 1905): 234–48.

111 in his pew: Harriotte Lee Taliaferro, "Mrs. Taliaferro's Memoir," in Ludwell Lee Montague, "Memoir of Mrs. Harriotte Lee Taliaferro Concerning Events in Virginia, April 11–21, 1861," *Virginia Magazine of History and Biography* 57, no. 4 (October 1949): 416–20.

111 wish he had: Abraham Lincoln to Erastus Corning and Others, Executive Mansion, Washington, DC, June 12, 1863, in Fehrenbacher, ed., *Abraham Lincoln: Speeches and Writings, 1859–1865*, 458.

111 "There is no": *Alexandria Gazette*, April 20, 1861, quoted in Freeman, *R. E. Lee*, vol. 1, 444–45.

111 received a summons: Thomas, *Robert E. Lee*, 189.

112 "Tell Custis": Robert E. Lee to Mary Custis Lee, Richmond, May 13, 1861, quoted in Lee, *General Lee*, 94.

112 a month: George Washington Custis Lee to John Letcher, Richmond, May 24,

1861, in H. W. Flournoy, ed., *Calendar of Virginia State Papers and Other Manuscripts* (Richmond, 1893), vol. 11, 133.

112 "were he": Lee, "War Time in Alexandria, Virginia."

112 headquarters: "Visit to the Federal Camps in Virginia," *New York Herald*, May 30, 1861.

Chapter 7: The Battle for Arlington

115 briefly served: Robert E. Lee to Charles Carter Lee, Cockspur, February 27, 1831, Robert E. Lee Papers, University of Virginia.

115 "I must remark": Joseph Mansfield to Winfield Scott, Headquarters, Department of Washington, May 3, 1861, in *O.R.*, series 1, vol. 2, 618–19.

115 Scott agreed: E. D. Townsend, *Anecdotes of the Civil War in the United States* (New York: D. Appleton, 1884), 32–33.

115 Virginians lugging: Nelligan, *Old Arlington*, 456.

115 "It is quite": Joseph Mansfield to Winfield Scott, Headquarters, Department of Washington, May 3, 1861, in *O.R.*, series 1, vol. 2, 619.

116 "not prepared": Eighth Day of Secret Session, *Proceedings of the Virginia State Convention of 1861*.

116 street orators: Sallie A. Brock, *Richmond During the War: Four Years of Personal Observation* (New York: G. W. Carleton, 1867), 21–22.

116 month's end: Leech, *Reveille in Washington, 1860–1865*, 68–69.

116 "bravado and boasting": Robert E. Lee to Mary Custis Lee, Richmond, May 13, 1861, quoted in Lee, *General Lee*, 94.

116 sister: Robert E. Lee to Anne Marshall, Arlington, Virginia, April 20, 1861, in Dowdey and Manarin, eds., *The Wartime Papers of Robert E. Lee*, 9–10.

116 General Scott: For anecdotes illustrating Lee's regard for Northern soldiers and General Scott, see Freeman, *R. E. Lee*, vol. 1, 475 and 478.

116 Virginia Mechanics Institute: Thomas, *Robert E. Lee*, 194.

116 "prolonged and bloody": Walter H. Taylor, *Four Years with General Lee* (New York: D. Appleton, 1878), 11.

116 "The war may": Robert E. Lee to Mary Custis Lee, Richmond, April 30, 1861, in Dowdey and Manarin, eds., *The Wartime Papers of Robert E. Lee*, 15.

116 fifty-one thousand: Robert E. Lee to John Letcher, Headquarters, Virginia Forces, Richmond, June 15, 1861, in ibid., 51.

116 twenty thousand: Thomas, *Robert E. Lee*, 194.

116 "zeal": Robert E. Lee to Daniel Ruggles, Headquarters, Virginia Forces, Richmond, May 10, 1861, in *O.R.*, series 1, vol. 2, 828–29.

116 "very much": Robert E. Lee to L. Pope Walker, Headquarters, Virginia Forces, Richmond, May 25, 1861, in ibid., 877.

116 "old flint-lock": Robert E. Lee to Joseph Brown, Headquarters, Virginia Forces, Richmond, May 26, 1861, in Dowdey and Manarin, eds., *The Wartime Papers of Robert E. Lee*, 37.

116 akin to what: Joseph T. Glatthaar, *General Lee's Army: From Victory to Collapse* (New York: Free Press, 2009), 259.

Notes

117   defense: Robert E. Lee to Thomas J. Jackson, Headquarters, Virginia Forces, Richmond, May 10, 1861, in *O.R.*, series 1, vol. 2, 825.

117   provided pathways: Robert E. Lee to John Letcher, Headquarters, Virginia Forces, Richmond, in Dowdey and Manarin, eds., *The Wartime Papers of Robert E. Lee*, 50–52.

117   "this section": Francis M. Boykin to Robert E. Lee, Grafton, Virginia, May 10, 1861, in *O.R.*, series 1, vol. 2, 827.

117   arranged: Hearn, *Six Years of Hell*, 50–51.

117   torched: Report of R. Jones, Carlisle Barracks, April 20, 1861, in *O.R.*, series 1, vol. 2, 4.

117   relocating: Robert E. Lee to Thomas J. Jackson, Headquarters, Virginia Forces, Richmond, May 1, 1861, in *O.R.*, series 1, vol. 2, 793–94; Thomas J. Jackson to Robert E. Lee, Division Headquarters, Harper's Ferry, May 7, 1861, in *O.R.*, series 1, vol. 2, 814–15.

117   "Every rifle": Robert E. Lee to Thomas J. Jackson, Headquarters Virginia Forces, Richmond, May 10, 1861, in *O.R.*, series 1, vol. 2, 825.

117   "a means": Ibid.

119   his own hand: "Death of Brig. Gen. Cocke," *Richmond Whig*, December 31, 1861; Ezra J. Warner, *Generals in Gray* (Baton Rouge: Louisiana State University Press, 2006), 56–57.

119   fifty thousand: Philip St. George Cocke to Daniel Ruggles, Headquarters, Potomac Department, Culpeper Court-House, May 2, 1861, in *O.R.*, series 1, vol. 2, 795–96.

119   "Should Virginia": Philip St. George Cocke, Headquarters, Potomac Department, Culpeper Court-House, May 5, 1861, in ibid., 805.

119   block by block: Philip St. George Cocke to A. S. Taylor, Culpeper Court-House, May 5, 1861, in ibid., 24.

119   "in my opinion": Robert E. Lee to Philip St. George Cocke, Headquarters, Virginia Forces, Richmond, May 15, 1861, in ibid., 845.

119   make a stand: Robert E. Lee to George H. Terrett, Headquarters, Virginia Forces, Richmond, May 15, 1861, in ibid., 845–46.

119   buy time: Robert E. Lee to Philip St. George Cocke, April 23, 1861, in Flournoy, ed., *Calendar of Virginia State Papers and Other Manuscripts*, vol. 11, 112.

119   "Among such": Robert E. Lee to Mary Custis Lee, Richmond, April 30, 1861, in Dowdey and Manarin, eds., *The Wartime Papers of Robert E. Lee*, 15.

120   "I want you": Robert E. Lee to Mary Custis Lee, Richmond, May 2, 1861, in ibid., 18.

120   warning: Robert E. Lee to Mary Custis Lee, Richmond, April 26, 1861, in ibid., 12–13.

120   routine: Mary Custis Lee, "My Reminiscences of the War," in deButts, "Mary Custis Lee's 'Reminiscences of the War.'"

120   "I never saw": Mary Custis Lee to Robert E. Lee, Arlington, May 9, 1861, DeButts-Ely Collection of Lee Family Papers, Library of Congress.

120   "You must pack": Mary Custis Lee, "My Reminiscences of the War," in deButts, "Mary Custis Lee's 'Reminiscences of the War.'"

120   town called Lexington: Robert E. Lee to Mary Custis Lee, Richmond, May 8, 1861, DeButts-Ely Collection of Lee Family Papers, Library of Congress;

Notes

Robert E. Lee to Mary Custis Lee, Richmond, May 13, 1861, Mary Custis Lee Papers, Virginia Historical Society.

120 "My sanguine": Mary Custis Lee, "My Reminiscences of the War," in deButts, "Mary Custis Lee's 'Reminiscences of the War.'"

120 "My beautiful home": Mary Custis Lee to Mildred Lee, Arlington, May 5, DeButts-Ely Collection of Lee Family Papers, Library of Congress.

120 went to Ravensworth: Mary Custis Lee, "My Reminiscences of the War," in deButts, "Mary Custis Lee's 'Reminiscences of the War'"; Mary Custis Lee to Robert E. Lee, Arlington, May 9, 1861, DeButts-Ely Collection of Lee Family Papers, Library of Congress.

120 hanging on the walls: "A Sketch of a Hasty Visit to Dear Old Arlington," Mary Custis Lee Papers, Virginia Historical Society.

120 "The rest": Mary Custis Lee to Mildred Lee, Arlington, May 5, DeButts-Ely Collection of Lee Family Papers, Library of Congress.

121 "The servants distress": Agnes Lee to Annie Lee, May 6, DeButts-Ely Collection of Lee Family Papers, Library of Congress.

121 seemed empty: Nelligan, *Old Arlington*, 459.

121 Union prison: Mary Custis Lee to Robert E. Lee, Arlington, May 9, 1861, DeButts-Ely Collection of Lee Family Papers, Library of Congress.

121 pet cat: Mary P. Coulling, *The Lee Girls* (Winston-Salem: John F. Blair, 1987), 87.

121 "may burst": Robert E. Lee to Mary Custis Lee, Richmond, May 11, 1861, in Dowdey and Manarin, eds., *The Wartime Papers of Robert E. Lee*, 25–26.

121 "piercing eye": Bernice-Marie Yates, *The Perfect Gentleman: The Life and Letters of George Washington Custis Lee* (Xulon Press, 2003), vol. 2, 74–75.

121 "Custis astonishes me": Mary Custis Lee to Robert E. Lee, Arlington, May 9, 1861, DeButts-Ely Collection of Lee Family Papers, Library of Congress.

121 "Were it not": Mary Custis Lee to Winfield Scott, Arlington, May 5, [1861], in Townsend, *Anecdotes of the Civil War in the United States*, 34.

121 "I would not": Mary Custis Lee to Mildred Lee, Arlington, May 5, DeButts-Ely Collection of Lee Family Papers, Library of Congress.

122 laughed: Mary Custis Lee to Robert E. Lee, Sunday, May 12, DeButts-Ely Collection of Lee Family Papers, Library of Congress.

122 "must be commencing": Mary Custis Lee to Robert E. Lee, Arlington, May 9, 1861, DeButts-Ely Collection of Lee Family Papers, Library of Congress.

122 spoke of returning: Mary Custis Lee, "My Reminiscences of the War," in deButts, "Mary Custis Lee's 'Reminiscences of the War.'"

122 keys: Robert M. Poole, *On Hallowed Ground: The Story of Arlington National Cemetery* (New York: Walker, 2009), 25 and 29.

122 weeping: Mary Custis Lee, "My Reminiscences of the War," in deButts, "Mary Custis Lee's 'Reminiscences of the War.'"

122 beautiful: Diary of Samuel P. Heintzelman, May 23, 1861, Samuel P. Heintzelman Papers, Library of Congress.

122 "Perhaps they've": *Boston Traveller*, May 4, 1861.

122 two o'clock in the morning: Report of Samuel P. Heintzelman, Headquarters, Department of Washington, July 20, 1863, in *O.R.*, series 1, vol. 2, 40.

122 taps: Poole, *On Hallowed Ground*, 26 and 41–42.

Notes

123 steamers for Alexandria: Report of S. C. Rowan, USS *Pawnee*, Off Alexandria, May 29, 1861, in United States Naval War Records Office, *Official Records of the Union and Confederate Navies in the War of the Rebellion* (Washington, DC: Government Printing Office, 1894–1922), series 1, vol. 4, 478–79.

123 "It would be": Report of George H. Terrett, Manassas Junction, Camp Pickens, May 28, 1861, in *O.R.*, series 1, vol. 2, 43–44.

123 Confederate flag: "The Death of Col. Ellsworth," *New York Times*, May 26, 1861.

123 lie in state: Adam Goodheart, "How Col. Ellsworth's Death Shocked the Union," Smithsonianmag.com, March 31, 2011, online.

123 "I stated": Report of Charles Sandford, Headquarters, First Division NYSM, Washington, May 28, 1861, in *O.R.*, series 1, vol. 2, 38.

123 shoveling: *New York Tribune*, May 25, 1861.

123 camp: *New York Times*, May 29, 1861.

123 "The place": *New York Times*, June 1, 1861.

124 Lafayette himself: Elliot, *Historical Sketches of the Ten Miles Square Forming the District of Columbia*, 292.

124 "It never": Mary Custis Lee to Charles Sandford, May 30, 1861, Robert E. Lee Family Collection, Museum of the Confederacy.

124 precipitous promotion: William C. Davis, *Battle at Bull Run: A History of the First Major Campaign of the Civil War* (Mechanicsburg, PA: Stackpole Books, 1995), 9–12.

124 "With respect": Irvin McDowell to Mary Custis Lee, Headquarters, Department of Northeastern Virginia, Arlington, May 30, 1861, Robert E. Lee Family Collection, Museum of the Confederacy.

125 "There is": Markie Williams to Mary Custis Lee, Washington, DC, July 13, 1861, DeButts-Ely Collection of Lee Family Papers, Library of Congress.

125 "I do not": Robert E. Lee to Mary Custis Lee, Richmond, May 25, 1861, in Dowdey and Manarin, eds., *The Wartime Papers of Robert E. Lee*, 36.

125 "much blood": Francis Pickens to John Floyd, State of South Carolina Headquarters, August 4, 1861, in *O.R.*, series 1, vol. 51, part 2, 213.

125 "If Lee": Davis, *Battle at Bull Run*, 32.

125 "stupidly": "Views of Current Events," *New York Times*, June 3, 1861.

126 now belonged: A Proclamation by the Governor of Virginia, Headquarters, Virginia Forces, Richmond, June 8, 1861, in *O.R.*, series 1, vol. 2, 911–12.

126 set up shop: William C. Davis, "Richmond Becomes the Capital," in William C. Davis and James I. Robertson Jr., eds., *Virginia at War, 1861* (Lexington: University Press of Kentucky, 2005), 127.

126 superseded Jackson: Joseph E. Johnston, *Narrative of Military Operations* (New York: D. Appleton, 1874), 14–25.

126 "When it": Robert E. Lee to John Letcher, Headquarters, Virginia Forces, Richmond, June 15, 1861, in Dowdey and Manarin, eds., *The Wartime Papers of Robert E. Lee*, 50–52.

127 "early at": Taylor, *General Lee*, 24–25.

127 "The city": John Augustine Washington III to Eliza Washington, Richmond, May 10, 1861, Mount Vernon.

127 fondness: Taylor, *General Lee*, 25–26; Brock, *Richmond During the War*, 50.

Notes

127 "I do not": Robert E. Lee to Mary Custis Lee, Richmond, June 9, 1861, in Dowdey and Manarin, eds., *The Wartime Papers of Robert E. Lee*, 46.

127 "I have never": Robert E. Lee to Mary Custis Lee, Richmond, July 12, 1861, DeButts-Ely Collection of Lee Family Papers, Library of Congress.

127 command in the field: Shelby Foote, *The Civil War: A Narrative* (New York: Vintage Books, 1986), vol. 1, 16–17.

127 "too hollow": William J. Cooper Jr., *Jefferson Davis, American* (New York: Vintage Books, 2001), 357–58.

127 subordinate his wishes: William C. Davis, *Jefferson Davis: The Man and His Hour* (Baton Rouge: Louisiana State University Press, 1996), 426–27.

127 "Where I": Robert E. Lee to Mary Custis Lee, Richmond, July 12, 1861, DeButts-Ely Collection of Lee Family Papers, Library of Congress.

127 adviser: Taylor, *Four Years with General Lee*, 15.

127 the strategy: Davis, *Battle at Bull Run*, 29–31.

127 "We could": P. G. T. Beauregard to Jefferson Davis, Headquarters, Manassas, Camp Pickens, June 12, 1861, in Alfred Roman, *The Military Operations of General Beauregard in the War Between the States, 1861–1865* (New York: Harper & Brothers, 1884), vol. 1, 77.

128 "Concurring fully": Jefferson Davis to P. G. T. Beauregard, Executive Department, Richmond, June 13, 1861, in *O.R.*, series 1, vol. 2, 922–23.

128 sauntered west: Foote, *The Civil War*, vol. 1, 70–71; MacDonald, *Mrs. Robert E. Lee*, 155–56.

128 ordered Lee: Robert E. Lee to Mary Custis Lee, Richmond, July 27, 1861, DeButts-Ely Collection of Lee Family Papers, Library of Congress.

128 came word: J. B. Jones, *A Rebel War Clerk's Diary at the Confederate States Capital* (Philadelphia: J. B. Lippincott, 1866), vol. 1, 64–65.

128 the stonewall: Foote, *The Civil War*, vol. 1, 74–82.

128 spirits lifted: William T. Sherman, *Memoirs of General William T. Sherman*, 2nd ed. (New York: D. Appleton, 1904), vol. 1, 217–18.

128 keep fighting: *New York Herald*, July 24, 1861.

129 "The battle": Robert E. Lee to Mary Custis Lee, Richmond, July 27, 1861, DeButts-Ely Collection of Lee Family Papers, Library of Congress.

129 Two aides: Taylor, *General Lee*, 27.

Chapter 8: The Last Heir

130 spacious: John Augustine Washington III to Gustavus Myers, Camp on Valley Mountain, August 12, 1861, Gustavus A. Myers Papers, Swem Library Digital Projects.

130 "some portion": Robert E. Lee to Mary Custis Lee, Camp on Valley Mountain, August 9, 1861, in Dowdey and Manarin, eds., *The Wartime Papers of Robert E. Lee*, 64.

130 "Have become": John Augustine Washington III to My Dear Aunt, Camp on Valley Mountain, August 31, 1861, Virginia Historical Society.

130 train: Taylor, *Four Years with General Lee*, 16.

Notes

130   "Sometimes we": John Augustine Washington III to Eliza Washington, Monterey, Highland County, August 1, 1861, Mount Vernon.

130   "If any one": Robert E. Lee to Mary Custis Lee, Huntersville, Virginia, August 4, 1861, in Dowdey and Manarin, eds., *The Wartime Papers of Robert E. Lee*, 61–62.

130   sympathies: Robert E. Lee to Mary Custis Lee, Camp at Valley Mountain, August 9, 1861, in ibid., 64.

131   developments: W. Hunter Lesser, *Rebels at the Gate: Lee and McClellan on the Front Line of a Nation Divided* (Naperville, IL: Sourcebooks, 2004), 78–79 and 126–29.

131   penetrating: Jefferson Davis to Joseph Johnston, Richmond, Virginia, August 1, 1861, in *O.R.*, series 1, vol. 5, 767.

131   mountain passes: Freeman, *R. E. Lee*, vol. 1, 543–51.

131   "to strike": Jefferson Davis to Joseph Johnston, Richmond, Virginia, August 1, 1861, in *O.R.*, series 1, vol. 5, 767.

131   commanders: Robert E. Lee to Mary Custis Lee, Huntersville, Virginia, August 4, 1861, in Dowdey and Manarin, eds., *The Wartime Papers of Robert E. Lee*, 61; Taylor, *Four Years with General Lee*, 16.

131   "could not": Long, *Memoirs of Robert E. Lee*, 112 and 120.

131   "The soldiers everywhere": Robert E. Lee to Mary Custis Lee, Huntersville, Virginia, August 4, 1861, in Dowdey and Manarin, eds., *The Wartime Papers of Robert E. Lee*, 61–62.

132   sidestepped: Freeman, *R. E. Lee*, vol. 1, 551–54; Long, *Memoirs of Robert E. Lee*, 120–21.

132   "I think": John Augustine Washington III to Ned Turner, Huntersville, August 5, 1861, Mount Vernon.

132   reached Valley Mountain: John Augustine Washington III to Maria Washington, Camp on Valley Mountain, August 7, 1861, Papers of Beverley Dandridge Tucker, University of Virginia.

132   "The mountains": Robert E. Lee to Mary Custis Lee, Camp at Valley Mountain, August 9, 1861, in Dowdey and Manarin, eds., *The Wartime Papers of Robert E. Lee*, 63.

132   guessed: Taylor, *General Lee*, 31–32; Marcus J. Wright, *General Officers of the Confederate Army: Officers of the Executive Departments of the Confederate States, Members of the Confederate Congress by States* (New York: Neale Publishing, 1911), 9–10.

132   "Gen. Lee": John Augustine Washington III to Maria Washington, Camp on Valley Mountain, August 7, 1861, Papers of Beverley Dandridge Tucker, University of Virginia.

132   not only his: John Augustine Washington III to Gustavus Myers, Camp on Valley Mountain, August 12, 1861, Gustavus A. Myers Papers, Swem Library Digital Projects.

132   "He always": Taylor, *General Lee*, 31–32.

132   Happiness: John Augustine Washington III to Gustavus Myers, Camp on Valley Mountain, August 12, 1861, Gustavus A. Myers Papers, Swem Library Digital Projects.

133   stewardship: Scott E. Casper, *Sarah Johnson's Mount Vernon: The Forgotten History of an American Shrine* (New York: Hill and Wang, 2008), 39.

Notes

133 reddish-brown: Arthur Herbert, *The Washington Address* (Lynchburg, VA: J. P. Bell, 1915), 4–5; Chernow, *Washington*, xxi and 29.

133 increase: Casper, *Sarah Johnson's Mount Vernon*, 44.

133 "pulling down": Jean B. Lee, "Historical Memory, Sectional Strife, and the American Mecca: Mount Vernon, 1783–1853," *Virginia Magazine of History and Biography* 109, no. 3 (2001): 255–300.

133 Souvenir: Ibid.; Casper, *Sarah Johnson's Mount Vernon*, 64 and 66.

133 "Mecca of Freemen": Lee, "Historical Memory, Sectional Strife, and the American Mecca."

133 talk of saving: Casper, *Sarah Johnson's Mount Vernon*, 67–71.

134 disappointed: Elswyth Thane, *Mount Vernon Is Ours: The Story of Its Preservation* (New York: Duell, Sloan, and Pearce, 1966), 73–74.

134 "Here we have": *New York Tribune*, December 27, 1858.

134 used the proceeds: Casper, *Sarah Johnson's Mount Vernon*, 73–74.

134 visited: Nelly Washington to John Augustine Washington III, Mount Vernon, April 19, 1860, Mount Vernon Ladies' Association Archives, Library of Virginia.

134 "perfectly well": Mary Custis Lee to Annie Lee, Arlington, October 21, DeButts-Ely Collection of Lee Family Papers, Library of Congress.

134 "He has seen": Cassius Lee to John Augustine Washington III, Alexandria, October 11, 1860, Alexandria Library.

134 fife and drum: John Augustine Washington III to Eliza Washington, Richmond, May 10, 1861, Mount Vernon.

135 seven children: Casper, *Sarah Johnson's Mount Vernon*, 77.

135 arrived at: "In Town," *Richmond Daily Dispatch*, May 2, 1861.

135 "When yet": John Augustine Washington to Daughter, Richmond, May 3, 1861, in John Lipscomb Johnson, *The University Memorial: Biographical Sketches of Alumni of the University of Virginia Who Fell in the Confederate War* (Baltimore: Turnbull Brothers, 1871), 59.

135 hated: Robert E. Lee to Mary Custis Lee, Valley Mountain, September 17, 1861, in Dowdey and Manarin, eds., *The Wartime Papers of Robert E. Lee*, 73.

135 "No greater": Herbert, *The Washington Address*, 6–7.

135 "The Yankees": John Augustine Washington III to Eliza Washington, Richmond, June 29, 1861, Mount Vernon.

135 one historian: Casper, *Sarah Johnson's Mount Vernon*, 83–84.

135 "belonging alike": Dorothy Troth Muir, *Mount Vernon: The Civil War Years* (Mount Vernon: Mount Vernon Ladies' Association, 1993), 49–50 and 53.

136 By the time: John Augustine Washington III to Gustavus Myers, Camp on Valley Mountain, August 12, 1861, Gustavus A. Myers Papers, Swem Library Digital Projects; Long, *Memoirs of Robert E. Lee*, 121.

136 three miles: John Augustine Washington III to Gustavus Myers, Camp on Valley Mountain, August 12, 1861, Gustavus A. Myers Papers, Swem Library Digital Projects.

136 "dashing through": Long, *Memoirs of Robert E. Lee*, 121–22.

136 mists: John Augustine Washington III to My Dear Aunt, Camp on Valley Mountain, August 31, 1861, Virginia Historical Society.

136 ten miles: John Augustine Washington III to Gustavus Myers, Camp on Valley

Notes

Mountain, August 12, 1861, Gustavus A. Myers Papers, Swem Library Digital Projects; Taylor, *Four Years with General Lee*, 21.

136 Seven miles: Lesser, *Rebels at the Gate*, 139–40.

136 Wagons: Taylor, *Four Years with General Lee*, 17.

136 "It rains": Robert E. Lee to Annie and Agnes Lee, Valley Mountain, August 29, 1861, in Dowdey and Manarin, eds., *The Wartime Papers of Robert E. Lee*, 67.

136 stalemate: Ibid., 67–68.

137 more than half: Robert E. Lee to George Washington Custis Lee, Valley Mountain, September 3, 1861, in ibid., 70.

137 "Those on": Robert E. Lee to Mary Custis Lee, Valley Mountain, September 1, 1861, in ibid., 68–69.

137 "They are worse": Robert E. Lee to Mary Custis Lee, Valley Mountain, September 17, 1861, in ibid., 74.

137 "Don't drink": Marcus B. Toney, *The Privations of a Private* (Nashville, 1905), 21.

137 concealed: John Augustine Washington III to My Dear Aunt, Camp on Valley Mountain, August 31, 1861, Virginia Historical Society.

137 fabricated: Freeman, *R. E. Lee*, vol. 1, 558.

137 "Do not": Robert E. Lee to Mary Custis Lee, Camp at Valley Mountain, September 9, 1861, in Dowdey and Manarin, eds., *The Wartime Papers of Robert E. Lee*, 71.

137 dispatch: John Augustine Washington III to My Dear Aunt, Camp on Valley Mountain, August 31, 1861, Virginia Historical Society.

137 sun: Robert E. Lee to George Washington Custis Lee, Valley Mountain, September 3, 1861, in Dowdey and Manarin, eds., *The Wartime Papers of Robert E. Lee*, 70.

137 side of the summit: Taylor, *Four Years with General Lee*, 22–23; Lesser, *Rebels at the Gate*, 185 and 187.

137 a second: Long, *Memoirs of Robert E. Lee*, 123.

137 any retreat: Taylor, *Four Years with General Lee*, 23–24.

137 "The enemy": Robert E. Lee to George Washington Custis Lee, Valley Mountain, September 3, 1861, in Dowdey and Manarin, eds., *The Wartime Papers of Robert E. Lee*, 69–70.

138 in their rear: Long, *Memoirs of Robert E. Lee*, 123–25; Taylor, *Four Years with General Lee*, 24–26.

138 "The eyes": Special Orders, Headquarters of the Forces, Valley Mountain, September 9, 1861, in *O.R.*, series 1, vol. 5, 192.

138 other farmlands: John Augustine Washington III to Eliza Washington, Camp on Valley Mountain, August 26, 1861, Mount Vernon; Casper, *Sarah Johnson's Mount Vernon*, 73 and 89.

138 confiscate: Muir, *Mount Vernon*, 78–84; *New York Times*, October 28, 1861.

138 "I want": John Augustine Washington III to My Dear Aunt, Camp on Valley Mountain, August 31, 1861, Virginia Historical Society.

138 "superfluous beef": John Augustine Washington III to W. Fontaine Alexander, Camp on Valley Mountain, September 6, 1861, in John A. Washington, "John Augustine Washington, III et al.," *Magazine of the Jefferson County Historical Society* 73 (December 2007): 24–34.

Notes

138 twice a day: Taylor, *General Lee*, 29.

138 "blessing": John Augustine Washington III to Eliza Washington, Camp on Valley Mountain, September 6, 1861, Mount Vernon.

138 "I know": Anne Lee Peyton, Commonplace Book, 1861, Peyton Family Papers, Virginia Historical Society.

139 "The rain": C. T. Quintard, *Doctor Quintard, Chaplain C.S.A. and Second Bishop of Tennessee: Being His Story of the War*, ed. Arthur Howard Noll (Sewanee, TN: The University Press, 1905), 22.

139 "All the projected": Robert E. Lee to S. Cooper, Headquarters, Valley Mountain, September 16, 1861, Robert E. Lee Papers, Virginia Historical Society.

139 signal: Robert E. Lee to Mary Custis Lee, Valley Mountain, September 17, 1861, in Dowdey and Manarin, eds., *The Wartime Papers of Robert E. Lee*, 73.

139 drowning: Lesser, *Rebels at the Gate*, 190.

139 "They had to": Robert E. Lee to Mary Custis Lee, Valley Mountain, September 17, 1861, in Dowdey and Manarin, eds., *The Wartime Papers of Robert E. Lee*, 73.

139 "I could see": Robert E. Lee to John Letcher, Valley Mountain, September 17, 1861, in ibid., 75.

139 Lee learn: Taylor, *Four Years with General Lee*, 23 and 28–29.

140 "All chance": Robert E. Lee to John Letcher, Valley Mountain, September 17, 1861, in Dowdey and Manarin, eds., *The Wartime Papers of Robert E. Lee*, 75.

140 pondered their options: Lesser, *Rebels at the Gate*, 199; Robert E. Lee to S. Cooper, Headquarters, Valley Mountain, September 16, 1861, Robert E. Lee Papers, Virginia Historical Society.

140 delivered orders: William Fitzhugh Lee, quoted in Johnson, *The University Memorial*, 60.

140 high rank: Yates, *The Perfect Gentlemen*, vol. 1, 228; Mary Bandy Daughtry, *Gray Cavalier: The Life and Wars of General W. H. F. "Rooney" Lee* (Cambridge, MA: Da Capo Press, 2002), 55.

140 nepotism: C. Vann Woodward, ed., *Mary Chesnut's Civil War* (New Haven, CT: Yale University Press, 1981), 138.

140 "I have enjoyed": Robert E. Lee to Mary Custis Lee, Camp at Valley Mountain, August 9, 1861, in Dowdey and Manarin, eds., *The Wartime Papers of Robert E. Lee*, 63.

140 220 pounds: Daughtry, *Gray Cavalier*, 54.

140 grinning: Johnson, *The University Memorial*, 60.

140 acquiesced: Robert E. Lee to Mary Custis Lee, Valley Mountain, September 17, 1861, in Dowdey and Manarin, eds., *The Wartime Papers of Robert E. Lee*, 74.

140 "We had to": William Fitzhugh Lee, quoted in Johnson, *The University Memorial*, 60.

140 "Oh no": Ibid., 60–61.

141 Rooney assumed: John Levering, "Lee's Advance and Retreat in the Cheat Mountain Campaign in 1861: Supplemented by the Tragic Death of Colonel John A. Washington of His Staff," in *Military Essays and Recollections* (Chicago: Cozzens & Beaton, 1907), vol. 4, 30–31.

141 few hundred yards: William Fitzhugh Lee, quoted in Johnson, *The University Memorial*, 60–61.

Notes

141 ride away: Robert E. Lee to John Letcher, Valley Mountain, September 17, 1861, in Dowdey and Manarin, eds., *The Wartime Papers of Robert E. Lee*, 75–76.

141 Three bullets: Levering, "Lee's Advance and Retreat in the Cheat Mountain Campaign in 1861," 31–32.

141 shoulder straps: "Latest from Western Virginia," *Cincinnati Daily Enquirer*, September 19, 1861.

141 "I shall": Levering, "Lee's Advance and Retreat in the Cheat Mountain Campaign in 1861," 32–34.

141 "I fear": Robert E. Lee to Mary Custis Lee, Valley Mountain, September 17, 1861, in Dowdey and Manarin, eds., *The Wartime Papers of Robert E. Lee*, 74.

141 "Lieutenant Colonel": Levering, "Lee's Advance and Retreat in the Cheat Mountain Campaign in 1861," 33.

141 "I saw him": Quintard, *Doctor Quintard, Chaplain C.S.A. and Second Bishop of Tennessee*, 30.

142 "My intimate": Robert E. Lee to Louisa Washington, Camp on Valley River, September 16, 1861, in Freeman, *R. E. Lee*, vol. 1, 569–70.

142 "Our enemies": Robert E. Lee to Edward C. Turner, Camp at Valley River, September 14, 1861, Robert E. Lee Papers, University of Virginia.

142 "hasty": Mary Custis Lee to Mildred Lee, Hot Springs, Saturday the 21st, DeButts-Ely Collection of Lee Family Papers, Library of Congress.

142 "He justly": "John A. Washington Dead," *Daily Cleveland Herald*, September 16, 1861.

142 "My wish": "Latest from Western Virginia," *Cincinnati Daily Enquirer*, September 19, 1861.

142 "While referring": *Daily National Intelligencer*, September 19, 1861.

143 "weaving ingenious": "The New Programme for Western Virginia," *Richmond Daily Dispatch*, September 26, 1861.

143 seventy-five miles: Lesser, *Rebels at the Gate*, 205–15.

143 "Why": Freeman, *R. E. Lee*, vol. 1, 577 and 602.

143 "I have": Robert E. Lee to Mildred Lee, Charleston, November 15, 1861, in Dowdey and Manarin, eds., *The Wartime Papers of Robert E. Lee*, 86.

143 "wiry": Robert E. Lee to Charlotte Lee, Dabb's, June 22, 1862, in ibid., 197.

143 "Granny Lee": Freeman, *R. E. Lee*, vol. 1, 602.

143 upset: Robert E. Lee to Mary Custis Lee, Camp at Valley Mountain, September 9, 1861, in Dowdey and Manarin, eds., *The Wartime Papers of Robert E. Lee*, 71.

143 "I am sorry": Robert E. Lee to Mary Custis Lee, Sewell's Mountain, October 7, 1861, in ibid., 80.

143 quarrelsome generals: Douglas Southall Freeman, *Lee's Lieutenants: A Study in Command* (New York: Charles Scribner's Sons, 1942–1944), vol. 1, 99–109 and 113–17.

144 "Though subjected": Jefferson Davis, *The Rise and Fall of the Confederate Government* (New York: D. Appleton, 1881), vol. 1, 436–37.

144 new aide: General Orders, No. 1, Headquarters, Coosawhatchie, South Carolina, November 8, 1861, in Dowdey and Manarin, eds., *The Wartime Papers of Robert E. Lee*, 84; "Colonel Thornton A. Washington," *New York Tribune*, July 12, 1894; Thornton Augustin Washington, ed., *A Genealogical History, Beginning with Col-*

onel John Washington, the Emigrant, and Head of the Washington Family in America (Washington, DC: McGill & Wallace, 1891), 44–45.

Chapter 9: White House Burning

145 abandon the place: Robert E. Lee to J. H. Trapier, Savannah, Georgia, February 24, 1862, in *O.R.*, series 1, vol. 6, 398–99; Report of S. F. Du Pont, Flagship *Wabash*, Off St. Augustine, Florida, March 13, 1862, in *Official Records of the Union and Confederate Navies in the War of the Rebellion*, series 1, vol. 12, 598.

145 concentrate troops: Robert E. Lee to J. H. Trapier, Savannah, Georgia, February 19, 1862, in *O.R.*, series 1, vol. 6, 393–94.

145 "accompany him": Long, *Memoirs of Robert E. Lee*, 22.

145 parlor: Robert E. Lee to Mary Custis Lee, Coosawhatchie, South Carolina, January 18, 1862, in Dowdey and Manarin, eds., *The Wartime Papers of Robert E. Lee*, 103–4.

145 "Passing on": Long, *Memoirs of Robert E. Lee*, 22–23.

145 "He died there": Robert E. Lee to Mary Custis Lee, Coosawhatchie, South Carolina, January 18, 1862, in Dowdey and Manarin, eds., *The Wartime Papers of Robert E. Lee*, 103.

145 the details: Pryor, *Reading the Man*, 29; Royster, *Light-Horse Harry Lee and the Legacy of the American Revolution*, 3–7.

146 marble slab: Robert E. Lee to Mary Custis Lee, Coosawhatchie, South Carolina, January 18, 1862, in Dowdey and Manarin, eds., *The Wartime Papers of Robert E. Lee*, 103.

146 approached alone: Long, *Memoirs of Robert E. Lee*, 23.

146 never before: Robert E. Lee to Mary Custis Lee, Coosawhatchie, South Carolina, January 18, 1862, in Dowdey and Manarin, eds., *The Wartime Papers of Robert E. Lee*, 103. For the debate over whether it was truly the first visit, see J. Anderson Thomson Jr. and Carlos Michael Santos, "The Mystery in the Coffin: Another View of Lee's Visit to His Father's Grave," *Virginia Magazine of History and Biography* 103, no. 1 (January 1995): 75–94, and John Morgan Dederer, "Robert E. Lee's First Visit to His Father's Grave," *Virginia Magazine of History and Biography* 102, no. 1 (January 1994): 73–88.

146 "I am much pleased": Robert E. Lee to Annie and Agnes Lee, Savannah, November 22, 1861, in Dowdey and Manarin, eds., *The Wartime Papers of Robert E. Lee*, 88–89.

146 "so desecrated": Robert E. Lee to Daughter, Coosawhatchie, South Carolina, December 25, 1861, in Jones, *Life and Letters of Robert Edward Lee*, 156.

146 Newspaper reports: "Interesting Relics of Gen. Washington," *Daily National Intelligencer*, January 22, 1862.

146 "This place": *Mount Vernon Relics*, 41st Cong., 2nd session, 1870, H. Rep. No. 36, 1–4.

146 "Nor is it": "Relics of the Washington Family," *New York Evening Post*, January 8, 1862.

146 "I suffer": Mary Custis Lee to Mildred Lee, Richmond, DeButts-Ely Collection of Lee Family Papers, Library of Congress.

Notes

146 celebrated: Robert E. Lee Jr. to Mildred Lee, University of Virginia, January 5, 1862, DeButts-Ely Collection of Lee Family Papers, Library of Congress.

147 "I am very glad": Robert E. Lee to Mary Custis Lee, Coosawhatchie, South Carolina, January 18, 1862, in Dowdey and Manarin, eds., *The Wartime Papers of Robert E. Lee*, 103.

147 Twelfth Night: Arthur Gray, "The White House: Washington's Marriage Place," *Virginia Magazine of History and Biography* 42, no. 3 (July 1934): 229–40.

147 two-story: Report of Charles S. Tripler, June 22, 1862, in "The White House Affair," *New York Times*, July 20, 1862.

147 brown than white: "A Trip Up York and Pamunkey," *Daily National Intelligencer*, June 3, 1862.

147 Washington's first: "The White House, New Kent County, Virginia," *Frank Leslie's Illustrated Newspaper*, June 7, 1862.

147 "The farm is": Robert E. Lee Jr. to Mildred Lee, University of Virginia, January 5, 1862, DeButts-Ely Collection of Lee Family Papers, Library of Congress.

147 Twenty-three miles: Report of Stewart Van Vliet, Quartermaster's Office, Washington, August 2, 1862, in *O.R.*, series 1, vol. 11, part 1, 159.

147 "The tide": Foote, *The Civil War*, vol. 1, 217–20.

148 "Wherever his fleet": Robert E. Lee to Samuel Cooper, Savannah, January 8, 1862, in Dowdey and Manarin, eds., *The Wartime Papers of Robert E. Lee*, 101.

148 more than 160,000: Foote, *The Civil War*, vol. 1, 99.

148 Lincoln's order: Donald, *Lincoln*, 334–35.

148 retreated: Freeman, *Lee's Lieutenants*, vol. 1, 140.

148 "look dark": Robert E. Lee to Annie Lee, Savannah, March 2, 1862, in Dowdey and Manarin, eds., *The Wartime Papers of Robert E. Lee*, 121.

148 "They have all": Robert E. Lee to George Washington Custis Lee, Coosawhatchie, South Carolina, December 29, 1861, in ibid., 98.

148 "Our people": Robert E. Lee to Annie Lee, Savannah, March 2, 1862, in ibid., 121–22.

148 Trouble recruiting: Robert E. Lee to Samuel Cooper, Savannah, January 8, 1862, in ibid., 101; Robert E. Lee to Judah Benjamin, Savannah, February 6, 1862, in ibid., 110.

148 "He thought": Charles Marshall, *An Aide-de-Camp of Lee*, ed. Frederick Maurice (Boston: Little, Brown, 1927), 32.

149 under fire: Davis, *Jefferson Davis*, 389–90; Jefferson Davis to Robert E. Lee, Richmond, Virginia, March 2, 1862, in *O.R.*, series 1, vol. 6, 400.

149 "the armies": General Orders, No. 14, Richmond, March 13, 1862, in Dowdey and Manarin, eds., *The Wartime Papers of Robert E. Lee*, 127.

149 assistant secretary of war: Marshall, *An Aide-de-Camp of Lee*, 6.

149 first conscription: Thomas, *Robert E. Lee*, 219.

149 personal correspondence: Marshall, *An Aide-de-Camp of Lee*, 6.

149 "I do not": Robert E. Lee to Mary Custis Lee, Richmond, March 14, 1861, in Dowdey and Manarin, eds., *The Wartime Papers of Robert E. Lee*, 127–28.

149 "The re-enforcements": Charles Collins to Sir, Cottage Home, March 24, 1862, in *O.R.*, series 1, vol. 11, part 3, 394.

149 "Nothing comparable": Stephen W. Sears, *To the Gates of Richmond: The Peninsula Campaign* (Boston: Mariner Books, 2001), 23–24.

Notes

149   guard a line: John Magruder to George Randolph, Headquarters, Department of the Peninsula, Lee's House, April 11, 1862, in *O.R.*, series 1, vol. 11, part 3, 436; John Magruder to George Randolph, Headquarters, Department of the Peninsula, Yorktown, March 24, 1862, in *O.R.*, series 1, vol. 11, part 3, 393.

150   steer McClellan: Sears, *To the Gates of Richmond*, 28.

150   "Should they select": Robert E. Lee to Mary Custis Lee, Richmond, April 4, 1861, in Dowdey and Manarin, eds., *The Wartime Papers of Robert E. Lee*, 142.

150   commandeered the old: Sears, *To the Gates of Richmond*, 48.

150   "These frowning": John Magruder to the Army of the Peninsula, Headquarters Army of the Peninsula, Yorktown, March 4, 1862, in *O.R.*, series 1, vol. 9, 53.

150   "Gen. McClellan obviously": "The Siege of Yorktown," *New York Times*, April 10, 1862.

150   army outnumbered: Sears, *To the Gates of Richmond*, 43.

150   "No one but": Joseph Johnston to Robert E. Lee, Headquarters, Lee's Farm, April 22, 1862, in *O.R.*, series, 1, vol. 11, part 3, 455–56.

150   remarkable meeting: Johnston, *Narrative of Military Operations*, 114–15.

151   "Though General J. E. Johnston": Davis, *The Rise and Fall of the Confederate Government*, vol. 2, 88.

151   humor the president: Johnston, *Narrative of Military Operations*, 116.

151   "The army commanded": "Yorktown in 1781 and 1862," *New York Times*, May 2, 1862.

151   that night: General Orders, Headquarters, Department of Northern Virginia, Lee's Farm, May 2, 1862, in *O.R.*, series 1, vol. 11, part 3, 489–90.

151   stunned: Jefferson Davis to Joseph Johnston, Richmond, May 1, 1862, in *O.R.*, series 1, vol. 11, part 3, 484–85.

151   "It is not known": Robert E. Lee to Joseph Johnston, Headquarters, Richmond, May 2, 1862, in *O.R.*, series 1, vol. 11, part 3, 488.

151   under the command: "The Advance of Gen. McClellan," *Daily National Intelligencer*, May 13, 1862; Mildred Lee and Mary Custis Lee to Mary Custis Lee (Daughter), Marlbourne, May 11, 1862, Mary Custis Lee Papers, Virginia Historical Society.

151   "great interest": Donald C. Caughey and Jimmy J. Jones, *The 6th United States Cavalry in the Civil War: A History and Roster* (Jefferson, NC: McFarland, 2013), 50.

152   "Northern soldiers": "The White House, New Kent County, Virginia," *Frank Leslie's Illustrated Newspaper*, June 7, 1862.

152   "How are": Robert E. Lee to Mary Custis Lee, Richmond, April 22, 1861, in Dowdey and Manarin, eds., *The Wartime Papers of Robert E. Lee*, 153–54.

152   "I have taken": George McClellan to Edwin Stanton, Headquarters, Army of the Potomac, White House, May 16, 1862, in *O.R.*, series 1, vol. 11, part 3, 175–76.

152   "Lady": "The White House, New Kent County, Virginia," *Frank Leslie's Illustrated Newspaper*, June 7, 1862.

152   massive supply base: Report of Stewart Van Vliet, Quartermaster's Office, Washington, August 2, 1862, in *O.R.*, series 1, vol. 11, part 1, 159.

152   170 tents: Charles Tripler to R. B. Marcy, Headquarters, Army of the Potomac, Medical Director's Office, June 22, 1862, in *O.R.*, series 1, vol. 11, part 1, 206.

152   "our final depot": Stewart Van Vliet to Montgomery Meigs, Within Two Miles of Chickahominy, May 23, 1862, in *O.R.*, series 1, vol. 11, part 1, 162.

152 "I cannot number": "A Trip Up York and Pamunkey," *Daily National Intelligencer*, June 3, 1862.

153 "Yankees would": *New York Herald*, June 3, 1862.

153 a surprise: Report of Robert Tyler, Camp Near Gaines' Landing, June 1, 1862, in *O.R.*, series 1, vol. 11, part 1, 737–38.

153 "The wife": William Kauffman Scarborough, ed., *The Diary of Edmund Ruffin: The Years of Hope, April 1861–June 1863* (Baton Rouge: Louisiana State University Press, 1976), 318.

153 assigned: A. V. Colburn to P. St. George Cooke, Headquarters, Army of the Potomac, Camp Near New Bridge, May 31, 1862, in *O.R.*, series 1, vol. 11, part 3, 203.

153 "nothing since": Robert E. Lee to Agnes Lee, Richmond, May 29, 1862, DeButts-Ely Collection of Lee Family Papers, Library of Congress.

153 "timid": Sears, *To the Gates of Richmond*, 57 and 195.

153 "Cheer after cheer": W. Roy Mason, "Origin of the Lee Tomatoes," in Johnson and Buel, eds., *Battles and Leaders of the Civil War*, vol. 2, 277.

153 gray coat: Robert E. Lee to Charlotte Lee, Dabb's, June 22, 1862, in Dowdey and Manarin, eds., *The Wartime Papers of Robert E. Lee*, 197.

153 insignia: Edward D. C. Campbell Jr., "The Fabric of Command: R. E. Lee, Confederate Insignia, and the Perception of Rank," *Virginia Magazine of History and Biography* 98, no. 2 (April 1990): 261–90.

154 "Johnston is": Edward A. Pollard, *The Early Life, Campaigns, and Public Services of Robert E. Lee: With a Record of the Campaigns and Heroic Deeds of his Companions in Arms* (New York, 1871), 343.

154 isolated Federals: Johnston, *Narrative of Military Operations*, 129–30 and 132.

154 a bullet: Sears, *To the Gates of Richmond*, 138.

154 reassigned: Davis, *The Rise and Fall of the Confederate Government*, vol. 2, 122–24 and 130.

154 "Army of Northern Virginia": Special Orders, No. 22, Headquarters, Richmond, Virginia, June 1, 1862, in Dowdey and Manarin, eds., *The Wartime Papers of Robert E. Lee*, 181–82.

154 six thousand: Sears, *To the Gates of Richmond*, 146 and 148.

154 "spires of Richmond": Ibid., 110.

154 sound of artillery: Brock, *Richmond During the War*, 132–33.

154 essential papers: Memorandum from the Secretary of War to Chiefs of Bureaus, May 28, 1862, in *O.R.*, series 1, vol. 11, part 3, 557.

155 "If we leave": Marshall, *An Aide-de-Camp of Lee*, 77.

155 without announcing: James Longstreet, *From Manassas to Appomattox: Memoirs of the Civil War in America* (Philadelphia: J. B. Lippincott, 1896), 112–13.

155 Traveller: Robert E. Lee to Jefferson Davis, Near Richmond, June 3, 1861, in Douglas Southall Freeman, ed., *Lee's Dispatches: Unpublished Letters of General Robert E. Lee to Jefferson Davis and the War Department of the Confederate States of America* (New York: G. P. Putnam's Sons, 1915), 3–5.

155 carping: Marshall, *An Aide-de-Camp of Lee*, 79–80.

155 black slaves: John Magruder to R. H. Chilton, Headquarters, Right Wing, Thorne's, Virginia, June 11, 1862, in *O.R.*, series 1, vol. 11, part 3, 593.

155 "Our people": Robert E. Lee to Jefferson Davis, Headquarters, near Richmond,

Notes

June 5, 1862, in Dowdey and Manarin, eds., *The Wartime Papers of Robert E. Lee*, 184.

156 right flank: Robert E. Lee to James Longstreet, Headquarters, June 6, 1862, in *O.R.*, series 1, vol. 11, part 3, 577; Marshall, *An Aide-de-Camp of Lee*, 80–81.

156 Stuart delivered: Marshall, *An Aide-de-Camp of Lee*, 82–83.

156 nearly see: William Fitzhugh Lee to Charlotte Lee, Near Richmond, June 25, 1862, DeButts-Ely Collection of Lee Family Papers, Library of Congress.

156 north side: Foote, *The Civil War*, vol. 1, 467.

156 link up: Irvin McDowell to George McClellan, Headquarters, Department of the Rappahannock, Opposite Fredericksburg, May 22, 1862, in *O.R.*, series 1, vol. 11, part 3, 186; George McClellan to Edwin Stanton, Headquarters, Army of the Potomac, June 12, 1862, in *O.R.*, series 1, vol. 11, part 3, 225.

156 major general: Freeman, *Lee's Lieutenants*, vol. 1, 122.

156 feint: Robert E. Lee to Thomas J. Jackson, Headquarters, Richmond, Virginia, May 16, 1862, in Dowdey and Manarin, eds., *The Wartime Papers of Robert E. Lee*, 174–75.

156 "An attack": Robert E. Lee to Thomas J. Jackson, Headquarters, Richmond, Virginia, April 21, 1862, in ibid., 151.

156 sending the missing: Abraham Lincoln to George McClellan, Washington, May 24, 1862, in *O.R.*, series 1, vol. 11, part 1, 30.

157 word of it: Allan, "Memoranda of Conversations with General Robert E. Lee," 15.

157 bluff: Sears, *To the Gates of Richmond*, 157–58.

157 92,400 soldiers: Ibid., 156.

157 "The sooner": Robert E. Lee to Thomas J. Jackson, Headquarters, Near Richmond, Virginia, June 16, 1862, in Dowdey and Manarin, eds., *The Wartime Papers of Robert E. Lee*, 194.

157 "dusty": Daniel H. Hill, "Lee's Attacks North of the Chickahominy," in Johnson and Buel, eds., *Battles and Leaders of the Civil War*, vol. 2, 347.

157 astonished: Marshall, *An Aide-de-Camp of Lee*, 84–85.

157 "The four divisions": General Orders, No. 75, Headquarters, Department of Northern Virginia, June 24, 1862, in Dowdey and Manarin, eds., *The Wartime Papers of Robert E. Lee*, 198–99.

157 "should behave": Davis, *The Rise and Fall of the Confederate Government*, vol. 2, 132.

157 "was to compel": Marshall, *An Aide-de-Camp of Lee*, 89.

158 deal: Horace Green, "Lincoln Breaks McClellan's Promise," *Century Magazine* 81, no. 4 (February 1911): 594–96.

158 Union lost: Foote, *The Civil War*, vol. 1, 350; Sears, *To the Gates of Richmond*, 147.

158 "Many were confined": Green, "Lincoln Breaks McClellan's Promise."

158 "Very urgent": Edwin Stanton to George McClellan, Washington, June 7, 1862, in *Occupation of the "White House," in Virginia*, 37th Cong., 2nd session, 1862, House Executive Doc. 145, 3.

158 "special directions": George McClellan to Edwin Stanton, Headquarters, Army of the Potomac, June 7, 1862, in *Occupation of the "White House," in Virginia*, 3–4.

159 "indifferent tents": *Congressional Globe*, 37th Cong., 2nd session, 2738 and 2739.

159 "He doesn't": Green, "Lincoln Breaks McClellan's Promise."

159 Stanton informed: Edwin Stanton to Galusha Grow, War Department, Washington, DC, June 18, 1862, in *White House on Pamunkey River*, 37th Cong., 2nd session, 1862, House Executive Doc. 135; Hill, "Lee's Attacks North of the Chickahominy," 348.

159 concealed behind: Marshall, *An Aide-de-Camp of Lee*, 91.

159 days earlier: Longstreet, *From Manassas to Appomattox*, 121–22.

159 senior: Freeman, *Lee's Lieutenants*, vol. 1, 495.

159 "ample": G. Moxley Sorrel, *Recollections of a Confederate Staff Officer* (New York: Neale Publishing, 1905), 23–24 and 37–38.

162 "his eyes": Sears, *To the Gates of Richmond*, 200.

162 thirty-six: Warner, *Generals in Gray*, 134–35.

162 By three: Report of A. P. Hill, Headquarters, Light Division, Camp Gregg, February 28, 1863, in *O.R.*, series 1, vol. 11, part 2, 835.

162 around five: Freeman, *R. E. Lee*, vol. 1, 129–30.

162 "About a mile": Report of Charles W. Field, Headquarters, First Brigade, Light Division, July 20, 1862, in *O.R.*, series 1, vol. 11, part 2, 841.

162 did not surprise: Marshall, *An Aide-de-Camp of Lee*, 83 and 89.

162 "In order": Allan, "Memoranda of Conversations with General Robert E. Lee," 16.

162 red shirt: Foote, *The Civil War*, vol. 1, 480.

162 "Apparently unaware": Fitz John Porter, "Hanover Court House and Gaines's Mill," in Johnson and Buel, eds., *Battles and Leaders of the Civil War*, vol. 2, 330.

163 "most destructive": Report of Charles W. Field, Headquarters, First Brigade, Light Division, July 20, 1862, in *O.R.*, series 1, vol. 11, part 2, 841.

163 dead Confederates: Marshall, *An Aide-de-Camp of Lee*, 95–96.

163 fourteen hundred: Sears, *To the Gates of Richmond*, 208.

163 thundered again: Report of A. P. Hill, Headquarters, Light Division, Camp Gregg, February 28, 1863, in *O.R.*, series 1, vol. 11, part 2, 836.

163 located: Report of Fitz John Porter, Headquarters, Fifth Provisional Corps, Camp at Harrison's Landing, Virginia, July 8, 1862, in *O.R.*, series 1, vol. 11, part 2, 222–23.

163 previous afternoon: Freeman, *Lee's Lieutenants*, vol. 1, 512–14.

163 repaired: Report of Winfield S. Featherston, Richmond, Virginia, July 12, 1862, in *O.R.*, series 1, vol. 11, part 2, 783.

163 stronger position: Freeman, *R. E. Lee*, vol. 2, 143–45.

163 Rows of: Report of A. P. Hill, Headquarters, Light Division, Camp Gregg, February 28, 1863, in *O.R.*, series 1, vol. 11, part 2, 836–37.

163 "principal part": Report of Robert E. Lee, Headquarters, Army of Northern Virginia, March 6, 1863, in *O.R.*, series 1, vol. 11, part 2, 492.

163 three-to-two: Foote, *The Civil War*, vol. 1, 488.

164 "I am very glad": Cooke, *A Life of Gen. Robert E. Lee*, 82–85.

164 "This must be": Hood, *Advance and Retreat*, 25–28.

164 "The enemy": Robert E. Lee to Jefferson Davis, Headquarters, June 27, 1862, in Dowdey and Manarin, eds., *The Wartime Papers of Robert E. Lee*, 202.

164 nearly eight thousand: Sears, *To the Gates of Richmond*, 249.

164 six miles: Freeman, *R. E. Lee*, vol. 1, 160–61.

Notes

164 attempt to save: Longstreet, *From Manassas to Appomattox*, 130.

164 twelve miles: Rufus Ingalls to Montgomery Meigs, Fort Monroe, June 29, 1862, in *O.R.*, series 1, vol. 11, part 3, 273.

164 clouds of smoke: Report of J. E. B. Stuart, Headquarters, Cavalry Brigade, Near Richmond, Virginia, July 14, 1862, in *O.R.*, series 1, vol. 11, part 2, 515–16.

165 chimneys: "Affairs Before Richmond," *New York Times*, July 2, 1862.

165 stench: John Esten Cooke, *Wearing of the Gray; Being Personal Portraits, Scenes and Adventures of the War* (New York: E. B. Treat, 1867), 467–69.

165 "An opportunity": Report of J. E. B. Stuart, Headquarters, Cavalry Brigade, Near Richmond, Virginia, July 14, 1862, in *O.R.*, series 1, vol. 11, part 2, 517.

165 military provisions: Report of Silas Casey, On Board Steamer *Knickerbocker*, In York River, June 29, 1862, in *O.R.*, series 1, vol. 11, part 2, 483.

165 Union private: Report of Henry Lansing, Harrison's Landing, Virginia, July 5, 1862, in *O.R.*, series 1, vol. 11, part 2, 333.

165 opposing the idea: *Occupation of the "White House," in Virginia*, 5–6.

165 "Provisions": Report of J. E. B. Stuart, Headquarters, Cavalry Brigade, Near Richmond, Virginia, July 14, 1862, in *O.R.*, series 1, vol. 11, part 2, 517.

165 eggs: Cooke, *Wearing of the Gray*, 470–71.

165 "In the quiet": G. W. Beale, *A Lieutenant of Cavalry in Lee's Army* (Boston: Gorham Press, 1918), 222.

166 "Yes": Freeman, *R. E. Lee*, vol. 2, 202.

166 disappointed: Robert E. Lee to Mary Custis Lee, June [*sic*] 9, 1862, Dabb's Farm, in Dowdey and Manarin, eds., *The Wartime Papers of Robert E. Lee*, 230.

166 "Today": General Orders, No. 75, Headquarters in the Field, July 7, 1862, in ibid., 210.

166 Northern newspapers: Cooke, *Wearing of the Gray*, 468.

166 "The rise": "Gen. Lee," *Richmond Daily Dispatch*, July 9, 1862.

166 3,494: Sears, *To the Gates of Richmond*, 343–45.

166 "The sorrow": Mary Custis Lee to W. H. Stiles, Richmond, July 5, 1862, Mackay-McQueen Family Papers, National Society Colonial Dames of America, Georgia Historical Society.

167 two corps: Long, *Memoirs of Robert E. Lee*, 178.

167 "Capital soldier": Robert E. Lee to Jefferson Davis, Headquarters, June 7, 1862, in Freeman, ed., *Lee's Dispatches*, 10–11.

167 fortified capital: Robert E. Lee to Jefferson Davis, Headquarters, Alexandria & Leesburg Road, Near Dranesville, September 3, 1862, in Dowdey and Manarin, eds., *The Wartime Papers of Robert E. Lee*, 293.

Chapter 10: Emancipation

168 most of the slaves: Mary Custis Lee to Charlotte Lee, Richmond, July 11, DeButts-Ely Collection of Lee Family Papers, Library of Congress.

168 loosely defined: Allen C. Guelzo, *Lincoln's Emancipation Proclamation: The End of Slavery in America* (New York: Simon & Schuster, 2004), 41 and 54.

168 "Old and young": *New York Herald*, July 2, 1862.

168 "thievish villains": Mary Custis Lee to W. H. Stiles, Richmond, July 5, 1862,

Mackay-McQueen Family Papers, National Society Colonial Dames of America, Georgia Historical Society.

168 "entitled": Circuit Court Ruling, May 25, 1859, in Exr. of George Washington Parke Custis vs. Mary Anna Randolph Custis Lee and Others, Arlington Chancery Records, Library of Virginia.

168 lawyer argued: "Note of Argument for Appellant," Custis's Exr v. Lee and Others, Supreme Court of Appeals of Virginia, Alexandria Library.

168 "to be worked": Will of G. W. P. Custis, in Prussing, *The Estate of George Washington, Deceased*, 477.

168 "The slaves": Orders of November 22, 1861, Order Books, Virginia Supreme Court of Appeals (Richmond Session), State Government Records Collection, Library of Virginia.

169 reversed: *Richmond Daily Dispatch*, November 25, 1861.

169 tempted: Robert E. Lee to George Washington Custis Lee, Coosawhatchie, January 4, 1862, in Dowdey and Manarin, eds., *The Wartime Papers of Robert E. Lee*, 99–100.

169 "The decision": Robert E. Lee to William Fitzhugh Lee, Savannah, February 16, 1862, George Bolling Lee Papers, Virginia Historical Society.

169 "It is the": Orders of November 22, 1861, Order Books, Virginia Supreme Court of Appeals (Richmond Session), State Government Records Collection, Library of Virginia.

169 "How I can": Robert E. Lee to George Washington Custis Lee, Coosawhatchie, January 4, 1862, in Dowdey and Manarin, eds., *The Wartime Papers of Robert E. Lee*, 100.

169 "The bonds": Robert E. Lee to George Washington Custis Lee, Coosawhatchie, South Carolina, January 19, 1862, in ibid., 105.

169 "If emancipated": Robert E. Lee to William Fitzhugh Lee, Savannah, February 16, 1862, George Bolling Lee Papers, Virginia Historical Society.

169 back in Illinois: "House Divided" Speech at Springfield, Illinois, June 16, 1858, in Fehrenbacher, ed., *Abraham Lincoln: Speeches and Writings, 1832–1858*, 426.

170 desperate: Guelzo, *Lincoln's Emancipation Proclamation*, 122–23.

170 forced back: Ibid., 151 and 153.

170 between September 4: Report of Robert E. Lee, Headquarters, August 19, 1863, in Dowdey and Manarin, eds., *The Wartime Papers of Robert E. Lee*, 313.

170 thousands: Robert E. Lee to Jefferson Davis, Headquarters, Alexandria & Leesburg Road, Near Dranesville, September 3, 1862, in Dowdey and Manarin, eds., *The Wartime Papers of Robert E. Lee*, 293.

170 "Were these": James V. Murfin, *The Gleam of Bayonets: The Battle of Antietam and Robert E. Lee's Maryland Campaign, September 1862* (Baton Rouge: Louisiana University Press, 2004), 108–9.

170 ambulance: Taylor, *General Lee*, 115.

170 "So much": Robert E. Lee to Jefferson Davis, Headquarters, Army of Northern Virginia, Hagerstown, Maryland, September 13, 1862, in Dowdey and Manarin, eds., *The Wartime Papers of Robert E. Lee*, 306.

171 "What was": Marshall, *An Aide-de-Camp of Lee*, 144.

171 threaten both: Report of Robert E. Lee, Headquarters, August 19, 1863, in Dowdey and Manarin, eds., *The Wartime Papers of Robert E. Lee*, 313.

Notes

171 "As long as": Robert E. Lee to Jefferson Davis, Headquarters, Alexandria & Leesburg Road, Near Dranesville, September 3, 1862, in ibid., 292–94.

171 off the land: Longstreet, *From Manassas to Appomattox*, 199–200; Freeman, *Lee's Lieutenants*, vol. 2, 151.

171 "Still": Robert E. Lee to Jefferson Davis, Headquarters, Alexandria & Leesburg Road, Near Dranesville, September 3, 1862, in Dowdey and Manarin, eds., *The Wartime Papers of Robert E. Lee*, 292–94.

171 "Confidence in": Davis, *Jefferson Davis*, 468.

171 often discussed: Robert E. Lee to Jefferson Davis, Headquarters, Near Richmond, June 5, 1862, in Dowdey and Manarin, eds., *The Wartime Papers of Robert E. Lee*, 183–84.

171 "If it": Robert E. Lee to Jefferson Davis, Headquarters, Alexandria & Leesburg Road, Near Dranesville, September 3, 1862, in ibid., 292–93.

172 his own voice: Longstreet, *From Manassas to Appomattox*, 199.

172 "The people of": Robert E. Lee to the People of Maryland, Headquarters, Army of Northern Virginia, Near Fredericktown, September 8, 1862, in Dowdey and Manarin, eds., *The Wartime Papers of Robert E. Lee*, 299.

172 doubted: Robert E. Lee to Jefferson Davis, Headquarters, Two Miles from Fredericktown, Maryland, September 7, 1862, in ibid., 298.

172 "About here": Walter Taylor to Mary Lou, Near Fredericktown, Maryland, September 7, 1862, in R. Lockwood Tower, ed., *Lee's Adjutant: The Wartime Letters of Colonel Walter Herron Taylor, 1862–1865* (Columbia: University of South Carolina Press, 1995), 43.

172 "The present posture": Robert E. Lee to Jefferson Davis, Headquarters, Near Fredericktown, Maryland, September 8, 1862, in Dowdey and Manarin, eds., *The Wartime Papers of Robert E. Lee*, 301.

172 cautioned against: Robert E. Lee to George Washington Custis Lee, Coosawhatchie, South Carolina, December 29, 1861, in ibid., 98.

172 might intervene: James M. McPherson, *Crossroads of Freedom: Antietam* (New York: Oxford University Press, 2002), 91–94.

173 "I went": Edward Clifford Gordon to William Allan, November 18, 1886, quoted in Edward Clifford Gordon, "Memorandum of a Conversation with General R. E. Lee," in Gallagher, ed., *Lee*, 27.

173 "There will": John G. Walker, "Jackson's Capture of Harper's Ferry," in Johnson and Buel, eds., *Battles and Leaders of the Civil War*, vol. 2, 604–5.

173 four parts: Special Orders, No. 191, Headquarters, Army of Northern Virginia, September 9, 1862, in Dowdey and Manarin, eds., *The Wartime Papers of Robert E. Lee*, 301–2.

173 fifty-five thousand: McPherson, *Crossroads of Freedom*, 100; Robert E. Lee to Jefferson Davis, Headquarters, Army of Northern Virginia, Hagerstown, Maryland, September 13, 1862, in Dowdey and Manarin, eds., *The Wartime Papers of Robert E. Lee*, 307.

173 "Are you acquainted": Walker, "Jackson's Capture of Harper's Ferry," 605–6.

174 Jackson embraced: James Longstreet, "The Invasion of Maryland," in Johnson and Buel, eds., *Battles and Leaders of the Civil War*, vol. 2, 663.

174 chewed up: Walker, "Jackson's Capture of Harper's Ferry," 606–7.

Notes

174 three cigars: Silas Colgrove, "The Finding of Lee's Lost Order," in Johnson and Buel, eds., *Battles and Leaders of the Civil War*, vol. 2, 603.

174 "Here is a paper": McPherson, *Crossroads of Freedom*, 108.

174 "The number increased": Longstreet, "The Invasion of Maryland," 667.

174 scarcely believe: Marshall, *An Aide-de-Camp of Lee*, 158.

174 thirteen miles: Stephen W. Sears, *Landscape Turned Red: The Battle of Antietam* (Boston: Mariner Books, 2003), 96.

174 informant: Ibid., 125.

174 mountain passes: Marshall, *An Aide-de-Camp of Lee*, 159.

175 numbered just: Freeman, *R. E. Lee*, vol. 2, 378.

175 Longstreet thought: Longstreet, "The Invasion of Maryland," 666.

175 sixty thousand: Sears, *Landscape Turned Red*, 163.

175 retreating: R. H. Chilton to Lafayette McLaws, Headquarters, Army of Northern Virginia, September 14, 1862, in Dowdey and Manarin, eds., *The Wartime Papers of Robert E. Lee*, 307–8.

175 "Through God's blessing": Thomas J. Jackson to Robert E. Lee, September 15, 1862, in *O.R.*, series 1, vol. 19, part 1, 951.

175 Union prisoners: Thomas J. Jackson to R. H. Chilton, Headquarters, Valley District, September 16, 1862, in *O.R.*, series 1, vol. 19, part 1, 951.

175 tempted him: Long, *Memoirs of Robert E. Lee*, 216; Freeman, *R. E. Lee*, vol. 2, 381.

175 stunned: Sears, *Landscape Turned Red*, 160–64.

175 "If he had": John G. Walker, "Sharpsburg," in Johnson and Buel, eds., *Battles and Leaders of the Civil War*, vol. 2, 675.

176 the odds: Sears, *Landscape Turned Red*, 173–74.

176 light rain: Longstreet, *From Manassas to Appomattox*, 236–38.

176 "Every stalk": Report of Joseph Hooker, Headquarters, First Corps, Washington, DC, November 8, 1862, in *O.R.*, series 1, vol. 19, part 1, 217–18.

176 trampling: Hood, *Advance and Retreat*, 42–44.

176 "Don't be": Sears, *Landscape Turned Red*, 214.

176 "If you insist": Longstreet, "The Invasion of Maryland," 671.

177 penned them: Foote, *The Civil War*, vol. 1, 693–94.

177 tear the line: Longstreet, "The Invasion of Maryland," 669; McPherson, *Crossroads of Freedom*, 123–24.

177 grimy-faced: Henry Kyd Douglas, "Stonewall Jackson in Maryland," in Johnson and Buel, eds., *Battles and Leaders of the Civil War*, vol. 2, 629.

177 "Yes, my son": Lee, *Recollections and Letters of General Robert E. Lee*, 78.

177 four times: Sears, *Landscape Turned Red*, 260–67 and 277.

177 "It is A. P. Hill": Freeman, *R. E. Lee*, vol. 2, 400–401.

177 seventeen-mile: Report of A. P. Hill, Headquarters, Light Division, Camp Gregg, Virginia, February 25, 1863, in *O.R.*, series 1, vol. 19, part 1, 981.

177 battle shirt: Foote, *The Civil War*, vol. 1, 699.

179 attack again: Report of Robert E. Lee, Headquarters, August 19, 1863, in Dowdey and Manarin, eds., *The Wartime Papers of Robert E. Lee*, 322.

179 casualties: Sears, *Landscape Turned Red*, 294–96.

179 "Thank God!": Walker, "Sharpsburg," 682.

179 Never having: Report of Robert E. Lee, Headquarters, August 19, 1863, in Dowdey and Manarin, eds., *The Wartime Papers of Robert E. Lee*, 322.

Notes

179 "On the field": Order of Robert E. Lee, quoted in Taylor, *General Lee*, 138–39.

180 "One of the bands": Walter Taylor to Mary Lou, Between Martinsburg and Winchester, September 28, 1862, in Tower, ed., *Lee's Adjutant*, 46.

180 full story: Sears, *Landscape Turned Red*, 349–52.

180 "Had the": Allan, "Memoranda of Conversations with General Robert E. Lee," 8.

180 "a great calamity": Robert E. Lee to D. H. Hill, Lexington, Virginia, February 21, 1868, in Hal Bridges, ed., "A Lee Letter on the 'Lost Dispatch' and the Maryland Campaign of 1862," *Virginia Magazine of History and Biography* 66, no. 2 (April 1958): 161–66.

180 "It looks as": Taylor, *General Lee*, 124–25.

180 "had decided": Guelzo, *Lincoln's Emancipation Proclamation*, 153.

180 Not until: Robert E. Lee to Mary Custis Lee, Camp near Winchester, October 19, 1862, DeButts-Ely Collection of Lee Family Papers, Library of Congress.

180 typhoid: Agnes Lee to Dear Sister, Richmond, October 27, DeButts-Ely Collection of Lee Family Papers, Library of Congress.

180 "I cannot express": Robert E. Lee to Mary Custis Lee, Camp near Winchester, October 26, 1862, DeButts-Ely Collection of Lee Family Papers, Library of Congress.

181 "His army": Taylor, *Four Years with General Lee*, 76–77.

181 "I hope you": Robert E. Lee to George Washington Custis Lee, Camp near Fredericksburg, November 28, 1862, in Dowdey and Manarin, eds., *The Wartime Papers of Robert E. Lee*, 350.

181 thick fog: Taylor, *Four Years with General Lee*, 80–81.

181 "Our batteries": Report of Robert E. Lee, Headquarters Army of Northern Virginia, April 10, 1863, in Dowdey and Manarin, eds., *The Wartime Papers of Robert E. Lee*, 372.

182 easier: Taylor, *Four Years with General Lee*, 81.

182 "It is well": Cooke, *A Life of Gen. Robert E. Lee*, 184.

182 Burnside's casualties: Foote, *The Civil War*, vol. 2, 44.

182 "suffered heavily": Robert E. Lee to Mary Custis Lee, Camp, Fredericksburg, December 16, 1862, in Dowdey and Manarin, eds., *The Wartime Papers of Robert E. Lee*, 365.

182 "The savage": Robert E. Lee to James A. Seddon, Headquarters, Army of Northern Virginia, January 10, 1863, in ibid., 390.

182 "as regards": Robert E. Lee to Mary Custis Lee, Camp, Fredericksburg, December 16, 1862, in ibid., 365.

182 "to do what": Robert E. Lee to Mary Custis Lee, Camp, Fredericksburg, December 21, 1862, in ibid., 379.

182 "Know all": Manumission Document, December 29, 1862, Online Gallery, Museum of the Confederacy.

182 inserted: Robert E. Lee to Mary Custis Lee, Camp, Fredericksburg, January 8, 1863, DeButts-Ely Collection of Lee Family Papers, Library of Congress.

183 "Those at Arlington": Robert E. Lee to Mary Custis Lee, Camp, Fredericksburg, December 21, 1862, in Dowdey and Manarin, eds., *The Wartime Papers of Robert E. Lee*, 379.

183 Critics: Guelzo, *Lincoln's Emancipation Proclamation*, 227.

183 absent: *Alexandria Gazette*, January 2, 1863.

183 "excepted": Final Emancipation Proclamation, January 1, 1863, in Fehrenbacher, ed., *Abraham Lincoln: Speeches and Writings, 1859–1865*, 425.

183 "an exception": *Alexandria Gazette*, January 3, 1863.

Chapter 11: The Indispensable Man

184 "Old General": "An English Picture of Confederate Headquarters," *Richmond Daily Dispatch*, April 27, 1863.

184 "not do": Abraham Lincoln to George McClellan, Executive Mansion, Washington, October 13, 1862, in Fehrenbacher, ed., *Abraham Lincoln: Speeches and Writings, 1859–1865*, 376.

184 "indispensable man": James Thomas Flexner, *Washington: The Indispensable Man* (New York: Back Bay Books, 1974), 116.

184 "as the man": Lee, *Funeral Oration*, 10.

184 "The country should": "Gen. Robert E. Lee," *Richmond Daily Dispatch*, December 13, 1862.

184 "direct and honest": "English Portraits of Confederate Generals," *Alexandria Gazette*, January 19, 1863.

185 "Whenever": Long, *Memoirs of Robert E. Lee*, 229.

185 "It does not": Freeman, *R. E. Lee*, vol. 2, 498.

185 many more men: McPherson, *Battle Cry of Freedom*, 322.

185 "awful": Doris Kearns Goodwin, *Team of Rivals: The Political Genius of Abraham Lincoln* (New York: Simon & Schuster, 2005), 486.

185 "The lives of": Robert E. Lee to James A. Seddon, Headquarters, Army of Northern Virginia, January 10, 1863, in Dowdey and Manarin, eds., *The Wartime Papers of Robert E. Lee*, 389–90.

185 During the Revolution: McPherson, *Battle Cry of Freedom*, 337; Chernow, *Washington*, 207–8.

185 social order: Robert E. Lee to James A. Seddon, Headquarters, Army of Northern Virginia, January 10, 1863, in Dowdey and Manarin, eds., *The Wartime Papers of Robert E. Lee*, 389–90.

185 "Nothing can": Robert E. Lee to George Washington Custis Lee, Camp, Fredericksburg, February 28, 1863, in ibid., 411.

186 "Our salvation": Robert E. Lee to George Washington Custis Lee, Camp, February 12, 1863, Robert E. Lee Papers, Duke University.

186 "I tremble": Robert E. Lee to Mary Custis Lee, Camp, Fredericksburg, December 2, 1862, DeButts-Ely Collection of Lee Family Papers, Library of Congress.

186 "Mr. F J": Robert E. Lee to Mary Custis Lee, Camp, Fredericksburg, February 23, 1863, in Dowdey and Manarin, eds., *The Wartime Papers of Robert E. Lee*, 407–8.

186 refused to occupy: Long, *Memoirs of Robert E. Lee*, 227.

186 "The only place": Robert E. Lee to Agnes Lee, Camp, Fredericksburg, February 6, 1863, in Dowdey and Manarin, eds., *The Wartime Papers of Robert E. Lee*, 400.

186 ten thousand papers: Glatthaar, *General Lee's Army*, 338.

186 "twist or jerk": Taylor, *General Lee*, 156.

Notes

186 "No man": Charles S. Venable, "General Lee in the Wilderness Campaign," in Johnson and Buel, ed., *Battles and Leaders of the Civil War*, vol. 4, 240.

186 "I never": Walter Taylor to Bettie, Camp near Orange Court House, August 8, 1863, in Tower, ed., *Lee's Adjutant*, 68.

186 "little stimulant": Taylor, *General Lee*, 158.

186 "You forget": Robert E. Lee to Mary Custis Lee, Camp, Fredericksburg, March 9, 1863, in Dowdey and Manarin, eds., *The Wartime Papers of Robert E. Lee*, 413.

187 "As usual": Robert E. Lee to Mary Custis Lee, Richmond, July 12, 1861, DeButts-Ely Collection of Lee Family Papers, Library of Congress.

187 "I have not been": Robert E. Lee to Mary Custis Lee, Near Fredericksburg, April 5, 1863, in Dowdey and Manarin, eds., *The Wartime Papers of Robert E. Lee*, 427–28.

187 Modern doctors: Marvin P. Rozear, E. Wayne Massey, Jennifer Horner, Erin Foley, and Joseph C. Greenfield Jr., "R. E. Lee's Stroke," *Virginia Magazine of History and Biography* 98, no. 2 (April 1990): 291–308.

187 bundled: Robert E. Lee to Mary Custis Lee, Near Fredericksburg, April 5, 1863, in Dowdey and Manarin, eds., *The Wartime Papers of Robert E. Lee*, 427–28.

187 pulse: Robert E. Lee to Mary Custis Lee, Fredericksburg, April 12, 1863, in ibid., 432.

187 150,000 troops: Robert E. Lee to James Longstreet, Headquarters, Army of Northern Virginia, April 27, 1863, in ibid., 440–41.

187 65,000 soldiers: Stephen W. Sears, *Chancellorsville* (Boston: Mariner Books, 1996), 95–96 and 112.

187 couple of divisions: Abstract from Return of the Army of Northern Virginia, March 1863, in *O.R.*, series 1, vol. 25, part 2, 696.

187 "The troops of": Robert E. Lee to James A. Seddon, Headquarters, Army of Northern Virginia, March 27, 1863, in *O.R.*, series 1, vol. 25, part 2, 687.

187 "feel oppressed": Robert E. Lee to Mary Custis Lee, Camp, Fredericksburg, April 24, 1863, in Dowdey and Manarin, eds., *The Wartime Papers of Robert E. Lee*, 440.

187 "I thought": James Power Smith, "Stonewall Jackson's Last Battle," in Johnson and Buel, eds., *Battles and Leaders of the Civil War*, vol. 3, 203.

188 concerned Lee: Report of Robert E. Lee, Headquarters, September 23, 1863, in Dowdey and Manarin, eds., *The Wartime Papers of Robert E. Lee*, 460; Robert E. Lee to Samuel Cooper, Fredericksburg, Virginia, April 29, 1863, in ibid., 442.

188 into focus: Sears, *Chancellorsville*, 160–75.

188 forty thousand soldiers: McPherson, *Battle Cry of Freedom*, 639.

188 copied: Walter Taylor to Mary Lou, May 8, 1863, in Tower, ed., *Lee's Adjutant*, 53.

188 12,400 troops: Sears, *Chancellorsville*, 198.

188 reasons lost: Darius N. Couch, "The Chancellorsville Campaign," in Johnson and Buel, eds., *Battles and Leaders of the Civil War*, vol. 3, 159–61.

188 Chancellor: Sears, *Chancellorsville*, 97 and 193.

188 mile and a half: Smith, "Stonewall Jackson's Last Battle," 204.

188 shrapnel: Justus Scheibert, *Seven Months in the Rebel States During the North American War, 1863*, trans. Joseph C. Hayes, ed. W. Stanley Hoole (Tuscaloosa, AL: Confederate Publishing, 1958), 60–61.

Notes

188 "How can we": T. M. R. Talcott, "General Lee's Strategy at the Battle of Chancellorsville," *Southern Historical Society Papers* 34 (1906): 1–27. For the best summary of the controversy over who proposed what, see Talcott.

188 inspecting: Fitzhugh Lee, "Chancellorsville," *Southern Historical Society Papers* 7, no. 12 (December 1879): 545–85.

188 "a position": Report of Robert E. Lee, Headquarters, Army of Northern Virginia, September 23, 1863, in Dowdey and Manarin, eds., *The Wartime Papers of Robert E. Lee*, 462.

189 "General, we": Lee, "Chancellorsville."

189 scouts: Robert E. Lee to Mary Anna Jackson, Lexington, Virginia, January 25, 1866, Letterbook No. 3, DeButts-Ely Collection of Lee Family Papers, Library of Congress.

189 Jackson sitting: Long, *Memoirs of Robert E. Lee*, 255 and 258; Smith, "Stonewall Jackson's Last Battle," 205.

189 "General Jackson": Jed Hotchkiss, quoted in Talcott, "General Lee's Strategy at the Battle of Chancellorsville."

189 13,915 infantrymen: Sears, *Chancellorsville*, 239.

189 "no question": Robert E. Lee to A. T. Bledsoe, Lexington, Virginia, October 28, 1867, Letterbook No. 4, DeButts-Ely Collection of Lee Family Papers, Library of Congress.

189 "Well": Jed Hotchkiss, quoted in Talcott, "General Lee's Strategy at the Battle of Chancellorsville."

190 "all the news": R. E. Wilbourn to C. J. Faulkner, Headquarters, Second Army Corps, May 1863, Virginia Historical Society, online.

190 charged out: Sears, *Chancellorsville*, 258 and 272–89.

190 sounds: Freeman, *R. E. Lee*, vol. 2, 530–32.

190 "Any victory": R. E. Wilbourn to C. J. Faulkner, Headquarters, Second Army Corps, May 1863, Virginia Historical Society, online.

190 "It is necessary": Robert E. Lee to J. E. B. Stuart, May 3, 1863, in *O.R.*, series 1, vol. 25, part 2, 769.

190 forward again: Report of Robert E. Lee, Headquarters, Army of Northern Virginia, September 23, 1863, in Dowdey and Manarin, eds., *The Wartime Papers of Robert E. Lee*, 464–65.

190 "frightful": Scheibert, *Seven Months in the Rebel States During the North American War, 1863*, 71–73 and 75–76.

191 long line: Freeman, *R. E. Lee*, vol. 2, 539–41.

191 ablaze: Sears, *Chancellorsville*, 365.

191 brown eyes: Lee, *General Lee*, 90.

191 "One long": Marshall, *An Aide-de-Camp of Lee*, 172–73.

191 doffed: Sears, *Chancellorsville*, 365.

191 "I thought": Marshall, *An Aide-de-Camp of Lee*, 173.

191 He shuttled: Report of Robert E. Lee, Headquarters, Army of Northern Virginia, September 23, 1863, in Dowdey and Manarin, eds., *The Wartime Papers of Robert E. Lee*, 465–68; Edward Porter Alexander, *Fighting for the Confederacy: The Personal Recollections of General Edward Porter Alexander*, ed. Gary W. Gallagher (Chapel Hill: University of North Carolina Press, 1989), 211–15.

191 "That is": Freeman, *R. E. Lee*, vol. 2, 557.

Notes

194 "The strength": Edward Porter Alexander, *Military Memoirs of a Confederate: A Critical Narrative* (New York: Charles Scribner's Sons, 1907), 357–58.

194 13,460 men: Sears, *Chancellorsville*, 442.

194 "He has lost": Freeman, *Lee's Lieutenants*, vol. 2, 581 and 669–82.

194 rivaled: Connelly, *The Marble Man*, 18–19.

194 "Our labor": Robert E. Lee to Charles Carter Lee, Fredericksburg, May 24, 1863, Robert E. Lee Papers, University of Virginia.

194 "I do not": Robert E. Lee to George Washington Custis Lee, Camp, May 11, 1863, in Dowdey and Manarin, eds., *The Wartime Papers of Robert E. Lee*, 484.

194 reorganized: Robert E. Lee to Jefferson Davis, Camp, Fredericksburg, May 20, 1863, in ibid., 488.

194 "Our loss": Henry Heth, "Letter from Major General Henry Heth, of A. P. Hill's Corps, A. N. V.," *Southern Historical Society Papers* 4, no. 4 (October 1877): 151–60.

194 "The enemy": James Longstreet, "Lee in Pennsylvania," in Gallagher, ed., *Lee*, 397; James Longstreet, "Lee's Right Wing at Gettysburg," in Johnson and Buel, eds., *Battles and Leaders of the Civil War*, vol. 3, 339.

194 burying: Allen C. Guelzo, *Gettysburg: The Last Invasion* (New York: Alfred A. Knopf, 2013), 104.

195 "Not more": Longstreet, "Lee in Pennsylvania," 409.

195 urgency: Robert E. Lee to Jefferson Davis, Opposite Williamsport, June 25, 1863, in *O.R.*, series 1, vol. 27, part 3, 931.

195 "You can": Robert E. Lee to James A. Seddon, Headquarters, Army of Northern Virginia, May 10, 1863, in *O.R.*, series 1, vol. 25, part 2, 790.

195 an offensive across: Robert E. Lee to James A. Seddon, Headquarters, Army of Northern Virginia, April 9, 1863, in *O.R.*, series 1, vol. 25, part 2, 713; Allan, "Memoranda of Conversations with General Robert E. Lee," 14; Marshall, *An Aide-de-Camp of Lee*, 186–87.

195 "It would very": Long, *Memoirs of Robert E. Lee*, 268–69.

195 pale-looking: Jones, *A Rebel War Clerk's Diary at the Confederate States Capital*, vol. 1, 325–26.

195 reluctantly: Allan, "Memoranda of Conversations with General Robert E. Lee," 17; Davis, *Jefferson Davis*, 504–5.

195 no more than: Stephen W. Sears, *Gettysburg* (Boston: Mariner Books, 2004), 95.

195 "old bull-dog": Arthur Fremantle, *Three Months in the Southern States, April–June, 1863* (New York: John Bradburn, 1864), 253.

195 to the west: William Garrett Piston, *Lee's Tarnished Lieutenant: James Longstreet and His Place in Southern History* (Athens, GA: University of Georgia Press, 1987), 44.

196 apparently struck Longstreet: Longstreet, "Lee in Pennsylvania," 384; Report of Robert E. Lee, Headquarters, Army of Northern Virginia, July 31, 1863, in *O.R.*, series 1, vol. 27, part 2, 308; Allan, "Memoranda of Conversations with General Robert E. Lee," 15.

196 more glamorous: Freeman, *Lee's Lieutenants*, vol. 3, 55–72.

196 "eye of the army": Freeman, *R. E. Lee*, vol. 3, 60.

196 stumbled: Report of Robert E. Lee, Headquarters, Army of Northern Virginia, July 31, 1863, in *O.R.*, series 1, vol. 27, part 2, 307–8.

Notes

196 "to press": Taylor, *Four Years with General Lee*, 95.

196 "practicable": Report of Robert E. Lee, Headquarters, Army of Northern Virginia, January 1864, in *O.R.*, series 1, vol. 27, part 2, 318.

196 Ewell's subordinates: Freeman, *Lee's Lieutenants*, vol. 3, 90–101.

196 reportedly: Ibid., 174–75.

196 "apathy": Sorrel, *Recollections of a Confederate Staff Officer*, 166–67.

196 debate later: Robert K. Krick, " 'If Longstreet . . . Says So, It Is Most Likely Not True': James Longstreet and the Second Day at Gettysburg," in Gary W. Gallagher, ed., *Three Days at Gettysburg: Essays on Confederate and Union Leadership* (Kent, OH: The Kent State University Press, 1999), 156–63; Piston, *Lee's Tarnished Lieutenant*, 51–58 and 118–36; Gary W. Gallagher, " 'If The Enemy Is There, We Must Attack Him': R. E. Lee and the Second Day at Gettysburg," in Gallagher, ed., *Lee*, 497–516; Sears, *Gettysburg*, 252–62; Freeman, *Lee's Lieutenants*, vol. 3, 106–28 and 173–76.

197 "If God": Issac R. Trimble, "The Battle and Campaign of Gettysburg," *Southern Historical Society Papers* 26 (1898): 116–28.

197 "Under these": Robert E. Lee to Jefferson Davis, Headquarters, Army of Northern Virginia, June 10, 1863, in Dowdey and Manarin, eds., *The Wartime Papers of Robert E. Lee*, 507–9.

197 agreed: Robert E. Lee to Jefferson Davis, Opposite Williamsport, June 25, 1863, in ibid., 530.

197 sail from: Alexander Stephens to S. P. Lee, C. S. Steamer Torpedo, On James River, July 4, 1863, in *O.R.*, series 2, vol. 6, 79–80; Alexander Stephens to Jefferson Davis, Richmond, July 8, 1863, in *O.R.*, series 2, vol. 6, 94.

197 expansive: Stephens, *A Constitutional View of the Late War Between the States*, vol. 2, 567–68.

197 advised maneuvering: Longstreet, "Lee's Right Wing at Gettysburg," 342–43.

197 "There never were": Robert E. Lee to John B. Hood, Camp, Fredericksburg, May 21, 1863, in Dowdey and Manarin, eds., *The Wartime Papers of Robert E. Lee*, 490.

197 "sanguine": Alexander, *Fighting for the Confederacy*, 255.

197 five hundred yards: Sears, *Gettysburg*, 383–95 and 419–20.

200 "It is my": Longstreet, "Lee in Pennsylvania," 397.

200 hundred guns: Sears, *Gettysburg*, 382–83 and 396.

200 American soil: Guelzo, *Gettysburg*, 396.

200 mile and a half: Sears, *Gettysburg*, 415.

200 hoisting their swords: Guelzo, *Gettysburg*, 409.

200 Onward: Sears, *Gettysburg*, 419–43; Alexander, *Fighting for the Confederacy*, 263.

200 "See what": F. M. Colston, "Gettysburg As I Saw It," *Confederate Veteran* 5, no. 11 (November 1897): 551–53.

200 slumped shoulders: Fremantle, *Three Months in the Southern States, April–June, 1863*, 266.

200 "no division": Freeman, *R. E. Lee*, vol. 3, 129.

200 returned unwounded: Sears, *Gettysburg*, 467–68.

200 "All this": Fremantle, *Three Months in the Southern States, April–June, 1863*, 267–69.

200 failing to inform: Report of Robert E. Lee, Headquarters, Army of Northern

Virginia, January 20, 1864, in Dowdey and Manarin, eds., *The Wartime Papers of Robert E. Lee*, 580.

201 "imperfect": Allan, "Memoranda of Conversations with General Robert E. Lee," 13–14 and 17–18.

201 "With the knowledge": Robert E. Lee to Jefferson Davis, Camp Culpeper, July 31, 1863, in Dowdey and Manarin, eds., *The Wartime Papers of Robert E. Lee*, 565.

201 "unavoidable": Report of Robert E. Lee, Headquarters, Army of Northern Virginia, July 31, 1863, in *O.R.*, series 1, vol. 27, part 2, 308; Report of Robert E. Lee, Headquarters, Army of Northern Virginia, January 20, 1864, in Dowdey and Manarin, eds., *The Wartime Papers of Robert E. Lee*, 576.

201 "Victory": Robert E. Lee to William M. McDonald, Lexington, Virginia, April 15, 1868, Letterbook No. 4, DeButts-Ely Collection of Lee Family Papers, Library of Congress.

201 "God willed": Robert E. Lee to Margaret Stuart, Camp Culpeper, July 26, 1863, in Dowdey and Manarin, eds., *The Wartime Papers of Robert E. Lee*, 561.

201 "No blame": Robert E. Lee to Jefferson Davis, Camp Culpeper, July 31, 1863, in ibid., 565.

201 "It has accomplished": Robert E. Lee to Mary Custis Lee, Camp Culpeper, July 26, 1863, in ibid., 560.

201 "There is no": Longstreet, "Lee in Pennsylvania," 400.

201 "I am becoming": Robert E. Lee to Jefferson Davis, Camp, Orange, August 8, 1863, in Dowdey and Manarin, eds., *The Wartime Papers of Robert E. Lee*, 589–90.

202 "The struggle": Robert E. Lee to Mildred Lee, Camp, Orange Court House, September 10, 1863, in ibid., 597.

202 "new birth": Address at Gettysburg, Pennsylvania, November 19, 1863, in Fehrenbacher, ed., *Abraham Lincoln: Speeches and Writings, 1859–1865*, 536.

202 stacked: Ulysses S. Grant, *Personal Memoirs of U. S. Grant*, ed. E. B. Long, 2nd ed. (New York: Da Capo Press, 2001), 295.

202 "hold no": Edwin Stanton to William Ludlow, Washington, July 4, 1863, in *O.R.*, series 2, vol. 6, 80.

202 "Canvas was": John D. Imboden, "The Confederate Retreat from Gettysburg," in Johnson and Buel, eds., *Battles and Leaders of the Civil War*, vol. 3, 423–24.

202 Union cavalry: Sears, *Gettysburg*, 480–81.

203 "Had the river": Robert E. Lee to Mary Custis Lee, Camp near Hagerstown, July 12, 1863, in Dowdey and Manarin, eds., *The Wartime Papers of Robert E. Lee*, 547–48.

203 Lincoln urged: Guelzo, *Gettysburg*, 447.

203 nervously: Alexander, *Military Memoirs of a Confederate*, 439.

203 waded across: Report of Robert E. Lee, Headquarters, Army of Northern Virginia, January 20, 1864, in Dowdey and Manarin, eds., *The Wartime Papers of Robert E. Lee*, 582–83.

203 "The death": Robert E. Lee to Charlotte Lee, Camp Culpeper, July 26, 1863, George Bolling Lee Papers, Virginia Historical Society.

203 casualties: Sears, *Gettysburg*, 95 and 498.

203 "To ask": Jefferson Davis to Robert E. Lee, Richmond, Virginia, August 11, 1863, in *O.R.*, series 1, vol. 29, part 2, 639–40.

Notes

Chapter 12: The Cemetery

204 irresistible theme: Guelzo, *Gettysburg*, 475–79.

204 "new nation": Address at Gettysburg, Pennsylvania, November 19, 1863, in Fehrenbacher, ed., *Abraham Lincoln: Speeches and Writings, 1859–1865*, 536.

204 packed: Poole, *On Hallowed Ground*, 48 and 56–57; "The Soldiers' Cemetery," *Daily National Intelligencer*, October 17, 1863.

204 "miserable": Report of James M. Moore, 1864, in *O.R.*, series 3, vol. 4, 902–5.

204 eleven hundred acres: Tax-Sale Certificate, Washington, DC, in Transcript of Record, Supreme Court of the United States, *The United States v. George W. P. C. Lee* and *Frederick Kaufman and Richard P. Strong v. George W. P. C. Lee* (July 28, 1879), 24.

204 law passed: Anthony J. Gaughan, *The Last Battle of the Civil War: United States Versus Lee, 1861–1883* (Baton Rouge: Louisiana State University Press, 2011), 20–24; "Collection of Taxes in Insurrectionary Districts; A Proclamation," *New York Times*, July 3, 1862.

204 "be sold": *Alexandria Gazette*, November 23, 1863.

205 years later: Robert E. Lee to William H. Hope, Lexington, Virginia, April 5, 1866, Letterbook No. 3, DeButts-Ely Collection of Lee Family Papers, Library of Congress.

205 captured: Lee, *Recollections and Letters of General Robert E. Lee*, 98–100.

205 "I hope": Robert E. Lee to Mary Custis Lee, Camp Culpeper, July 26, 1863, in Dowdey and Manarin, eds., *The Wartime Papers of Robert E. Lee*, 559.

205 hostage: Daughtry, *Gray Cavalier*, 146–63.

205 scaffold: Coulling, *The Lee Girls*, 122–25.

205 "I see": Robert E. Lee to Mary Custis Lee, Headquarters, June 14, 1863, DeButts-Ely Collection of Lee Family Papers, Library of Congress.

205 suffered: Robert E. Lee to Mary Custis Lee, Camp, Orange, Christmas Night, 1863, in Dowdey and Manarin, eds., *The Wartime Papers of Robert E. Lee*, 644; Robert E. Lee to Mary Custis Lee, Camp, Rappahannock, October 28, 1863, in ibid., 615.

205 "It would be": Walter Taylor to Bettie, Camp near Orange, December 20, 1863, in Tower, ed., *Lee's Adjutant*, 101.

205 "Thus dear": Robert E. Lee to Mary Custis Lee, December 27, 1863, in Dowdey and Manarin, eds., *The Wartime Papers of Robert E. Lee*, 645.

205 "Union man": Testimony of R. Fendall, in Transcript of Record, Supreme Court of the United States, *The United States v. George W. P. C. Lee* and *Frederick Kaufman and Richard P. Strong v. George W. P. C. Lee*.

205 number of Lee's: C. F. Lee to P. R. Fendall, November 27, 1863, Philip Fendall Papers, Duke University; Deposition of William L. Marshall, in Transcript of Record, Supreme Court of the United States, *The United States v. George W. P. C. Lee* and *Frederick Kaufman and Richard P. Strong v. George W. P. C. Lee*, 93–94; *Alexandria Gazette*, November 23, 1863; Francis L. Smith to Mary Custis Lee, Alexandria, Virginia, February 23, 1871, Mary Custis Lee Papers, Virginia Historical Society.

206 rule: Enoch Aquila Chase, "The Arlington Case: George Washington Custis

Notes

Lee Against the United States of America," *Records of the Columbia Historical Society* 31/32 (1930): 175–207.

206 "said they": Testimony of E. W. Janney, in Transcript of Record, Supreme Court of the United States, *The United States v. George W. P. C. Lee and Frederick Kaufman and Richard P. Strong v. George W. P. C. Lee*, 96–97.

206 early biographer: MacDonald, *Mrs. Robert E. Lee,* 173.

206 "estate, lately": Tax-Sale Certificate, Washington, Transcript of Record, Supreme Court of the United States, *The United States v. George W. P. C. Lee and Frederick Kaufman and Richard P. Strong v. George W. P. C. Lee*, 24–26.

206 January 11, 1864: *Daily National Intelligencer*, January 13, 1864.

206 lieutenant general: Jean Edward Smith, *Grant* (New York: Simon & Schuster, 2001), 284–86.

206 "the invaders": Guelzo, *Gettysburg*, 447.

207 "In your": Sears, *Chancellorsville*, 14 and 116.

207 "man": Smith, *Grant*, 259.

207 "Lee's army": Grant, *Personal Memoirs of U.S. Grant*, 369.

207 "recall a single": Horace Porter, "The Surrender at Appomattox Court House," in Johnson and Buel, eds., *Battles and Leaders of the Civil War*, vol. 4, 737.

207 "He will find": Walter Taylor to Bettie, Camp, Orange Courthouse, March 15 and 20, 1864, in Tower, ed., *Lee's Adjutant*, 139.

207 "He had been": Walter Taylor to Bettie, Camp, Orange County, April 3, 1864, in ibid., 148.

207 "If Richmond": Robert E. Lee to Jefferson Davis, Headquarters, April 15, 1864, in Dowdey and Manarin, eds., *The Wartime Papers of Robert E. Lee*, 699–700.

208 steal: Venable, "General Lee in the Wilderness Campaign," 240.

208 "The commanding general": General Orders, No. 7, Headquarters, Army of Northern Virginia, January 22, 1864, in Dowdey and Manarin, eds., *The Wartime Papers of Robert E. Lee*, 659.

208 how much more: Robert E. Lee to Jefferson Davis, Headquarters, April 12, 1864, in ibid., 698.

208 "The time": Robert E. Lee to George Washington Custis Lee, Camp, Orange Court House, March 29, 1864, in ibid., 685–86.

208 tickle: Lee, *Recollections and Letters of General Robert E. Lee*, 9–10.

208 "I am again": Robert E. Lee to Mary Custis Lee, Camp, March 27, 1864, in DeButts-Ely Collection of Lee Family Papers, Library of Congress.

208 soldiers in camp: Freeman, *R. E. Lee*, vol. 3, 270.

208 75,000 soldiers: Robert E. Lee to Jefferson Davis, Headquarters, April 18, 1864, in *O.R.*, series 1, vol. 33, 1290.

208 amassing 120,000: Foote, *The Civil War*, vol. 3, 18.

208 "We cannot": Robert E. Lee to William Fitzhugh Lee, Camp, Orange, April 24, 1864, Gilder Lehrman Collection, online.

209 caught: Venable, "General Lee in the Wilderness Campaign," 240–41.

209 "Go back": Clifford Dowdey, *Lee's Last Campaign: The Story of Lee and His Men Against Grant—1864* (New York: Skyhorse Publishing, 2011), 153–54 and 206–11.

209 lost many: Ibid., 166–67 and 219–23.

Notes

209 "We must": C. S. Venable, "The Campaign from the Wilderness to Petersburg," *Southern Historical Society Papers* 14 (1886): 522–42.

209 supply base: Ulysses S. Grant to Henry Halleck, Headquarters, Armies of the United States, Quarles' Mill, May 26, 1864, in *O.R.*, series 1, vol. 36, part 3, 207; Report of Thomas A. McParlin, Headquarters, Army of the Potomac Medical Director's Office, November 28, 1864, in *O.R.*, series 1, vol. 36, part 1, 243 and 249.

210 its crown: "The Statue of the Capitol Dome," *Washington Evening Union*, December 1, 1863; David W. Miller, *Second Only to Grant: Quartermaster General Montgomery C. Meigs* (Shippensburg, PA: White Mane Books, 2000), 34, 46, and 79.

210 early as 1853: Miller, *Second Only to Grant*, 27.

210 "capable & qualified,": Robert E. Lee to George Washington Custis Lee, San Antonio, Texas, November 24, 1860, Robert E. Lee Papers, Duke University.

210 "the model": Miller, *Second Only to Grant*, 13.

210 "No man": Ibid., 89–90.

210 "Arlington Heights": Ibid., 92.

210 fifty thousand casualties: Foote, *The Civil War*, 291–92, 297, and 310.

211 stench: Ernest B. Furguson, *Freedom Rising: Washington in the Civil War* (New York: Alfred A. Knopf, 2004), 299–301.

211 "exhausted": Report of James M. Moore, 1864, in *O.R.*, series 3, vol. 4, 903.

211 "The bodies of all": Poole, *On Hallowed Ground*, 61.

211 avoid disturbing: Ibid.

211 half mile: "Dedication of the New Chapel," *Boston Recorder*, December 18, 1863.

211 "encircling": Nelligan, *Old Arlington*, 490–92.

211 "How appropriate": "Gen. Lee's Land," *Liberator*, July 15, 1864.

211 glass cases: "Curiosities at the Patent Office," *Philadelphia Age*, February 17, 1864.

211 "Here Lafayette": "The Arlington Mansion," *Boston Daily Advertiser*, August 17, 1864.

212 "Do you recollect": Robert E. Lee to Mary Custis Lee, Camp, Petersburg, June 30, 1864, in Dowdey and Manarin, eds., *The Wartime Papers of Robert E. Lee*, 812.

212 "will incur": Robert E. Lee to Mary Custis Lee, Gaines's Mill, June 8, 1864, in ibid., 769.

212 buried: McCaslin, *Lee in the Shadow of Washington*, 204.

212 burned: Report of David Hunter, Headquarters, Department of West Virginia, Harper's Ferry, August 8, 1864, in *O.R.*, series 1, vol. 37, part 1, 97; Jubal A. Early, *A Memoir of the Last Year of the War for Independence, in the Confederate States of America* (Lynchburg: Charles W. Button, 1867), 48.

212 back to the valley: Early, *A Memoir of the Last Year of the War for Independence*, 40–41; Freeman, *R. E. Lee*, vol. 3, 396 and 401.

212 Davis wondered: Robert E. Lee to Jefferson Davis, Riddell's Shop, Charles City Road, June 15 [*sic*], 1864, in Dowdey and Manarin, eds., *The Wartime Papers of Robert E. Lee*, 782–83.

212 vanished: Robert E. Lee to James A. Seddon, Headquarters, Army of Northern Virginia, June 13, 1864, in ibid., 777.

212 "broken up": Robert E. Lee to James A. Seddon, Headquarters, Army of Northern Virginia, June 14, 1864, in ibid., 780.

212 speculated: Robert E. Lee to Jefferson Davis, Headquarters, Army of Northern Virginia, June 14, 1864, in ibid., 777–78.

213 worried Lee: Thomas, *Robert E. Lee*, 335–38.

213 already pointed: Dowdey, *Lee's Last Campaign*, 350–51; Freeman, *R. E. Lee*, vol. 3, 425 and 448.

213 every point: Robert E. Lee to Jefferson Davis, Headquarters, Army of Northern Virginia, Near Petersburg, Virginia, June 19, 1864, in Dowdey and Manarin, eds., *The Wartime Papers of Robert E. Lee*, 794–95; Long, *Memoirs of Robert E. Lee*, 390–91.

213 For a time: Thomas, *Robert E. Lee*, 340.

213 "We must destroy": Early, *The Campaigns of Gen. Robert E. Lee*, 42.

213 "I still think": Robert E. Lee to Jefferson Davis, Petersburg, June 29, 1864, in *O.R.*, series 1, vol. 37, part 1, 769–70.

214 discovered: Robert E. Lee to Jefferson Davis, Headquarters, Army of Northern Virginia, June 26, 1864, in *O.R.*, series 1, vol. 37, part 1, 768.

214 "threaten": Marc Leepson, *Desperate Engagement: How a Little-Known Civil War Battle Saved Washington, DC, and Changed American History* (New York: Thomas Dunne, 2007), 52.

214 twelve thousand Confederate: Ibid., 54.

214 "The prisoners": Robert E. Lee to Jefferson Davis, Headquarters, Army of Northern Virginia, June 26, 1864, in *O.R.*, series 1, vol. 37, part 1, 767–68.

214 inform Early: Lee, *Recollections and Letters of General Robert E. Lee*, 131–32; Jubal A. Early, *Lieutenant General Jubal Anderson Early, C.S.A.: Autobiographical Sketch and Narrative of the War Between the States* (Philadelphia: J. B. Lippincott, 1912), 385.

214 "The position": *New York Herald*, July 8, 1864.

214 "The people": Robert E. Lee to Jefferson Davis, Camp, July 10, 1864, in Freeman, ed., *Lee's Dispatches*, 279–80.

214 about one-third: Leepson, *Desperate Engagement*, 148 and 152–54.

215 Early crossed: Early, *Lieutenant General Jubal Anderson Early, C.S.A.*, 389–92.

215 "a very conspicuous": Donald, *Lincoln*, 519.

215 armed government workers: Leepson, *Desperate Engagement*, 167.

215 "Undoubtedly": John B. Gordon, *Reminiscences of the Civil War* (New York: Charles Scribner's Sons, 1911), 314; Leepson, *Desperate Engagement*, 176–77.

215 "would take": Jedediah Hotchkiss, *Make Me a Map of the Valley: The Civil War Journal of Stonewall Jackson's Topographer*, ed. Archie P. McDonald (Dallas: Southern Methodist University Press, 1973), 215.

215 tired the men: Early, *Lieutenant General Jubal Anderson Early, C.S.A.*, 389–92.

215 barely missed: Leepson, *Desperate Engagement*, 199–204.

215 compromised: Early, *Lieutenant General Jubal Anderson Early, C.S.A.*, 394–95.

216 "Washington can": Report of Jubal A. Early, Leesburg, July 14, 1864, in *O.R.*, series 1, vol. 37, part 1, 349.

216 modest success: Report of Robert E. Lee, Headquarters, Army of Northern Virginia, July 19, 1864, in *O.R.*, series 1, vol. 37, part 1, 346.

216 "Those poor": Walter Taylor to Bettie, Camp at Violet Bank, September 4, 1864, in Tower, ed., *Lee's Adjutant*, 189–90.

Notes

216 "Where are we": Robert E. Lee to George Washington Custis Lee, Camp, July 24, 1864, in Dowdey and Manarin, eds., *The Wartime Papers of Robert E. Lee*, 825.

216 "natural military": Robert E. Lee to James A. Seddon, Headquarters, Army of Northern Virginia, August 23, 1864, in ibid., 844.

216 "As far as": Robert E. Lee to Jefferson Davis, Camp, Petersburg, July 6, 1864, Robert E. Lee Papers, Duke University.

217 deployed black: Robert E. Lee to Mary Custis Lee, Chaffins, October 9, 1864, DeButts-Ely Collections of Lee Family Papers, Library of Congress; Andrew Hunter to Robert E. Lee, Richmond, January 7, 1865, in *O.R.*, series 4, vol. 3, 1007–8.

217 "We must": Robert E. Lee to Andrew Hunter, Headquarters, Army of Northern Virginia, January 11, 1865, in *O.R.*, series 4, vol. 3, 1013.

217 "If successful": Robert E. Lee to Mary Custis Lee, Camp, Fredericksburg, April 19, 1863, in Dowdey and Manarin, eds., *The Wartime Papers of Robert E. Lee*, 438.

217 "will have secured": Memorandum on Probable Failure of Re-election, Executive Mansion, Washington, August 23, 1864, in Fehrenbacher, ed., *Abraham Lincoln: Speeches and Writings, 1859–1865*, 624.

217 all but three: McPherson, *Battle Cry of Freedom*, 805.

217 "I think you": Robert E. Lee to Mary Custis Lee, Petersburg, November 12, 1864, DeButts-Ely Collection of Lee Family Papers, Library of Congress.

217 "In the latter": *Richmond Daily Dispatch*, December 28, 1864.

218 "Our old Chief": Walter Taylor to Bettie, Edge Hill, February 20, 1865, in Tower, ed., *Lee's Adjutant*, 225.

218 "The arrangement": Robert E. Lee to Jefferson Davis, Headquarters, Army of Northern Virginia, January 19, 1865, in Dowdey and Manarin, eds., *The Wartime Papers of Robert E. Lee*, 884.

218 "without meat": Robert E. Lee to James A. Seddon, Headquarters, Army of Northern Virginia, February 8, 1865, in ibid., 890.

218 assumed the role: Robert E. Lee to Jefferson Davis, Headquarters, Petersburg, February 9, 1865, in ibid., 892; Robert E. Lee to Mary Custis Lee (daughter), Camp, Petersburg, February 3, 1865, Mary Custis Lee Papers, Virginia Historical Society.

218 "It may be": Robert E. Lee to John C. Breckinridge, Headquarters, Petersburg, February 19, 1865, in Dowdey and Manarin, eds., *The Wartime Papers of Robert E. Lee*, 904–5.

218 "calamity": Robert E. Lee to James A. Seddon, Headquarters, Army of Northern Virginia, February 8, 1865, in ibid., 890.

218 warned Davis: Davis, *The Rise and Fall of the Confederate Government*, vol. 2, 648.

218 "While the military": Robert E. Lee to John C. Breckinridge, Headquarters, Confederate States Armies, March 9, 1865, in Dowdey and Manarin, eds., *The Wartime Papers of Robert E. Lee*, 913.

219 "Mister Custis": George Taylor Lee, "Reminiscences of General Robert E. Lee, 1865–1868," *South Atlantic Quarterly* 26 (1927), Lee Family Digital Archive, Washington and Lee University.

219 "My belief": Robert E. Lee to Jefferson Davis, Near Petersburg, March 2, 1865, Robert E. Lee Papers, Duke University.

Notes

219 "weary": Robert E. Lee to Agnes Lee, March 31, 1865, in Dowdey and Manarin, eds., *The Wartime Papers of Robert E. Lee*, 92.

219 "He appears": Robert E. Lee to Mary Custis Lee, Petersburg, March 28, 1865, DeButts-Ely Collections of Lee Family Papers, Library of Congress.

219 picked the site: Marshall, *An Aide-de-Camp of Lee*, 268–69.

219 called for reinforcements: Long, *Memoirs of Robert E. Lee*, 420–21.

219 thirty thousand infantrymen: Thomas, *Robert E. Lee*, 356 and 359; Freeman, *R. E. Lee*, vol. 4, 58, 93, and 118.

220 bark: Marshall, *An Aide-de-Camp of Lee*, 259–60.

220 "There is nothing": Long, *Memoirs of Robert E. Lee*, 421.

220 "How easily": Cooke, *A Life of Gen. Robert E. Lee*, 461.

220 "rabbits and partridges": Alexander, *Military Memoirs of a Confederate*, 605.

220 "obeying emotions": Marshall, *An Aide-de-Camp of Lee*, 256–58.

220 half an hour: Ibid., 269.

220 what punishment: Longstreet, *From Manassas to Appomattox*, 624–28.

220 granduncle: Marshall, *An Aide-de-Camp of Lee*, xiii and 269.

221 "silver gray": Porter, "The Surrender at Appomattox Court House," 737.

221 gilt-wrapped: Lee, *General Lee*, 393–94.

221 looked down: Porter, "The Surrender at Appomattox Court House," 738.

221 "Each officer": U. S. Grant to Robert E. Lee, Headquarters, Armies of the United States, Appomattox Court-House, Virginia, April 9, 1865, in *O.R.*, series 1, vol. 46, part 3, 665.

221 "was evidently": Porter, "The Surrender at Appomattox Court House," 739.

221 "As he was": Grant, *Personal Memoirs of U. S. Grant*, 555.

221 darker hue: George A. Forsyth, "The Closing Scene at Appomattox Court House," *Harper's New Monthly Magazine* 96, no. 575 (April 1898): 700–711.

221 lifted his hat: Porter, "The Surrender at Appomattox Court House," 743.

221 "worthy citizens": Long, *Memoirs of Robert E. Lee*, 423–24.

222 new residents: Poole, *On Hallowed Ground*, 53, 64, and 85; McPherson, *Battle Cry of Freedom*, 854.

Chapter 13: Washington and Lee

225 cheered: "Arrival of the Rebel General Lee," *New York Herald*, April 18, 1865.

225 charred: Brock, *Richmond During the War*, 369–70.

225 had approached: Charles Bracelen Flood, *Lee: The Last Years* (Boston: Mariner Book, 1998), 42; MacDonald, *Mrs. Robert E. Lee*, 196.

225 "I wish": Mary Custis Lee to Louisa, Richmond, April 16, 1865, in Pryor, *Reading the Man*, 427.

225 "malice toward none": Second Inaugural Address, March 4, 1865, in Fehrenbacher, ed., *Abraham Lincoln: Speeches and Writings, 1859–1865*, 686.

225 condemned: *New York Herald*, April 29, 1865.

225 Brooding alone: Robins, "Mrs. Lee During the War," 341; Flood, *Lee*, 54.

225 "useless": Robert E. Lee to Jefferson Davis, Richmond, April 20, 1865, Letterbook No. 3, DeButts-Ely Collection of Lee Family Papers, Library of Congress.

225 "Why shouldn't": Robins, "Mrs. Lee During the War," 342.

Notes

226   needed her sons: *New York Herald*, April 29, 1865.

226   in his view: Robert E. Lee to Ulysses S. Grant, Richmond, June 13, 1865, Letterbook No. 3, DeButts-Ely Collection of Lee Family Papers, Library of Congress.

226   "Altho' the": Robert E. Lee to Richard L. Maury, Near Cartersville, July 31, 1865, Letterbook No. 3, DeButts-Ely Collection of Lee Family Papers, Library of Congress.

226   "are entitled": Robert E. Lee to Mary Custis Lee, City of Mexico, February 13, 1848, DeButts-Ely Collection of Lee Family Papers, Library of Congress.

226   "There was not": Grant, *Personal Memoirs of U. S. Grant*, 559.

226   hesitation: Marshall, *An Aide-de-Camp of Lee*, 274–75.

226   a model: George Washington Custis Lee to Robert E. Lee Jr., in Lee, *Recollections and Letters of General Robert E. Lee*, 165.

226   applied: Robert E. Lee to Josiah Tatnall, Near Cartersville, Virginia, September 7, 1865, Letterbook No. 3, DeButts-Ely Collection of Lee Family Papers, Library of Congress.

226   "The questions": Robert E. Lee to John Letcher, Near Cartersville, Virginia, August 28, 1865, Letterbook No. 3, DeButts-Ely Collection of Lee Family Papers, Library of Congress.

227   "I need not": Robert E. Lee to P. G. T. Beauregard, Lexington, Virginia, October 3, 1865, Letterbook No. 3, DeButts-Ely Collection of Lee Family Papers, Library of Congress.

227   "I am looking": Robert E. Lee to A. L. Long, in Long, *Memoirs of Robert E. Lee*, 439.

227   Grant had voiced: Jones, *Life and Letters of Robert E. Lee*, 384–86.

227   "We may expect": Robert E. Lee to William Fitzhugh Lee, Near Cartersville, Cumberland County, Virginia, July 29, 1865, in Lee, *Recollections and Letters of General Robert E. Lee*, 177–78.

228   "We are all": Robert E. Lee to Robert E. Lee Jr., Near Cartersville, July 10, 1865, DeButts-Ely Collection of Lee Family Papers, Library of Congress.

228   a traveler: Alexander L. Nelson, "How Lee Became a College President," in Riley, ed., *General Robert E. Lee After Appomattox*, 1–4.

228   "chagrin": Lee, *Recollections and Letters of General Robert E. Lee*, 180–82.

228   Everett's biography: Everett, *The Life of George Washington*, 157–58.

228   "No circumstance": Prussing, *The Estate of George Washington, Deceased*, 173–83.

229   pelting: Ollinger Crenshaw, *General Lee's College: Rise and Growth of Washington and Lee* (Lexington, VA: Unpublished Typescript, 1973), Special Collections, Washington and Lee University, vol. 1, 519–21.

229   "But the damage": Annual Report of the Faculty, 1864, Trustees Papers, Washington and Lee University.

229   accounted for: Report of the Committee on Finance, 1865, Trustees Papers, Washington and Lee University; Robert E. Lee to Townsend Wade, Lexington, Virginia, January 18, 1866, Letterbook No. 3, DeButts-Ely Collection of Lee Family Papers, Library of Congress.

229   forty-five: Annual Report of the Faculty, 1865, Trustees Papers, Washington and Lee University.

229   "How could they": Nelson, "How Lee Became a College President," 1–2.

230   "The cause gave": Lee, *Recollections and Letters of General Robert E. Lee*, 182.

Notes

230 "So greatly": Ibid., 210.

230 "great ability": Robert E. Lee to Gentlemen, Powhatan County, August 24, 1865, Robert E. Lee Papers, Washington and Lee University.

230 take a different view: Board Resolutions, Lexington, August 31, 1865, Trustees Papers, Washington and Lee University.

230 rejected: Freeman, *R. E. Lee*, vol. 4, 244.

231 insisted on keeping: *New York Herald*, October 7, 1865.

231 unbeknownst: Ulysses S. Grant to Robert E. Lee, Headquarters, Armies of the United States, Washington, June 20, 1865, in Jones, *Life and Letters of Robert E. Lee*, 385–86.

231 "I, Robert E. Lee": Robert E. Lee's Amnesty Oath, October 2, 1865, National Archives, online.

231 "And here": *New York Herald*, October 7, 1865.

231 108 miles: Robert E. Lee to Mary Custis Lee, Rockbridge Baths, September 25, 1865, DeButts-Ely Collection of Lee Family Papers, Library of Congress.

231 twenty-three-mile: Freeman, *R. E. Lee*, vol. 4, 395.

231 "the easiest": Lee, *Recollections and Letters of General Robert E. Lee*, 202–3.

231 cherished the mountain: Robert E. Lee to Mary Custis Lee, Lexington, October 3, 1865, DeButts-Ely Collection of Lee Family Papers, Library of Congress.

231 "Lexington I fear": Mary Custis Lee to Betty Poulson, Derwent, September 21, 1865, Robert E. Lee Family Collection, Museum of the Confederacy.

231 "General Lee's College": Crenshaw, *General Lee's College*, vol. 1, 554–58.

232 "His education": Lemuel P. Conner to Robert E. Lee, Near Natchez, December 27, 1865, Lee Family Digital Archive, Washington and Lee University.

232 tripled: Robert E. Lee to Board of Trustees, Washington College, June 1866, Robert E. Lee Papers, Washington and Lee University.

232 begged: Crenshaw, *General Lee's College*, vol. 1, 559–60.

232 looked for them: Freeman, *R. E. Lee*, vol. 4, 282; Flood, *Lee*, 105; C. A. Graves, "General Lee at Lexington," in Riley, ed., *General Robert E. Lee After Appomattox*, 26–27.

232 Boys falling: Freeman, *R. E. Lee*, vol. 4, 279–80 and 287–88.

232 "the commercial": Paragraph on Education, Lee Letterbook, Robert E. Lee Papers, Washington and Lee University.

232 "Such a course": Robert E. Lee to Cyrus McCormick, Lexington, Virginia, November 28, 1865, Letterbook No. 3, DeButts-Ely Collection of Lee Family Papers, Library of Congress.

232 ten thousand: Crenshaw, *General Lee's College*, vol. 1, 630.

232 salary: Freeman, *R. E. Lee*, vol. 4, 215.

232 "massive": *New York Herald*, October 7, 1865.

233 "bright and even": Lee, *Recollections and Letters of General Robert E. Lee*, 203–4.

233 "It is better": Robert E. Lee to Mary Custis Lee, October 19, 1865, in ibid., 190.

233 "All accounts": Robert E. Lee to Mary Custis Lee, Lexington, Virginia, October 9, 1865, DeButts-Ely Collection of Lee Family Papers, Library of Congress.

233 "It was a beautiful": Poole, *On Hallowed Ground*, 68–69.

233 "that the house": Ibid., 69.

233 "are just": "A Sketch of a Hasty Visit to Dear Old Arlington," Mary Custis Lee Papers, Virginia Historical Society.

Notes

233 "My heart yearns": Mary Custis Lee to Varina Davis, Lexington, February 6, 1867, Robert E. Lee Family Collection, Museum of the Confederacy.

233 "The whole Yankee": Mary Custis Lee to Betty Poulson, Derwent, September 21, 1865, Robert E. Lee Family Collection, Museum of the Confederacy.

234 resolved to restore: Lee, *Recollections and Letters of General Robert E. Lee*, 161; Robert E. Lee Jr. to Agnes Lee, Romancoke, November 7, 1867, DeButts-Ely Collection of Lee Family Papers, Library of Congress.

234 consider those plantations: Robert E. Lee to Robert E. Lee Jr., Lexington, May 26, 1866, DeButts-Ely Collections of Lee Family Papers, Library of Congress; Robert E. Lee to John A. Simkins, Lexington, Virginia, January 10, 1867, Letterbook No. 4, DeButts-Ely Collection of Lee Family Papers, Library of Congress.

234 Virginia Military Institute: Robert E. Lee to Mary Custis Lee, Lexington, October 3, 1865, DeButts-Ely Collections of Lee Family Papers, Library of Congress.

234 discovered: Robert E. Lee to William H. Hope, Lexington, Virginia, April 5, 1866, Letterbook No. 3, DeButts-Ely Collections of Lee Family Papers, Library of Congress.

234 "I have refrained": Robert E. Lee to Francis L. Smith, Lexington, April 6, 1866, Letterbook No. 3, DeButts-Ely Collections of Lee Family Papers, Library of Congress.

234 resurface: Elmer Oris Parker, "Why Was Lee Not Pardoned?" *Prologue* 2, no. 3 (Winter 1970): 181.

234 catalogued items: Mary Custis Lee to Philip Fendall, Lexington, November 12, 1866, Philip Fendall Papers, Duke University.

234 Selina Gray: Mary Custis Lee, Lexington, September 12, 1866, Philip Fendall Papers, Duke University.

234 "I do not suppose": Mary Custis Lee to Philip Fendall, Private, Philip Fendall Papers, Duke University.

234 one relic: Mary Custis Lee to Benson Lossing, Lexington, April 4, 1867, Custis-Lee Family Papers, Library of Congress.

235 about the paintings: Benson Lossing to Mary Custis Lee, Poughkeepsie, New York, May 14, 1867, Custis-Lee Family Papers, Library of Congress; Mary Custis Lee to Benson Lossing, Lexington, May 22, 1867, Custis-Lee Family Papers, Library of Congress.

235 retrieved the heirlooms: Lee, *Recollections and Letters of General Robert E. Lee*, 204–5; Coulling, *The Lee Girls*, 160.

235 sank: Lee, *Recollections and Letters of General Robert E. Lee*, 354; Mary Custis Lee to George Kinnear, August 16, 1873, Robert E. Lee Papers, Washington and Lee University.

235 water damage: *Alexandria Gazette*, August 16, 1873.

235 "relating to Washington": Will of G. W. P. Custis, in Prussing, *The Estate of George Washington, Deceased*, 477.

235 dull-looking: Long, *Memoirs of Robert E. Lee*, 469; "More Reminiscences of Miss Mary Custis Lee," *New Orleans Times-Picayune*, April 6, 1902.

235 granted her request: Department of the Interior to Mary Custis Lee, Washington, DC, February 24, 1869, Mary Custis Lee Papers, Virginia Historical Society.

235 "As the country": Robert E. Lee to George W. Jones, Lexington, Virginia,

Notes

March 22, 1869, Letterbook No. 4, DeButts-Ely Collection of Lee Family Papers, Library of Congress.

235   more respect: *Report of the Joint Committee on Reconstruction*, 39th Cong., 1st session, 1866, part 2, 7, 43, 48, 87, 126, and 129.

236   "I am considered": Robert E. Lee to Markie Williams, Lexington, Virginia, April 7, 1866, in Craven, ed., *"To Markie,"* 68–69.

236   clear view: Coulling, *The Lee Girls*, 37.

236   "I do not know": Robert E. Lee to Amanda Parks, Lexington, Virginia, March 9, 1866, Lee Letterbook No. 3, DeButts-Ely Collection of Lee Family Papers, Library of Congress.

236   "I think it would": *Report of the Joint Committee on Reconstruction*, part 2, 129–36.

236   conservative counterbalance: Eric Foner, *A Short History of Reconstruction, 1863–1877* (New York: Harper & Row, 1990), 104–29.

237   "The country": Mary Custis Lee to Mrs. Chilton, March 10, 1867, Robert E. Lee Family Collection, Museum of the Confederacy.

237   "All that the": Robert E. Lee to C. Chauncey Burr, Lexington, Virginia, January 5, 1866, Lee Letterbook No. 3, DeButts-Ely Collection of Lee Family Papers, Library of Congress.

237   prepared a draft: Charles Carter Lee to Robert E. Lee, Fine Creek, July 26, 1866, Mary Custis Lee Papers, Virginia Historical Society; Early Draft of "Life of General Henry Lee," Mary Custis Lee Papers, Virginia Historical Society.

237   borrowed: Franklin L. Riley, "What General Lee Read After the War," in Riley, ed., *General Robert E. Lee After Appomattox*, 168.

237   "I earnestly beg": Charles Carter Lee to Robert E. Lee, Fine Creek, July 26, 1866, Mary Custis Lee Papers, Virginia Historical Society.

237   "It is that": Charles Carter Lee to Robert E. Lee, Fine Creek, August 27, 1866, Mary Custis Lee Papers, Virginia Historical Society.

237   most troubled: Robert E. Lee to Charles Carter Lee, Lexington, Virginia, March 14, 1867, Robert E. Lee Papers, Washington and Lee University.

237   "distressing contrast": Early Draft of "Life of General Henry Lee," Mary Custis Lee Papers, Virginia Historical Society.

238   "I see no": Robert E. Lee to Charles Carter Lee, Lexington, Virginia, March 14, 1867, Robert E. Lee Papers, Washington and Lee University.

238   retained: Lee, "Life of General Henry Lee," 43 and 45–46.

238   "the leading men": Robert E. Lee to Lord Acton, Lexington, Virginia, December 15, 1866, in Riley, ed., *General Robert E. Lee After Appomattox*, 237–41.

239   deathbed: Envelope with Memoranda on Various Subjects, Mary Custis Lee Papers, Virginia Historical Society.

239   shredding: Robert E. Lee, "War," Mary Custis Lee Papers, Virginia Historical Society.

239   persists: Robert E. Lee, "Govt." Mary Custis Lee Papers, Virginia Historical Society.

239   legacy open: Robert E. Lee, "Memo," Mary Custis Lee Papers, Virginia Historical Society.

239   made no other: Freeman, *R. E. Lee*, vol. 1, 447.

239   "There were powerful": Allan, "Memoranda of Conversations with General Robert E. Lee," 12.

239 granted amnesty: Freeman, *R. E. Lee*, vol. 4, 381–82; Flood, *Lee*, 188–89.

239 met briefly: "The Rival Leaders of the Civil War in Conference," *New York Herald*, May 2, 1869.

239 "What shall": Lee, *Recollections and Letters of General Robert E. Lee*, 373.

239 freed his mind: Lee, "Reminiscences of General Robert E. Lee, 1865–1868."

239 "sorrow": John B. Collyar, "A College Boy's Observation of General Lee," in Riley, ed., *General Robert E. Lee After Appomattox*, 67.

239 thoughts traveled: Lee, *Recollections and Letters of General Robert E. Lee*, 279.

240 "impatient": M. W. Humphreys, "Reminiscences of General Lee as President of Washington College," in Riley, ed., *General Robert E. Lee After Appomattox*, 34–39.

240 "to do their duty": Ibid., 38.

240 "a gentleman": Collyar, "A College Boy's Observation of General Lee," 66.

240 "should be allowed": Paragraph on Education, Lee Letterbook, Robert E. Lee Papers, Washington and Lee University.

240 "one of the first": Flood, *Lee*, 112.

240 expanded offerings: Freeman, *R. E. Lee*, vol. 4, 426–27; Flood, *Lee*, 204–6.

240 enrollment: Robert E. Lee to the Board of Trustees, Washington College, Lexington, Virginia, June 16, 1868, Robert E. Lee Papers, Washington and Lee University.

240 Construction: Freeman, *R. E. Lee*, vol. 4, 366–67 and 408–9.

240 miniature portraits: MacDonald, *Mrs. Robert E. Lee*, 225.

240 "habitually sad": R. L. Madison and H. T. Barton to Dear Sir, Lexington, Virginia, October 21, 1870, in "Letter from Lexington, Va.," *Richmond and Louisville Medical Journal* 9 and 10 (1870): 516–23.

241 "If he did not": William Preston Johnston, "Memoranda of Conversations with General R. E. Lee," in Gallagher, ed., *Lee*, 30–32.

241 exhausted: Ibid., 31; Robert E. to Mary Custis Lee, Savannah, Georgia, April 11, 1870, DeButts-Ely Collection of Lee Family Papers, Library of Congress.

241 ached: Robert E. Lee to Mary Custis Lee, Savannah, Georgia, April 18, 1870, in Lee, *Recollections and Letters of General Robert E. Lee*, 399; Robert E. Lee to Mary Custis Lee, Brandon, May 7, 1870, in ibid., 402.

241 pulse: R. L. Madison and H. T. Barton to Dear Sir, Lexington, Virginia, October 21, 1870, in "Letter from Lexington, Va."

241 "My interest": Robert E. Lee to Markie Williams, Lexington, Virginia, January 1, 1868, in Craven, ed., *"To Markie,"* 78.

241 the chance: Lee, *Recollections and Letters of General Robert E. Lee*, 384–401.

241 "not promising": Robert E. Lee to Mary Custis Lee, Alexandria, July 15, 1870, in ibid., 414.

241 still wished: Johnston, "Memoranda of Conversations with General R. E. Lee," 31.

241 named another: Daughtry, *Gray Cavalier*, 284–89.

241 less cause: Mary Custis Lee to Caroline, January 16, 1867, Robert E. Lee Papers, Washington and Lee University.

241 shunned parties: Robert E. Lee to Markie Williams, Lexington, Virginia, January 1, 1868, in Craven, ed., *"To Markie,"* 79.

Notes

241 "You need not": Robert E. Lee to Charlotte Haxall, Lexington, Virginia, September 27, 1867, DeButts-Ely Collection of Lee Family Papers, Library of Congress.

241 celebrated the news: Robert E. Lee to Charlotte Haxall, Hot Springs, Bath County, Virginia, August 12, 1870, DeButts-Ely Collection of Lee Family Papers, Library of Congress.

241 "He was apt": Mildred Lee, "My Recollections of My Father's Death," Lexington, August 21, 1888, Journal of Agnes Lee, Virginia Historical Society.

241 "Experience will": Robert E. Lee to Mildred Lee, Lexington, DeButts-Ely Collection of Lee Family Papers, Library of Congress.

242 not wanted: Flood, *Lee*, 255–56.

242 "cold and damp": William Preston Johnston, "Death of General Lee," in Jones, *Personal Reminiscences, Anecdotes, and Letters of Gen. Robert E. Lee*, 447–48.

242 hat and cloak: Mary Custis Lee to Charles Carter Lee, October 7, 1870, Ethel Armes Collection of Lee Family Papers, Library of Congress.

242 Usually he: Lee, *Recollections and Letters of General Robert E. Lee*, 12.

242 "Where have": Mary Custis Lee to Charles Carter Lee, October 7, 1870, Ethel Armes Collection of Lee Family Papers, Library of Congress.

242 "He essayed": Mary Custis Lee to R. H. Chilton, Lexington, December 12, 1870, Robert E. Lee Family Collection, Museum of the Confederacy.

242 ten minutes: Mary Custis Lee to Charles Carter Lee, October 7, 1870, Ethel Armes Collection of Lee Family Papers, Library of Congress; Rozear, Massey, Horner, Foley, and Greenfield Jr., "R. E. Lee's Stroke."

242 "Nature seemed": Mary Custis Lee to Mary Jones, November 1870, DeButts-Ely Collection of Lee Family Papers, Library of Congress.

243 nine inches: *Staunton Spectator*, October 4, 1870.

243 swollen James: "The Great Flood," *Richmond Whig*, October 4, 1870.

243 Harpers Ferry: "The Great Flood," *Alexandria Gazette*, October 3, 1870.

243 rain stopped: Mary Custis Lee to Mary Jones, November 1870, DeButts-Ely Collection of Lee Family Papers, Library of Congress.

243 "less drowsy": R. L. Madison and H. T. Barton to Dear Sir, Lexington, Virginia, October 21, 1870, in "Letter from Lexington, Va."

243 "He never smiled": Mary Custis Lee to Virginia, November 20, 1870, Robert E. Lee Papers, Washington and Lee University.

243 "strike the tent": Johnston, "Death of General Lee," 451. For the debate over Lee's last words, see Flood, *Lee*, 261 and 292; Pryor, *Reading the Man*, 615; Rozear, Massey, Horner, Foley, and Greenfield Jr., "R. E. Lee's Stroke."

243 squeeze: Mary Custis Lee to R. H. Chilton, Lexington, December 12, 1870, Robert E. Lee Family Collection, Museum of the Confederacy; Mary Custis Lee to Mary Meade, October 12, 1870, in "Funeral of Mrs. G. W. P. Custis and Death of General R. E. Lee," *Virginia Magazine of History and Biography* 35, no. 1 (January 1927): 22–26.

243 "his rapid": R. L. Madison and H. T. Barton to Dear Sir, Lexington, Virginia, October 21, 1870, in "Letter from Lexington, Va."

243 "deepdrawn": Mary Custis Lee to Virginia, November 20, 1870, Robert E. Lee Papers, Washington and Lee University.

243 "her almost": Lee, *General Lee*, 415.

243 rolled over: R. L. Madison and H. T. Barton to Dear Sir, Lexington, Virginia, October 21, 1870, in "Letter from Lexington, Va."

243 "that the name": "The Late Robert E. Lee," *New York Times*, October 15, 1870.

244 swept away: "The Great Flood," *Washington Evening Star*, October 3, 1870.

Epilogue: The Bridge

245 wrong impression: Gaughan, *The Last Battle of the Civil War*, 43.

245 "Had he been": Mary Custis Lee to Virginia, November 20, 1870, Robert E. Lee Papers, Washington and Lee University.

245 "first in war": Address of Wade Hampton in Columbia, South Carolina, in Cooke, *A Life of Gen. Robert E. Lee*, 545; "Tribute of Respect to Gen. Lee," *Houston Union*, October 20, 1870; "Memorial Exercises in Honor of Gen. R. E. Lee," *Columbus Daily Enquirer*, October 16, 1870; "The Meeting in Washington," *Richmond Whig*, October 18, 1870.

245 "His unobtrusive": "Gen. Robert E. Lee," *New York Times*, October 13, 1870.

245 "The son of": *Congressional Globe*, 41st Cong., 3rd session, 73–74.

245 "Radical invectives": "Lee in the Senate," *New York Herald*, December 15, 1870.

246 "immediate connection": *Congressional Globe*, 41st Cong., 3rd session, 74 and 79. For more about the debate, see Gaughan, *The Last Battle of the Civil War*, 43–49.

246 sixteen thousand bodies: Poole, *On Hallowed Ground*, 83.

246 "He meant": *Congressional Globe*, 41st Cong., 3rd session, 79.

246 monetary compensation: Francis L. Smith to Mary Custis Lee, Alexandria, Virginia, February 5, 1871, Mary Custis Lee Papers, Virginia Historical Society.

246 Despite what: *Congressional Globe*, 41st. Cong., 3rd session, 74.

246 his assets: Estate of R. E. Lee, Rockbridge County Will Book 21, 250–52, Library of Virginia.

246 "After driving": "Mrs. Lee Revisits Arlington," *New York Commercial Advertiser*, June 7, 1873.

246 daughter heard: MacDonald, *Mrs. Robert E. Lee*, 296–99.

246 to court: Gaughan, *The Last Battle of the Civil War*, 74, 131–33, and 164–66.

247 moved to purchase: Report on Legislation Necessary to Secure Title to Arlington, 47th Cong., 2nd session, 1883, S. Rep. 993, 1–3.

247 "I have therefore": Robert Todd Lincoln to George Edmunds, January 15, 1883, Robert Todd Lincoln Letterpress Volumes, vol. 8, roll 10, 170, Abraham Lincoln Presidential Library and Museum; Jason Emerson, *Giant in the Shadows: The Life of Robert T. Lincoln* (Carbondale: Southern Illinois University Press, 2012), 243.

247 "the ownership": *Annual Report of the Secretary of War for the Year 1883* (Washington, DC: Government Printing Office, 1883), vol. 1, 12 and 576–77.

247 advised returning: Acting Attorney General to William McKinley, Department of Justice, Washington, DC, April 8, 1901, Mary Custis Lee Papers, Virginia Historical Society.

247 "It will afford": William McKinley to John W. Daniel, Executive Mansion, Washington, DC, April 25, 1901, in *Washington Star*, April 26, 1901, Mary Custis Lee Papers, Virginia Historical Society.

247 dredged: Gordon Chappell, *Historic Resource Study: West Potomac Park* (Denver:

Notes

National Park Service, 1973); Frederick Gutheim and Antoinette J. Lee, *Worthy of the Nation: Washington, DC, from L'Enfant to the National Capital Planning Commission*, 2nd ed. (Baltimore: Johns Hopkins University Press, 2006), 83 and 89–97.

247 commission overseeing: *The Improvement of the Park System of the District of Columbia*, 57th Cong., 1st session, 1902, S. Rep. 166, 51–52 and 56.

247 "Who is to": Charles Francis Adams, "Shall Cromwell Have a Statue?" *Southern Historical Society Papers* 30 (1902): 1–33; Merrill D. Peterson, *Lincoln in American Memory* (New York: Oxford University Press, 1994), 193–94.

248 "should stand": *The Improvement of the Park System of the District of Columbia*, 51–52.

248 would go: Peterson, *Lincoln in American Memory*, 206–8 and 214.

248 softened enough: Connelly, *The Marble Man*, 116–18 and 126; Nagel, *The Lees of Virginia*, 302–4.

248 "had gone out": Poole, *On Hallowed Ground*, 162–67.

248 Custis had favored: Nelligan, *Old Arlington*, 76–77.

248 Custis had heard: Ibid., 338.

248 "Before us": *Daily National Intelligencer*, July 8, 1851.

248 seventy-five years: Donald Beekman Myer, *Bridges and the City of Washington* (Washington, DC: US Commission of Fine Arts, 1974), 17–21.

249 stated purpose: *Report of the Arlington Memorial Bridge Commission*, 68th Cong., 1st session, 1924, S. Doc. 95, 5.

249 bicentennial: "Potomac Span Honors Memory of Washington," *Christian Science Monitor*, January 18, 1932; "Memorial Bridge Opened Informally," *Washington Post*, January 17, 1932.

249 "connects the": "Bridge of Lincoln and Lee," *Washington Post*, September 12, 1927.

249 Senate resolution: Charles Moore to Ulysses S. Grant III, July 2, 1929, Arlington Memorial Bridge Project Files, Records of the Commission of Fine Arts, National Archives.

249 "the impersonal": "Hits Grant-Lee Proposal," *New York Times*, November 11, 1929.

250 "I have no": Undelivered First Inaugural Address, in Crackel, ed., *The Papers of George Washington Digital Edition*.

Appendix: Custis–Lee Family Tree

254 Custis-Lee Family Tree: Armes, *Stratford Hall*; Brady, *Martha Washington*; Lee, *Lee of Virginia*; Nagel, *The Lees of Virginia*; Custis Family Bible, Custis-Lee Family Papers, Library of Congress.

Selected Bibliography

In researching this book, the author used archival collections from the Abraham Lincoln Presidential Library and Museum, the Alexandria Library, the Alexandria Circuit Court Clerk's Office, Duke University's David M. Rubenstein Rare Book and Manuscript Library, the Fred W. Smith National Library for the Study of George Washington at Mount Vernon, the Georgia Historical Society, the Library of Congress, the Library of Virginia, the Museum of the Confederacy's Eleanor S. Brockenbrough Archives, the National Archives, the University of Virginia Library, Tudor Place, the Virginia Historical Society, Washington and Lee University's James G. Leyburn Library, William and Mary's Swem Library, and other institutions cited in the notes. Research was also conducted using period newspaper articles from the *Alexandria Gazette, Daily National Intelligencer, Frank Leslie's Illustrated Newspaper, New York Herald, New York Times, New York Tribune, Richmond Daily Dispatch, Richmond Enquirer, Richmond Whig, Washington Evening Star, Washington Post,* and many other newspapers cited in the notes. What follows is a noncomprehensive list of books, articles, and published documents cited.

Achenbach, Joel. *The Grand Idea: George Washington's Potomac and the Race to the West.* New York: Simon & Schuster, 2004.

Adams, Charles Francis. *Charles Francis Adams, 1835–1915: An Autobiography.* Boston: Houghton Mifflin, 1916.

———. "Shall Cromwell Have a Statue?" *Southern Historical Society Papers* 30 (1902): 1–33.

Adams, Francis Raymond Jr. *An Annotated Edition of the Personal Letters of Robert E. Lee, April, 1855–April, 1861.* University of Maryland Dissertation, 1955.

Adams, Henry. *The Education of Henry Adams.* New York: Modern Library, 1918. Repr., Boston: First Mariner Books, 2000.

Alexander, Edward Porter. *Fighting for the Confederacy: The Personal Recollections of General Edward Porter Alexander.* Edited by Gary W. Gallagher. Chapel Hill: University of North Carolina Press, 1989.

———. *Military Memoirs of a Confederate: A Critical Narrative.* New York: Charles Scribner's Sons, 1907.

Allan, William. "Memoranda of Conversations with General Robert E. Lee." In Gallagher, ed., *Lee: The Soldier,* 7–24.

Selected Bibliography

Ambrose, Stephen E. *Duty, Honor, Country: A History of West Point*. Baltimore: Johns Hopkins University Press, 1999.

Anderson, Charles. *Texas, Before, and on the Eve of the Rebellion*. Cincinnati: Peter G. Thomson, 1884.

Anderson, Osborne P. *A Voice from Harper's Ferry: A Narrative of Events at Harper's Ferry*. Boston, 1861.

Andrews, Marietta Minnigerode. *Memoirs of a Poor Relation: Being the Story of a Post-War Southern Girl and Her Battle with Destiny*. New York: E. P. Dutton, 1927.

———. *Scraps of Paper*. New York: E. P. Dutton, 1929.

Annals of the Congress of the United States.

Annual Report of the Secretary of War for the Year 1883. Vol. 1. Washington, DC: Government Printing Office, 1883.

Armes, Ethel. *Stratford Hall: The Great House of the Lees*. Richmond: Garrett and Massie, 1936.

Artemel, Janice G., Elizabeth A. Crowell, and Jeff Parker. *The Alexandria Slave Pen: The Archaeology of Urban Captivity*. Washington, DC: Engineering-Science, October 1987.

Bailey, Worth. *Historic American Buildings Survey: Potts-Fitzhugh House*. Edited by Antoinette J. Lee. Washington, DC, 1975.

Beale, G. W. *A Lieutenant of Cavalry in Lee's Army*. Boston: Gorham Press, 1918.

Berry, Kate. "How Can An American Woman Serve Her Country." *Godey's Lady's Book* 43 (1851): 362–65.

Boteler, Alexander R. "Recollections of the John Brown Raid by a Virginian who Witnessed the Fight." *Century Magazine* 26, no. 3 (July 1883): 399–411.

Bowden, J. J. *The Exodus of Federal Forces from Texas*. Austin: Eakin Press, 1986.

Boyd, Thomas. *Light-Horse Harry Lee*. New York: Charles Scribner's Sons, 1931.

Brady, Patricia. *Martha Washington: An American Life*. New York: Viking, 2005.

Bridges, Hal, ed. "A Lee Letter on the 'Lost Dispatch' and the Maryland Campaign of 1862." *Virginia Magazine of History and Biography* 66, no. 2 (April 1958): 161–66.

Brock, R. A., ed. *Gen. Robert Edward Lee: Soldier, Citizen, and Christian Patriot*. Richmond: B. F. Johnson, 1897.

Brock, Sallie A. *Richmond During the War: Four Years of Personal Observation*. New York: G. W. Carleton, 1867.

Bryan, Helen. *Martha Washington: First Lady of Liberty*. New York: John Wiley & Sons, 2002.

Bryan, Thomas B. "War Memories." In *Military Essays and Recollections*. Vol. 3. Chicago: The Dial Press, 1899.

Bryan, William A. "George Washington: Symbolic Guardian of the Republic, 1850–1861." *William and Mary Quarterly* 7, no. 1 (January 1950): 53–63.

Campbell, Edward D. C. Jr. "The Fabric of Command: R. E. Lee, Confederate Insignia, and the Perception of Rank." *Virginia Magazine of History and Biography* 98, no. 2 (April 1990): 261–90.

Casper, Scott E. *Sarah Johnson's Mount Vernon: The Forgotten History of an American Shrine*. New York: Hill and Wang, 2008.

Caughey, Donald C., and Jimmy J. Jones. *The 6th United States Cavalry in the Civil War: A History and Roster*. Jefferson, NC: McFarland, 2013.

Chappell, Gordon. *Historic Resource Study: West Potomac Park*. Denver: National Park Service, 1973.

Chase, Enoch Aquila. "The Arlington Case: George Washington Custis Lee Against the United States of America." *Records of the Columbia Historical Society* 31/32 (1930): 175–207.

———. "The Restoration of Arlington House." *Records of the Columbia Historical Society* 33/34 (1932): 239–65.

Chernow, Ron. *Washington: A Life*. New York: Penguin Books, 2010.

Childe, Edward Lee. *The Life and Campaigns of General Lee*. Translated by George Litting. London: Chatto and Windus, 1875.

Colgrove, Silas. "The Finding of Lee's Lost Order." In Johnson and Buel, eds., *Battles and Leaders of the Civil War*, vol. 2, 603.

Collyar, John B. "A College Boy's Observation of General Lee." In Riley, ed., *General Robert E. Lee After Appomattox*, 65–68.

Colston, F. M. "Gettysburg As I Saw It." *Confederate Veteran* 5, no. 11 (November 1897): 551–53.

Congressional Globe.

Connelly, Thomas L. *The Marble Man: Robert E. Lee and His Image in American Society*. Baton Rouge: Louisiana State University Press, 1977.

Cooke, John Esten. *A Life of Gen. Robert E. Lee*. New York: D. Appleton, 1871.

———. *Wearing of the Gray; Being Personal Portraits, Scenes and Adventures of the War*. New York: E. B. Treat, 1867.

Cooper, William J. Jr. *Jefferson Davis, American*. New York: Vintage Books, 2001.

Correspondence Relating to the Insurrection at Harper's Ferry, October 17, 1859. Annapolis, 1860.

Couch, Darius N. "The Chancellorsville Campaign." In Johnson and Buel, eds., *Battles and Leaders of the Civil War*, vol. 3, 154–71.

Coulling, Mary P. *The Lee Girls*. Winston-Salem: John F. Blair, 1987.

Crackel, Theodore J., et al., eds. *The Papers of George Washington Digital Edition*, Charlottesville: University of Virginia Press, Rotunda, 2007.

Craven, Avery, ed. *"To Markie": The Letters of Robert E. Lee to Martha Custis Williams*. Cambridge: Harvard University Press, 1933.

Crenshaw, Ollinger. *General Lee's College: Rise and Growth of Washington and Lee*. 2 vols. Lexington, VA: Unpublished Typescript, 1973. Special Collections, Washington and Lee.

Crist, Lynda L., Suzanne Scott Gibbs, Brady L. Hutchison, and Elizabeth Henson Smith, eds. *The Papers of Jefferson Davis*. Vol. 12. Baton Rouge: Louisiana State University Press, 2008.

Critcher, John. "Secession Convention." *Virginia Magazine of History and Biography* 5, no. 2 (October 1897): 220–21.

Crothers, A. Glenn. "The 1846 Retrocession of Alexandria: Protecting Slavery and the Slave Trade in the District of Columbia." In *In the Shadow of Freedom: The Politics of Slavery in the National Capital*, edited by Paul Finkelman and Donald R. Kennon. Athens, OH: Ohio University Press, 2011, 141–68.

Custis, George Washington Parke. *Recollections and Private Memoirs of Washington*. New York: Derby & Jackson, 1860. Repr., Bridgewater, VA: American Foundation Publications, 1999.

Selected Bibliography

Cuthbert, Norma B. "To Molly: Five Early Letters from Robert E. Lee to His Wife, 1832–1835." *Huntington Library Quarterly* 15, no. 3 (May 1952): 257–76.

Darrow, Caroline Baldwin. "Recollections of the Twiggs Surrender." In Johnson and Buel, eds., *Battles and Leaders of the Civil War*, vol. 1, 33–39.

Daughtry, Mary Bandy. *Gray Cavalier: The Life and Wars of General W. H. F. "Rooney" Lee.* Cambridge, MA: Da Capo Press, 2002.

Davis, Jefferson. *The Rise and Fall of the Confederate Government.* 2 vols. New York: D. Appleton, 1881.

Davis, William C. *Battle at Bull Run: A History of the First Major Campaign of the Civil War.* Mechanicsburg, PA: Stackpole Books, 1995.

———. *Jefferson Davis: The Man and His Hour.* Baton Rouge: Louisiana State University Press, 1996.

Davis, William C., and James I. Robertson Jr., eds. *Virginia at War, 1861.* Lexington: University Press of Kentucky, 2005.

deButts, Mary Custis Lee, ed. *Growing Up in the 1850s: The Journal of Agnes Lee.* Chapel Hill: University of North Carolina Press, 1984.

deButts, Robert E. L. Jr. "Lee in Love: Courtship and Correspondence in Antebellum Virginia." *Virginia Magazine of History and Biography* 115, no. 4 (2007): 486–575.

———. "Mary Custis Lee's 'Reminiscences of the War.'" *Virginia Magazine of History and Biography* 109, no. 3 (2001): 301–25.

Dederer, John Morgan. "Robert E. Lee's First Visit to His Father's Grave." *Virginia Magazine of History and Biography* 102, no. 1 (January 1994): 73–88.

Dickens, Charles. *American Notes for General Circulation.* Vol. 1. London: Chapman and Hall, 1842.

Donald, David Herbert. *Lincoln.* New York: Simon & Schuster, 1995.

Douglas, Henry Kyd. "Stonewall Jackson in Maryland." In Johnson and Buel, eds., *Battles and Leaders of the Civil War*, vol. 2, 620–29.

Dowdey, Clifford. *Lee's Last Campaign: The Story of Lee and His Men Against Grant—1864.* New York: Skyhorse Publishing, 2011.

Dowdey, Clifford, and Louis H. Manarin, eds. *The Wartime Papers of Robert E. Lee.* Boston: Da Capo Press, 1961.

Early, Jubal A. *A Memoir of the Last Year of the War for Independence, in the Confederate States of America.* Lynchburg: Charles W. Button, 1867.

———. *Lieutenant General Jubal Anderson Early, C.S.A.: Autobiographical Sketch and Narrative of the War Between the States.* Philadelphia: J. B. Lippincott, 1912.

———. *The Campaigns of Gen. Robert E. Lee.* Baltimore: John Murphy, 1872.

Elliot, Jonathan. *Historical Sketches of the Ten Miles Square Forming the District of Columbia: With a Picture of Washington, Describing Objects of General Interest or Curiosity at the Metropolis of the Union.* Washington, DC: J. Elliot Jr., 1830.

Ellis, Joseph J. *Founding Brothers: The Revolutionary Generation.* New York: Vintage Books, 2002.

———. *His Excellency: George Washington.* New York: Alfred A. Knopf, 2004.

Emerson, Jason. *Giant in the Shadows: The Life of Robert T. Lincoln.* Carbondale: Southern Illinois University Press, 2012.

Everett, Edward. *The Life of George Washington.* New York: Sheldon, 1860.

Fehrenbacher, Don E., ed. *Abraham Lincoln: Speeches and Writings, 1832–1858.* New York: Library of America, 1989.

Selected Bibliography

———. *Abraham Lincoln: Speeches and Writings, 1859–1865*. New York: Library of America, 1989.

Fitzpatrick, John C., ed. *The Writings of George Washington from the Original Manuscript Sources, 1745–1799*. Charlottesville: University of Virginia Library, 2001. Online.

Flexner, James Thomas. *Washington: The Indispensable Man*. New York: Back Bay Books, 1974.

Flood, Charles Bracelen. *Lee: The Last Years*. Boston: Mariner Books, 1998.

Flournoy, H. W., ed. *Calendar of Virginia State Papers and Other Manuscripts*. Vol. 11. Richmond, 1893.

Foner, Eric. *A Short History of Reconstruction, 1863–1877*. New York: Harper & Row, 1990.

Foote, Henry S. *Casket of Reminiscences*. Washington, DC: Chronicle Publishing, 1874.

Foote, Shelby. *The Civil War: A Narrative*. 3 vols. New York: Vintage Books, 1986.

Forgie, George B. *Patricide in the House Divided: A Psychological Interpretation of Lincoln and His Age*. New York: W. W. Norton, 1979.

Forsyth, George A. "The Closing Scene at Appomattox Court House." *Harper's New Monthly Magazine* 96, no. 575 (April 1898): 700–711.

Freeman, Douglas Southall. *Lee's Lieutenants: A Study in Command*. 3 vols. New York: Charles Scribner's Sons, 1942–1944.

———. *R. E. Lee*. 4 vols. New York: Charles Scribner's Sons, 1934–1935. Repr., Safety Harbor, FL: Simon Publications, 2001.

Freeman, Douglas Southall, ed. *Lee's Dispatches: Unpublished Letters of General Robert E. Lee to Jefferson Davis and the War Department of the Confederate States of America*. New York: G. P. Putnam's Sons, 1915.

Fremantle, Arthur. *Three Months in the Southern States, April–June, 1863*. New York: John Bradburn, 1864.

"Funeral of Mrs. G. W. P. Custis and Death of General R. E. Lee." *Virginia Magazine of History and Biography* 35, no. 1 (January 1927): 22–26.

Furgurson, Ernest B. *Freedom Rising: Washington in the Civil War*. New York: Alfred A. Knopf, 2004.

Gallagher, Gary W. " 'If The Enemy Is There, We Must Attack Him': R. E. Lee and the Second Day at Gettysburg." In Gallagher, ed., *Lee: The Soldier*, 497–521.

Gallagher, Gary W., ed. *Lee: The Soldier*. Lincoln: University of Nebraska Press, 1996.

Gaughan, Anthony J. *The Last Battle of the Civil War: United States Versus Lee, 1861–1883*. Baton Rouge: Louisiana State University Press, 2011.

Glatthaar, Joseph T. *General Lee's Army: From Victory to Collapse*. New York: Free Press, 2009.

Goodheart, Adam. "How Col. Ellsworth's Death Shocked the Union." Smithsonianmag .com, March 31, 2011. Online.

———. "The War for (George) Washington." Disunion. *New York Times*, February 21, 2011. Online.

Goodwin, Doris Kearns. *Team of Rivals: The Political Genius of Abraham Lincoln*. New York: Simon & Schuster, 2005.

Gordon, Edward Clifford. "Memorandum of a Conversation with General R. E. Lee." In Gallagher, ed., *Lee: The Soldier*, 25–27.

———. "Recollections of General Robert E. Lee's Administration as President of

Selected Bibliography

Washington College, Virginia." In Riley, ed., *General Robert E. Lee After Appomattox*, 75–105.

Gordon, John B. *Reminiscences of the Civil War*. New York: Charles Scribner's Sons, 1911.

Grant, Ulysses S. *Personal Memoirs of U. S. Grant*. Edited by E. B. Long. 2nd ed. New York: Da Capo Press, 2001.

Graves, C. A. "General Lee at Lexington." In Riley, ed., *General Robert E. Lee After Appomattox*, 22–31.

Gray, Arthur. "The White House: Washington's Marriage Place." *Virginia Magazine of History and Biography* 42, no. 3 (July 1934): 229–40.

Green, Horace. "Lincoln Breaks McClellan's Promise." *Century Magazine* 81, no. 4 (February 1911): 594–96.

Guelzo, Allen C. *Gettysburg: The Last Invasion*. New York: Alfred A. Knopf, 2013.

———. *Lincoln's Emancipation Proclamation: The End of Slavery in America*. New York: Simon & Schuster, 2004.

Gutheim, Frederick. *The Potomac*. Baltimore: Johns Hopkins University Press, 1986.

Gutheim, Frederick, and Antoinette J. Lee. *Worthy of the Nation: Washington, DC, from L'Enfant to the National Capital Planning Commission*. 2nd ed. Baltimore: Johns Hopkins University Press, 2006.

Gwynne, S. C. *Empire of the Summer Moon: Quanah Parker and the Rise and Fall of the Comanches, the Most Powerful Indian Tribe in American History*. New York: Scribner, 2011.

Hallowell, Benjamin. *Autobiography of Benjamin Hallowell*. Philadelphia: Friends' Book Association, 1883.

Hampton, Wade. *Address on the Life and Character of Gen. Robert E. Lee*. Baltimore: John Murphy, 1871.

Hearn, Chester G. *Six Years of Hell: Harpers Ferry During the Civil War*. Baton Rouge: Louisiana State University Press, 1996.

Herbert, Arthur. *The Washington Address*. Lynchburg, VA: J. P. Bell, 1915.

Heth, Henry. "Letter from Major General Henry Heth, of A. P. Hill's Corps, A. N. V." *Southern Historical Society Papers* 4, no. 4 (October 1877): 151–60.

Hill, Daniel H. "Lee's Attacks North of the Chickahominy." In Johnson and Buel, eds., *Battles and Leaders of the Civil War*, vol. 2, 347–62.

Hirschfeld, Fritz. *George Washington and Slavery: A Documentary Portrayal*. Columbia: University of Missouri Press, 1998.

Hood, J. B. *Advance and Retreat: Personal Experiences in the United States and Confederate States Armies*. New Orleans: G. T. Beauregard, 1880.

Horwitz, Tony. *Midnight Rising: John Brown and the Raid That Sparked the Civil War*. New York: Henry Holt, 2011.

Hotchkiss, Jedediah. *Make Me a Map of the Valley: The Civil War Journal of Stonewall Jackson's Topographer*. Edited by Archie P. McDonald. Dallas: Southern Methodist University Press, 1973.

Howe, Daniel Walker. *What Hath God Wrought: The Transformation of America, 1815–1848*. New York: Oxford University Press, 2007.

Hoyt, William D. Jr. "Self-Portrait: Eliza Custis, 1808." *Virginia Magazine of History and Biography* 53, no. 2 (April 1945): 89–100.

Hoyt, William D. Jr., ed. "The Calvert-Stier Correspondence: Letters from America to the Low Countries, 1797–1828." *Maryland Historical Magazine* 38, no. 2 (June 1943): 123–40.

Humphreys, M. W. "Reminiscences of General Lee as President of Washington College." In Riley, ed., *General Robert E. Lee After Appomattox*, 32–39.

Imboden, John D. "The Confederate Retreat from Gettysburg." In Johnson and Buel, eds., *Battles and Leaders of the Civil War*, vol. 3, 420–29.

Inquiry in the Case of Major General Pillow. 30th Cong., 1st session, 1848. Senate Executive Doc. 65.

The Improvement of the Park System of the District of Columbia. 57th Cong., 1st session, 1902. S. Rep. 166.

James, Marquis. *The Raven: A Biography of Sam Houston.* Indianapolis: Bobbs-Merrill, 1929. Repr., Norwalk, CT: Easton Press, 1988.

Johnson, John Lipscomb. *The University Memorial: Biographical Sketches of Alumni of the University of Virginia Who Fell in the Confederate War.* Baltimore: Turnbull Brothers, 1871.

Johnson, Robert Underwood, and Clarence Clough Buel, eds. *Battles and Leaders of the Civil War.* 4 vols. New York: The Century, 1887.

Johnson, R. W. *A Soldier's Reminiscences in Peace and War.* Philadelphia: J. B. Lippincott, 1886.

Johnson, Timothy D. *Winfield Scott: The Quest for Military Glory.* Lawrence: University Press of Kansas, 1998.

Johnston, Joseph E. *Narrative of Military Operations.* New York: D. Appleton, 1874.

Johnston, William Preston. "Death of General Lee." In Jones, *Personal Reminiscences, Anecdotes, and Letters of Gen. Robert E. Lee*, 446–59.

———. "Memoranda of Conversations with General R. E. Lee." In Gallagher, ed., *Lee: The Soldier*, 29–34.

Jones, J. B. *A Rebel War Clerk's Diary at the Confederate States Capital.* 2 vols. Philadelphia: J. B. Lippincott, 1866.

Jones, J. William. *Life and Letters of Robert Edward Lee: Soldier and Man.* New York: Neale Publishing, 1906.

———. *Personal Reminiscences, Anecdotes, and Letters of Gen. Robert E. Lee.* New York: D. Appleton, 1874.

Kaminski, John P., Gaspare J. Saladino, Richard Leffler, Charles H. Schoenleber, Margaret A. Hogan, eds. *The Documentary History of Ratification of the Constitution Digital Edition.* Charlottesville: University of Virginia Press, 2009.

Keyes, E. D. *Fifty Years' Observation of Men and Events, Civil and Military.* New York: Charles Scribner's Sons, 1884.

Krick, Robert K. " 'If Longstreet . . . Says So, It Is Most Likely Not True': James Longstreet and the Second Day at Gettysburg." In *Three Days at Gettysburg: Essays on Confederate and Union Leadership.* Edited by Gary W. Gallagher. Kent, OH: Kent State University Press, 1999, 147–68.

Lee, Edmund Jennings. "The Character of General Lee." In Brock, ed., *Gen. Robert Edward Lee: Soldier, Citizen and Christian Patriot*, 379–413.

———. *Lee of Virginia, 1642–1892.* Philadelphia, 1895. Repr., Westminster, MD: Heritage Books, 2008.

Lee Family Digital Archive. Washington and Lee University. Online.

Lee, Fitzhugh. "Chancellorsville." *Southern Historical Society Papers* 7, no. 12 (December 1879): 545–85.

———. *General Lee*. New York: The University Society, 1905.

Lee, George Taylor. "Reminiscences of General Robert E. Lee, 1865–1868." *South Atlantic Quarterly* 26 (1927). In Lee Family Digital Archive, online.

Lee, Henry, III. *Funeral Oration*. Philadelphia, 1800.

———. *The Revolutionary Memoirs of General Henry Lee*. Edited by Robert E. Lee. New York, 1869. Repr. New York: Da Capo Press, 1998.

Lee, Jean B. "Historical Memory, Sectional Strife, and the American Mecca: Mount Vernon, 1783–1853." *Virginia Magazine of History and Biography* 109, no. 3 (2001): 255–300.

Lee, Jean B., ed. *Experiencing Mount Vernon: Eyewitness Accounts, 1784–1865*. Charlottesville: University of Virginia Press, 2006.

Lee, Mary Custis. "Memoir of George Washington Parke Custis." In Custis, *Recollections and Private Memoirs of Washington*, 7–72.

"A Lee Miscellany." *Virginia Magazine of History and Biography* 33, no. 4 (October 1925): 371.

Lee, Robert E. "Life of General Henry Lee." In Lee, *The Revolutionary Memoirs of General Henry Lee*, 11–79.

Lee, Robert E. Jr. *Recollections and Letters of General Robert E. Lee*. New York: Doubleday, Page, 1904.

Lee, S. L. "War Time in Alexandria, Virginia." *South Atlantic Quarterly* 4, no. 3 (July 1905): 234–48.

Leech, Margaret. *Reveille in Washington, 1860–1865*. New York: New York Review of Books, 1941.

Leepson, Marc. *Desperate Engagement: How a Little-Known Civil War Battle Saved Washington, DC, and Changed American History*. New York: Thomas Dunne, 2007.

Lengel, Edward G. *Inventing George Washington: America's Founder, in Myth and Memory*. New York: Harper, 2011.

Lesser, W. Hunter. *Rebels at the Gate: Lee and McClellan on the Front Line of a Nation Divided*. Naperville, IL: Sourcebooks, 2004.

"Letter from Lexington, Va." *Richmond and Louisville Medical Journal* 9 and 10 (1870): 516–23.

Levasseur, A. *Lafayette in America in 1824 and 1825; or, Journal of a Voyage to the United States*. Translated by John D. Godman. 2 vols. Philadelphia: Carey and Lea, 1829.

Levering, John. "Lee's Advance and Retreat in the Cheat Mountain Campaign in 1861: Supplemented by the Tragic Death of Colonel John A. Washington of His Staff." In *Military Essays and Recollections*. Vol. 4. Chicago: Cozzens & Beaton, 1907.

Link, William A. *Roots of Secession: Slavery and Politics in Antebellum Virginia*. Edited by Gary W. Gallagher. Chapel Hill: University of North Carolina Press, 2003.

Lomax, Elizabeth Lindsay. *Leaves from an Old Washington Diary, 1854–1863*. Edited by Lindsay Lomax Wood. New York: E. P. Dutton, 1943.

Long, A. L. *Memoirs of Robert E. Lee: His Military and Personal History*. Edited by Marcus J. Wright. London: Sampson Low, Marston, Searle, and Rivington, 1886.

Longstreet, James. *From Manassas to Appomattox: Memoirs of the Civil War in America*. Philadelphia: J. B. Lippincott, 1896.

———. "Lee in Pennsylvania." In Gallagher, ed., *Lee: The Soldier*, 381–414.

———. "Lee's Right Wing at Gettysburg." In Johnson and Buel, eds., *Battles and Leaders of the Civil War*, vol. 3, 339–54.

———. "The Invasion of Maryland." In Johnson and Buel, eds., *Battles and Leaders of the Civil War*, vol. 2, 663–74.

Lossing, Benson J. "Arlington House: The Seat of G. W. P. Custis, Esq." *Harper's New Monthly Magazine* 7, no. 40 (September 1853): 433–54.

MacDonald, Rose Mortimer Ellzey. *Mrs. Robert E. Lee*. Boston: Ginn, 1939.

Marshall, Charles. *An Aide-de-Camp of Lee*. Edited by Frederick Maurice. Boston: Little, Brown, 1927.

Mason, Emily V. *Popular Life of Gen. Robert Edward Lee*. Baltimore: John Murphy, 1872.

Mason, W. Roy. "Origin of the Lee Tomatoes." In Johnson and Buel, eds., *Battles and Leaders of the Civil War*, vol. 2, 277.

May, Gary. *John Tyler*. New York: Times Books, 2008.

McCaslin, Richard B. *Lee in the Shadow of Washington*. Baton Rouge: Louisiana State University Press, 2001.

McCullough, David. *John Adams*. New York: Simon & Schuster, 2001.

McPherson, James M. *Battle Cry of Freedom: The Civil War Era*. New York: Ballantine Books, 1989.

———. *Crossroads of Freedom: Antietam*. New York: Oxford University Press, 2002.

Message from the President of the United States. 30th Cong., 1st session, 1847. Executive Doc. 1.

Miller, David W. *Second Only to Grant: Quartermaster General Montgomery C. Meigs*. Shippensburg, PA: White Mane Books, 2000.

Montague, Ludwell Lee. "Memoir of Mrs. Harriotte Lee Taliaferro Concerning Events in Virginia, April 11–21, 1861." *Virginia Magazine of History and Biography* 57, no. 4 (October 1949): 416–20.

Moore, Gay Montague. *Seaport in Virginia: George Washington's Alexandria*. Richmond: Garrett and Massie, 1949.

Morgan, Edmund S. *American Slavery, American Freedom*. New York: W. W. Norton, 2003.

Morgan, Philip D. " 'To Get Quit of Negroes': George Washington and Slavery." *Journal of American Studies* 39, no. 3 (December 2005): 403–29.

Mosby, John Singleton. *The Memoirs of Colonel John S. Mosby*. Edited by Charles Wells Russell. Boston: Little, Brown, and Company, 1917.

Mount Vernon Relics. 41st Cong., 2nd session, 1870. H. Rep. No. 36.

Muir, Dorothy Troth. *Mount Vernon: The Civil War Years*. Mount Vernon, VA: Mount Vernon Ladies' Association, 1993.

Murfin, James V. *The Gleam of Bayonets: The Battle of Antietam and Robert E. Lee's Maryland Campaign, September 1862*. Baton Rouge: Louisiana University Press, 2004.

Myer, Donald Beekman. *Bridges and the City of Washington*. Washington, DC: US Commission of Fine Arts, 1974.

Nagel, Paul C. *The Lees of Virginia: Seven Generations of an American Family*. New York: Oxford University Press, 1992.

Napier, Elers. *The Life and Correspondence of Admiral Sir Charles Napier, K.C.B., From Personal Recollections, Letters, and Official Documents.* Vol. 1. London: Hurst and Blackett, 1862.

Nelligan, Murray H. *Old Arlington: The Story of the Lee Mansion National Memorial.* Columbia University Dissertation, 1953.

Nelson, Alexander L. "How Lee Became a College President." In Riley, ed., *General Robert E. Lee After Appomattox*, 1–4.

Nicolay, John G., and John Hay. *Abraham Lincoln: A History.* Vol. 4. New York: The Century, 1890.

Oates, Stephen B. *The Fires of Jubilee: Nat Turner's Fierce Rebellion.* New York: Harper & Row, 1975.

———. *To Purge This Land with Blood: A Biography of John Brown.* 2nd ed. Amherst: University of Massachusetts Press, 1984.

Occupation of the "White House," in Virginia. 37th Cong., 2nd session, House Executive Doc. 145.

Packard, Joseph. *Recollections of a Long Life.* Edited by Thomas J. Packard. Washington, DC: Byron S. Adams, 1902.

Parker, Elmer Oris. "Why Was Lee Not Pardoned?" *Prologue* 2, no. 3 (Winter 1970): 181.

Peterson, Merrill D. *Lincoln in American Memory.* New York: Oxford University Press, 1994.

———. *The Great Triumvirate: Webster, Clay, and Calhoun.* New York: Oxford University Press, 1987.

Piston, William Garrett. *Lee's Tarnished Lieutenant: James Longstreet and His Place in Southern History.* Athens: University of Georgia Press, 1987.

Pitch, Antony S. *The Burning of Washington: The British Invasion of 1814.* Annapolis: Naval Institute Press, 1998.

Pollard, Edward A. *The Early Life, Campaigns, and Public Services of Robert E. Lee: With a Record of the Campaigns and Heroic Deeds of His Companions in Arms.* New York: E. B. Treat, 1871.

Poole, Robert M. *On Hallowed Ground: The Story of Arlington National Cemetery.* New York: Walker, 2009.

Porter, Fitz John. "Hanover Court House and Gaines's Mill." In Johnson and Buel, eds., *Battles and Leaders of the Civil War*, vol. 2, 319–43.

Porter, Horace. "The Surrender at Appomattox Court House." In Johnson and Buel, eds., *Battles and Leaders of the Civil War*, vol. 4, 729–46.

Potter, David M. *The Impending Crisis: America Before the Civil War, 1848–1861.* Edited by Don E. Fehrenbacher. New York: Harper & Row, 1976. Repr., New York: Harper Perennial, 2011.

Powell, Mary G. *The History of Old Alexandria, Virginia.* Richmond: William Byrd Press, 1928. Repr., Westminster, MD: Willow Bend Books, 2000.

Prussing, Eugene E. *The Estate of George Washington, Deceased.* Boston: Little, Brown, 1927.

Pryor, Elizabeth Brown. *Reading the Man: A Portrait of Robert E. Lee Through His Private Letters.* New York: Viking, 2007.

———. "Thou Knowest Not the Time of Thy Visitation." *Virginia Magazine of History and Biography* 119, no. 3 (2011): 277–96.

Selected Bibliography

Quintard, C. T. *Doctor Quintard, Chaplain C.S.A. and Second Bishop of Tennessee: Being His Story of the War*. Edited by Arthur Howard Noll. Sewanee, TN: The University Press, 1905.

Reed, John C., Robert S. Sigafoos, and George W. Fisher. *The River and the Rocks: The Geologic Story of Great Falls and the Potomac River Gorge*. Washington, DC: Government Printing Office, 1980.

Report of the Arlington Memorial Bridge Commission. 68th Cong., 1st session, 1924. S. Doc. 95.

Report of the Joint Committee on the Harpers Ferry Outrages. Virginia General Assembly, 1860, No. 57.

Report of the Select Committee on the Harper's Ferry Invasion, 36th Cong., 1st session, 1860. S. Rep. 278.

Report of the Joint Committee on Reconstruction. 39th Cong., 1st session, 1866.

Report on Legislation Necessary to Secure Title to Arlington. 47th Cong., 2nd session, 1883. S. Rep. 993.

Rhodehamel, John, ed. *George Washington: Writings*. New York: Library of America, 1997.

Richard, Mark David. "The Debates over the Retrocession of the District of Columbia, 1801–2004." *Washington History* 16 (Spring/Summer 2004): 55–82.

Riley, Franklin L. "What General Lee Read After the War." In Riley, ed., *General Robert E. Lee After Appomattox*, 157–81.

Riley, Franklin L., ed. *General Robert E. Lee After Appomattox*. New York: MacMillan, 1922.

Robert, Joseph C. "Lee the Farmer." *Journal of Southern History* 3, no. 3 (November 1937): 422–40.

Robertson, James I. Jr. *Stonewall Jackson: The Man, the Soldier, the Legend*. New York: Macmillan, 1997.

Robins, Sally Nelson. "Mrs. Lee During the War." In Brock, ed., *Gen. Robert Edward Lee: Soldier, Citizen and Christian Patriot*, 322–49.

Roman, Alfred. *The Military Operations of General Beauregard in the War Between the States, 1861–1865*. Vol. 1. New York: Harper & Brothers, 1884.

Royster, Charles. *Light-Horse Harry Lee and the Legacy of the American Revolution*. Baton Rouge: Louisiana State University Press, 1994.

Rozear, Marvin P., E. Wayne Massey, Jennifer Horner, Erin Foley, and Joseph C. Greenfield Jr. "R. E. Lee's Stroke." *Virginia Magazine of History and Biography* 98, no. 2 (April 1990): 291–308.

Rutland, Robert A., and Charles F. Hobson, eds. *The Papers of James Madison*. Vol. 11. Charlottesville: University Press of Virginia, 1977.

Sanborn, Margaret. *Robert E. Lee: A Portrait, 1807–1861*. Philadelphia: J. B. Lippincott, 1966.

Scarborough, William Kauffman, ed. *The Diary of Edmund Ruffin: The Years of Hope, April 1861–June 1863*. Baton Rouge: Louisiana State University Press, 1976.

Scheibert, Justus. *Seven Months in the Rebel States During the North American War, 1863*. Translated by Joseph C. Hayes. Edited by W. Stanley Hoole. Tuscaloosa, AL: Confederate Publishing, 1958.

Schwartz, Barry. *George Washington: The Making of an American Symbol*. New York: Free Press, 1987.

Selected Bibliography

Scott, W. W. "Some Personal Memories of General Robert E. Lee." *William and Mary Quarterly* 6, no. 4 (October 1926): 277–88.

Sears, Stephen W. *Chancellorsville*. Boston: Mariner Books, 1996.

———. *Gettysburg*. Boston: Mariner Books, 2004.

———. *Landscape Turned Red: The Battle of Antietam*. Boston: Mariner Books, 2003.

———. *To the Gates of Richmond: The Peninsula Campaign*. Boston: Mariner Books, 2001.

Secession: Virginia and the Crisis of Union, 1861. University of Richmond. Online.

Sherman, William T. *Memoirs of General William T. Sherman*, 2nd ed. Vol. 1. New York: D. Appleton, 1904.

Sibley, Marilyn McAdams, ed. "Robert E. Lee to Albert Sidney Johnston, 1857." *Journal of Southern History* 29, no. 1 (February 1963): 100–107.

Smith, James Power. "Stonewall Jackson's Last Battle." In Johnson and Buel, eds., *Battles and Leaders of the Civil War*, vol. 3, 203–14.

Smith, Jean Edward. *Grant*. New York: Simon & Schuster, 2001.

Smith, Merritt Roe. "George Washington and the Establishment of the Harpers Ferry Armory." *Virginia Magazine of History and Biography* 81, no. 4 (October 1973): 415–36.

Snell, Charles W. "Construction of Arlington House, 1802–1818." In *Arlington House: Historic Structures Report*. Edited by Harlan D. Unrau. Denver: National Park Service, 1985. Online.

Sorrel, G. Moxley. *Recollections of a Confederate Staff Officer*. New York: Neale Publishing, 1905.

Stephens, Alexander H. *A Constitutional View of the Late War Between the States; Its Causes, Character, Conduct and Results*. Vol. 2. Philadelphia: National Publishing, 1870.

Talcott, T. M. R. "General Lee's Strategy at the Battle of Chancellorsville." *Southern Historical Society Papers* 34 (1906): 1–27.

Taylor, Walter H. *Four Years with General Lee*. New York: D. Appleton, 1878.

———. *General Lee: His Campaigns in Virginia, 1861–1865*. Norfolk, VA: Nusbaum Book and News, 1906.

Templin, Thomas E. *Henry "Light Horse Harry" Lee: A Biography*. University of Kentucky Dissertation, 1975.

Thane, Elswyth. *Mount Vernon Is Ours: The Story of Its Preservation*. New York: Duell, Sloan, and Pearce, 1966.

Thomas, Emory M. *Robert E. Lee*. New York: Norton, 1997.

———. " 'The Greatest Service I Rendered the State': J. E. B. Stuart's Account of the Capture of John Brown." *Virginia Magazine of History and Biography* 94, no. 3 (July 1986): 345–57.

Thomson, J. Anderson, Jr., and Carlos Michael Santos. "The Mystery in the Coffin: Another View of Lee's Visit to His Father's Grave." *Virginia Magazine of History and Biography* 103, no. 1 (January 1995): 75–94.

Toney, Marcus B. *The Privations of a Private*. Nashville, 1905.

Torrence, Clayton. "Arlington and Mount Vernon, 1856." *Virginia Magazine of History and Biography* 57, no. 2 (April 1949): 140–75.

Tower, R. Lockwood, ed. *Lee's Adjutant: The Wartime Letters of Colonel Walter Herron Taylor, 1862–1865*. Columbia: University of South Carolina Press, 1995.

Selected Bibliography

Townsend, E. D. *Anecdotes of the Civil War in the United States*. New York: D. Appleton, 1884.

Transcript of Record. Supreme Court of the United States. *The United States v. George W. P. C. Lee* and *Frederick Kaufman and Richard P. Strong v. George W. P. C. Lee*. July 28, 1879.

Trimble, Issac R. "The Battle and Campaign of Gettysburg." *Southern Historical Society Papers* 26 (1898): 116–28.

Unger, Harlow Giles. *Lafayette*. New York: John Wiley & Sons, 2002.

United States Naval War Records Office. *Official Records of the Union and Confederate Navies in the War of the Rebellion*. Washington, DC: Government Printing Office, 1894–1922.

United States War Department. *The War of the Rebellion: A Compilation of the Official Records of the Union and Confederate Armies*. Washington, DC: Government Printing Office, 1880–1901.

Upshur, George Lyttleton. *As I Recall Them; Memories of Crowded Years*. New York: Wilson-Erickson, 1936.

Valentine, Edward V. "Reminiscences of General Lee." In Riley, ed., *General Robert E. Lee After Appomattox*, 146–56.

Van Alstyne, Richard W. *Genesis of American Nationalism*. Waltham, MA: Blaisdell Publishing, 1970.

Venable, Charles S. "General Lee in the Wilderness Campaign." In Johnson and Buel, eds., *Battles and Leaders of the Civil War*, vol. 4, 240–46.

———. "The Campaign from the Wilderness to Petersburg." *Southern Historical Society Papers* 14 (1886): 522–42.

Villard, Oswald Garrison. *John Brown, 1800–1859: A Biography Fifty Years After*. Boston: Houghton Mifflin, 1911.

Wagner, Anthony R. "The Queen of England's American Ancestry and Cousinship to Washington and Lee." *New York Genealogical and Biographical Record* 70, no. 3 (July 1939): 201–6.

Walker, John G. "Jackson's Capture of Harper's Ferry." In Johnson and Buel, eds., *Battles and Leaders of the Civil War*, vol. 2, 604–11.

———. "Sharpsburg," In Johnson and Buel, eds., *Battles and Leaders of the Civil War*, vol. 2, 675–82.

Warner, Ezra J. *Generals in Gray*. Baton Rouge: Louisiana State University Press, 2006.

Washington, John A. "John Augustine Washington, III et al." *Magazine of the Jefferson County Historical Society* 73 (December 2007): 24–34.

Washington, Thornton Augustin, ed. *A Genealogical History, Beginning with Colonel John Washington, the Emigrant, and Head of the Washington Family in America*. Washington, DC: McGill & Wallace, 1891.

Watson, Walter A. *Notes on Southside Virginia*. Edited by Constance T. Watson. Richmond, 1925. Repr., Baltimore: Genealogical Publishing, 1977.

Weems, M. L. *The Life of George Washington; With Curious Anecdotes, Equally Honourable to Himself and Exemplary to His Young Countrymen*. 10th ed. Philadelphia: Mathew Carey, 1810.

White House on Pamunkey River. 37th Cong., 2nd session, 1862. House Executive Doc. 135.

Selected Bibliography

Whitman, Walt. *I Sit and Look Out: Editorials from the Brooklyn Daily Times*. Edited by Emory Holloway and Vernolian Schwarz. New York: Columbia University Press, 1932.

Wiencek, Henry. *An Imperfect God: George Washington, His Slaves, and the Creation of America*. New York: Farrar, Straus and Giroux, 2003.

Wood, Gordon S. *Empire of Liberty: A History of the Early Republic, 1789–1815*. New York: Oxford University Press, 2009.

Woodward, C. Vann, ed. *Mary Chesnut's Civil War*. New Haven: Yale University Press, 1981.

Wright, Marcus J. *General Officers of the Confederate Army: Officers of the Executive Departments of the Confederate States, Members of the Confederate Congress by States*. New York: Neale Publishing, 1911.

Yates, Bernice-Marie. *The Perfect Gentleman: The Life and Letters of George Washington Custis Lee*. 2 vols. Xulon Press, 2003.

Zimmer, Anne Carter. *The Robert E. Lee Family Cooking and Housekeeping Book*. Chapel Hill: University of North Carolina Press, 1997.

Map and Illustration Credits

Map and Graphic Credits:

1. Jeff Ward.
2. Courtesy of the Geography and Map Division, Library of Congress.
3. Courtesy of the *Atlas to Accompany the Official Records of the Union and Confederate Armies*, Geography and Map Division, Library of Congress.
4. Courtesy of the *Atlas to Accompany the Official Records of the Union and Confederate Armies*, Geography and Map Division, Library of Congress.
5. Courtesy of the *Atlas to Accompany the Official Records of the Union and Confederate Armies*, Geography and Map Division, Library of Congress.
6. Courtesy of the *Atlas to Accompany the Official Records of the Union and Confederate Armies*, Geography and Map Division, Library of Congress.
7. Custis-Lee Family Tree designed by Erich Hobbing.

Illustration Credits:

1. Courtesy of the Washington-Custis-Lee Collection, Washington and Lee University, Lexington, Virginia.
2. Courtesy of the National Gallery of Art, Washington, DC.
3. Courtesy of Independence National Historical Park.
4. Courtesy of the Washington-Custis-Lee Collection, Washington and Lee University, Lexington, Virginia.
5. Courtesy of the Washington-Custis-Lee Collection, Washington and Lee University, Lexington, Virginia.
6. Courtesy of the Prints & Photographs Division, Library of Congress.
7. Courtesy of the Prints & Photographs Division, Library of Congress.
8. Courtesy of the Museum of the Confederacy.
9. Courtesy of the Prints & Photographs Division, Library of Congress.
10. Courtesy of the Prints & Photographs Division, Library of Congress.
11. Author's collection.
12. Courtesy of the Prints & Photographs Division, Library of Congress.
13. Courtesy of Mount Vernon Ladies' Association.

14. Courtesy of the Prints & Photographs Division, Library of Congress.
15. Courtesy of the Prints & Photographs Division, Library of Congress.
16. Courtesy of the Prints & Photographs Division, Library of Congress.
17. Courtesy of the Prints & Photographs Division, Library of Congress.
18. Courtesy of the Prints & Photographs Division, Library of Congress.
19. Courtesy of the Prints & Photographs Division, Library of Congress.
20. Courtesy of Special Collections and Archives, James G. Leyburn Library, Washington and Lee University.
21. Courtesy of the Prints & Photographs Division, Library of Congress.
22. Courtesy of the Museum of the Confederacy.
23. Courtesy of the Prints & Photographs Division, Library of Congress.
24. Courtesy of the Historic American Engineering Record, Prints & Photographs Division, Library of Congress.

Index

Index

Index

Index

legacy of, 69, 78, 94

memoirs of, 93–94, 235

personality/character of, 53, 73

and preservation of Washington's legacy, 38, 42, 47–48, 54, 61, 69, 93, 120, 235

slavery and, 69–71, 72, 73, 75–78, 168–69, 181, 182–83

and Washington-Lee (Harry) relationship, 47–48

as Washington's adopted son, 35, 36–37, 38–39, 53, 67, 75, 99

and Washington's Birthday parades, 104

and Washington's farewell address, 82

and Washington's personal bequest to Lee, 110

Washington's personal relationship with, 37, 94

and Washington's sword, 81, 235

and Washington's views about marriage, 46–47

will/estate of, 68, 69–78, 168–69, 181, 182–83, 233–34, 235, 241

writings about Washington by, 47–48, 93

See also Arlington

Custis, Jacky, 36, 37

Custis, Martha Dandridge. *See* Washington, Martha Custis

Custis, Mary Anna Randolph. *See* Lee, Mary Anna Randolph Custis (wife)

Custis, Mary Lee Fitzhugh (mother-in-law)

and Custis-Lee relationship, 53

and Custis's birth, 55

death of, 69

Lee family relationship to, 34

and Lee-Mary courtship and wedding, 46, 50

and Mary and Lee at Fort Monroe, 51–52

Mary's (daughter) relationship with, 51–52, 53

and Mary's reaction to Fitzhugh's death, 45

religion and, 70–71

slavery and, 70–71, 75

Custis, Nelly, 36, 37, 40, 50–51

Custis, Patsy, 36

Dabbs house: as Lee's headquarters, 155, 157, 159

Daily Cleveland Herald, 142

Daily Dispatch, 143, 166, 169, 217–18

Daily National Intelligencer, 47–48, 81, 93, 142, 152–53

Davis, Jefferson

battlefront tour of, 154

as commander in chief of Confederate forces, 127, 149

and Confederate raid against Washington, DC, 214

criticisms of, 149

and defense of Richmond, 155, 157, 218

and Early's troops in Shenandoah Valley, 212, 213

flight from Richmond of, 225

and Fort Sumter, 107

headquarters of, 126

inauguration of, 147

Johnston, Lee, and Randolph meeting with, 150–51

and Johnston's retreat from Yorktown, 151

and Lee as adviser to Davis, 127, 149

Lee (Custis) as aide to, 140

and Lee as battlefield commander, 129, 154

and Lee as replacement for Johnston, 153, 154

and Lee's authority, 131, 149, 154, 218

and Lee's cavalry assignment, 65–66

and Lee's command of coastal fortifications, 144

and Lee's concerns about Confederate Army, 218

and Lee's health, 201

and Lee's invasion of Maryland, 171, 172

Index

Index

Index

Index

Index

Index

Index

Index

Index

Index

Index

Index

Index

Index

About the Author

Jonathan Horn is a former White House presidential speechwriter. He has appeared as a commentator on MSNBC and BBC radio, and his writing has appeared in *The New York Times'* Disunion series, *The Weekly Standard*, and other outlets. A graduate of Yale University, he lives in Bethesda, Maryland, with his wife, Caroline.